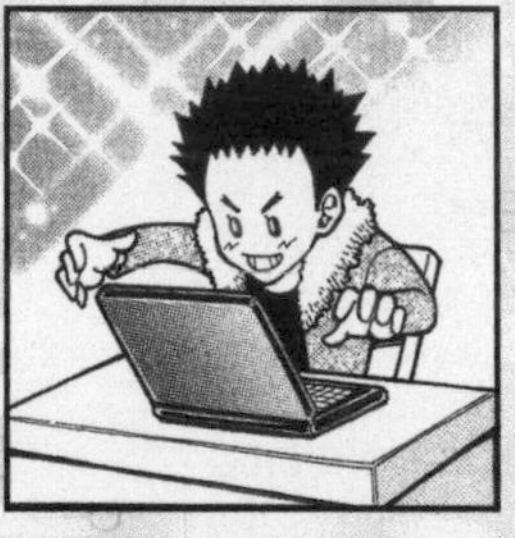

MASAHIRO HIKOKUBO

Before I knew it, all the characters from the anime had shown up in the manga... What's that you say? There are some characters you haven't seen yet? Oh, I bet they're having a blast Turbo Dueling somewhere in the world.

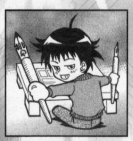

MASASHI SATO

When the series reached Chapter 50, my friends threw me a surprise party to celebrate!! I'll keep right on putting my soul into every line!!

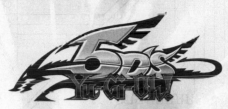

Volume 7
SHONEN JUMP Manga Edition

Story by **MASAHIRO HIKOKUBO**
Art by **MASASHI SATO**
Production Assistance **STUDIO DICE**

Translation & English Adaptation **TAYLOR ENGEL AND IAN REID, HC LANGUAGE SOLUTIONS**
Touch-up Art & Lettering **JOHN HUNT**
Designer **SHAWN CARRICO**
Editor **MIKE MONTESA**

YU-GI-OH! 5D's © 2009 by Masahiro Hikokubo, Masashi Sato
All rights reserved.
First published in Japan in 2009 by SHUEISHA Inc., Tokyo.
English translation rights arranged by SHUEISHA Inc.

Based on Animation TV series YU-GI-OH! 5D's
© 1996 Kazuki Takahashi
© 2008 NAS • TV TOKYO

Printed in the U.S.A.

Published by VIZ Media, LLC
P.O. Box 77010
San Francisco, CA 94107

10 9 8 7 6 5 4 3 2 1
First printing, March 2015

www.viz.com

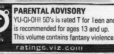

www.shonenjump.com

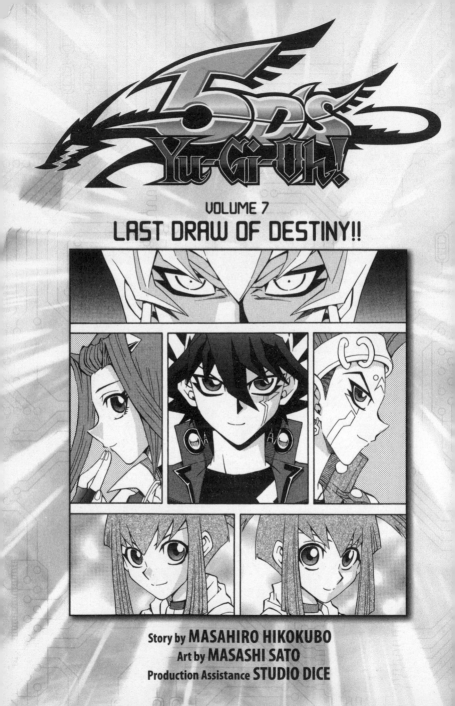

Yu-Gi-Oh! 5D's

VOLUME 7
LAST DRAW OF DESTINY!!

Story by MASAHIRO HIKOKUBO
Art by MASASHI SATO
Production Assistance STUDIO DICE

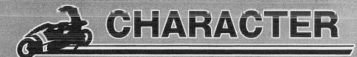

CHARACTER

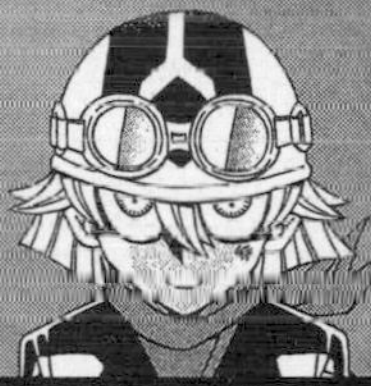

SECT IJUIN

He's like a kid brother to Yusei. His goal is to defeat Yusei in a Turbo Duel. He's been possessed by Shadowsense.

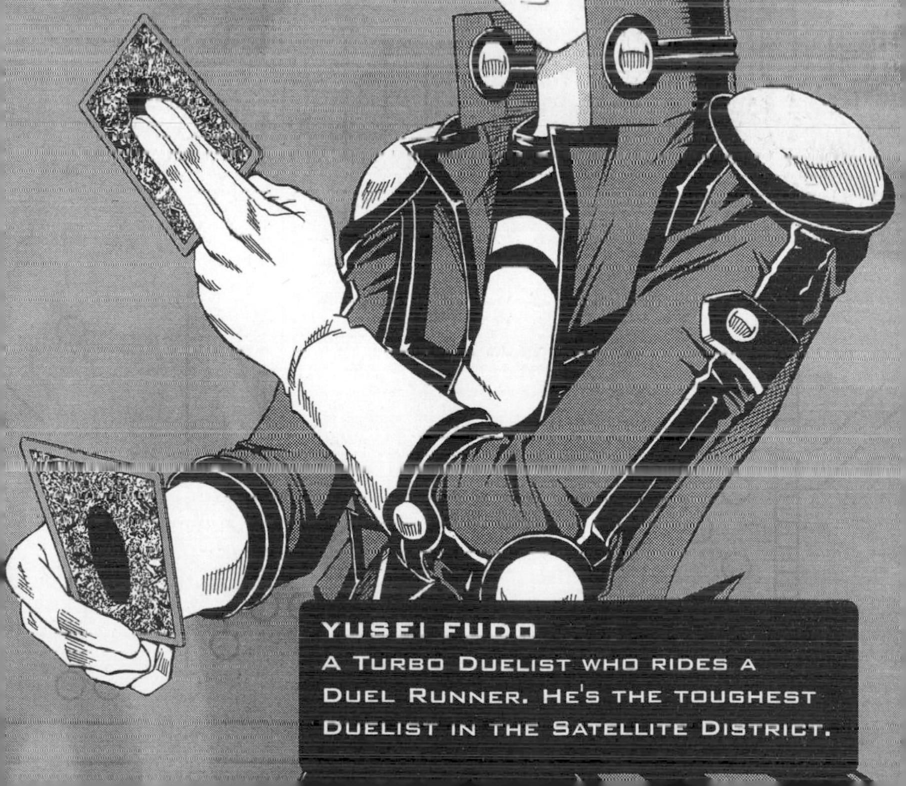

YUSEI FUDO

A Turbo Duelist who rides a Duel Runner. He's the toughest Duelist in the Satellite District.

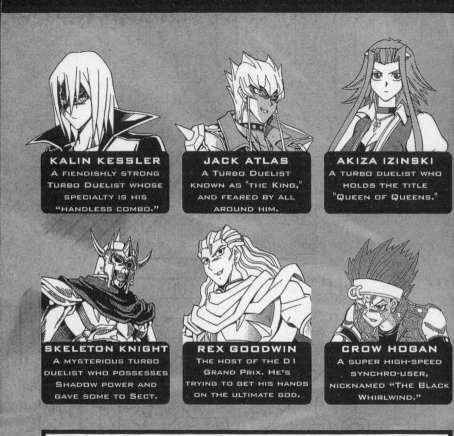

KALIN KESSLER
A fiendishly strong Turbo Duelist whose specialty is his "handless combo."

JACK ATLAS
A Turbo Duelist known as "the King," and feared by all around him.

AKIZA IZINSKI
A turbo duelist who holds the title "Queen of Queens."

SKELETON KNIGHT
A mysterious turbo duelist who possesses Shadow power and gave some to Sect.

REX GOODWIN
The host of the D1 Grand Prix. He's trying to get his hands on the ultimate god.

CROW HOGAN
A super high-speed synchro-user, nicknamed "The Black Whirlwind."

🏍 STORY

In New Domino City, in the year 20XX, Turbo Duels fought from the seats of motorcycle-shaped duel disks called "Duel Runners" are the hottest game in town.

Yusei Fudo, the toughest duelist in Satellite, suffered a painful loss to Jack Atlas. In order to duel Jack again, Yusei entered the D1 Grand Prix, the battle to determine the toughest duelist in the world!! As the strongmen of the dueling world slugged it out, Yusei fought his way into the second round, where he beat Crow, Leo and Luna, and won his own Duel Dragon, Stardust Spark Dragon! In Seibal's Corridor of the Northern Sky, he found himself facing the Skeleton Knight. Meanwhile, in the Corridor of the Southern Sky, Jack and Rex squared off. Who will win and reach Sect?

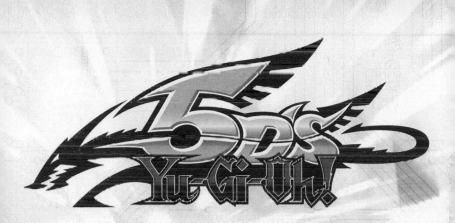

VOLUME 7
LAST DRAW OF DESTINY!!

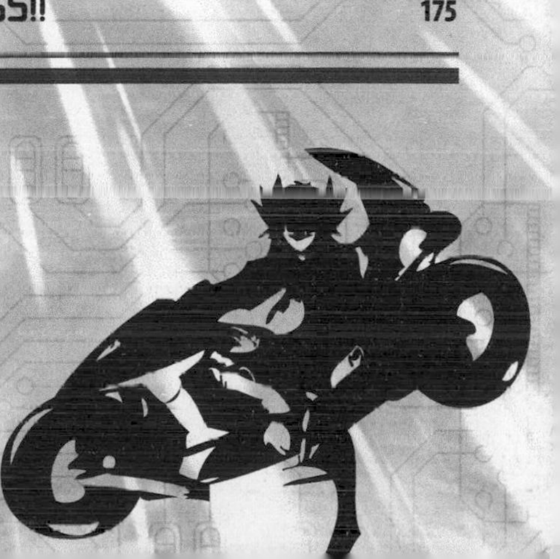

RIDE-47

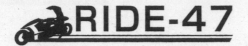

SOUTHERN CORRIDOR SPRINT!!

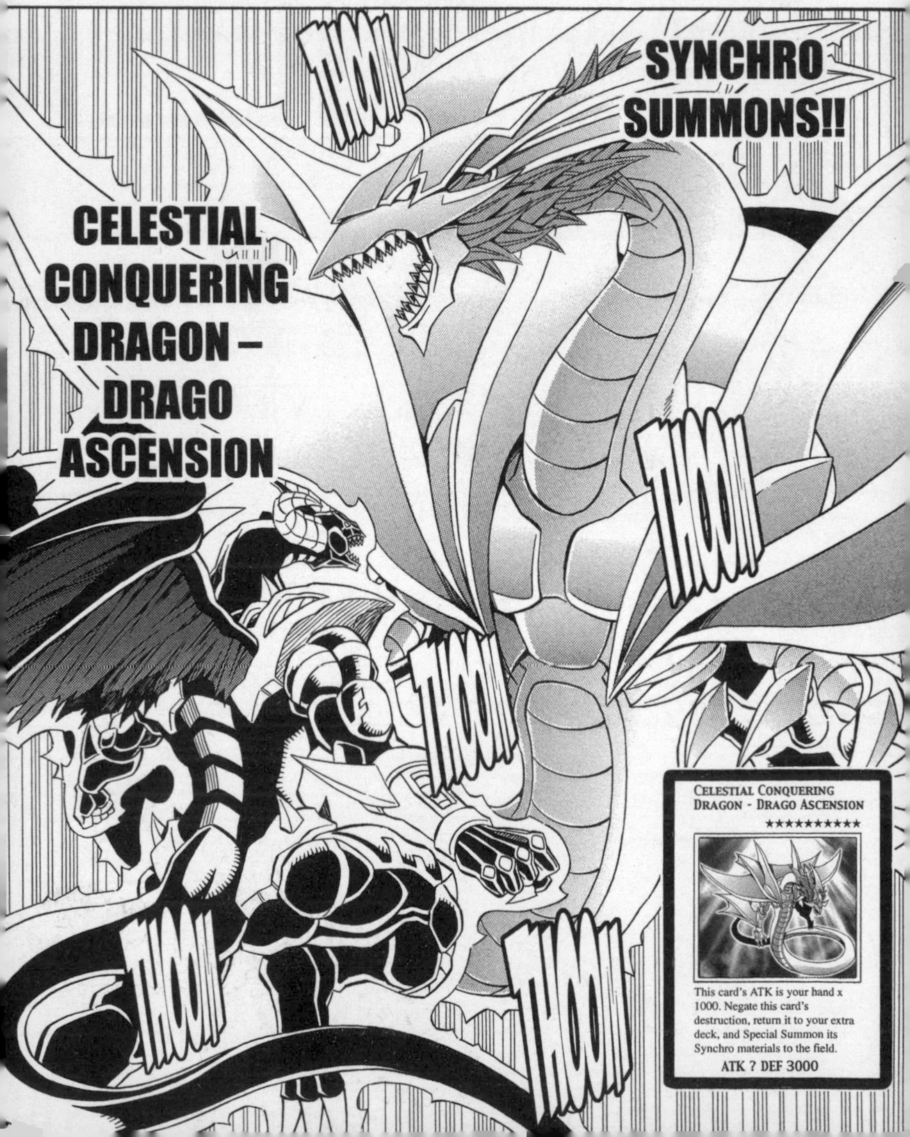

SYNCHRO SUMMONS!!
THOOM
CELESTIAL CONQUERING DRAGON – DRAGO ASCENSION
THOOM
THOOM
CELESTIAL CONQUERING DRAGON - DRAGO ASCENSION
★★★★★★★★★★★
This card's ATK is your hand x 1000. Negate this card's destruction, return it to your extra deck, and Special Summon its Synchro materials to the field.
ATK ? DEF 3000
THOOM
THOOM

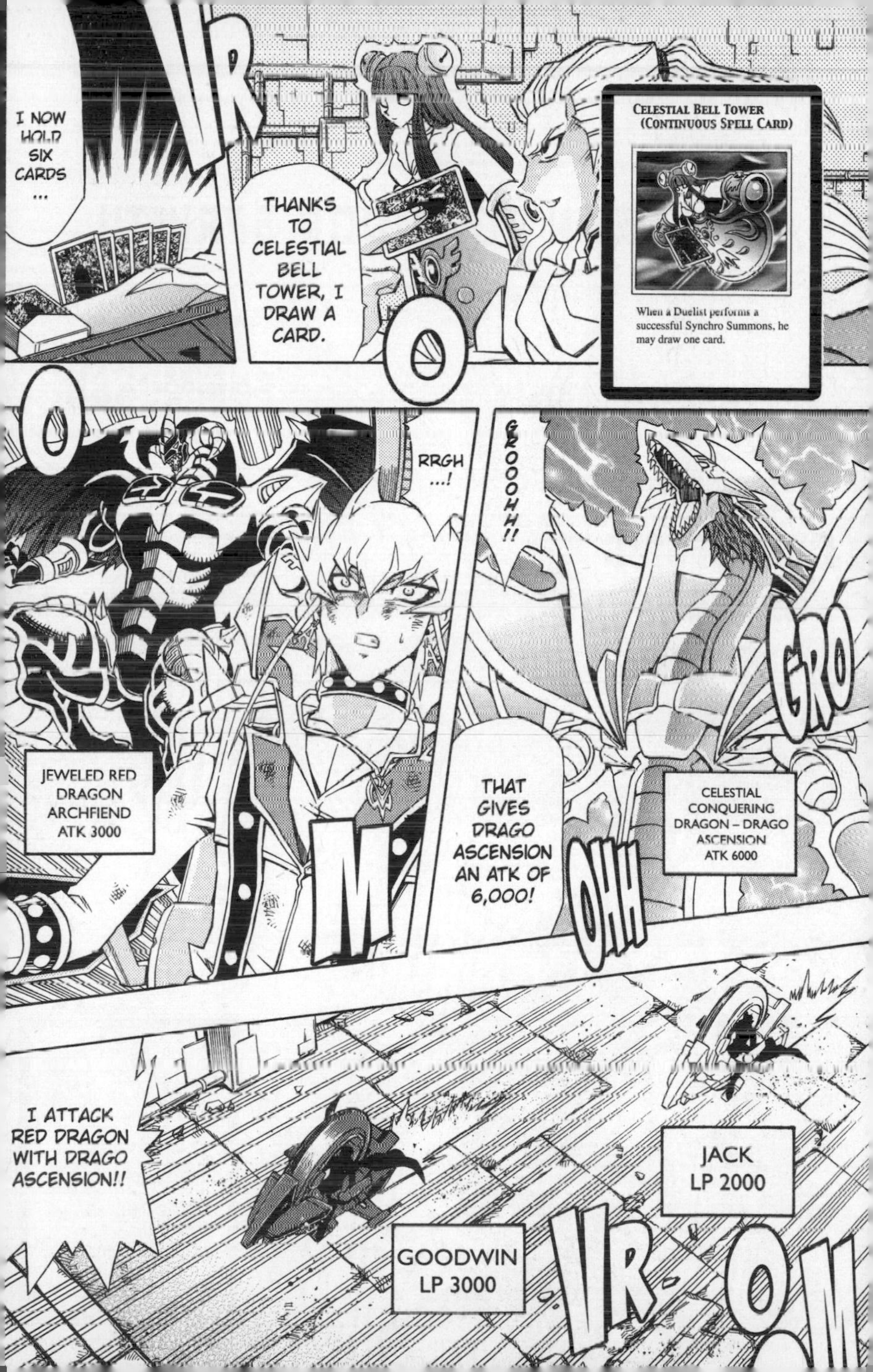
THANKS TO CELESTIAL BELL TOWER, I DRAW A CARD.
CELESTIAL BELL TOWER
(CONTINUOUS SPELL CARD)
When a Duelist performs a successful Synchro Summons, he may draw one card.
VR
O
O
I NOW HOLD SIX CARDS ...
GROOOOHH!!
GRO
OHH
CELESTIAL CONQUERING DRAGON – DRAGO ASCENSION ATK 6000
THAT GIVES DRAGO ASCENSION AN ATK OF 6,000!
RRGH ...!
M
JEWELED RED DRAGON ARCHFIEND ATK 3000
JACK LP 2000
VR
OM
GOODWIN LP 3000
I ATTACK RED DRAGON WITH DRAGO ASCENSION!!

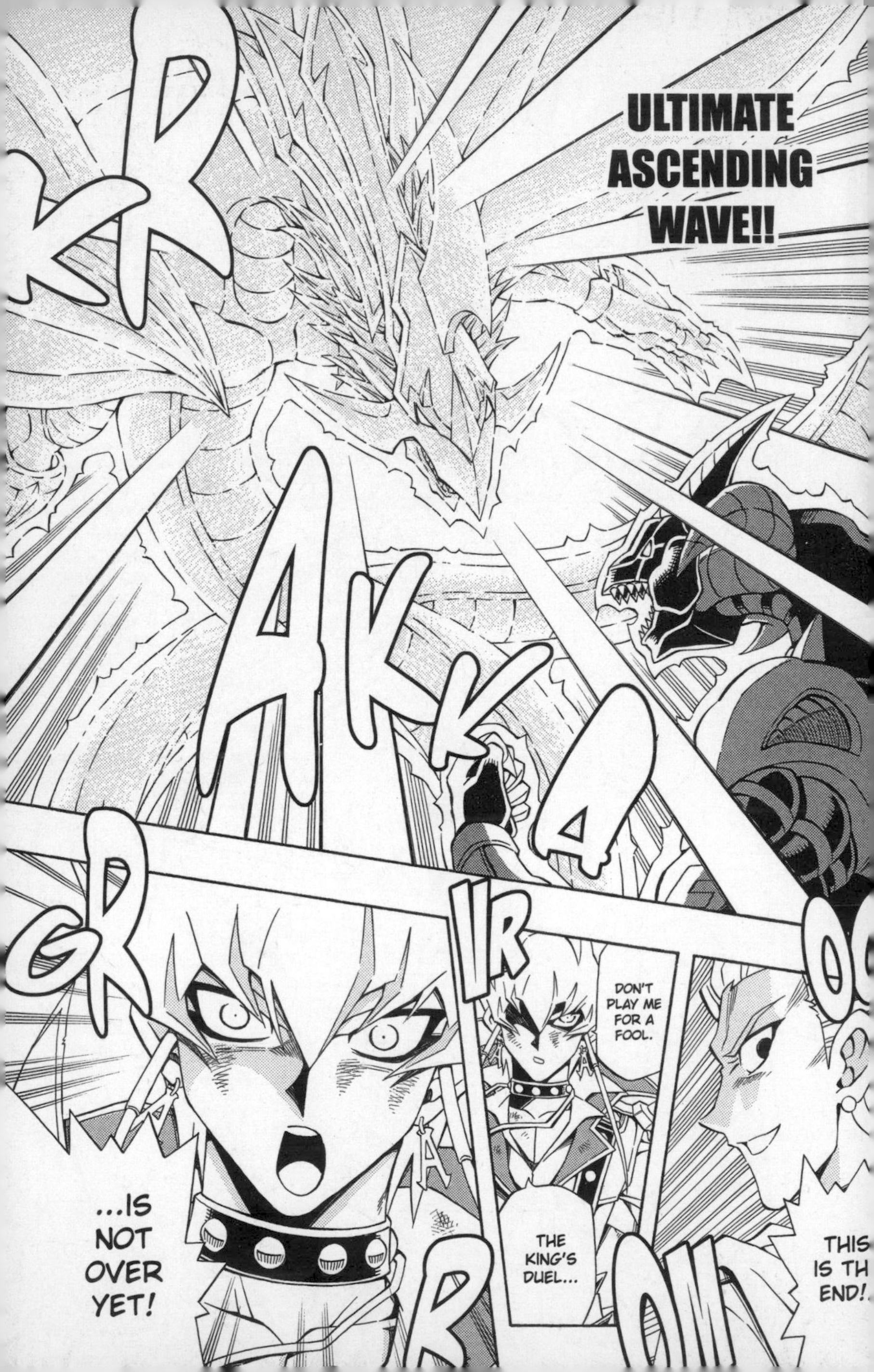
ULTIMATE ASCENDING WAVE!!
THIS IS TH END!
DON'T PLAY ME FOR A FOOL.
THE KING'S DUEL...
...IS NOT OVER YET!

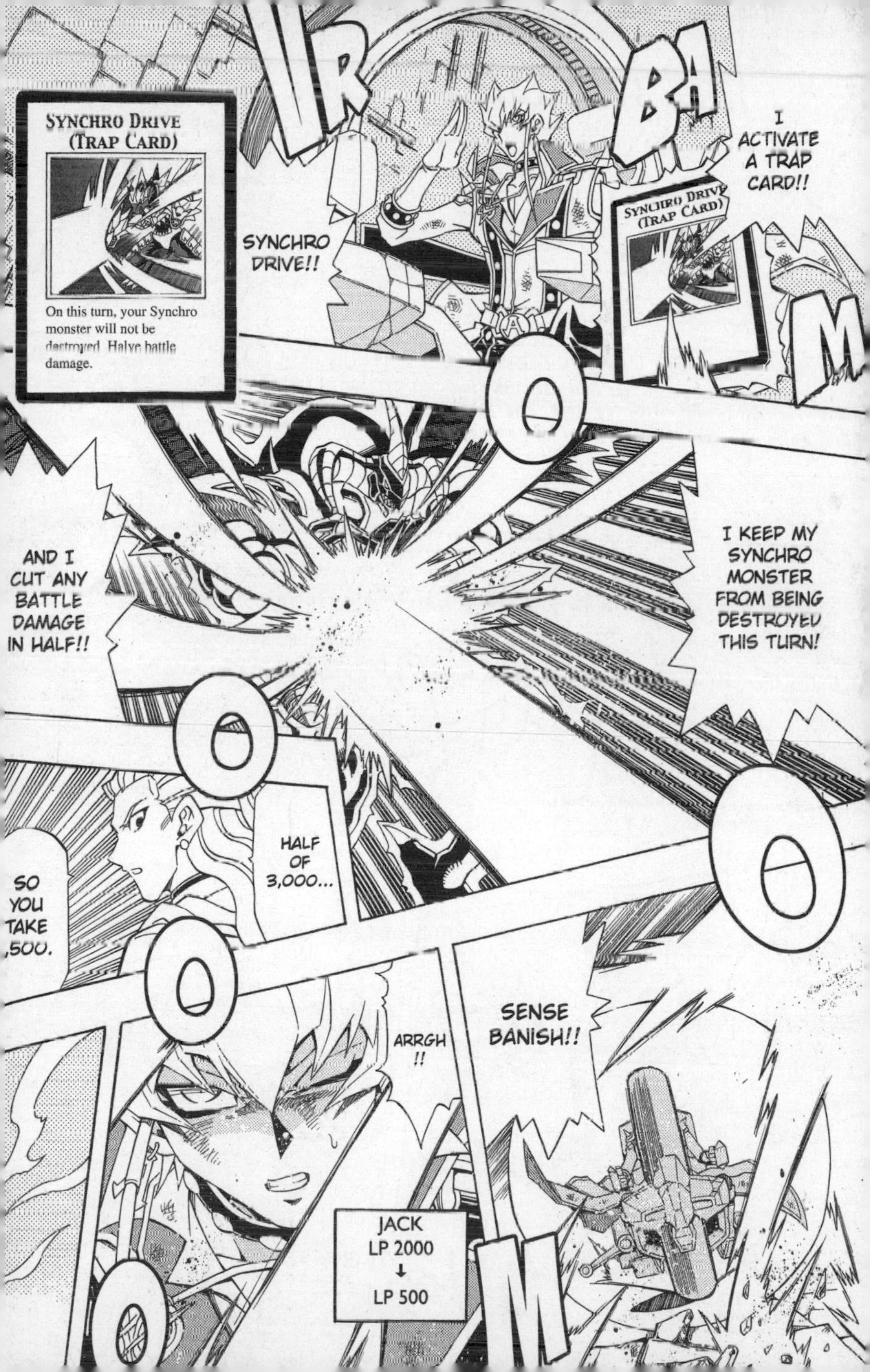
I ACTIVATE A TRAP CARD!!
SYNCHRO DRIVE!!
SYNCHRO DRIVE (TRAP CARD)
SYNCHRO DRIVE
(TRAP CARD)
On this turn, your Synchro monster will not be destroyed. Halve battle damage.
I KEEP MY SYNCHRO MONSTER FROM BEING DESTROYED THIS TURN!
AND I CUT ANY BATTLE DAMAGE IN HALF!!
HALF OF 3,000...
SO YOU TAKE ,500.
SENSE BANISH!!
ARRGH !!
JACK LP 2000 ↓ LP 500

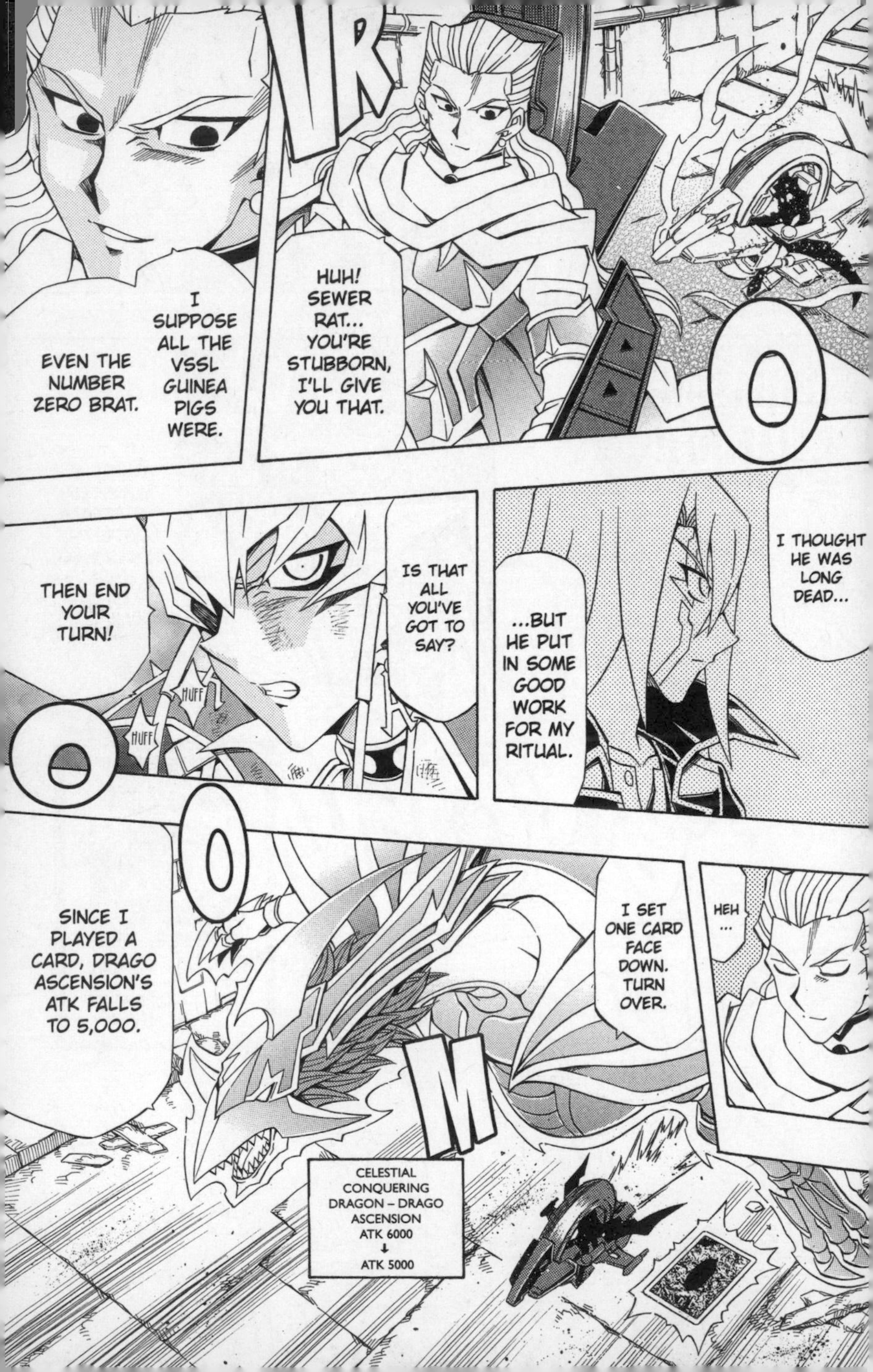
VR
O
HUH! SEWER RAT... YOU'RE STUBBORN, I'LL GIVE YOU THAT.
I SUPPOSE ALL THE VSSL GUINEA PIGS WERE.
EVEN THE NUMBER ZERO BRAT.
I THOUGHT HE WAS LONG DEAD...
...BUT HE PUT IN SOME GOOD WORK FOR MY RITUAL.
IS THAT ALL YOU'VE GOT TO SAY?
HUFF
HUFF
THEN END YOUR TURN!
O
HEH...
I SET ONE CARD FACE DOWN. TURN OVER.
O
SINCE I PLAYED A CARD, DRAGO ASCENSION'S ATK FALLS TO 5,000.
M
CELESTIAL CONQUERING DRAGON – DRAGO ASCENSION ATK 6000 ↓ ATK 5000

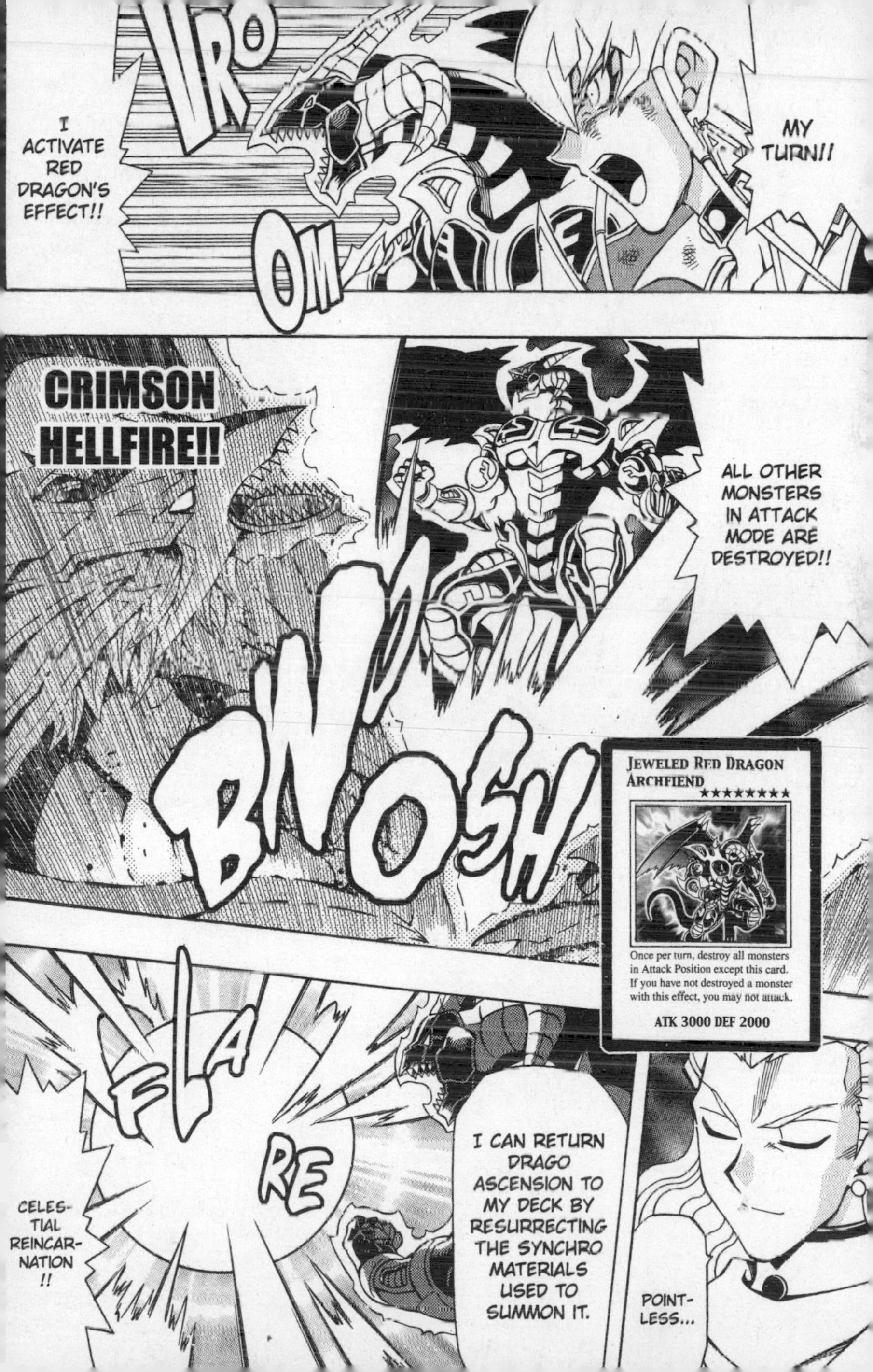
MY TURN!!
VROOM
I ACTIVATE RED DRAGON'S EFFECT!!
ALL OTHER MONSTERS IN ATTACK MODE ARE DESTROYED!!
CRIMSON HELLFIRE!!
BWOSH
JEWELED RED DRAGON ARCHFIEND
★★★★★★★★
Once per turn, destroy all monsters in Attack Position except this card. If you have not destroyed a monster with this effect, you may not attack.
ATK 3000 DEF 2000
POINTLESS...
I CAN RETURN DRAGO ASCENSION TO MY DECK BY RESURRECTING THE SYNCHRO MATERIALS USED TO SUMMON IT.
FLARE
CELESTIAL REINCARNATION!!

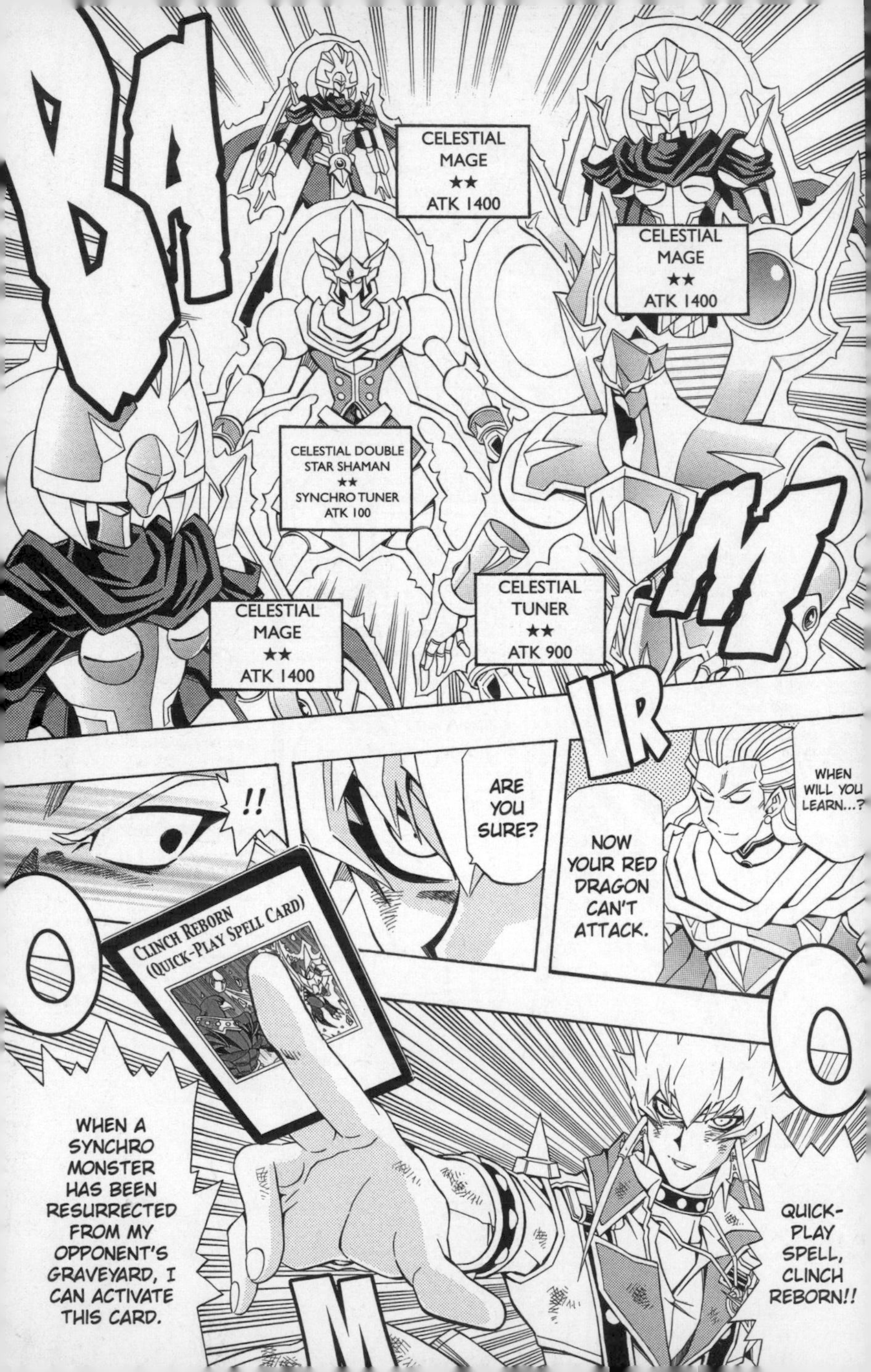
CELESTIAL MAGE ★★ ATK 1400
CELESTIAL MAGE ★★ ATK 1400
CELESTIAL DOUBLE STAR SHAMAN ★★ SYNCHRO TUNER ATK 100
CELESTIAL TUNER ★★ ATK 900
CELESTIAL MAGE ★★ ATK 1400
BA
M
VR
WHEN WILL YOU LEARN...?
NOW YOUR RED DRAGON CAN'T ATTACK.
ARE YOU SURE?
!!
QUICK-PLAY SPELL, CLINCH REBORN!!
CLINCH REBORN (QUICK-PLAY SPELL CARD)
WHEN A SYNCHRO MONSTER HAS BEEN RESURRECTED FROM MY OPPONENT'S GRAVEYARD, I CAN ACTIVATE THIS CARD.
M

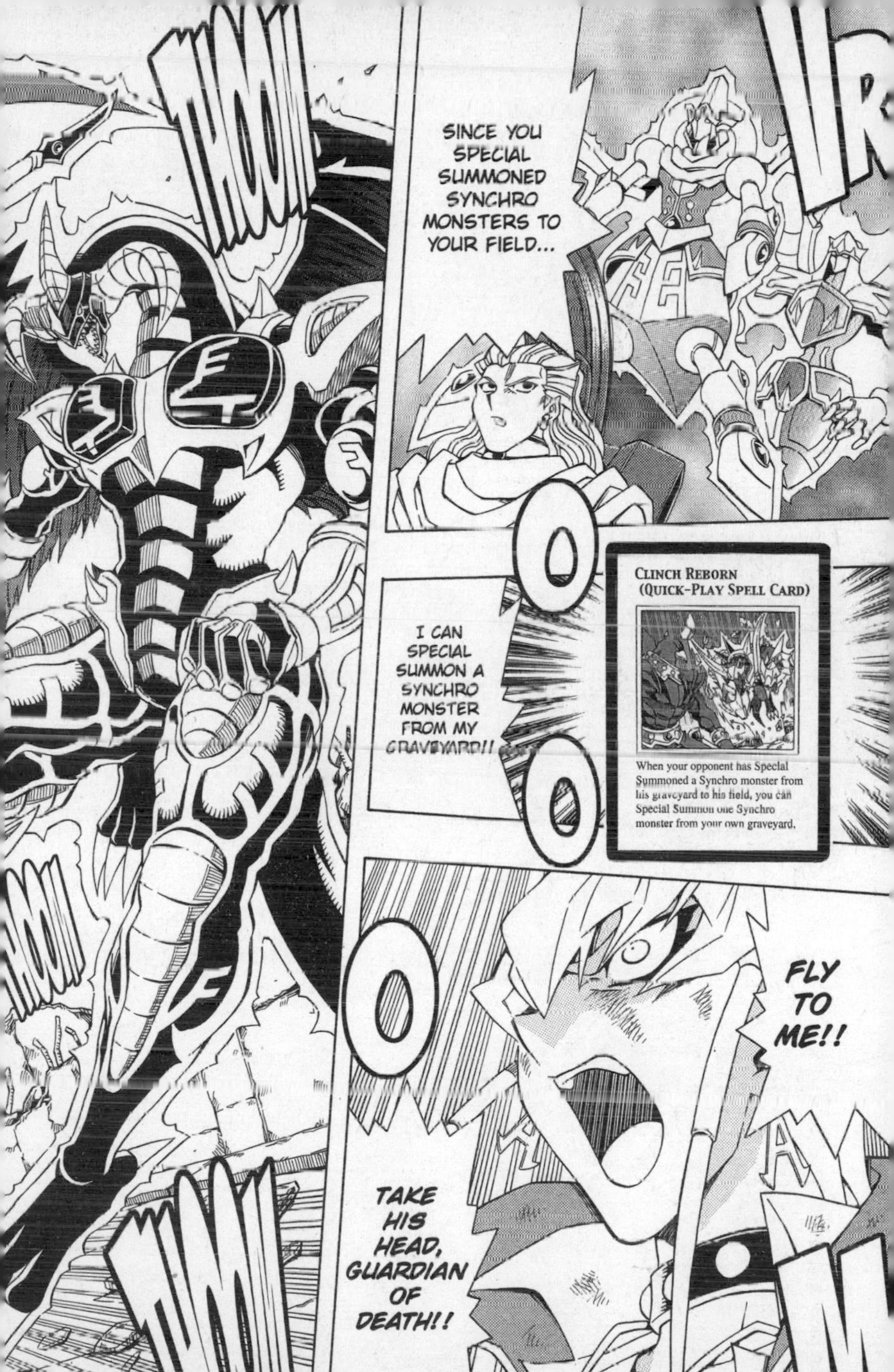
SINCE YOU SPECIAL SUMMONED SYNCHRO MONSTERS TO YOUR FIELD...
I CAN SPECIAL SUMMON A SYNCHRO MONSTER FROM MY GRAVEYARD!!
CLINCH REBORN
(QUICK-PLAY SPELL CARD)
When your opponent has Special Summoned a Synchro monster from his graveyard to his field, you can Special Summon one Synchro monster from your own graveyard.
FLY TO ME!!
TAKE HIS HEAD, GUARDIAN OF DEATH!!
THOOM!
THOOM
THOOM

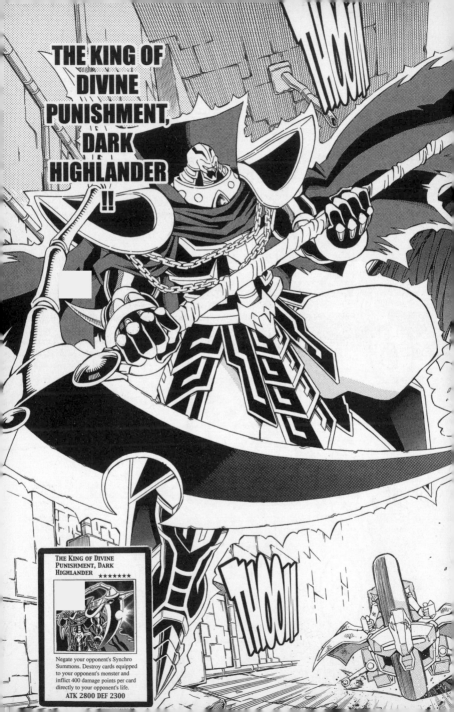

THE KING OF DIVINE PUNISHMENT, DARK HIGHLANDER!!

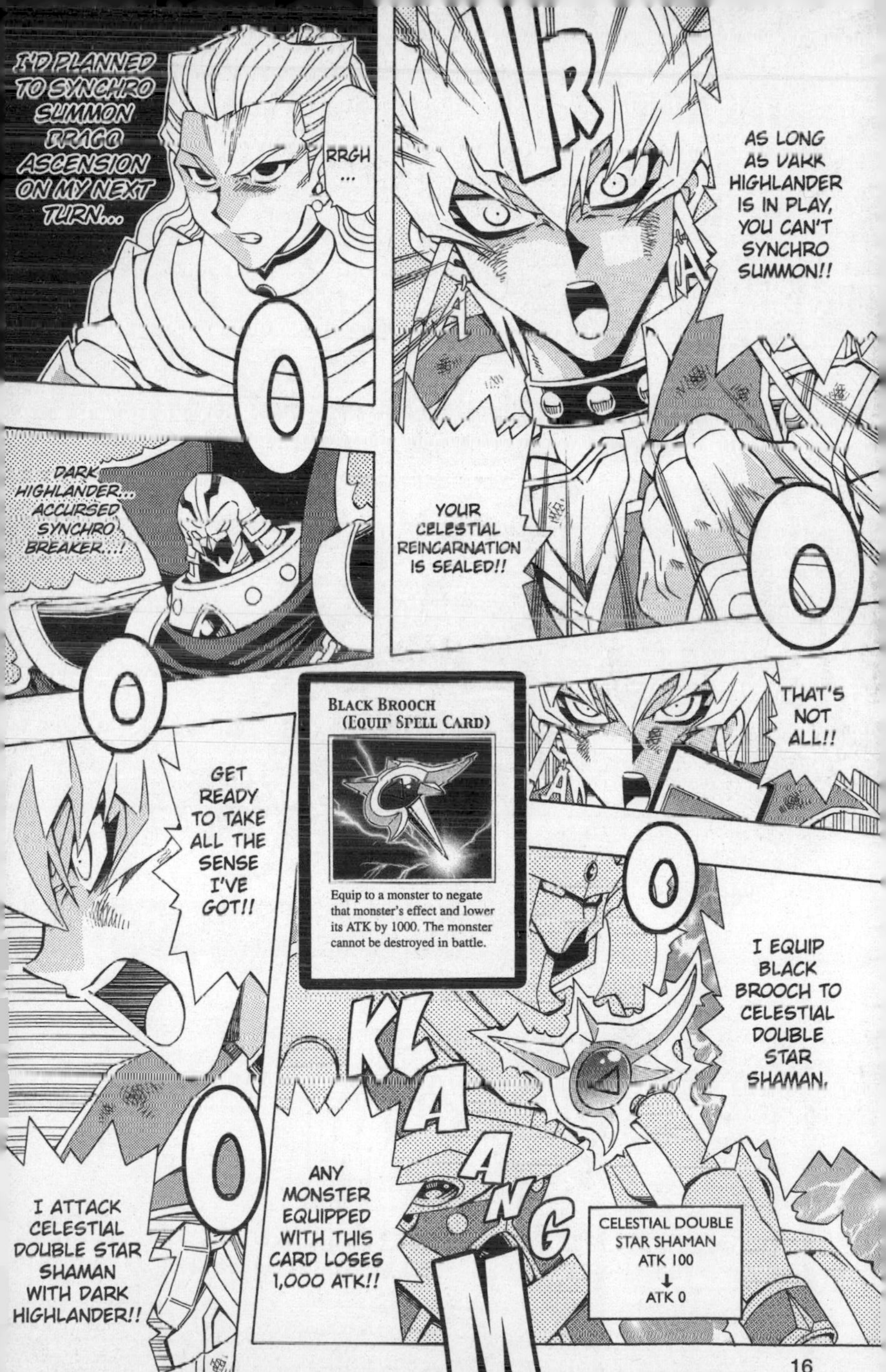
VRR
AS LONG AS DARK HIGHLANDER IS IN PLAY, YOU CAN'T SYNCHRO SUMMON!!
YOUR CELESTIAL REINCARNATION IS SEALED!!
RRGH...
I'D PLANNED TO SYNCHRO SUMMON DRAGO ASCENSION ON MY NEXT TURN...
DARK HIGHLANDER... ACCURSED SYNCHRO BREAKER...!
THAT'S NOT ALL!!
BLACK BROOCH (EQUIP SPELL CARD)
Equip to a monster to negate that monster's effect and lower its ATK by 1000. The monster cannot be destroyed in battle.
I EQUIP BLACK BROOCH TO CELESTIAL DOUBLE STAR SHAMAN.
KLAANGM
CELESTIAL DOUBLE STAR SHAMAN ATK 100 ↓ ATK 0
ANY MONSTER EQUIPPED WITH THIS CARD LOSES 1,000 ATK!!
GET READY TO TAKE ALL THE SENSE I'VE GOT!!
I ATTACK CELESTIAL DOUBLE STAR SHAMAN WITH DARK HIGHLANDER!!

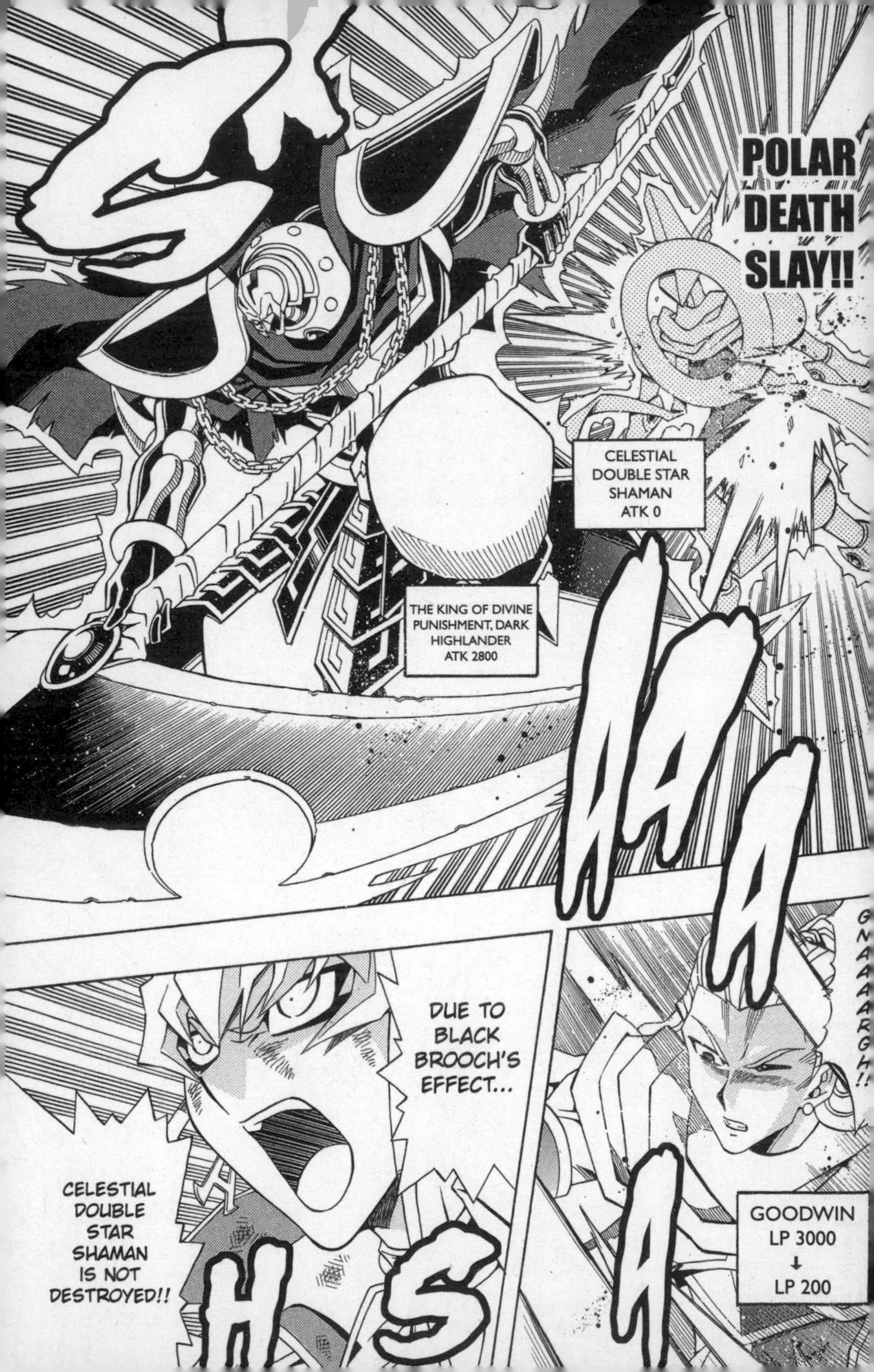
POLAR DEATH SLAY!!
CELESTIAL DOUBLE STAR SHAMAN ATK 0
THE KING OF DIVINE PUNISHMENT, DARK HIGHLANDER ATK 2800
GNAAAAARGH!!
GOODWIN LP 3000 ↓ LP 200
DUE TO BLACK BROOCH'S EFFECT...
CELESTIAL DOUBLE STAR SHAMAN IS NOT DESTROYED!!

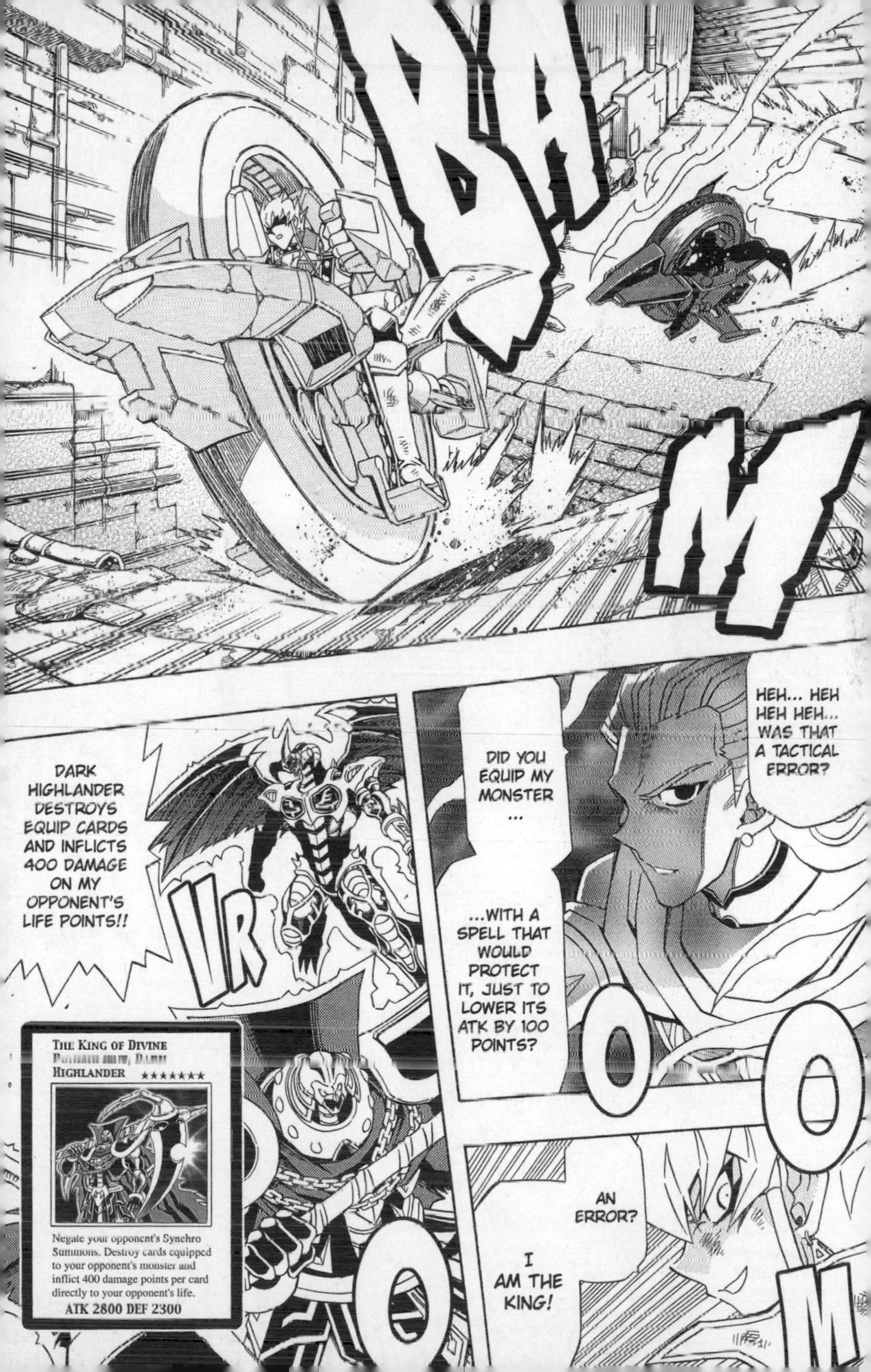

BAM
HEH... HEH HEH HEH... WAS THAT A TACTICAL ERROR?
DID YOU EQUIP MY MONSTER ...
...WITH A SPELL THAT WOULD PROTECT IT, JUST TO LOWER ITS ATK BY 100 POINTS?
AN ERROR?
I AM THE KING!
DARK HIGHLANDER DESTROYS EQUIP CARDS AND INFLICTS 400 DAMAGE ON MY OPPONENT'S LIFE POINTS!!
VROOOOM
THE KING OF DIVINE
HIGHLANDER ★★★★★★★
Negate your opponent's Synchro Summons. Destroy cards equipped to your opponent's monster and inflict 400 damage points per card directly to your opponent's life.
ATK 2800 DEF 2300

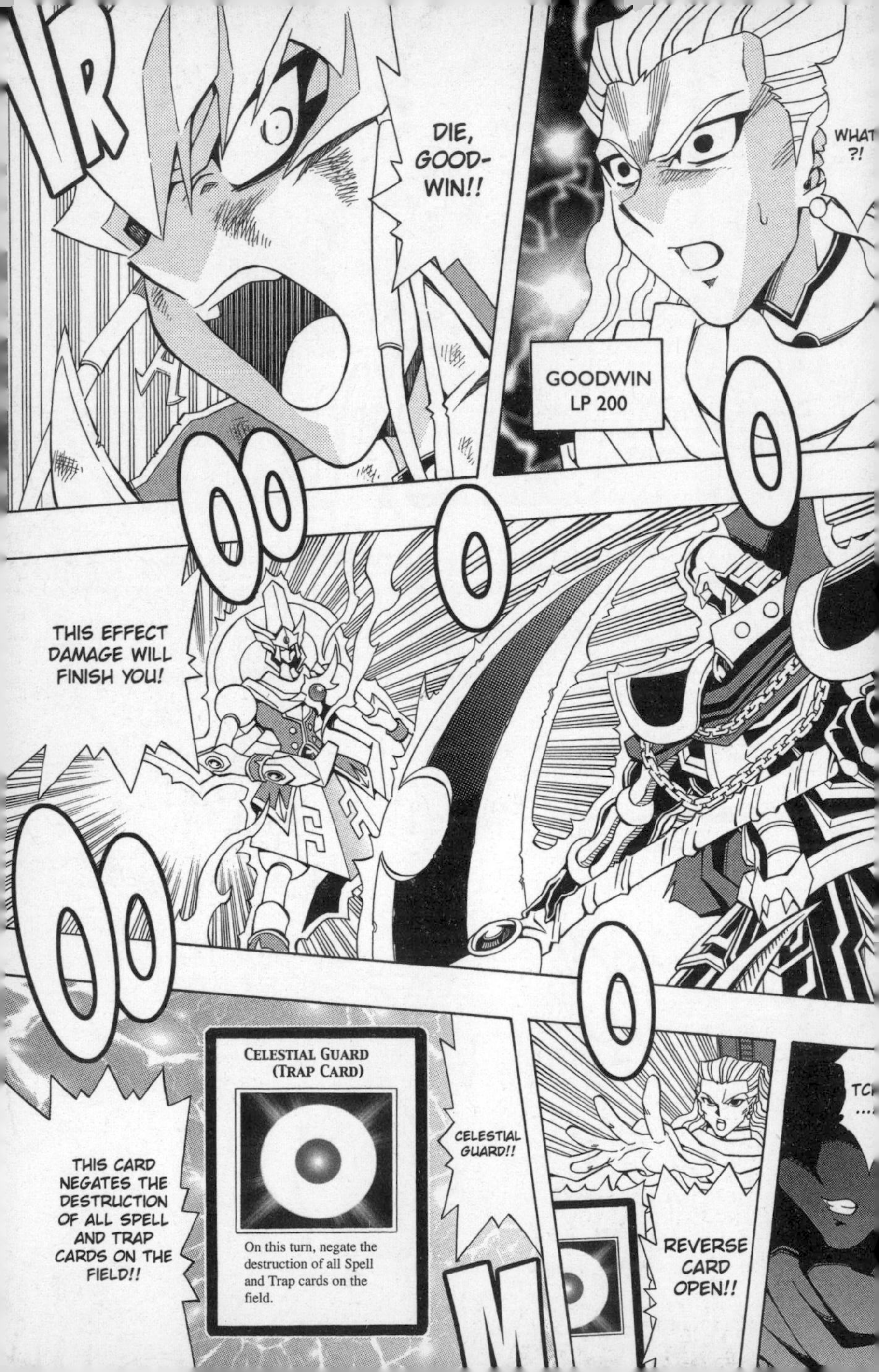

WHAT ?!
GOODWIN LP 200
DIE, GOOD-WIN!!
THIS EFFECT DAMAGE WILL FINISH YOU!
REVERSE CARD OPEN!!
CELESTIAL GUARD!!
CELESTIAL GUARD (TRAP CARD)
On this turn, negate the destruction of all Spell and Trap cards on the field.
THIS CARD NEGATES THE DESTRUCTION OF ALL SPELL AND TRAP CARDS ON THE FIELD!!

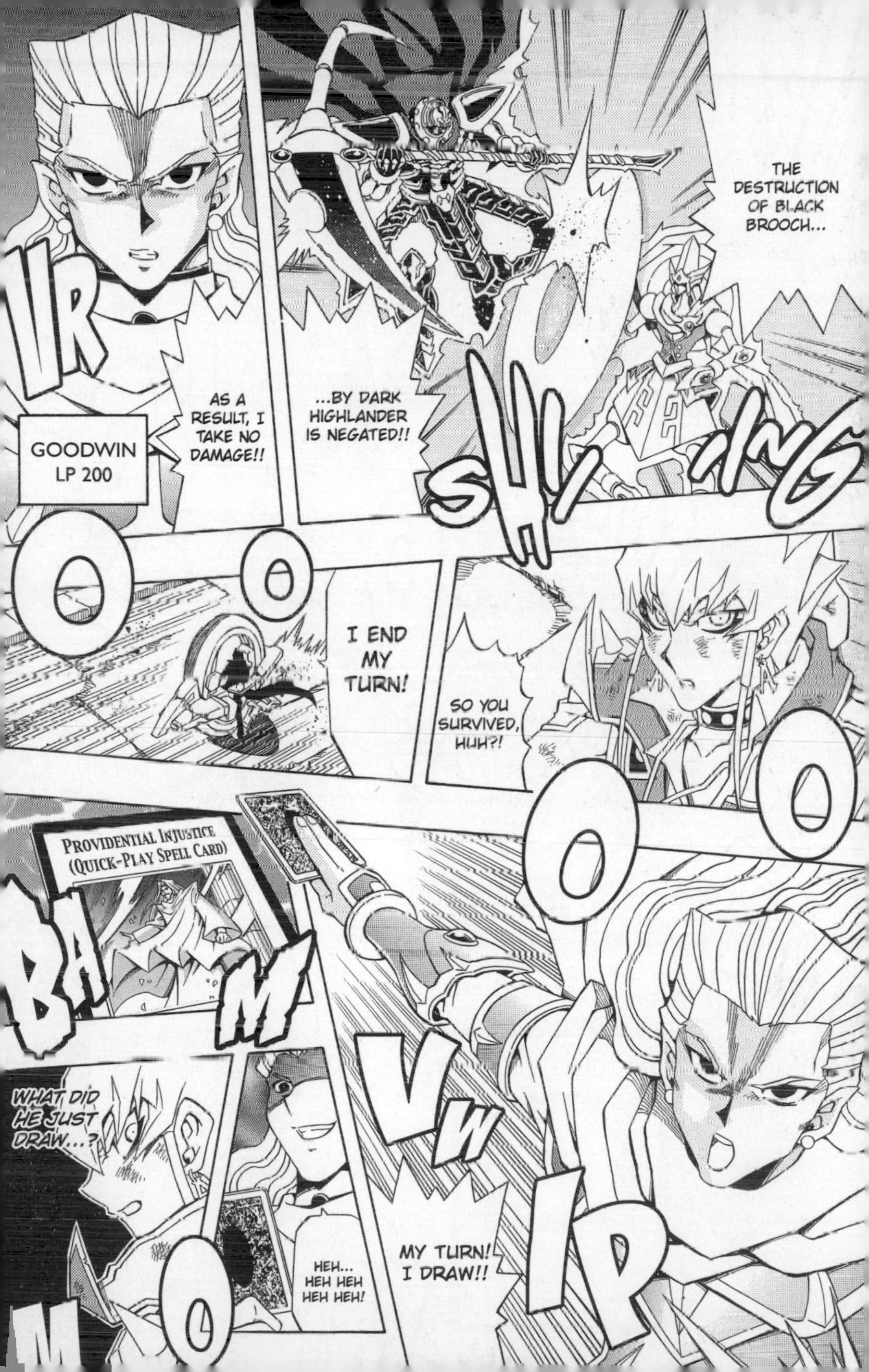
THE DESTRUCTION OF BLACK BROOCH...
...BY DARK HIGHLANDER IS NEGATED!!
SHING
AS A RESULT, I TAKE NO DAMAGE!!
GOODWIN LP 200
SO YOU SURVIVED, HUH?!
I END MY TURN!
MY TURN! I DRAW!!
VWIP
PROVIDENTIAL INJUSTICE (QUICK-PLAY SPELL CARD)
BAM
HEH... HEH HEH HEH HEH!
WHAT DID HE JUST DRAW...?

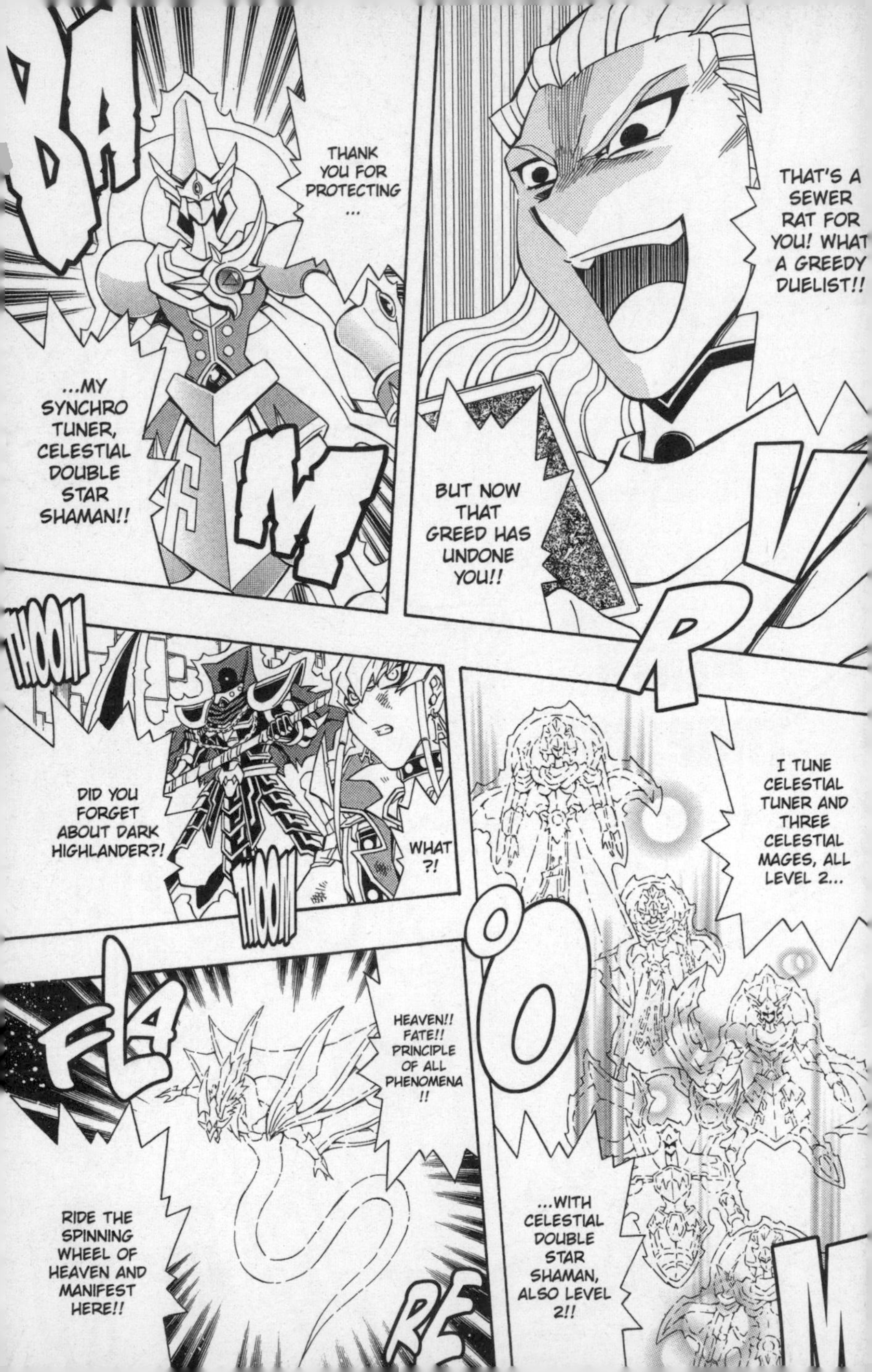
THAT'S A SEWER RAT FOR YOU! WHAT A GREEDY DUELIST!!
BUT NOW THAT GREED HAS UNDONE YOU!!
THANK YOU FOR PROTECTING ...
...MY SYNCHRO TUNER, CELESTIAL DOUBLE STAR SHAMAN!!
I TUNE CELESTIAL TUNER AND THREE CELESTIAL MAGES, ALL LEVEL 2...
...WITH CELESTIAL DOUBLE STAR SHAMAN, ALSO LEVEL 2!!
THOOM
WHAT ?!
DID YOU FORGET ABOUT DARK HIGHLANDER?!
THOOM
HEAVEN!! FATE!! PRINCIPLE OF ALL PHENOMENA !!
RIDE THE SPINNING WHEEL OF HEAVEN AND MANIFEST HERE!!

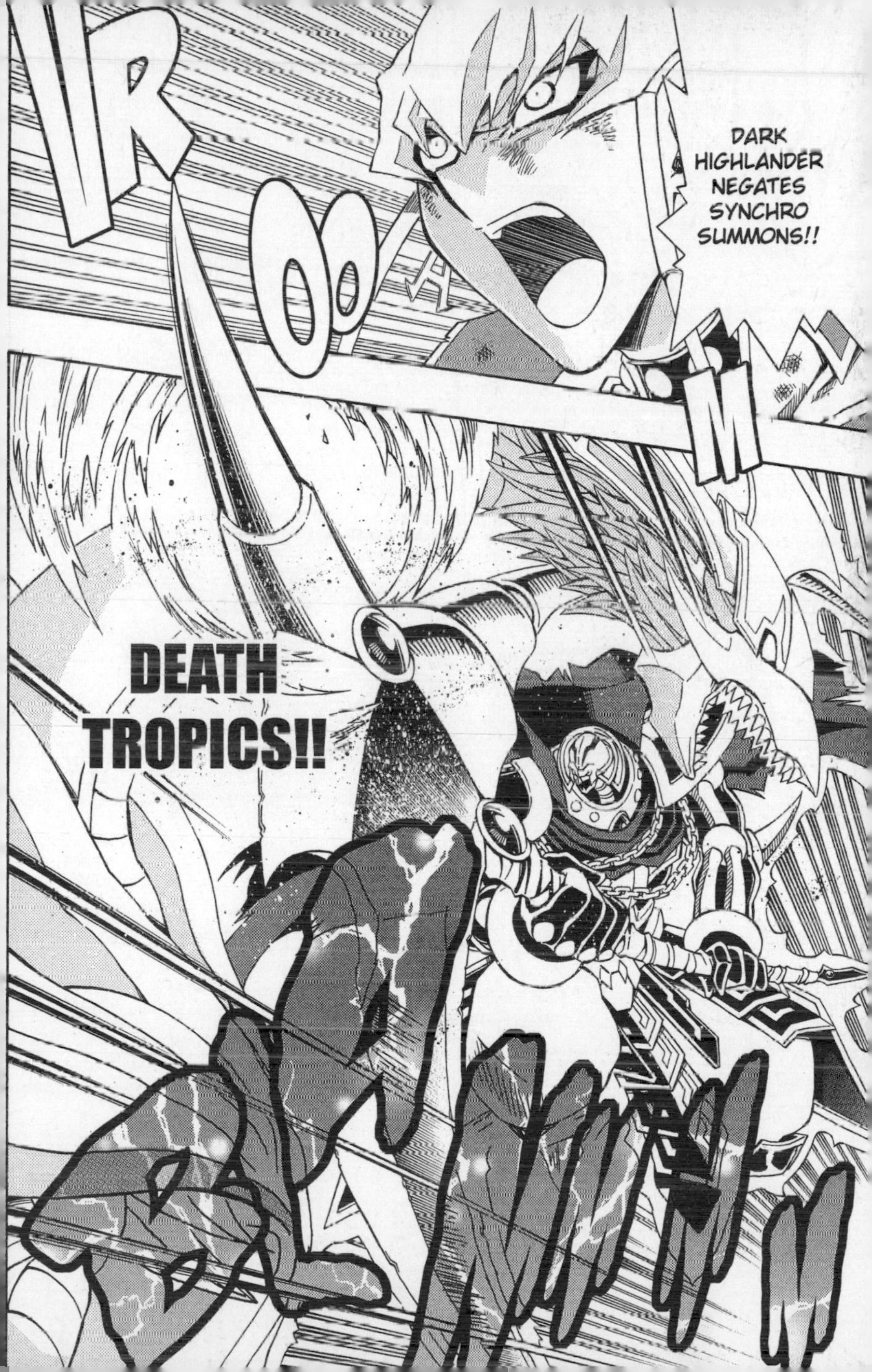
DARK HIGHLANDER NEGATES SYNCHRO SUMMONS!!
DEATH TROPICS!!

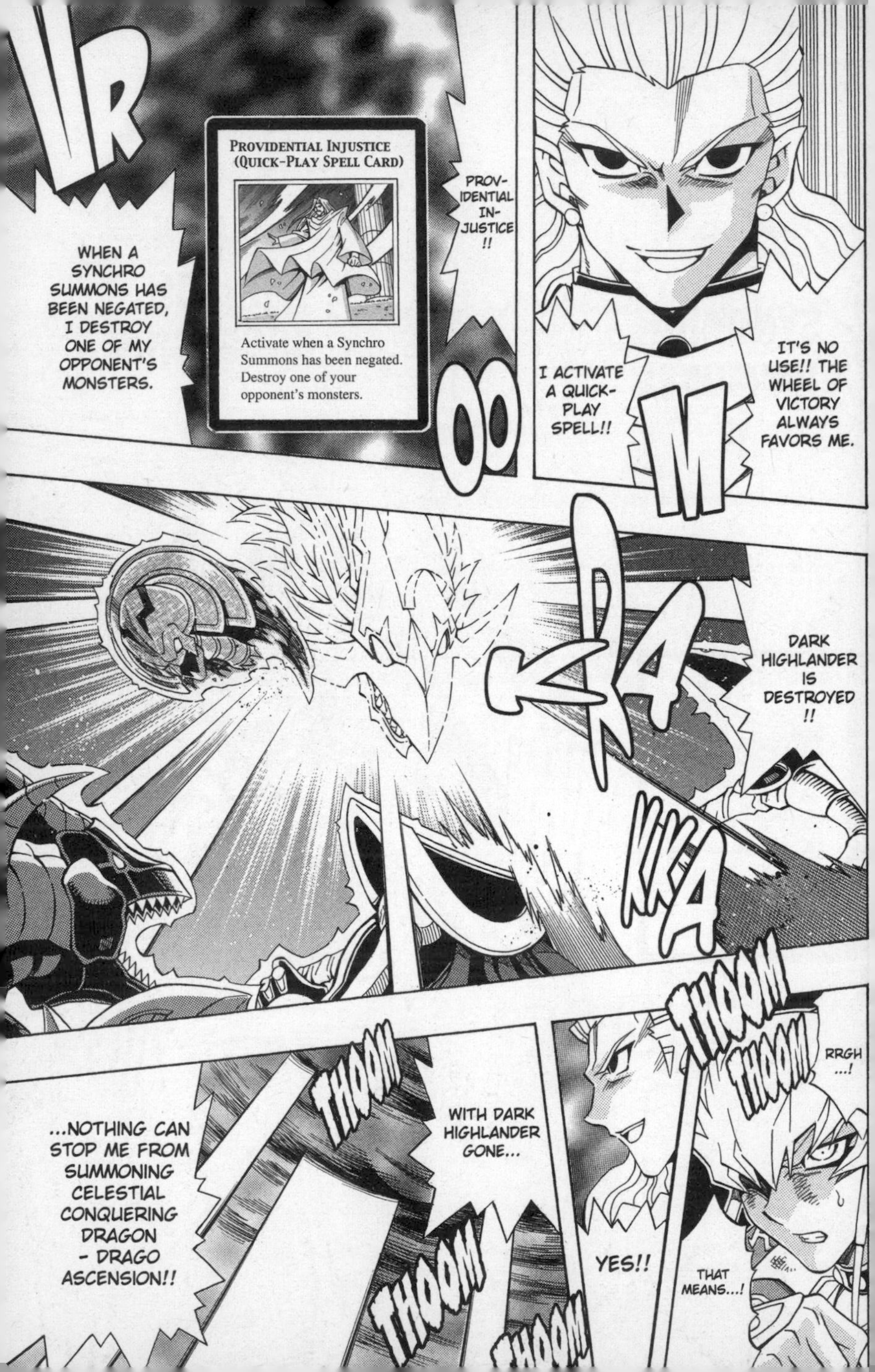
IT'S NO USE!! THE WHEEL OF VICTORY ALWAYS FAVORS ME.
I ACTIVATE A QUICK-PLAY SPELL!!
M
PROV-IDENTIAL IN-JUSTICE!!
OO
VR
PROVIDENTIAL INJUSTICE (QUICK-PLAY SPELL CARD)
Activate when a Synchro Summons has been negated. Destroy one of your opponent's monsters.
WHEN A SYNCHRO SUMMONS HAS BEEN NEGATED, I DESTROY ONE OF MY OPPONENT'S MONSTERS.
DARK HIGHLANDER IS DESTROYED!!
KRA
KKA
RRGH...!
THOOM
THOOM
YES!!
THAT MEANS...!
THOOM
WITH DARK HIGHLANDER GONE...
...NOTHING CAN STOP ME FROM SUMMONING CELESTIAL CONQUERING DRAGON - DRAGO ASCENSION!!
THOOM

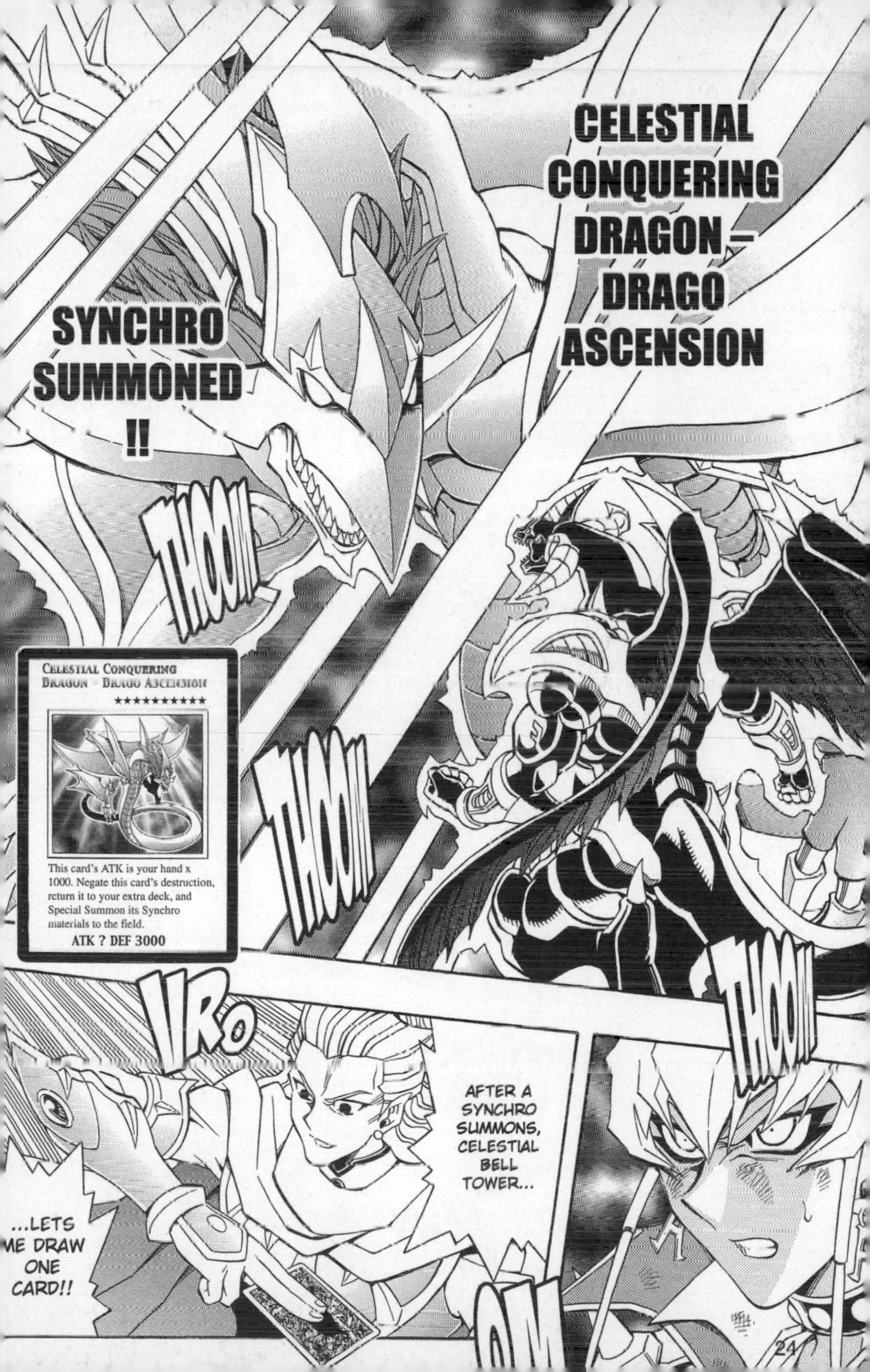
CELESTIAL CONQUERING DRAGON – DRAGO ASCENSION
SYNCHRO SUMMONED!!
THOOM
THOOM
THOOM
CELESTIAL CONQUERING DRAGON – DRAGO ASCENSION
★★★★★★★★★★★
This card's ATK is your hand x 1000. Negate this card's destruction, return it to your extra deck, and Special Summon its Synchro materials to the field.
ATK ? DEF 3000
AFTER A SYNCHRO SUMMONS, CELESTIAL BELL TOWER...
VRO
...LETS ME DRAW ONE CARD!!

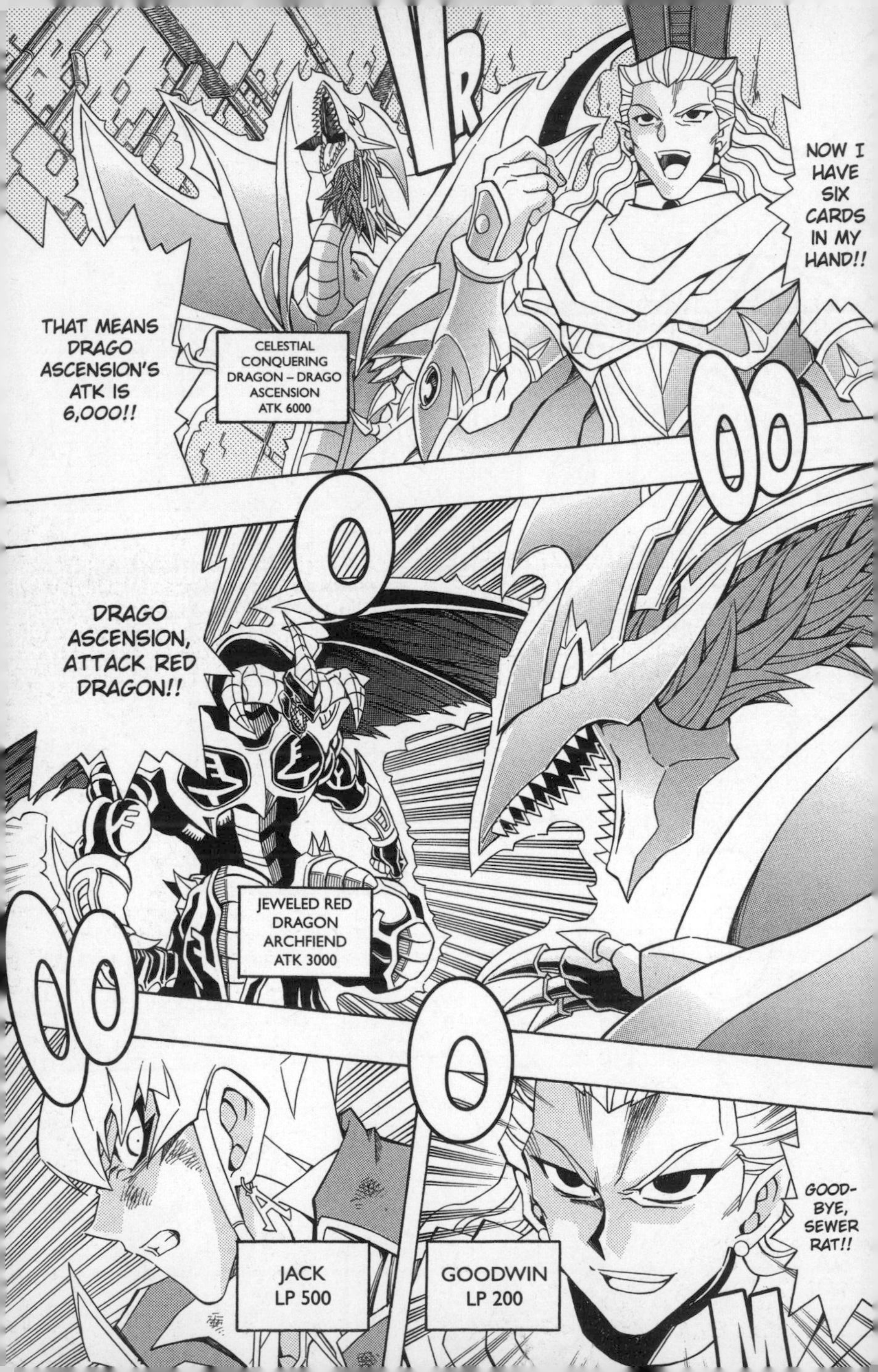
NOW I HAVE SIX CARDS IN MY HAND!!
THAT MEANS DRAGO ASCENSION'S ATK IS 6,000!!
CELESTIAL CONQUERING DRAGON – DRAGO ASCENSION ATK 6000
DRAGO ASCENSION, ATTACK RED DRAGON!!
JEWELED RED DRAGON ARCHFIEND ATK 3000
GOOD-BYE, SEWER RAT!!
GOODWIN LP 200
JACK LP 500

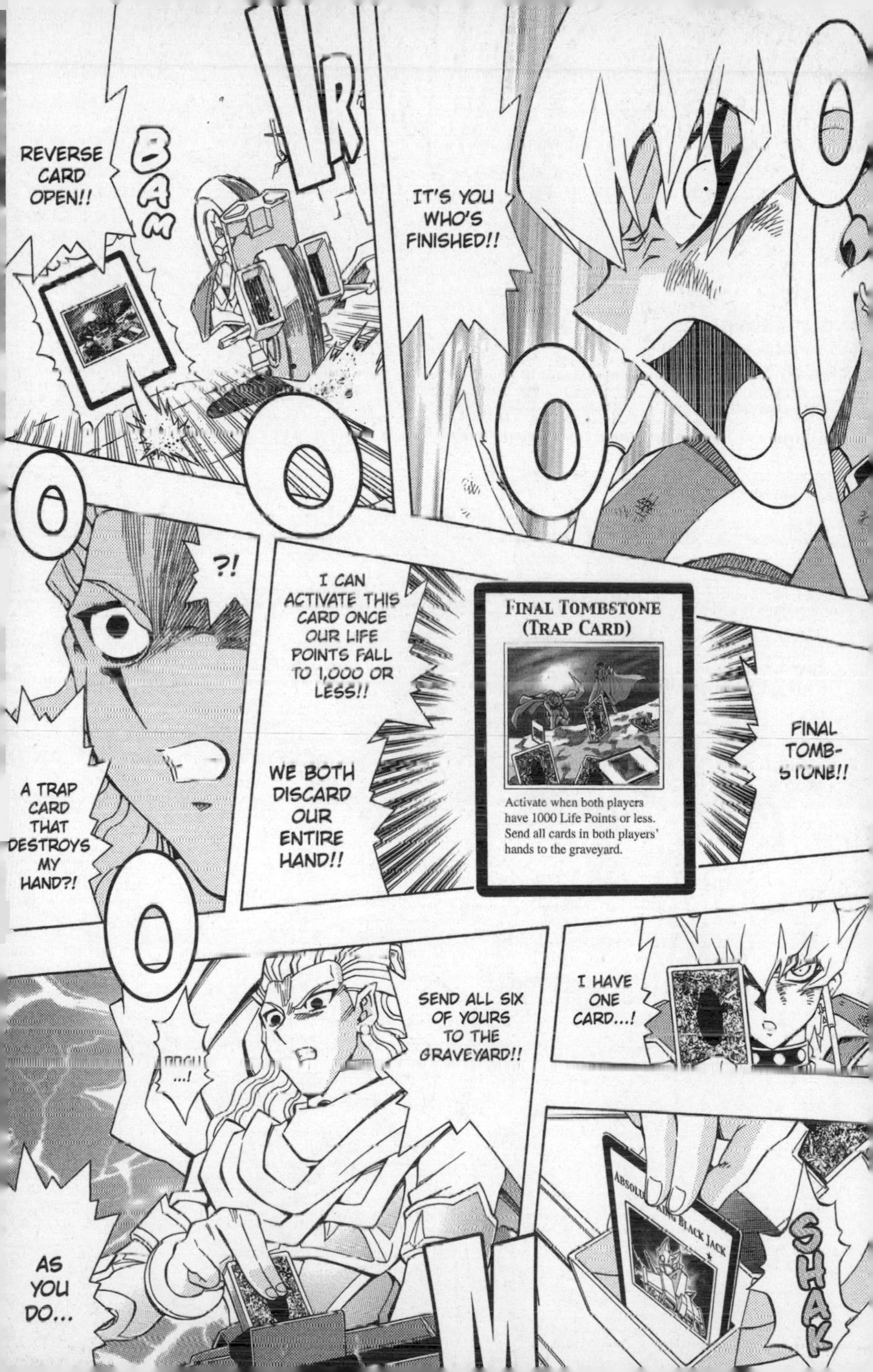
IT'S YOU WHO'S FINISHED!!
REVERSE CARD OPEN!!
BAM
FINAL TOMB-STONE!!
FINAL TOMBSTONE (TRAP CARD)
Activate when both players have 1000 Life Points or less. Send all cards in both players' hands to the graveyard.
I CAN ACTIVATE THIS CARD ONCE OUR LIFE POINTS FALL TO 1,000 OR LESS!!
WE BOTH DISCARD OUR ENTIRE HAND!!
?!
A TRAP CARD THAT DESTROYS MY HAND?!
I HAVE ONE CARD...!
SEND ALL SIX OF YOURS TO THE GRAVEYARD!!
AS YOU DO...
SHAK

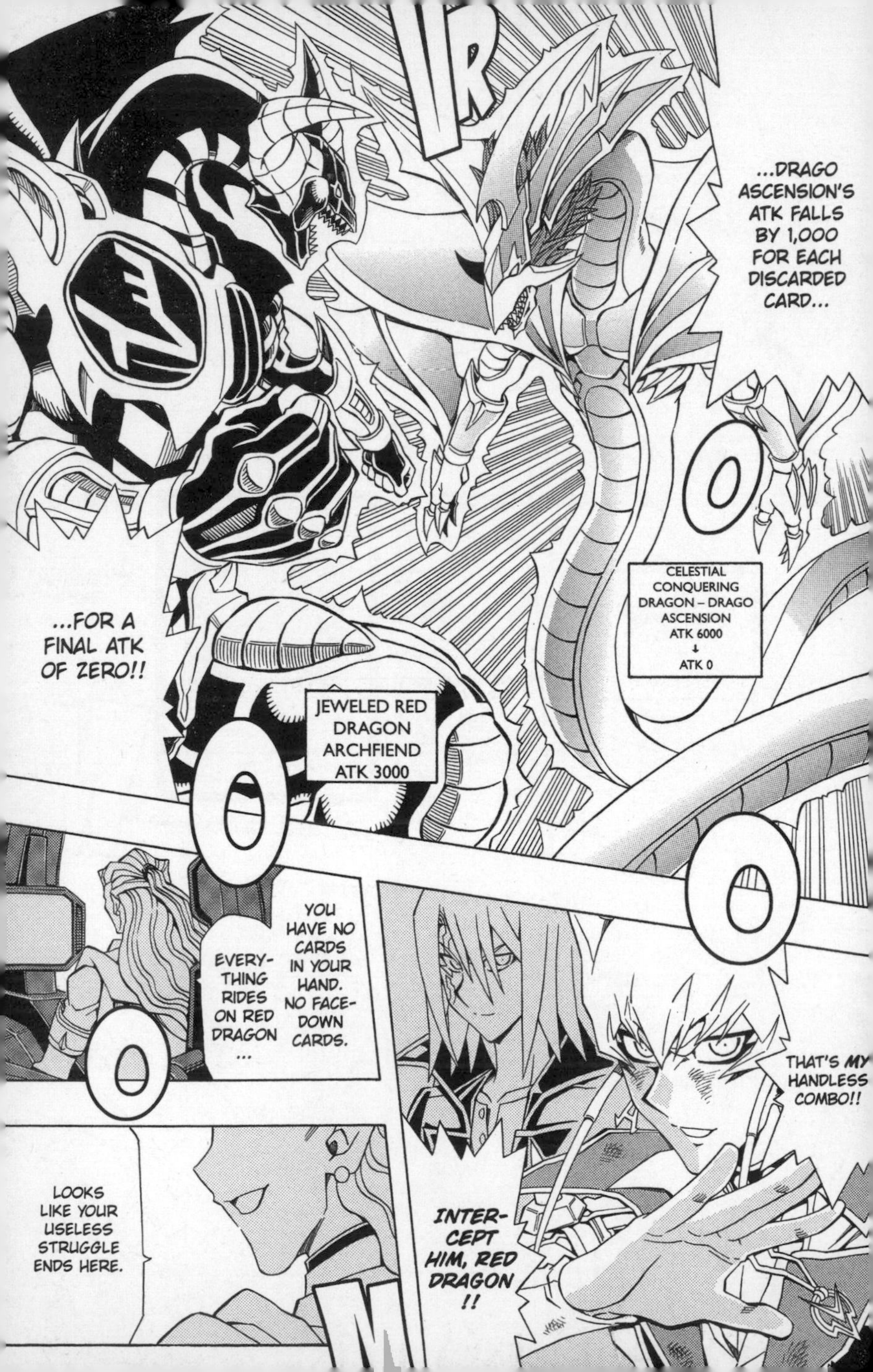
VR
...DRAGO ASCENSION'S ATK FALLS BY 1,000 FOR EACH DISCARDED CARD...
CELESTIAL CONQUERING DRAGON – DRAGO ASCENSION ATK 6000 ↓ ATK 0
JEWELED RED DRAGON ARCHFIEND ATK 3000
...FOR A FINAL ATK OF ZERO!!
O
O
O
O
THAT'S MY HANDLESS COMBO!!
INTERCEPT HIM, RED DRAGON!!
YOU HAVE NO CARDS IN YOUR HAND. NO FACE-DOWN CARDS.
EVERYTHING RIDES ON RED DRAGON...
LOOKS LIKE YOUR USELESS STRUGGLE ENDS HERE.
M

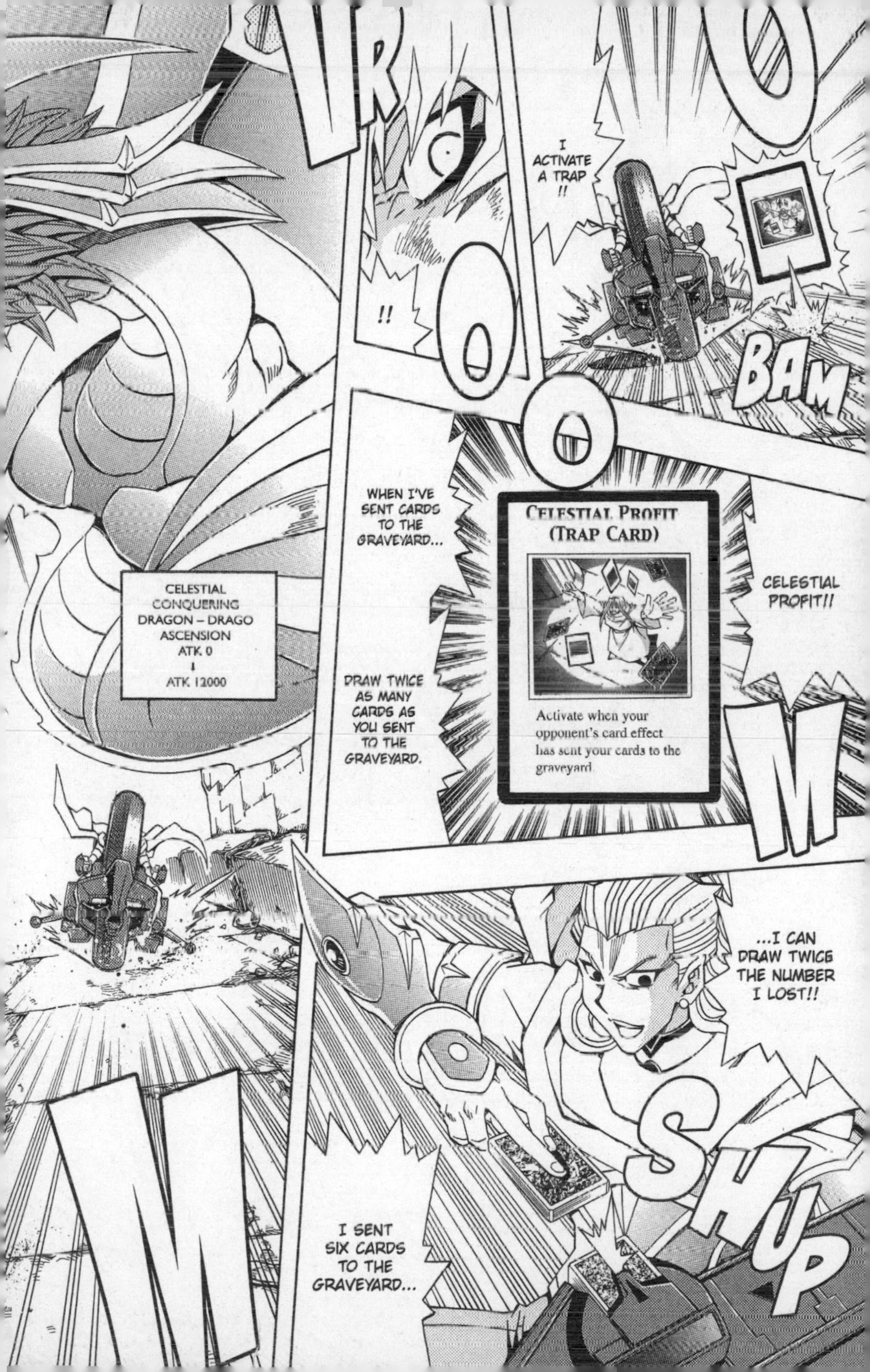

I ACTIVATE A TRAP!!
BAM
!!
CELESTIAL PROFIT!!
WHEN I'VE SENT CARDS TO THE GRAVEYARD...
CELESTIAL PROFIT (TRAP CARD)
Activate when your opponent's card effect has sent your cards to the graveyard.
DRAW TWICE AS MANY CARDS AS YOU SENT TO THE GRAVEYARD.
...I CAN DRAW TWICE THE NUMBER I LOST!!
SHUP
I SENT SIX CARDS TO THE GRAVEYARD...
CELESTIAL CONQUERING DRAGON – DRAGO ASCENSION ATK 0 ↓ ATK 12000

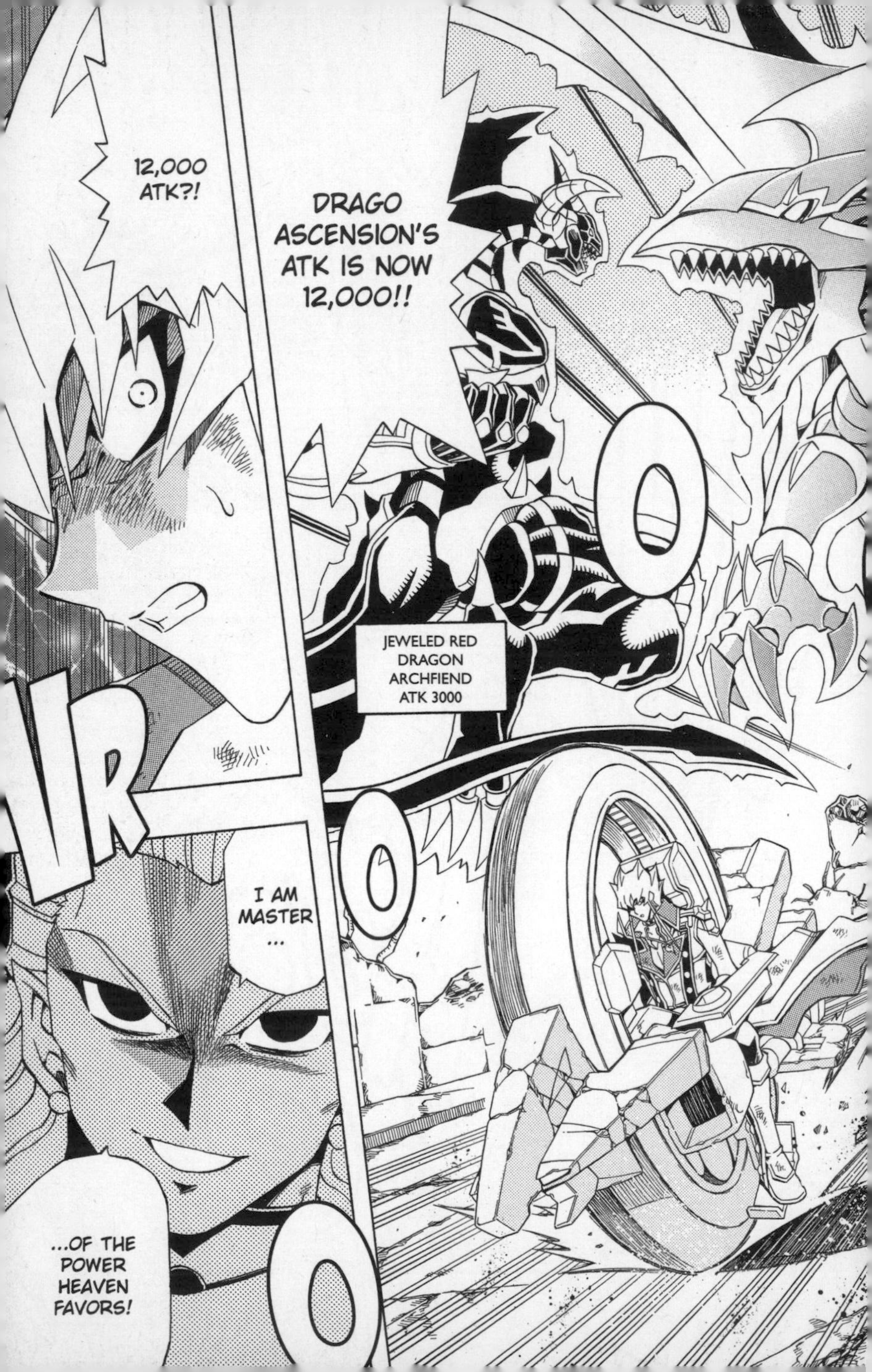
DRAGO ASCENSION'S ATK IS NOW 12,000!!
JEWELED RED DRAGON ARCHFIEND ATK 3000
12,000 ATK?!
VR
I AM MASTER ...
...OF THE POWER HEAVEN FAVORS!

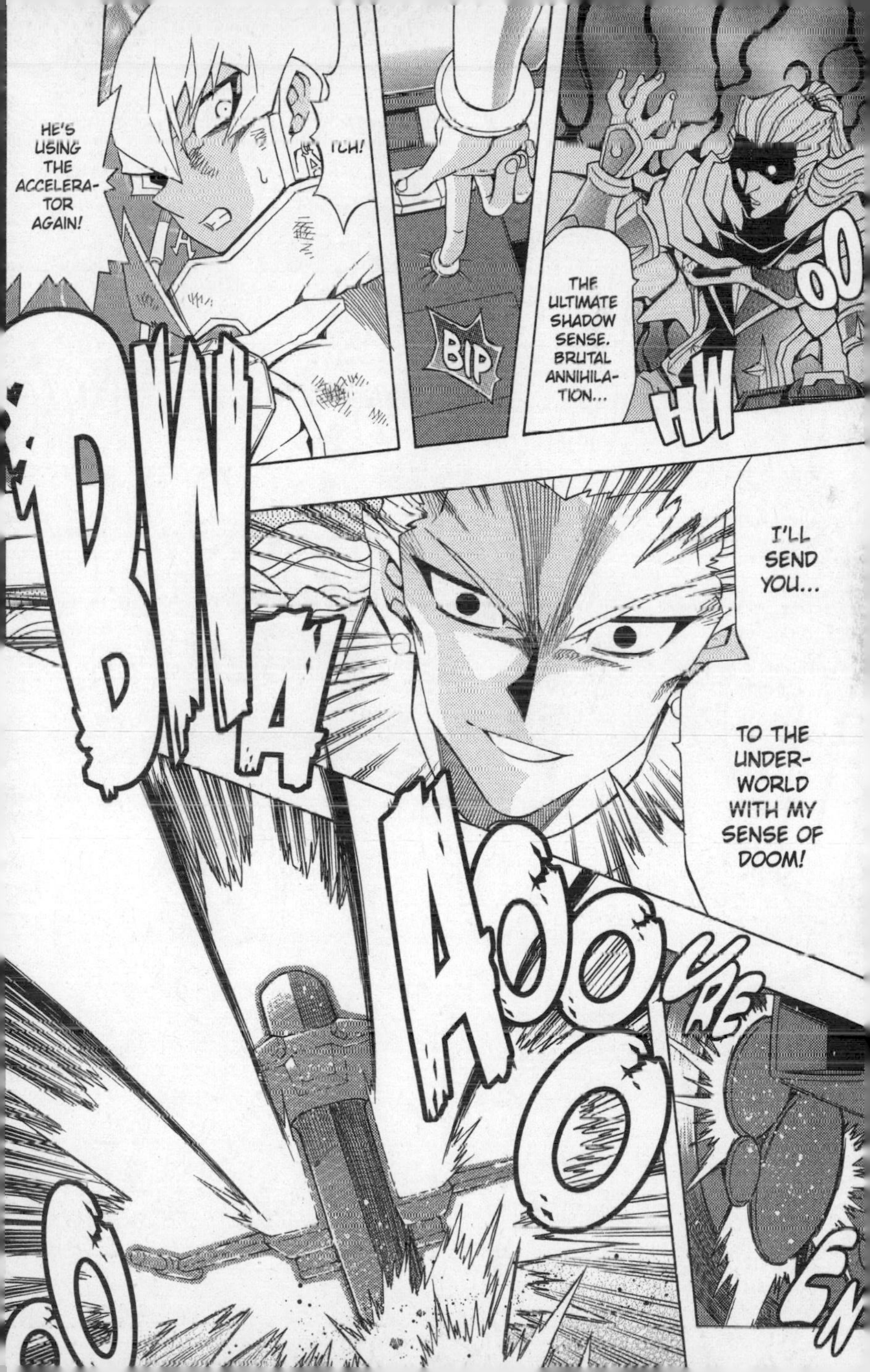
THE ULTIMATE SHADOW SENSE. BRUTAL ANNIHILATION...
BIP
HE'S USING THE ACCELERATOR AGAIN!
ICH!
I'LL SEND YOU...
TO THE UNDERWORLD WITH MY SENSE OF DOOM!

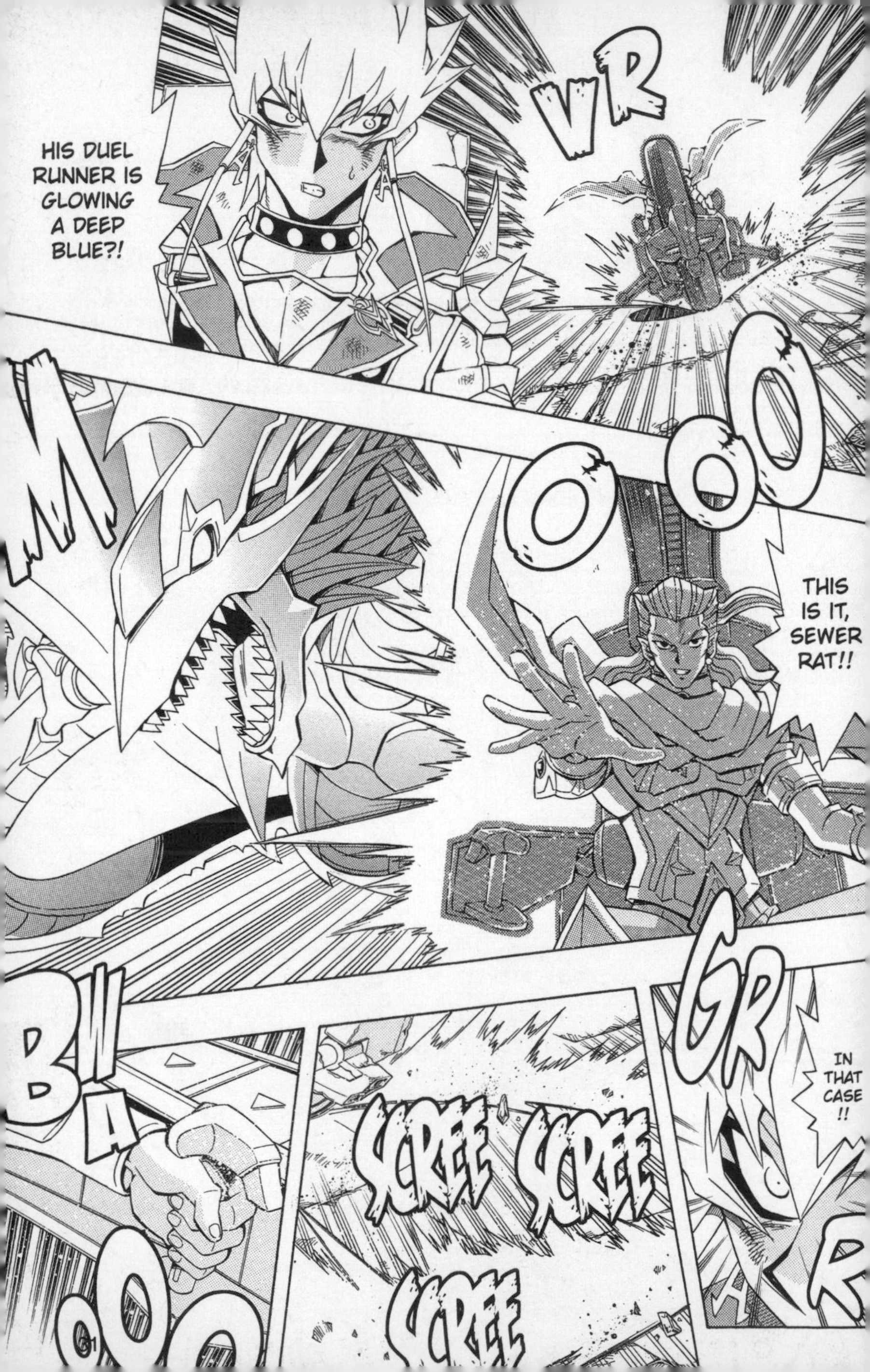
VR
HIS DUEL RUNNER IS GLOWING A DEEP BLUE?!
OOO
THIS IS IT, SEWER RAT!!
M
GR
IN THAT CASE!!
R
SCREE
SCREE
SCREE

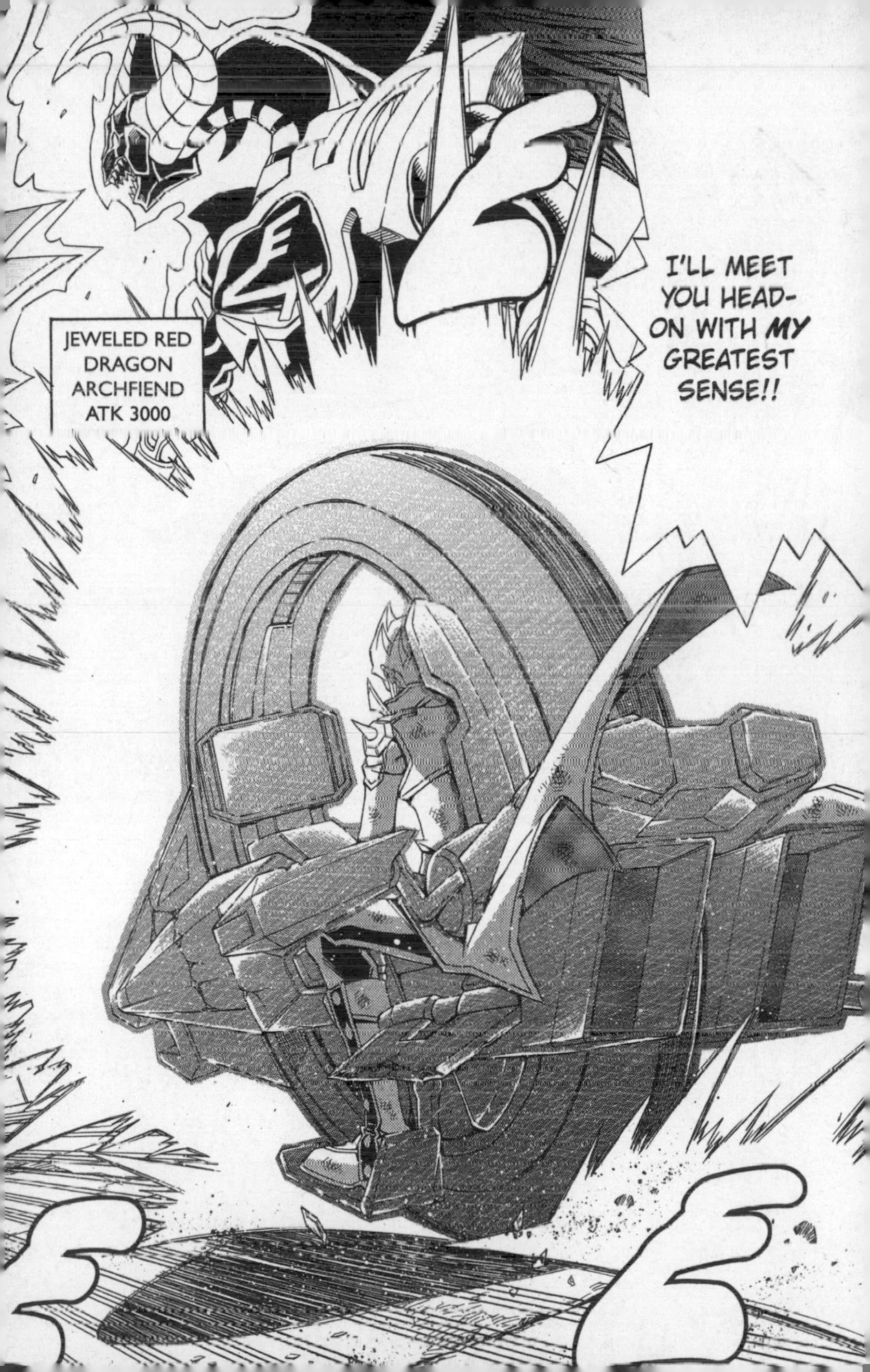
I'LL MEET YOU HEAD-ON WITH *MY* GREATEST SENSE!!
JEWELED RED DRAGON ARCHFIEND ATK 3000

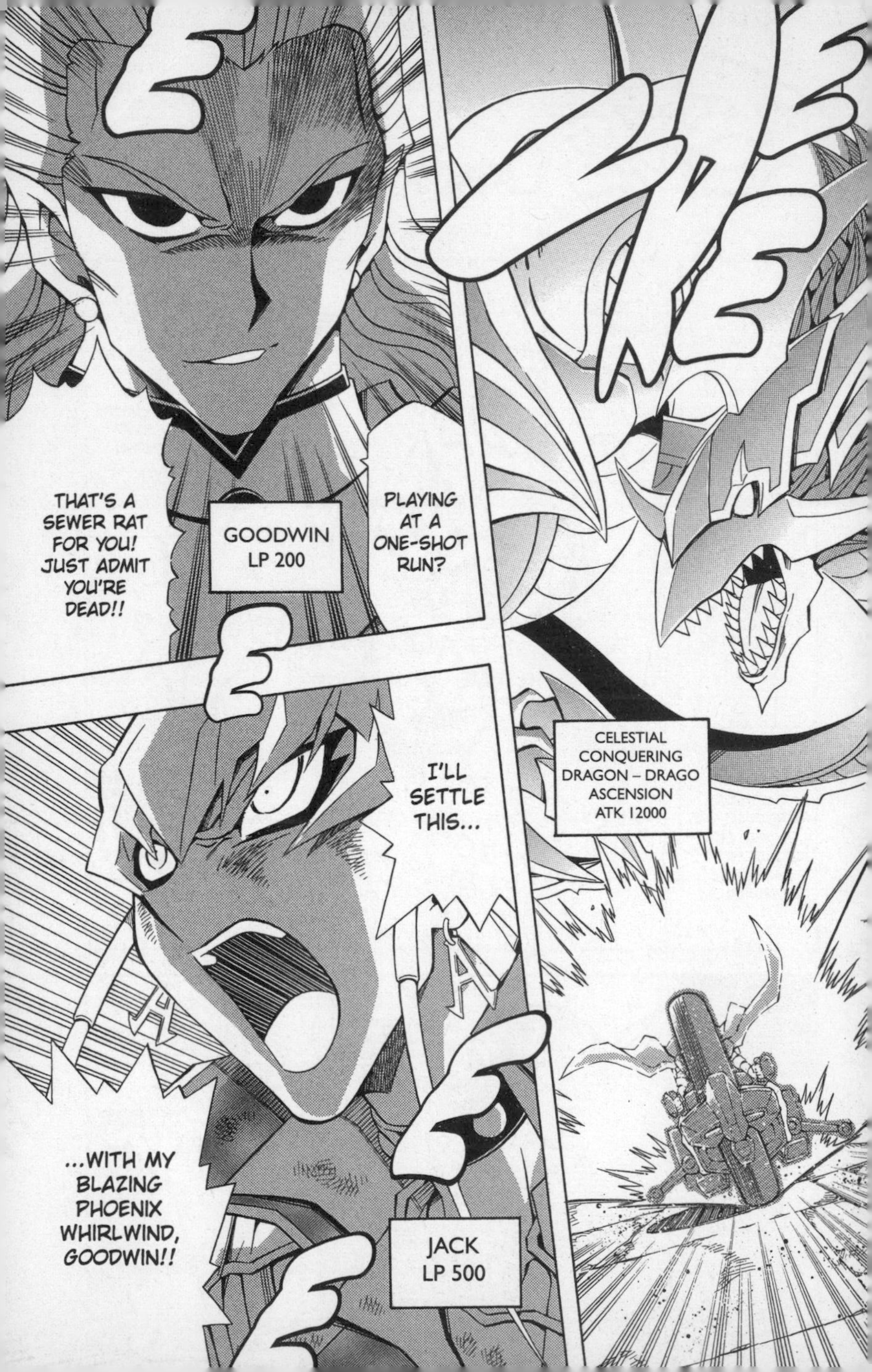
CELESTIAL CONQUERING DRAGON – DRAGO ASCENSION ATK 12000
PLAYING AT A ONE-SHOT RUN?
GOODWIN LP 200
THAT'S A SEWER RAT FOR YOU! JUST ADMIT YOU'RE DEAD!!
I'LL SETTLE THIS...
JACK LP 500
...WITH MY BLAZING PHOENIX WHIRLWIND, GOODWIN!!

5D's TRACKS

THE 46TH

BY SATOMASA

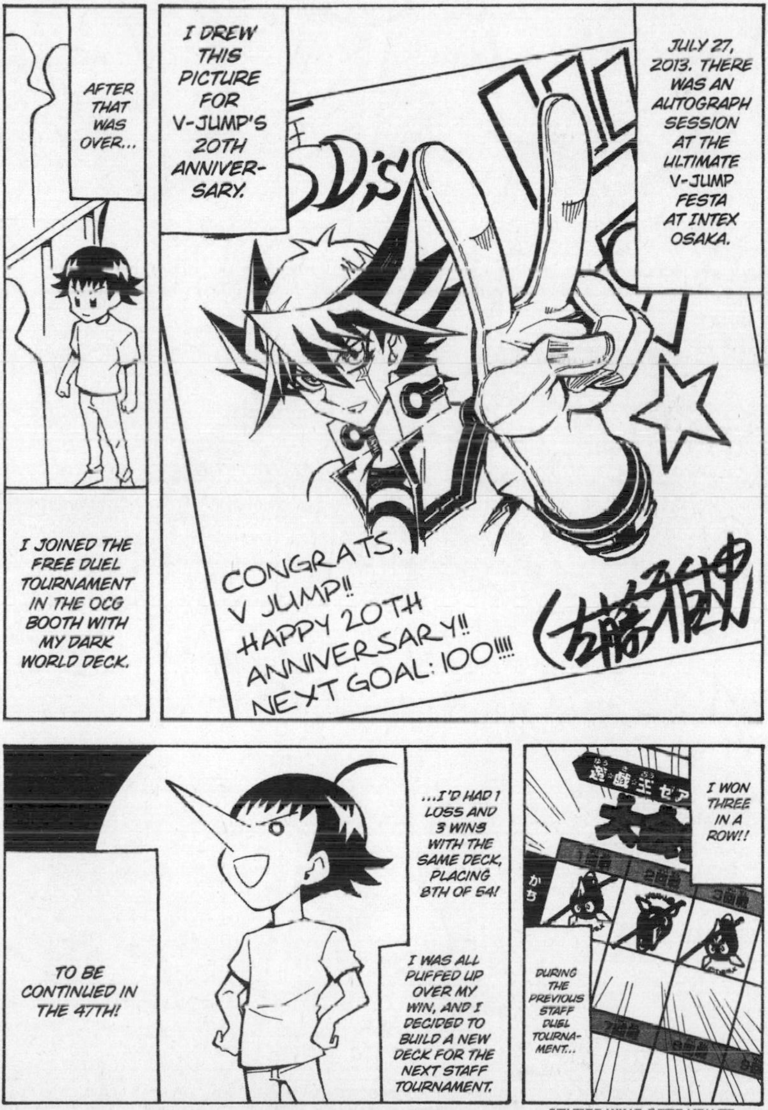

JULY 27, 2013. THERE WAS AN AUTOGRAPH SESSION AT THE ULTIMATE V-JUMP FESTA AT INTEX OSAKA.
I DREW THIS PICTURE FOR V-JUMP'S 20TH ANNIVERSARY.
5D's
CONGRATS, V JUMP!! HAPPY 20TH ANNIVERSARY!! NEXT GOAL: 100!!!!
AFTER THAT WAS OVER...
I JOINED THE FREE DUEL TOURNAMENT IN THE OCG BOOTH WITH MY DARK WORLD DECK.
I WON THREE IN A ROW!!
DURING THE PREVIOUS STAFF DUEL TOURNAMENT...
...I'D HAD 1 LOSS AND 3 WINS WITH THE SAME DECK, PLACING 8TH OF 54!
I WAS ALL PUFFED UP OVER MY WIN, AND I DECIDED TO BUILD A NEW DECK FOR THE NEXT STAFF TOURNAMENT.
TO BE CONTINUED IN THE 47TH!

*THREE WINS GETS YOU TO THE NEXT ROUND.

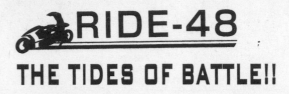

RIDE-48

THE TIDES OF BATTLE!!

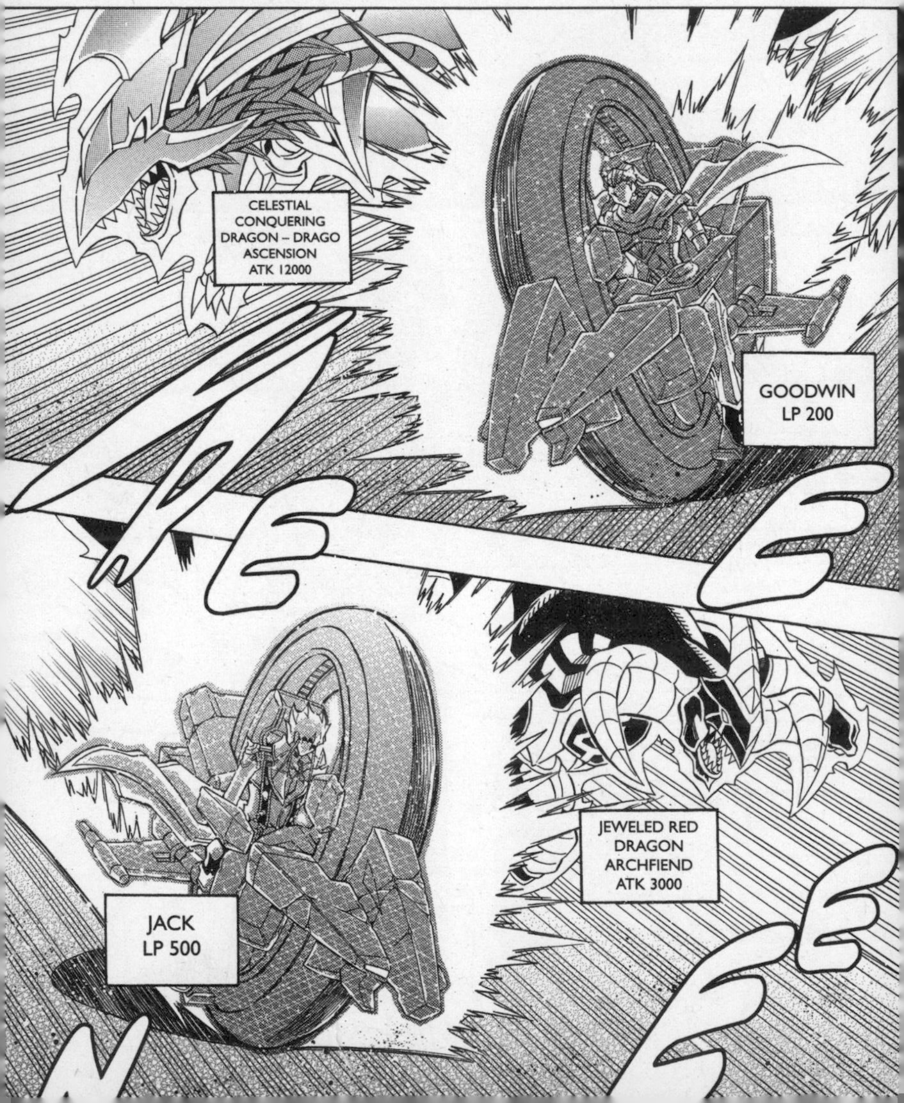

GOODWIN
LP 200
CELESTIAL CONQUERING DRAGON – DRAGO ASCENSION
ATK 12000
JEWELED RED DRAGON ARCHFIEND
ATK 3000
JACK
LP 500

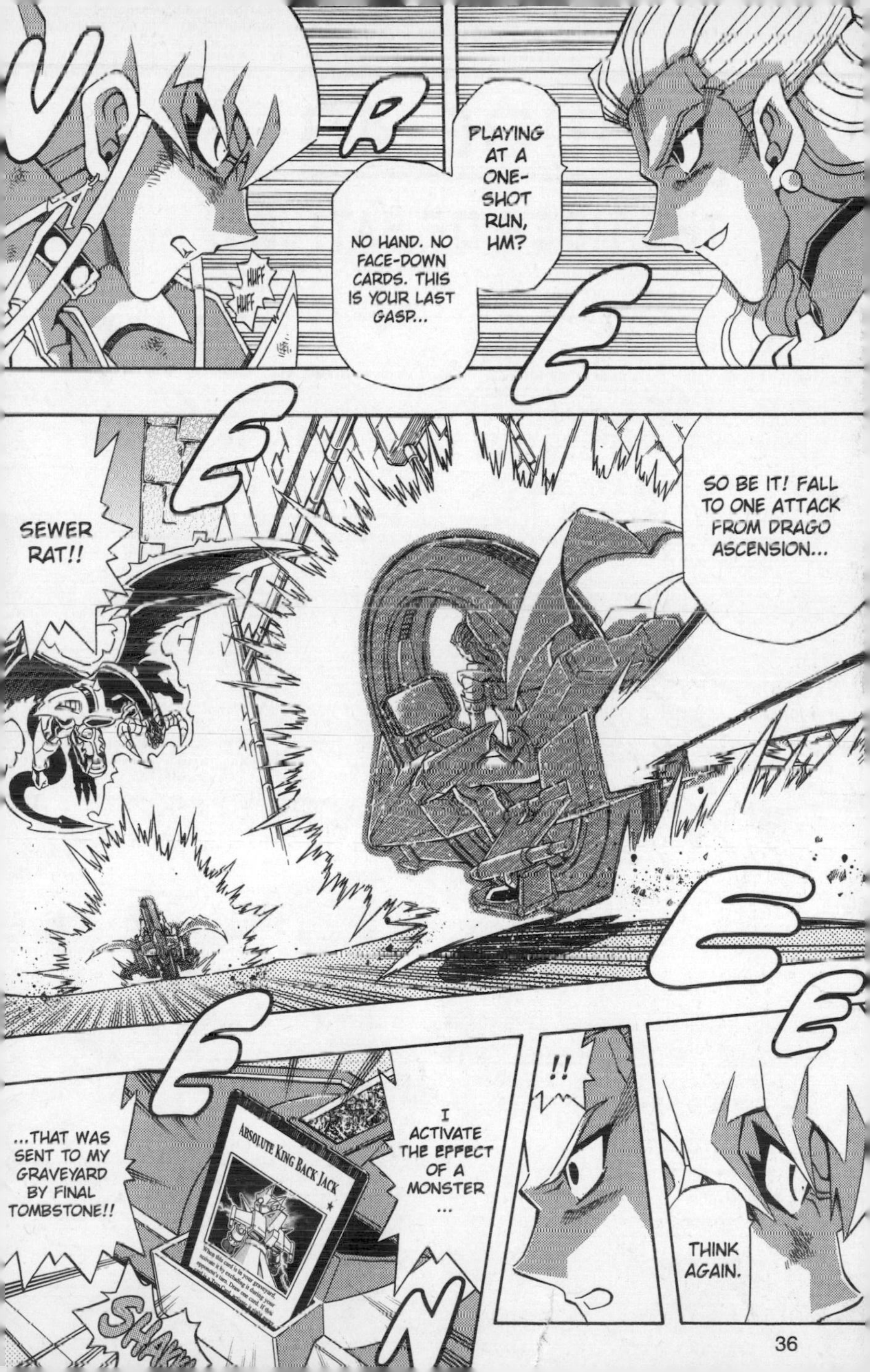
PLAYING AT A ONE-SHOT RUN, HM?
NO HAND. NO FACE-DOWN CARDS. THIS IS YOUR LAST GASP...
HUFF HUFF
SO BE IT! FALL TO ONE ATTACK FROM DRAGO ASCENSION...
SEWER RAT!!
THINK AGAIN.
!!
I ACTIVATE THE EFFECT OF A MONSTER ...
...THAT WAS SENT TO MY GRAVEYARD BY FINAL TOMBSTONE!!
ABSOLUTE KING BACK JACK

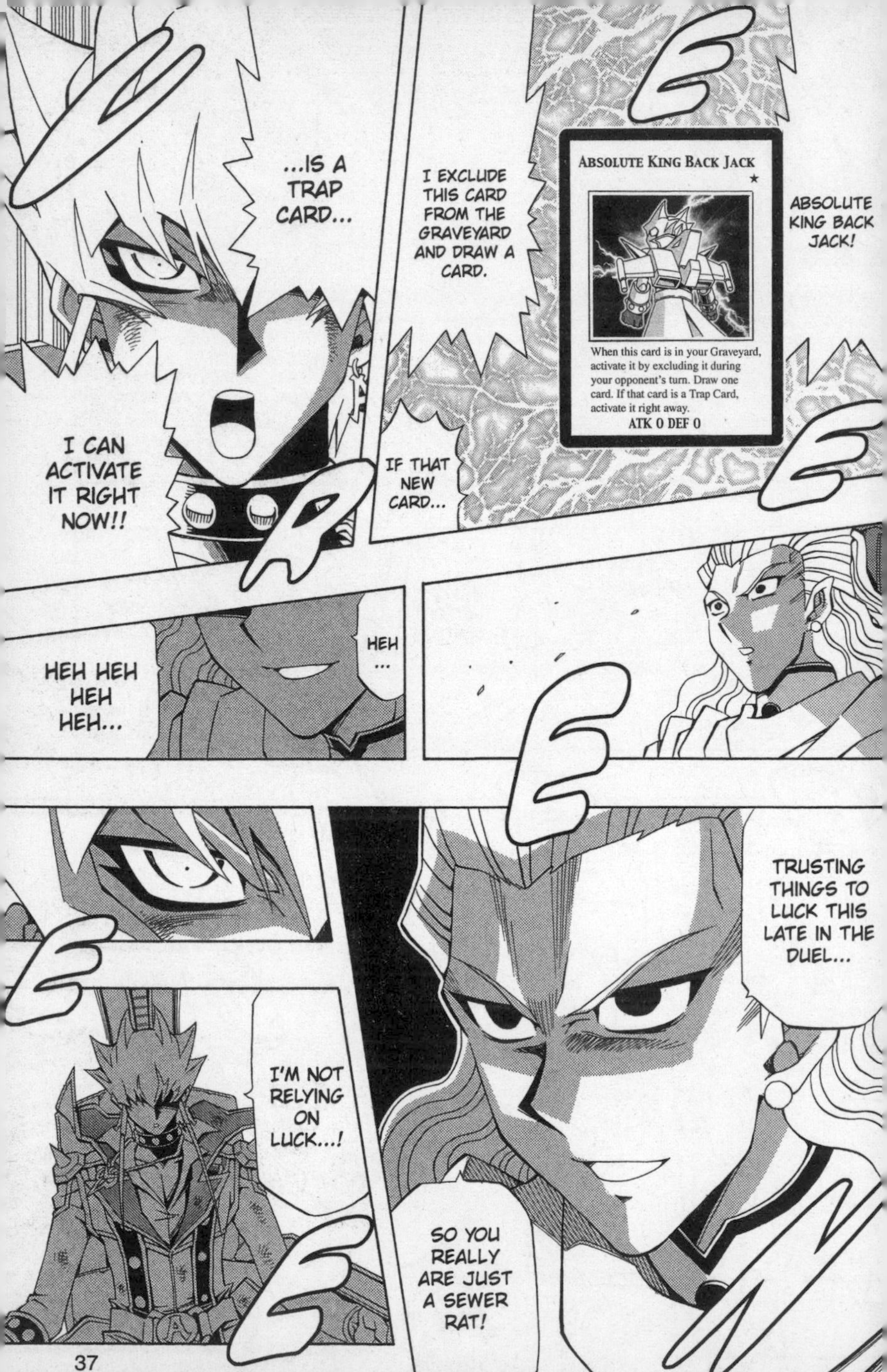
ABSOLUTE KING BACK JACK!
ABSOLUTE KING BACK JACK
When this card is in your Graveyard, activate it by excluding it during your opponent's turn. Draw one card. If that card is a Trap Card, activate it right away.
ATK 0 DEF 0
I EXCLUDE THIS CARD FROM THE GRAVEYARD AND DRAW A CARD.
IF THAT NEW CARD...
...IS A TRAP CARD...
I CAN ACTIVATE IT RIGHT NOW!!
HEH ...
HEH HEH HEH HEH...
TRUSTING THINGS TO LUCK THIS LATE IN THE DUEL...
SO YOU REALLY ARE JUST A SEWER RAT!
I'M NOT RELYING ON LUCK...!

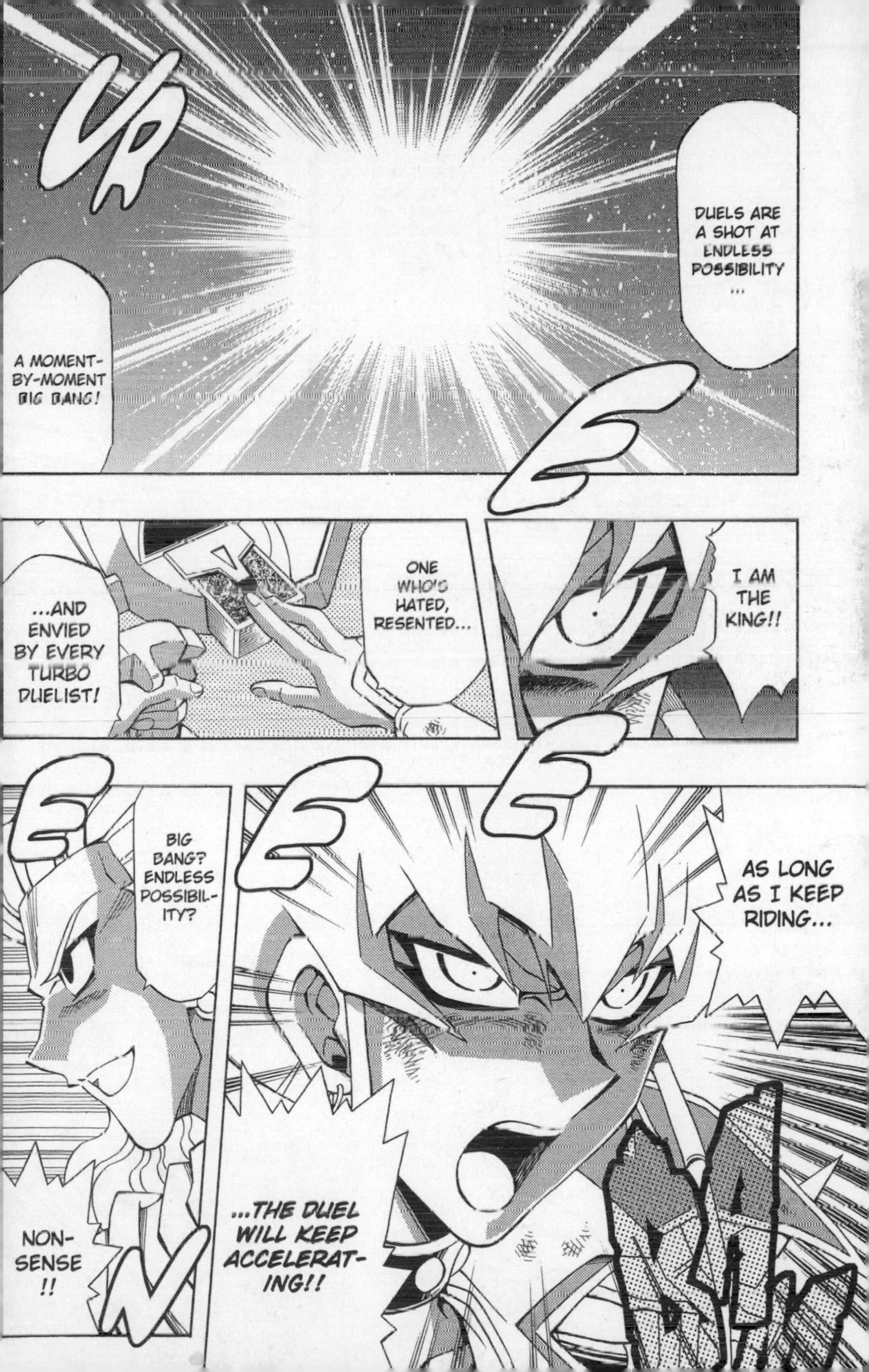
DUELS ARE A SHOT AT ENDLESS POSSIBILITY...
A MOMENT-BY-MOMENT BIG BANG!
I AM THE KING!!
ONE WHO'S HATED, RESENTED...
...AND ENVIED BY EVERY TURBO DUELIST!
AS LONG AS I KEEP RIDING...
...THE DUEL WILL KEEP ACCELERATING!!
BIG BANG? ENDLESS POSSIBILITY?
NONSENSE!!

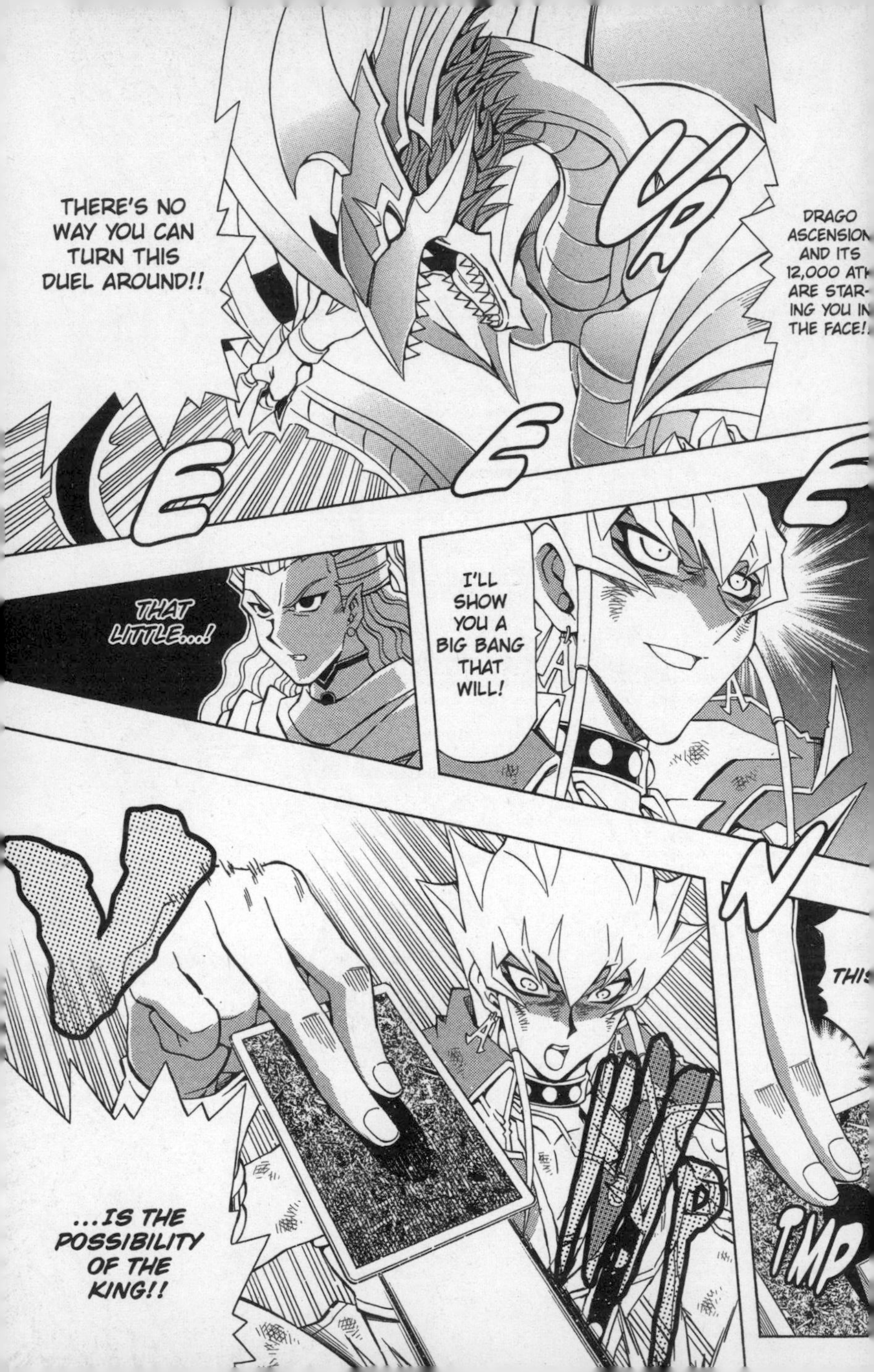
DRAGO ASCENSION AND ITS 12,000 ATK ARE STAR-ING YOU IN THE FACE!!
THERE'S NO WAY YOU CAN TURN THIS DUEL AROUND!!
I'LL SHOW YOU A BIG BANG THAT WILL!
THAT LITTLE...!
THIS
...IS THE POSSIBILITY OF THE KING!!
TMP

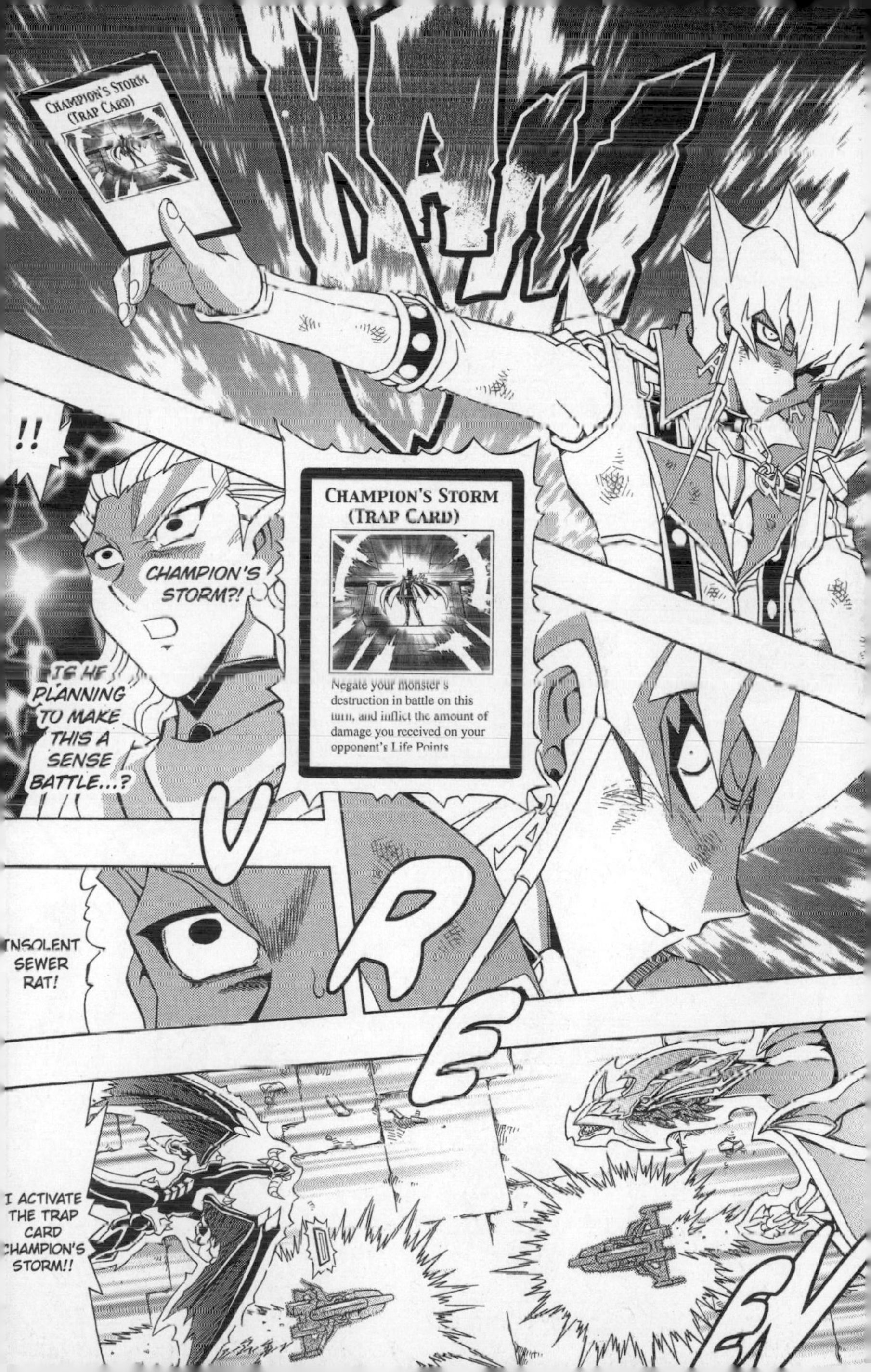
CHAMPION'S STORM
(TRAP CARD)
CHAMPION'S STORM
(TRAP CARD)
Negate your monster's destruction in battle on this turn, and inflict the amount of damage you received on your opponent's Life Points
!!
CHAMPION'S STORM?!
IS HE PLANNING TO MAKE THIS A SENSE BATTLE...?
INSOLENT SEWER RAT!
I ACTIVATE THE TRAP CARD CHAMPION'S STORM!!

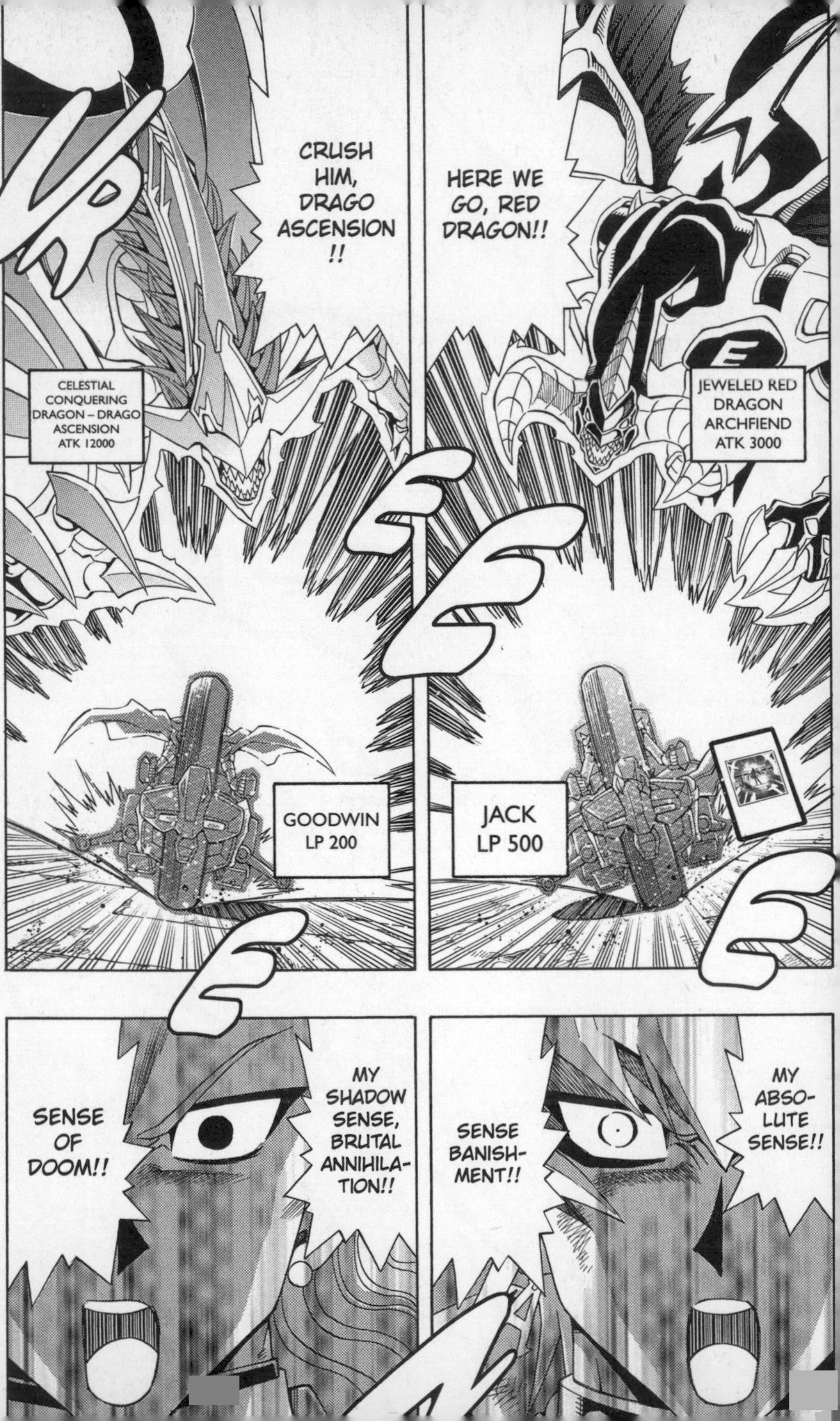
HERE WE GO, RED DRAGON!!
JEWELED RED DRAGON ARCHFIEND ATK 3000
JACK LP 500
CRUSH HIM, DRAGO ASCENSION!!
CELESTIAL CONQUERING DRAGON – DRAGO ASCENSION ATK 12000
GOODWIN LP 200
MY ABSOLUTE SENSE!!
SENSE BANISHMENT!!
MY SHADOW SENSE, BRUTAL ANNIHILATION!!
SENSE OF DOOM!!

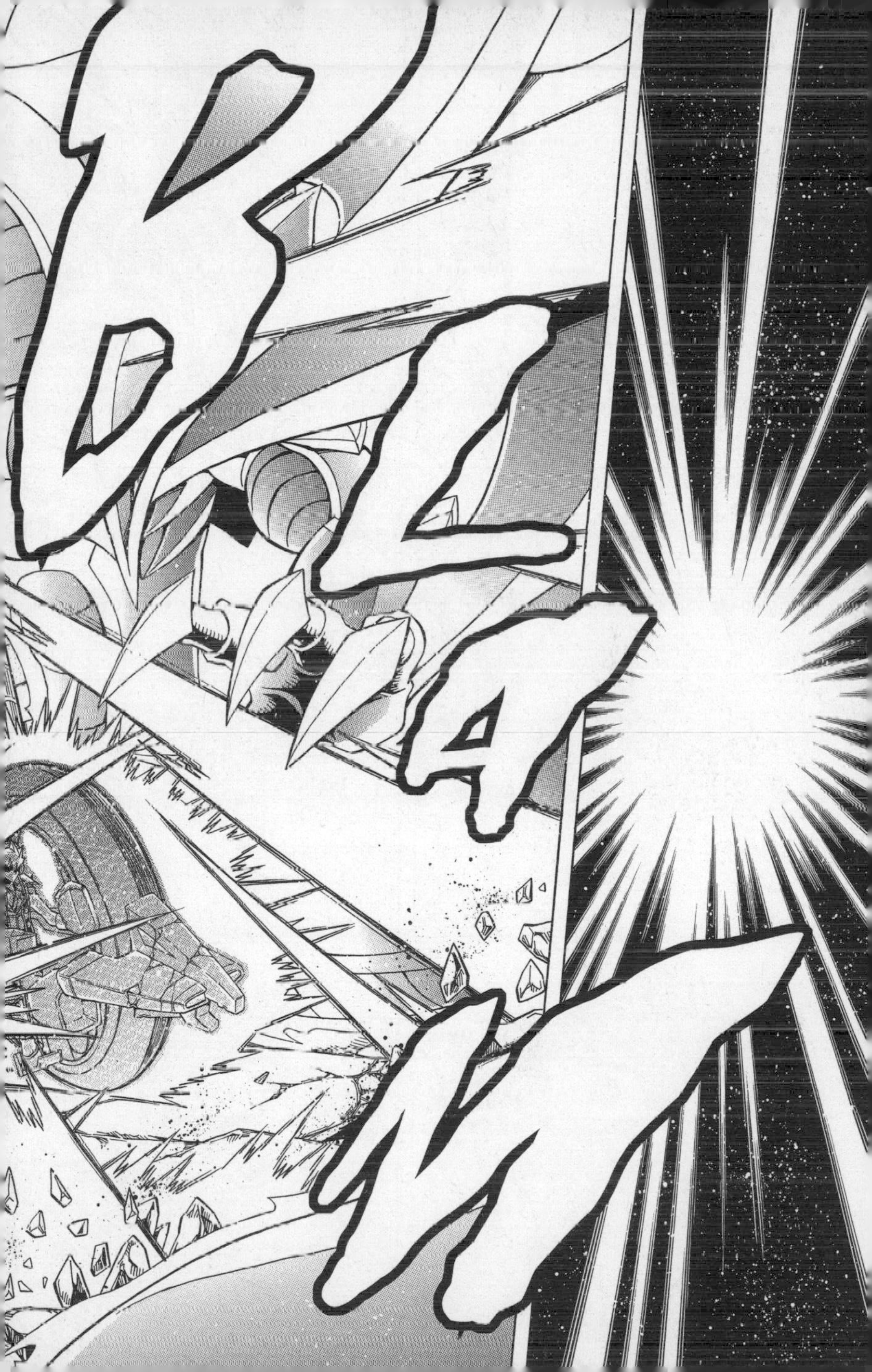
BLAM

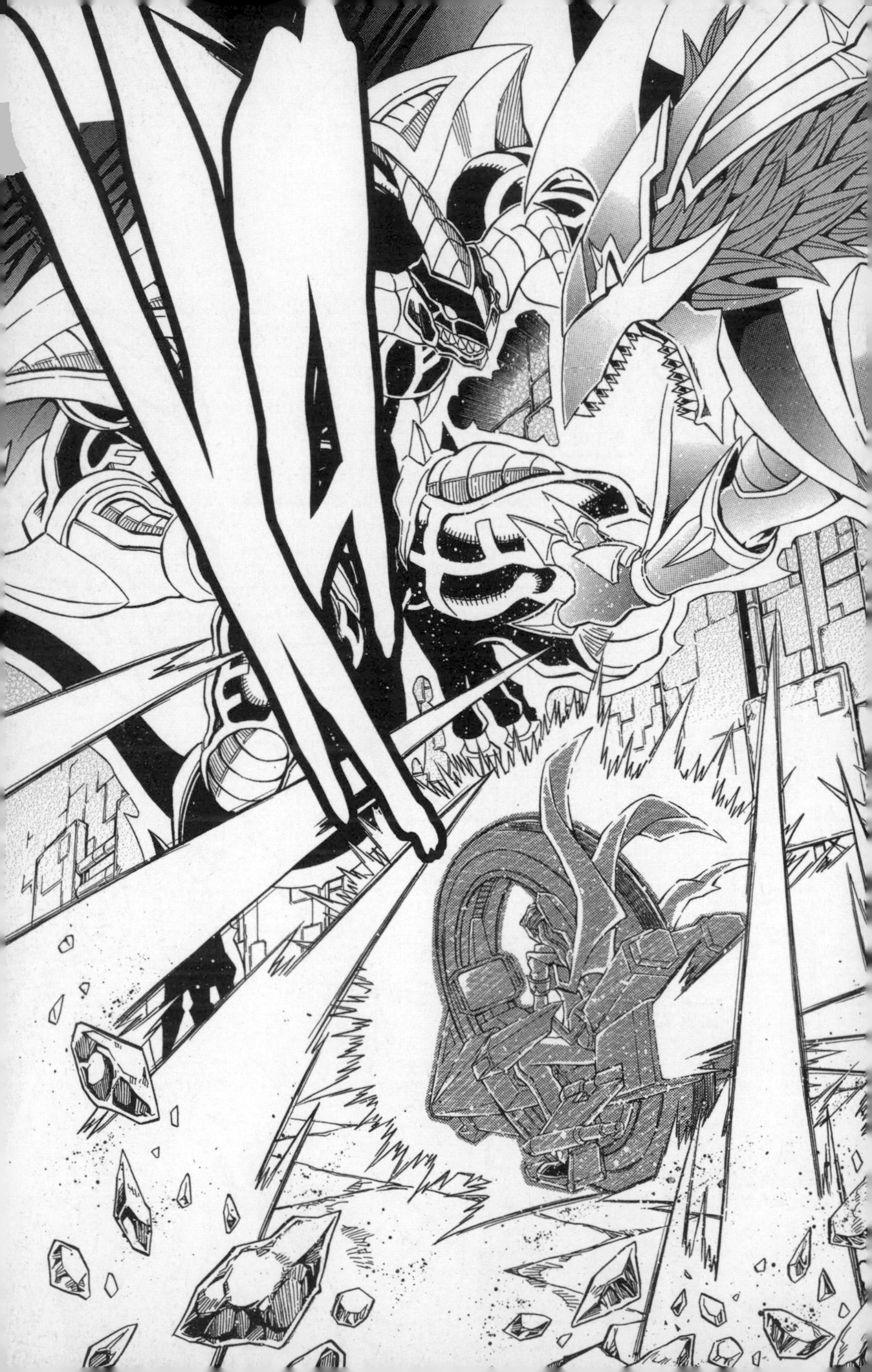

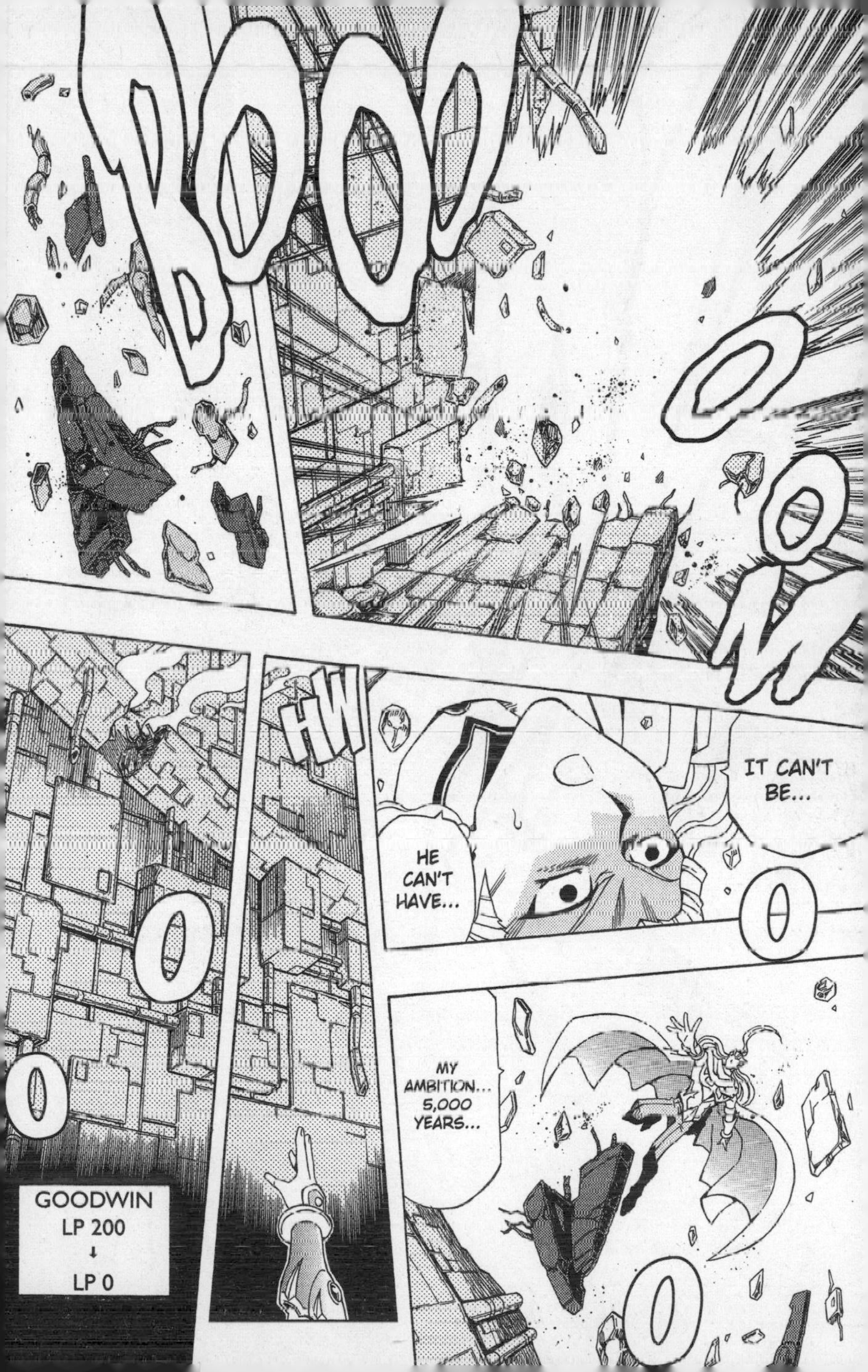
BOOOO
OOM
IT CAN'T BE...
HE CAN'T HAVE...
O
MY AMBITION... 5,000 YEARS...
O
HW
O
O
GOODWIN LP 200 ↓ LP 0

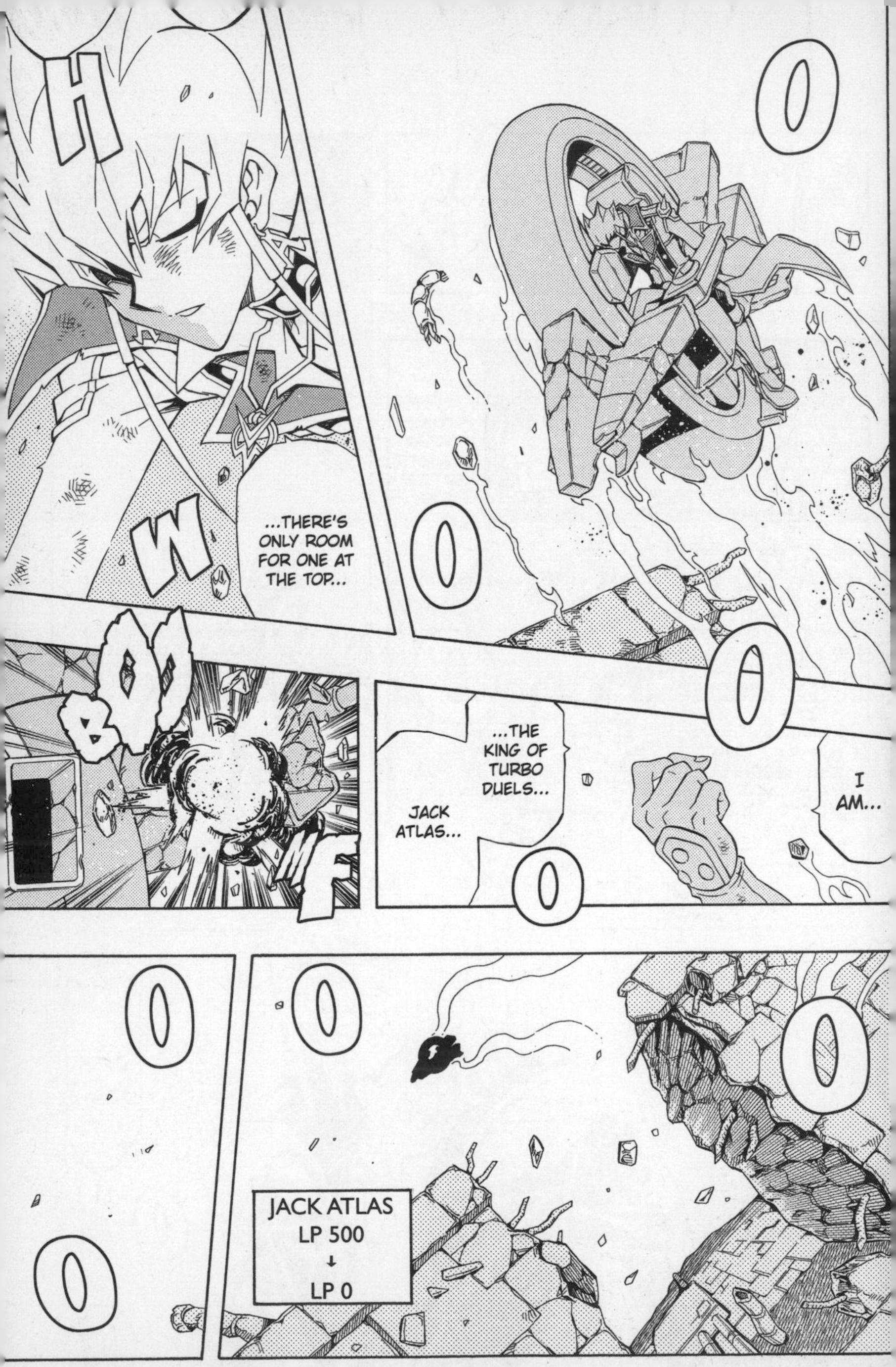
HWOOOOOOOO
...THERE'S ONLY ROOM FOR ONE AT THE TOP...
I AM...
...THE KING OF TURBO DUELS...
JACK ATLAS...
BOOF
JACK ATLAS
LP 500
↓
LP 0

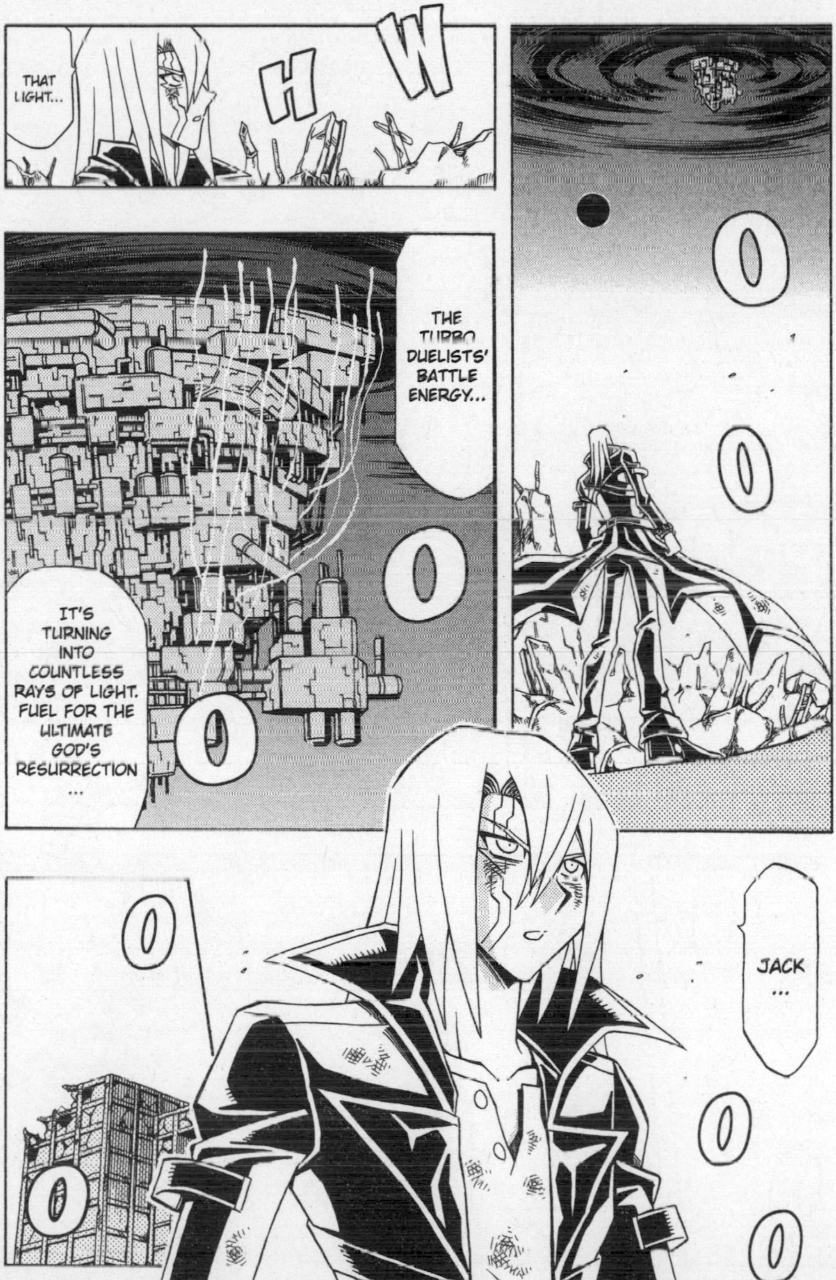
THAT LIGHT...
WHOOOOOOOO
THE TURBO DUELISTS' BATTLE ENERGY...
IT'S TURNING INTO COUNTLESS RAYS OF LIGHT. FUEL FOR THE ULTIMATE GOD'S RESURRECTION ...
JACK ...

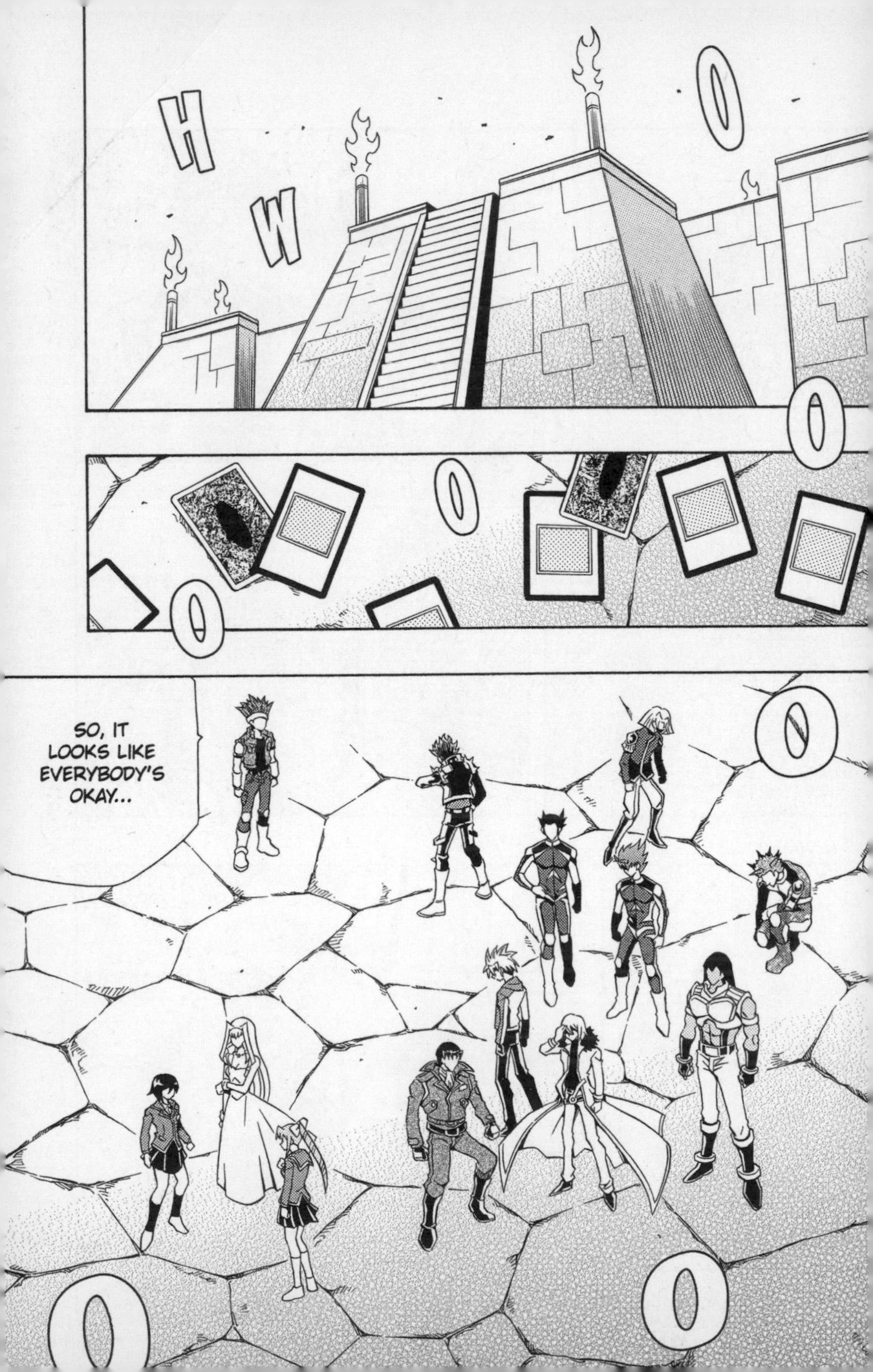
HWOOOOOOO
SO, IT LOOKS LIKE EVERYBODY'S OKAY...

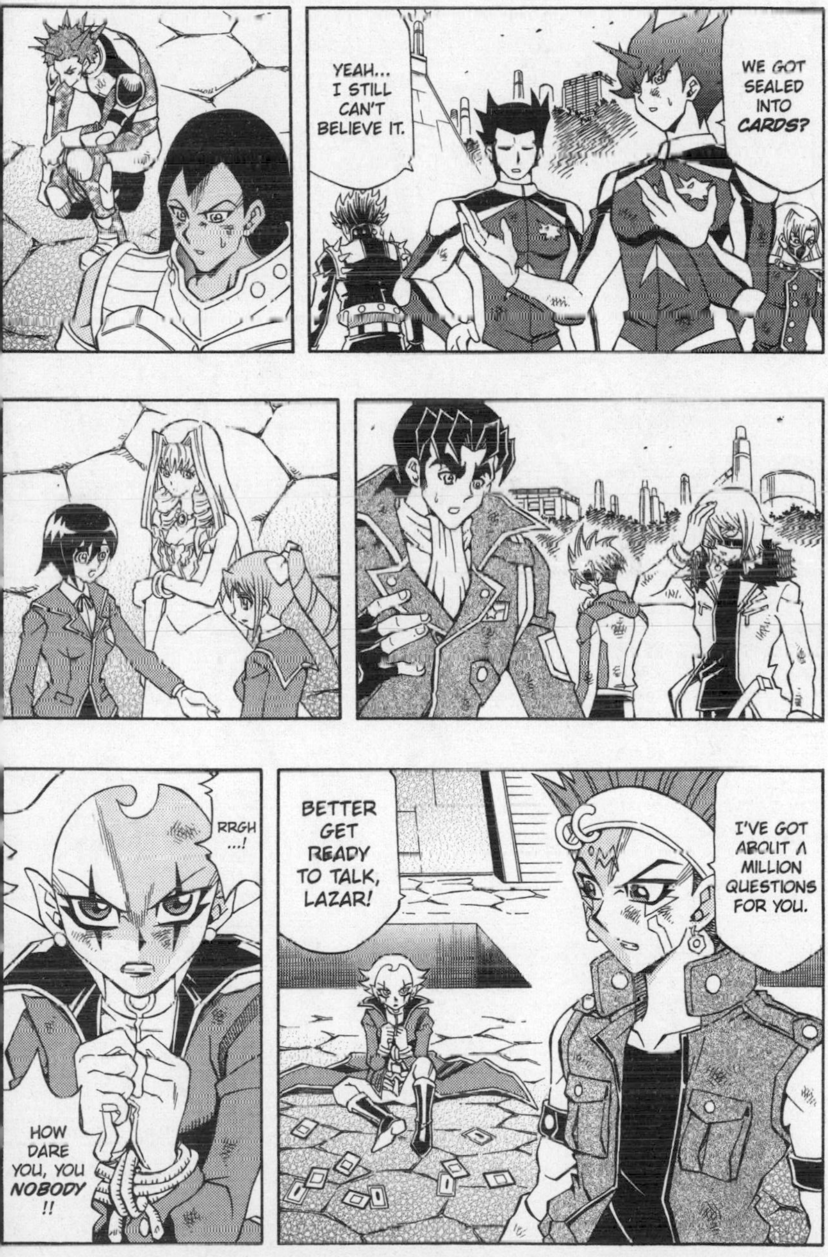
WE GOT SEALED INTO *CARDS?*
YEAH... I STILL CAN'T BELIEVE IT.
I'VE GOT ABOUT A MILLION QUESTIONS FOR YOU.
BETTER GET READY TO TALK, LAZAR!
RRGH ...!
HOW DARE YOU, YOU *NOBODY* !!

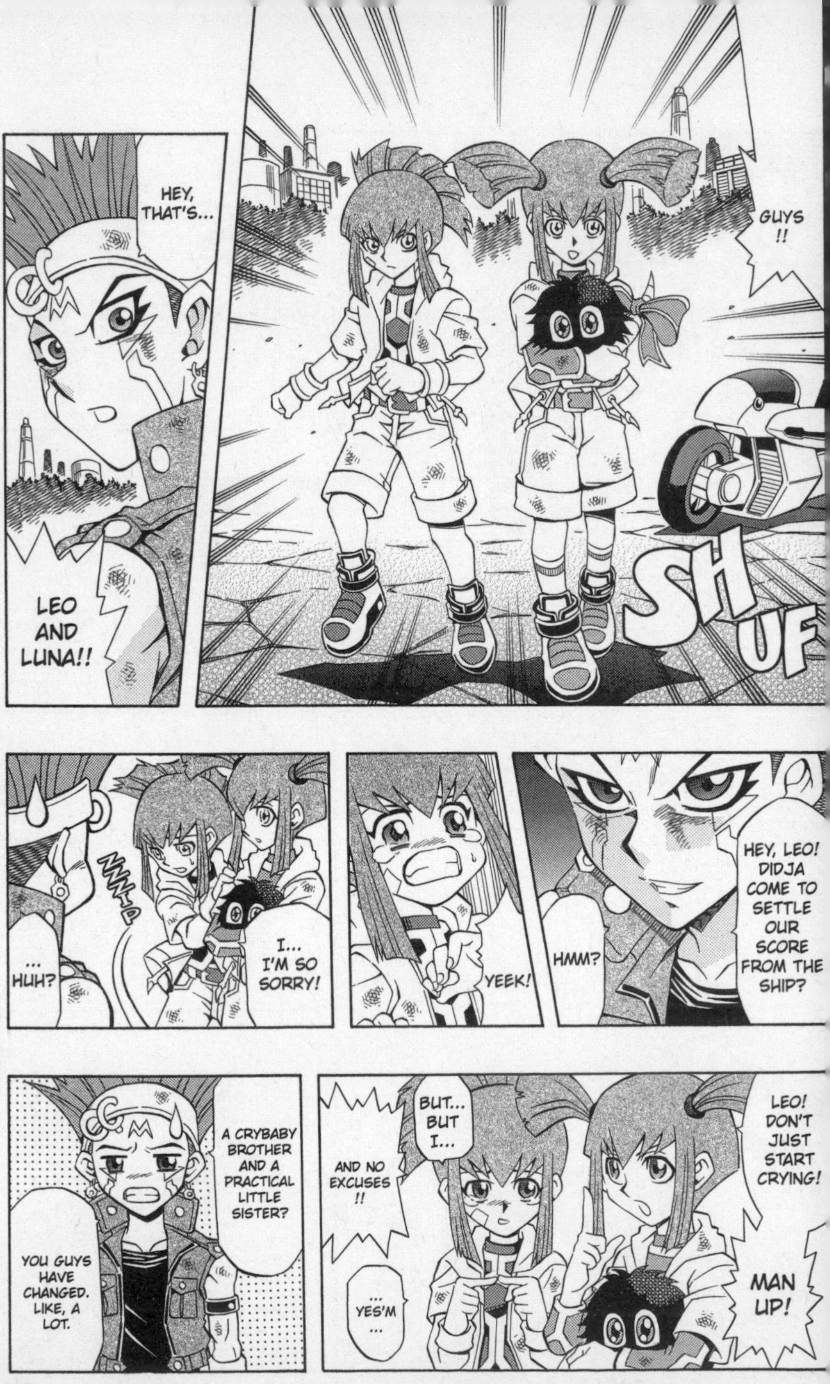

GUYS !!
SHUF
HEY, THAT'S...
LEO AND LUNA!!
HEY, LEO! DIDJA COME TO SETTLE OUR SCORE FROM THE SHIP?
HMM?
YEEK!
... HUH?
I... I'M SO SORRY!
LEO! DON'T JUST START CRYING!
BUT... BUT I...
AND NO EXCUSES !!
... YES'M ...
MAN UP!
A CRYBABY BROTHER AND A PRACTICAL LITTLE SISTER?
YOU GUYS HAVE CHANGED. LIKE, A LOT.

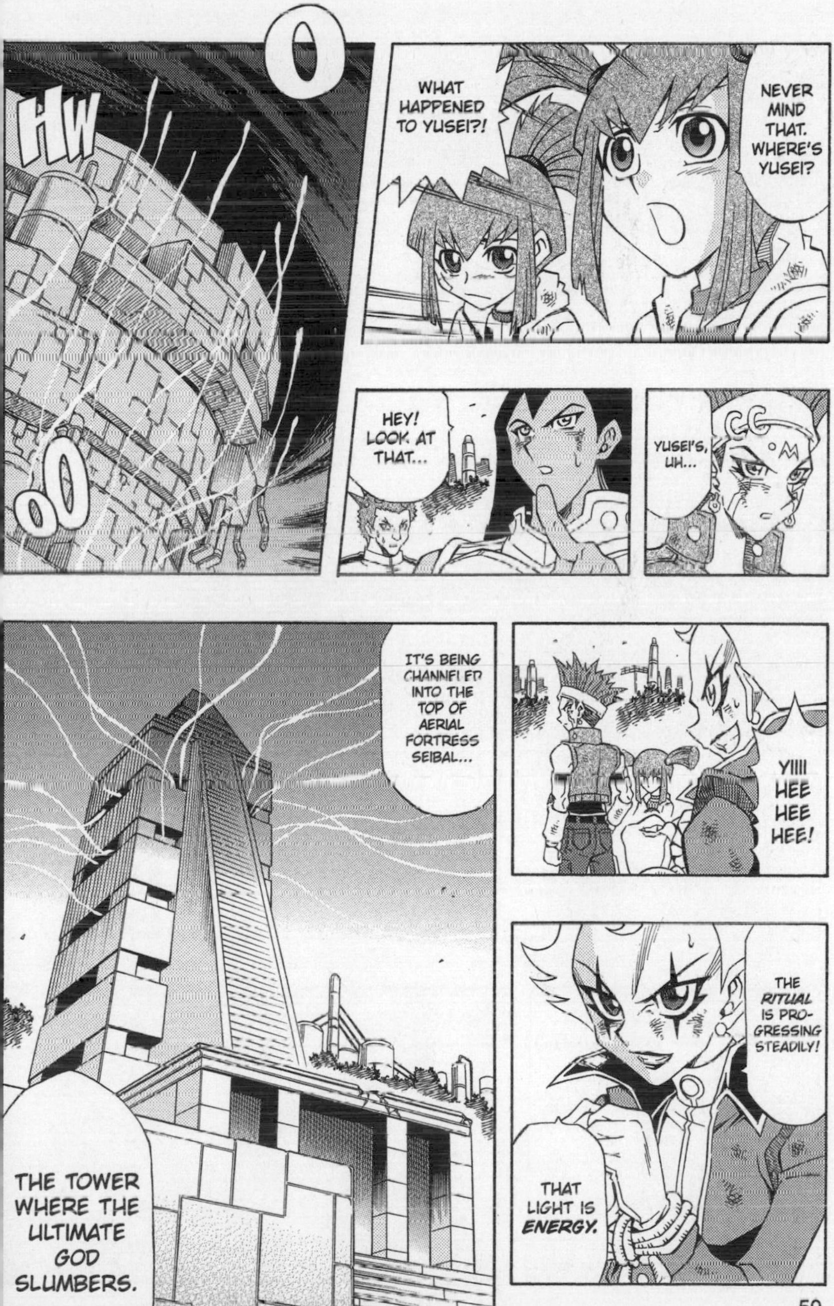
NEVER MIND THAT. WHERE'S YUSEI?
WHAT HAPPENED TO YUSEI?!
YUSEI'S, UH...
HEY! LOOK AT THAT...
HW
O
OO
YIIII HEE HEE HEE!
THE RITUAL IS PRO-GRESSING STEADILY!
THAT LIGHT IS ENERGY.
IT'S BEING CHANNELED INTO THE TOP OF AERIAL FORTRESS SEIBAL...
THE TOWER WHERE THE ULTIMATE GOD SLUMBERS.

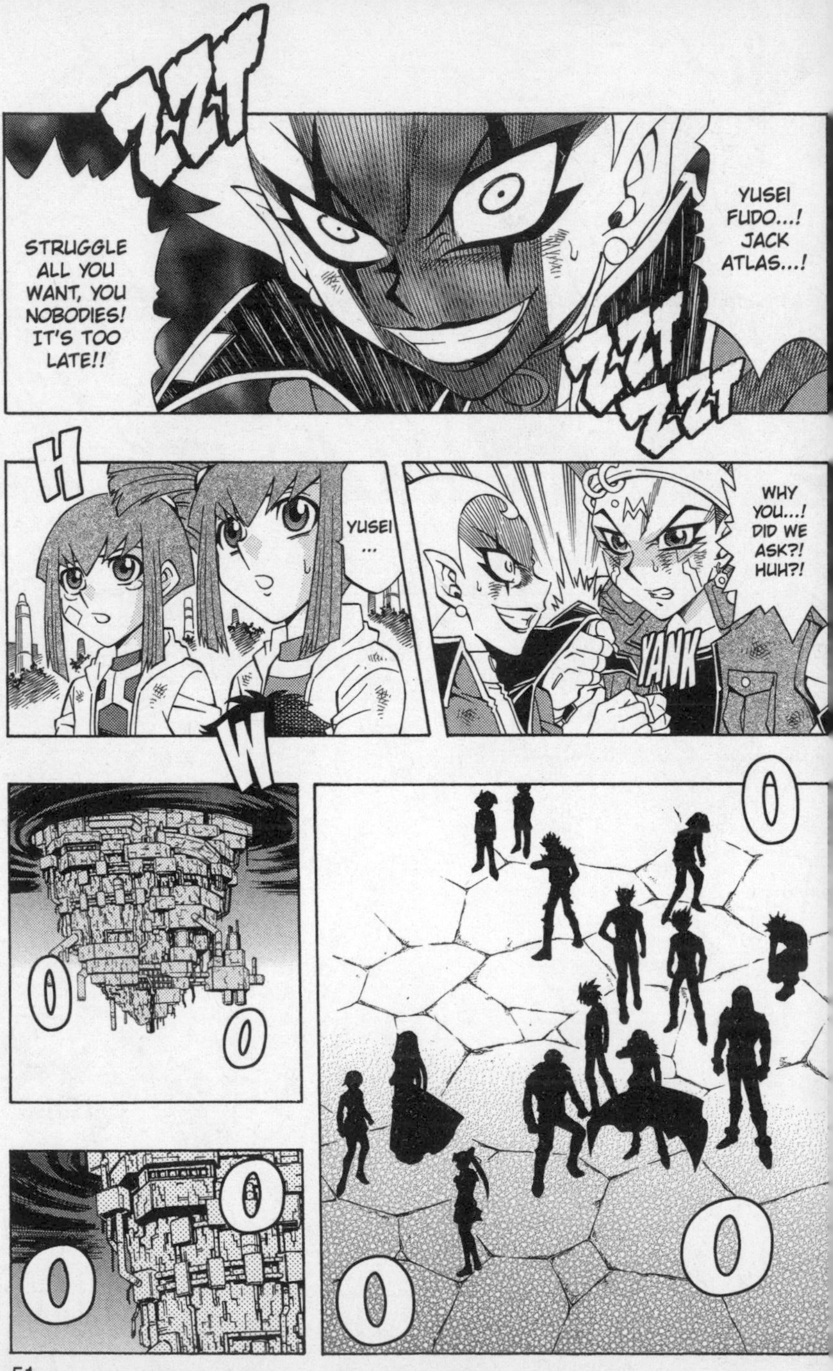
ZZZT
YUSEI FUDO...! JACK ATLAS...!
STRUGGLE ALL YOU WANT, YOU NOBODIES! IT'S TOO LATE!!
ZZZT
ZZZT
WHY YOU...! DID WE ASK?! HUH?!
YANK
YUSEI...
H
W
O
O
O
O
O
O
O

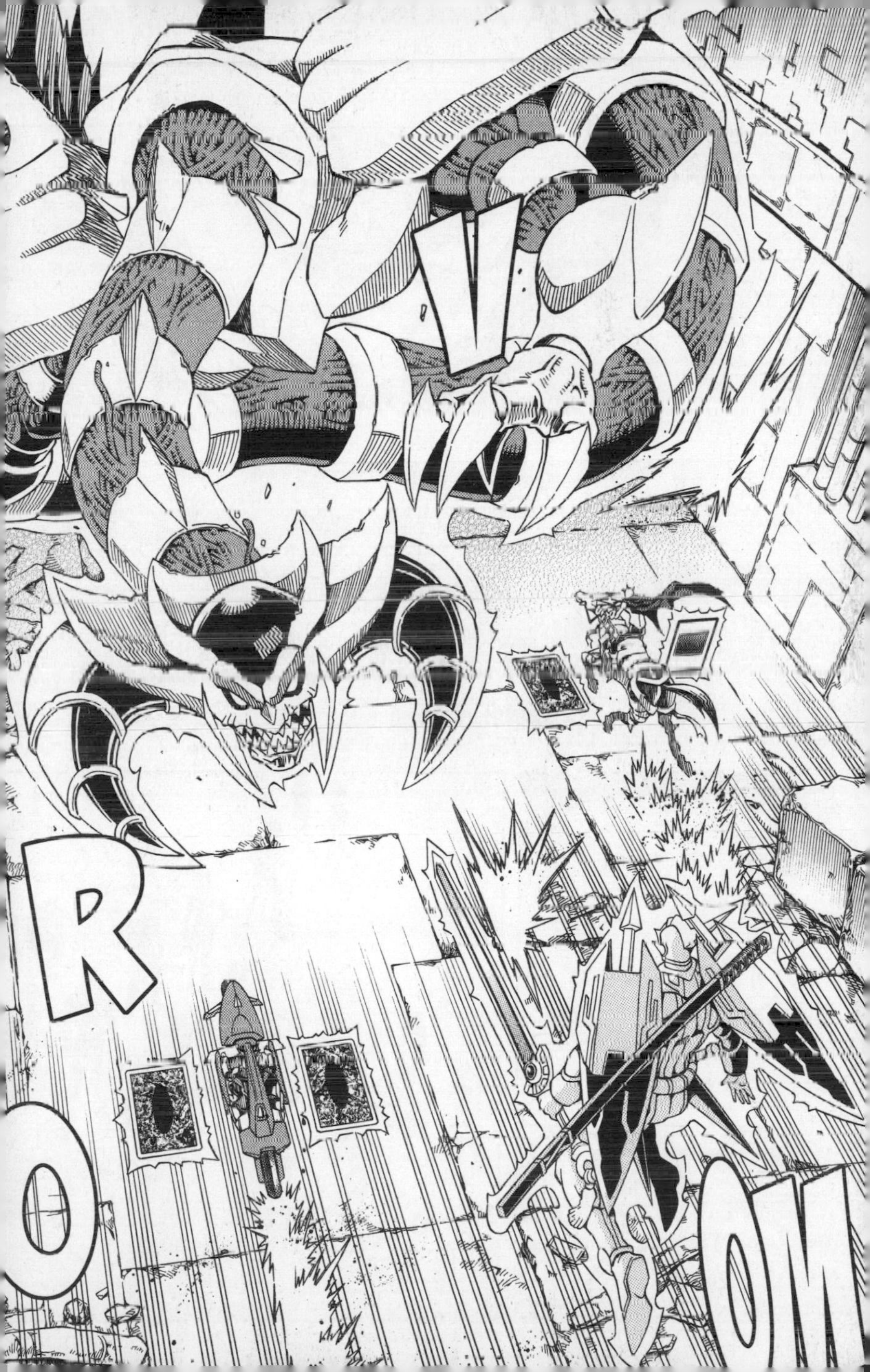
VROOM

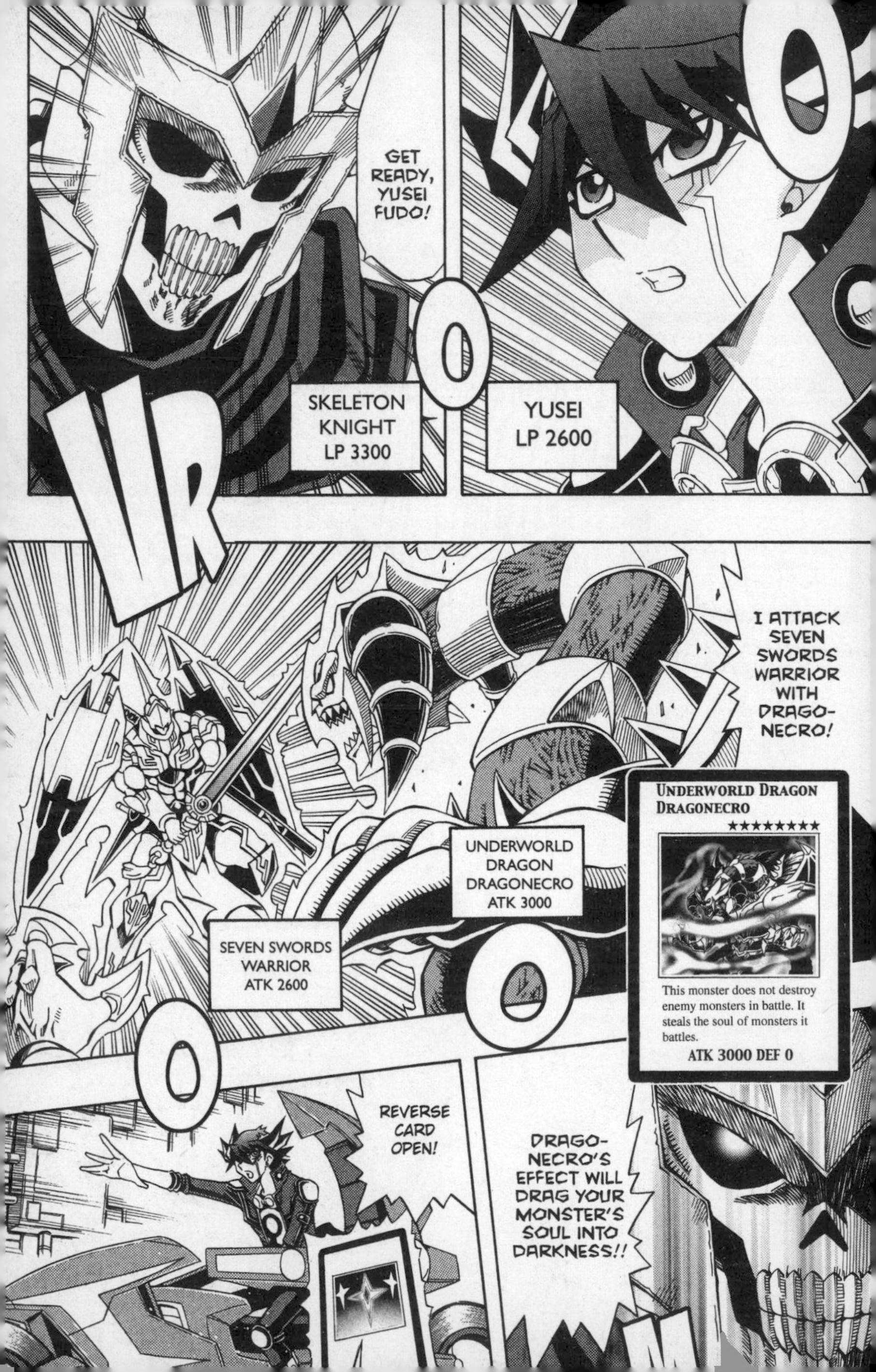
YUSEI
LP 2600
GET READY, YUSEI FUDO!
SKELETON KNIGHT
LP 3300
VR
I ATTACK SEVEN SWORDS WARRIOR WITH DRAGO-NECRO!
UNDERWORLD DRAGON DRAGONECRO
★★★★★★★★
This monster does not destroy enemy monsters in battle. It steals the soul of monsters it battles.
ATK 3000 DEF 0
UNDERWORLD DRAGON DRAGONECRO ATK 3000
SEVEN SWORDS WARRIOR ATK 2600
DRAGO-NECRO'S EFFECT WILL DRAG YOUR MONSTER'S SOUL INTO DARKNESS!!
REVERSE CARD OPEN!

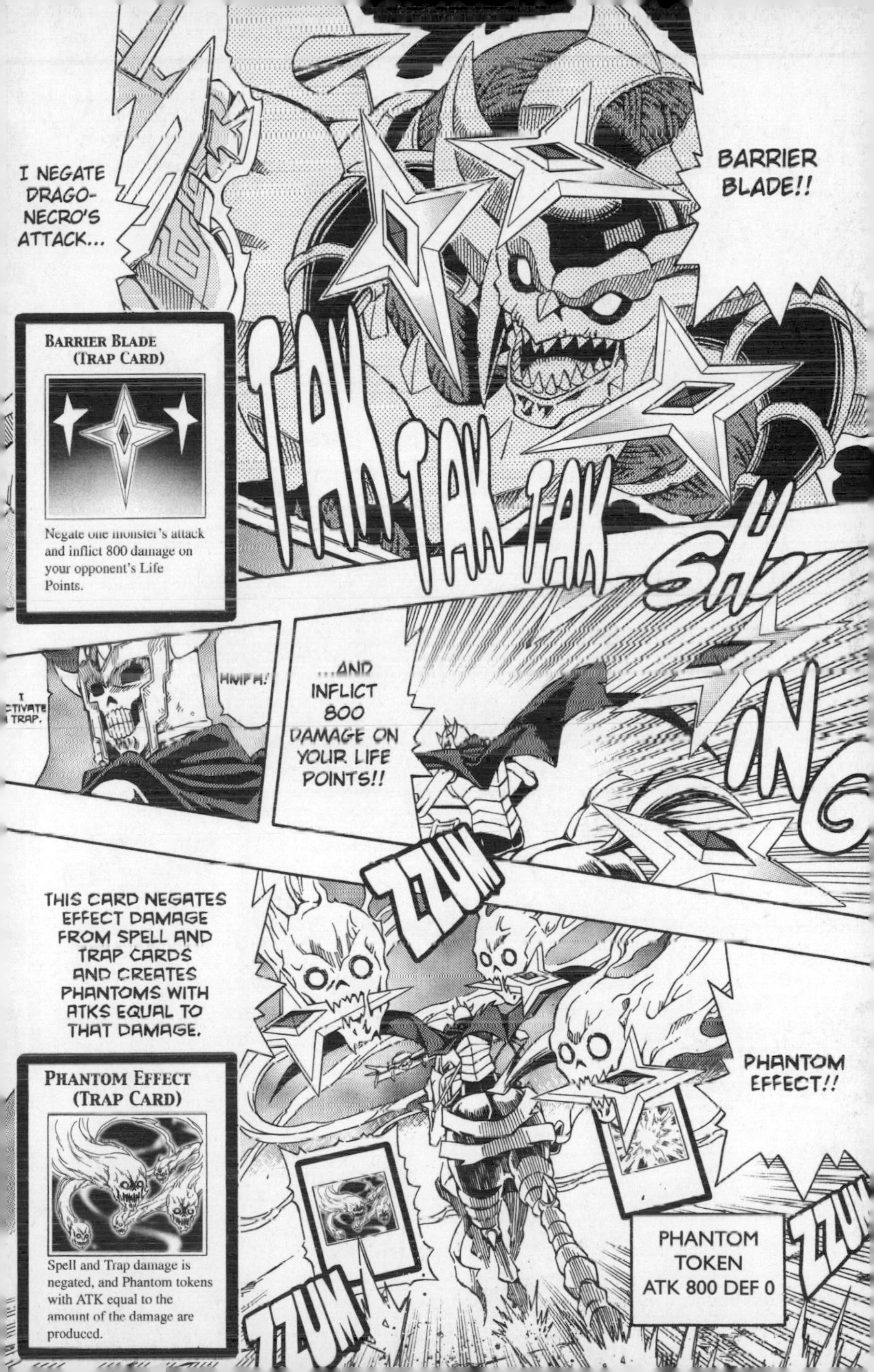
BARRIER BLADE!!
I NEGATE DRAGO-NECRO'S ATTACK...
BARRIER BLADE (TRAP CARD)
Negate one monster's attack and inflict 800 damage on your opponent's Life Points.
TAK TAK TAK
SH
ONG
...AND INFLICT 800 DAMAGE ON YOUR LIFE POINTS!!
HMPH!
I
CTIVATE
TRAP.
ZZUM
PHANTOM EFFECT!!
PHANTOM TOKEN ATK 800 DEF 0
ZZUM
THIS CARD NEGATES EFFECT DAMAGE FROM SPELL AND TRAP CARDS AND CREATES PHANTOMS WITH ATKS EQUAL TO THAT DAMAGE.
PHANTOM EFFECT (TRAP CARD)
Spell and Trap damage is negated, and Phantom tokens with ATK equal to the amount of the damage are produced.
ZZUM

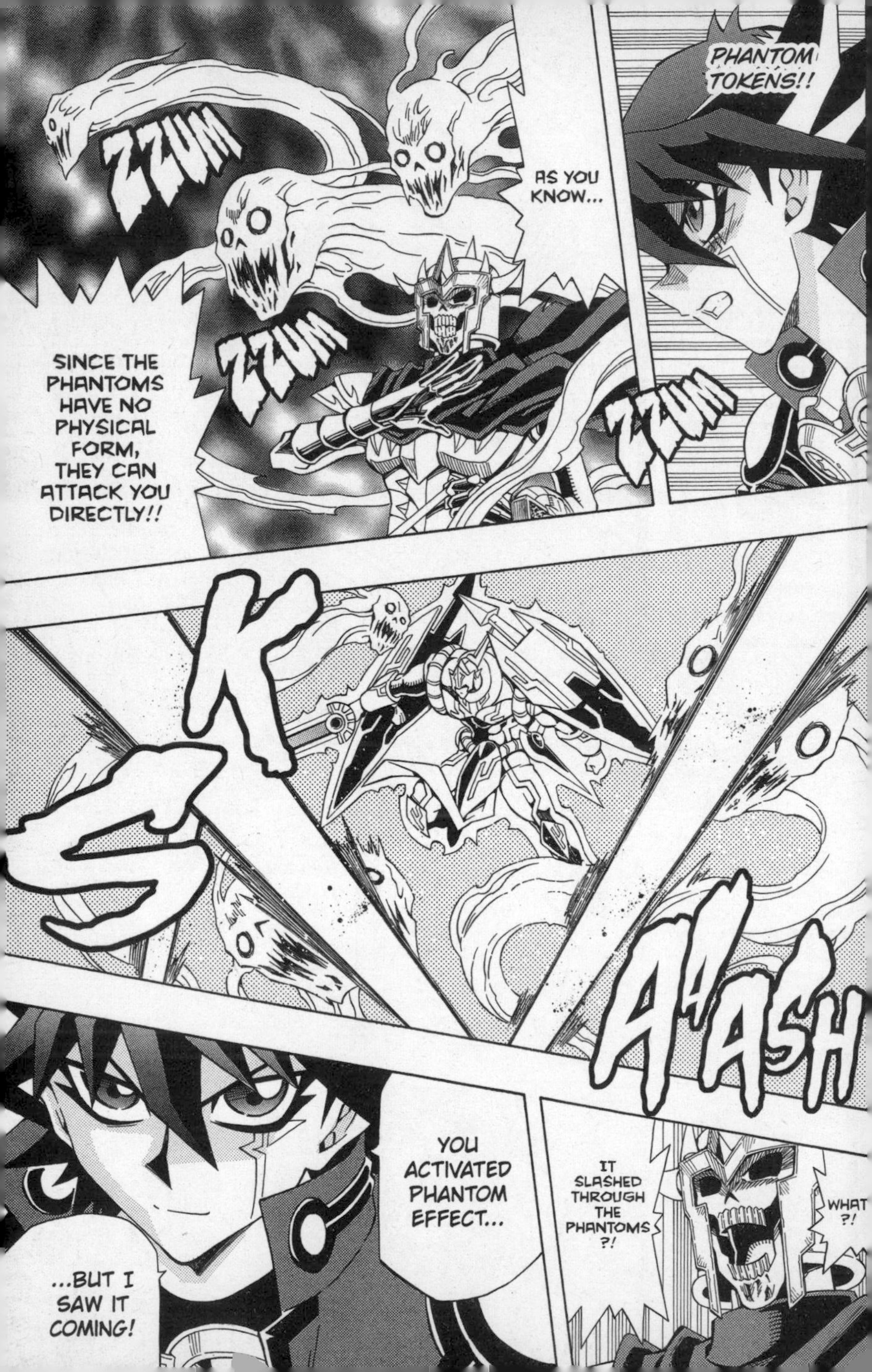
PHANTOM TOKENS!!
AS YOU KNOW...
ZZUM
ZZUM
ZZUM
SINCE THE PHANTOMS HAVE NO PHYSICAL FORM, THEY CAN ATTACK YOU DIRECTLY!!
KS
AAASH
WHAT?!
IT SLASHED THROUGH THE PHANTOMS?!
YOU ACTIVATED PHANTOM EFFECT...
...BUT I SAW IT COMING!

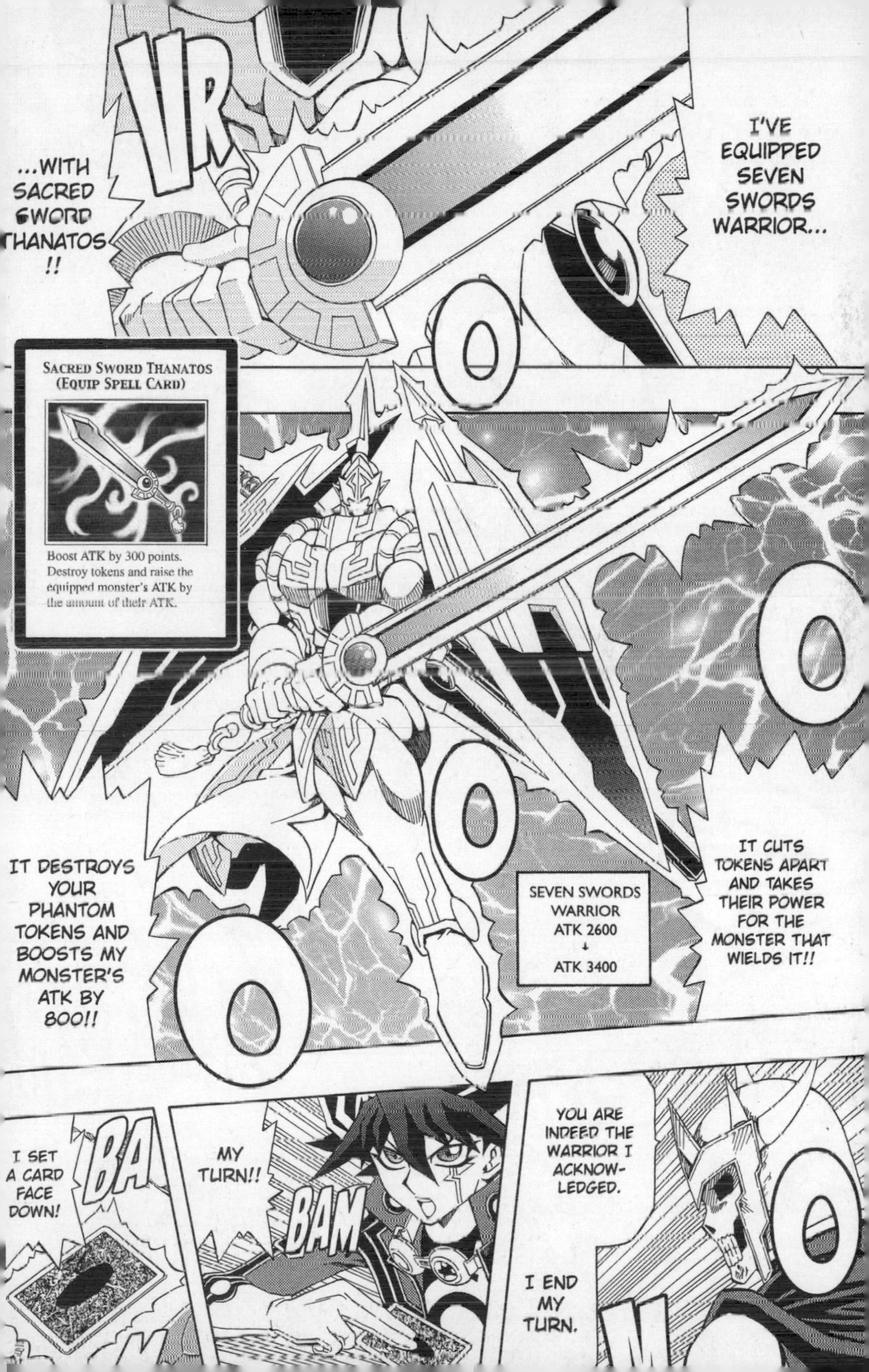

I'VE EQUIPPED SEVEN SWORDS WARRIOR...
...WITH SACRED SWORD THANATOS!!
VR
SACRED SWORD THANATOS (EQUIP SPELL CARD)
Boost ATK by 300 points. Destroy tokens and raise the equipped monster's ATK by the amount of their ATK.
IT CUTS TOKENS APART AND TAKES THEIR POWER FOR THE MONSTER THAT WIELDS IT!!
SEVEN SWORDS WARRIOR ATK 2600 → ATK 3400
IT DESTROYS YOUR PHANTOM TOKENS AND BOOSTS MY MONSTER'S ATK BY 800!!
YOU ARE INDEED THE WARRIOR I ACKNOWLEDGED.
I END MY TURN.
MY TURN!!
BAM
I SET A CARD FACE DOWN!
BA

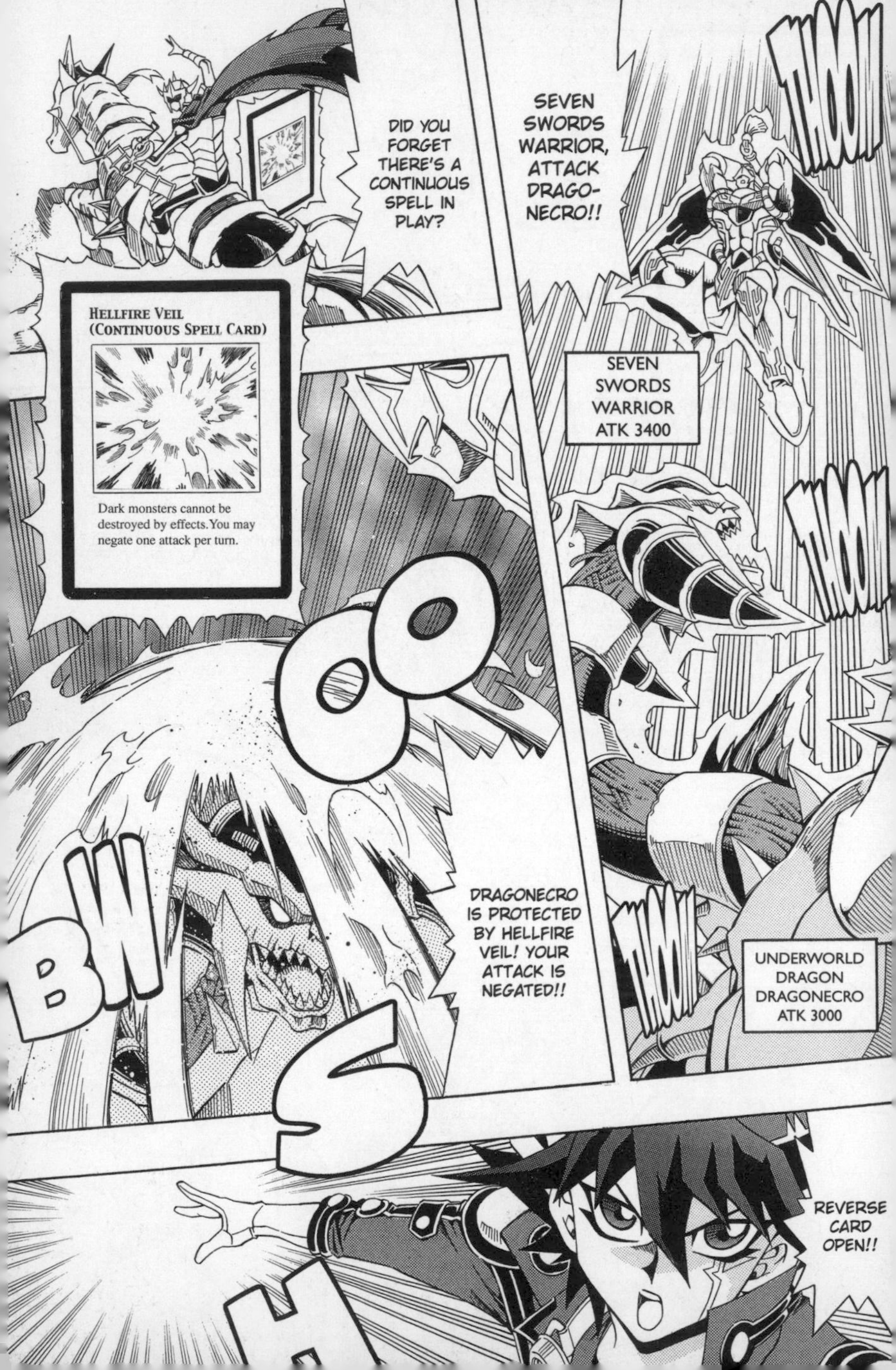
THOOM
SEVEN SWORDS WARRIOR, ATTACK DRAGO-NECRO!!
SEVEN SWORDS WARRIOR ATK 3400
THOOM
THOOM
UNDERWORLD DRAGON DRAGONECRO ATK 3000
DID YOU FORGET THERE'S A CONTINUOUS SPELL IN PLAY?
HELLFIRE VEIL (CONTINUOUS SPELL CARD)
Dark monsters cannot be destroyed by effects. You may negate one attack per turn.
DRAGONECRO IS PROTECTED BY HELLFIRE VEIL! YOUR ATTACK IS NEGATED!!
BWOOSH
REVERSE CARD OPEN!!

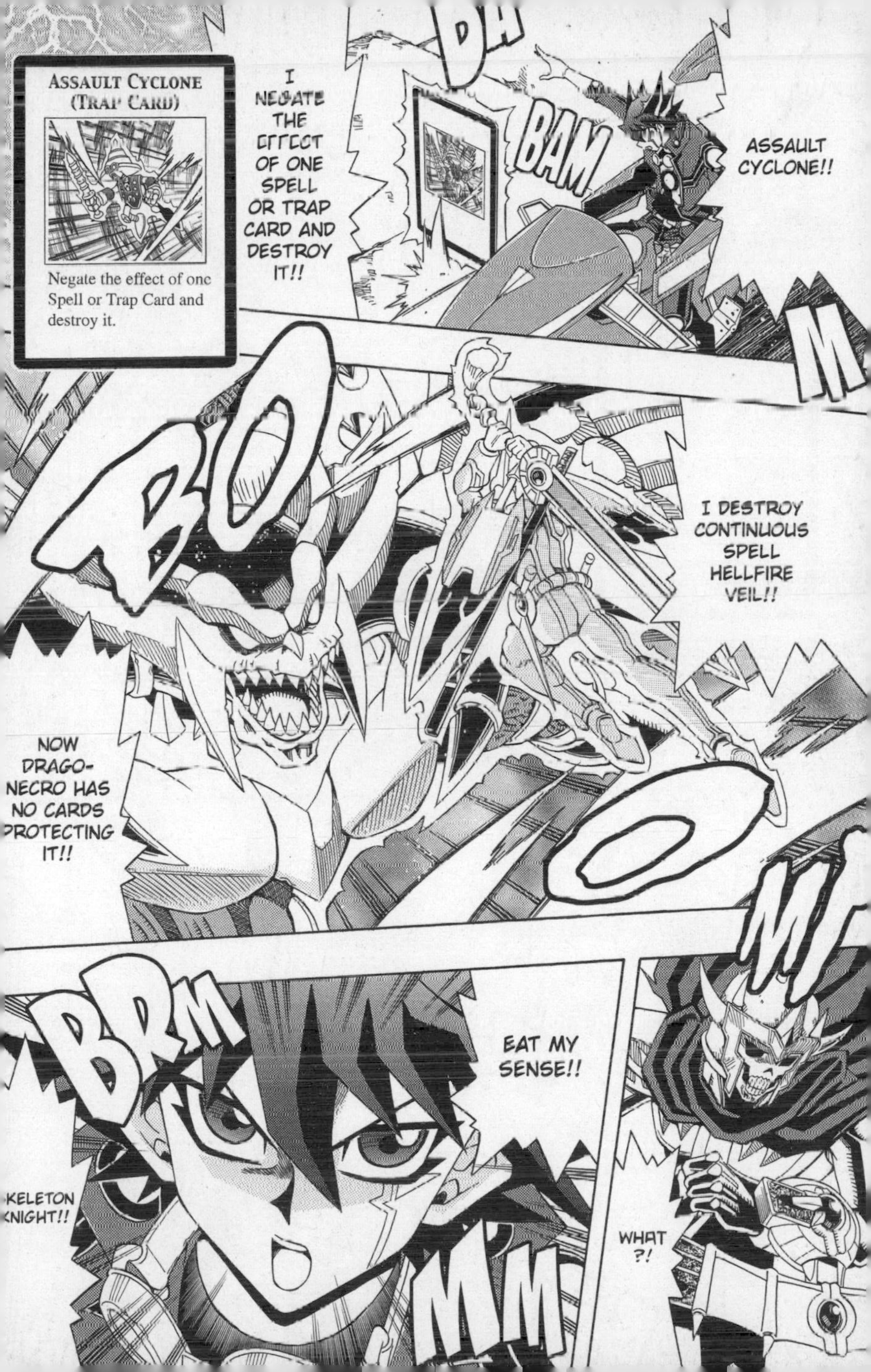
DA
BAM
ASSAULT CYCLONE!!
I NEGATE THE EFFECT OF ONE SPELL OR TRAP CARD AND DESTROY IT!!
ASSAULT CYCLONE (TRAP CARD)
Negate the effect of one Spell or Trap Card and destroy it.
M
I DESTROY CONTINUOUS SPELL HELLFIRE VEIL!!
BOOM
NOW DRAGO-NECRO HAS NO CARDS PROTECTING IT!!
M
WHAT ?!
BRM
EAT MY SENSE!!
KELETON NIGHT!!
MMM

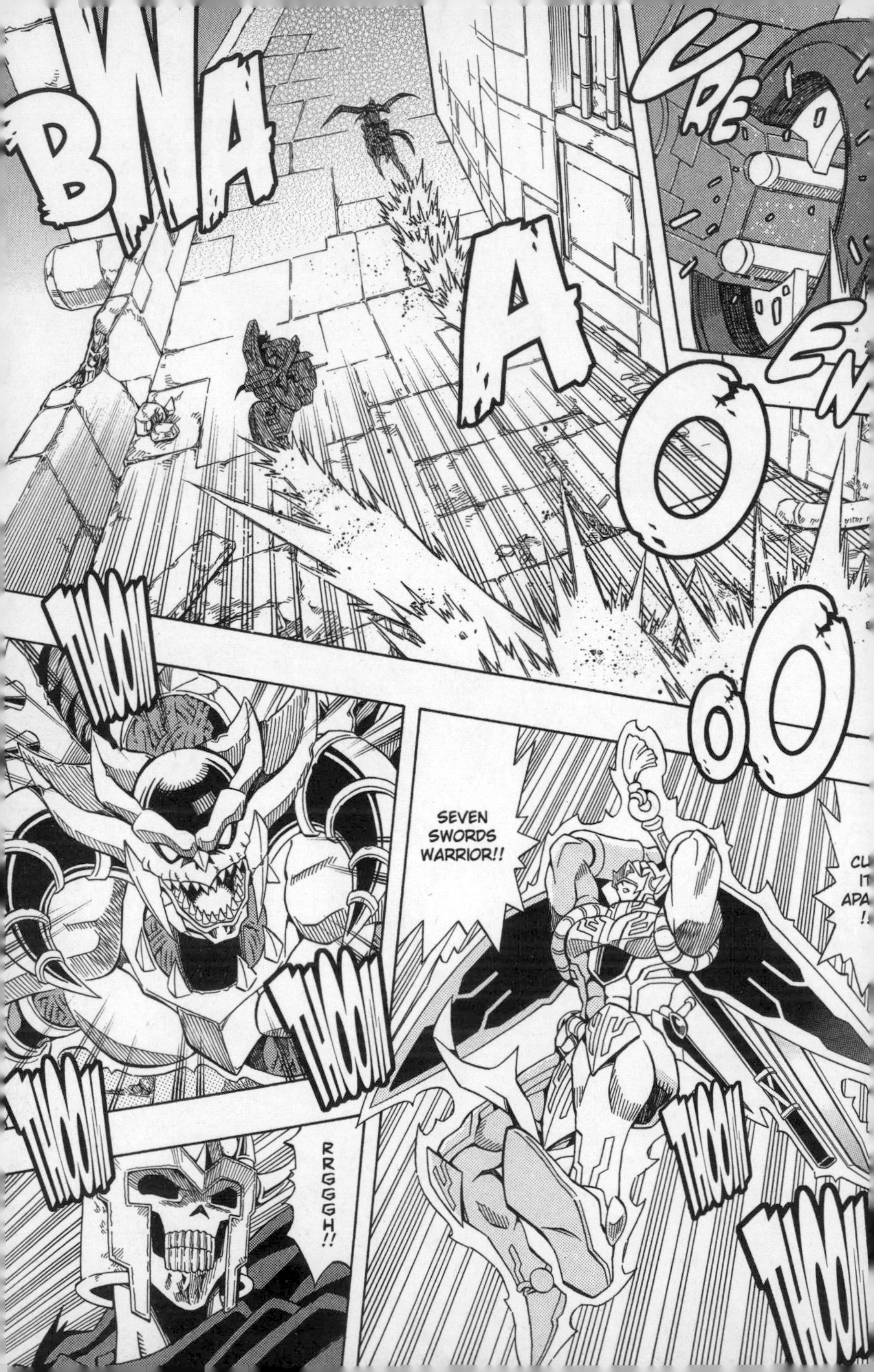
BWAAOOOO
CU
IT
APA
!!
SEVEN SWORDS WARRIOR!!
THOOM
THOOM
THOOM
THOOM
THOOM
THOOM
RRGGGH!!

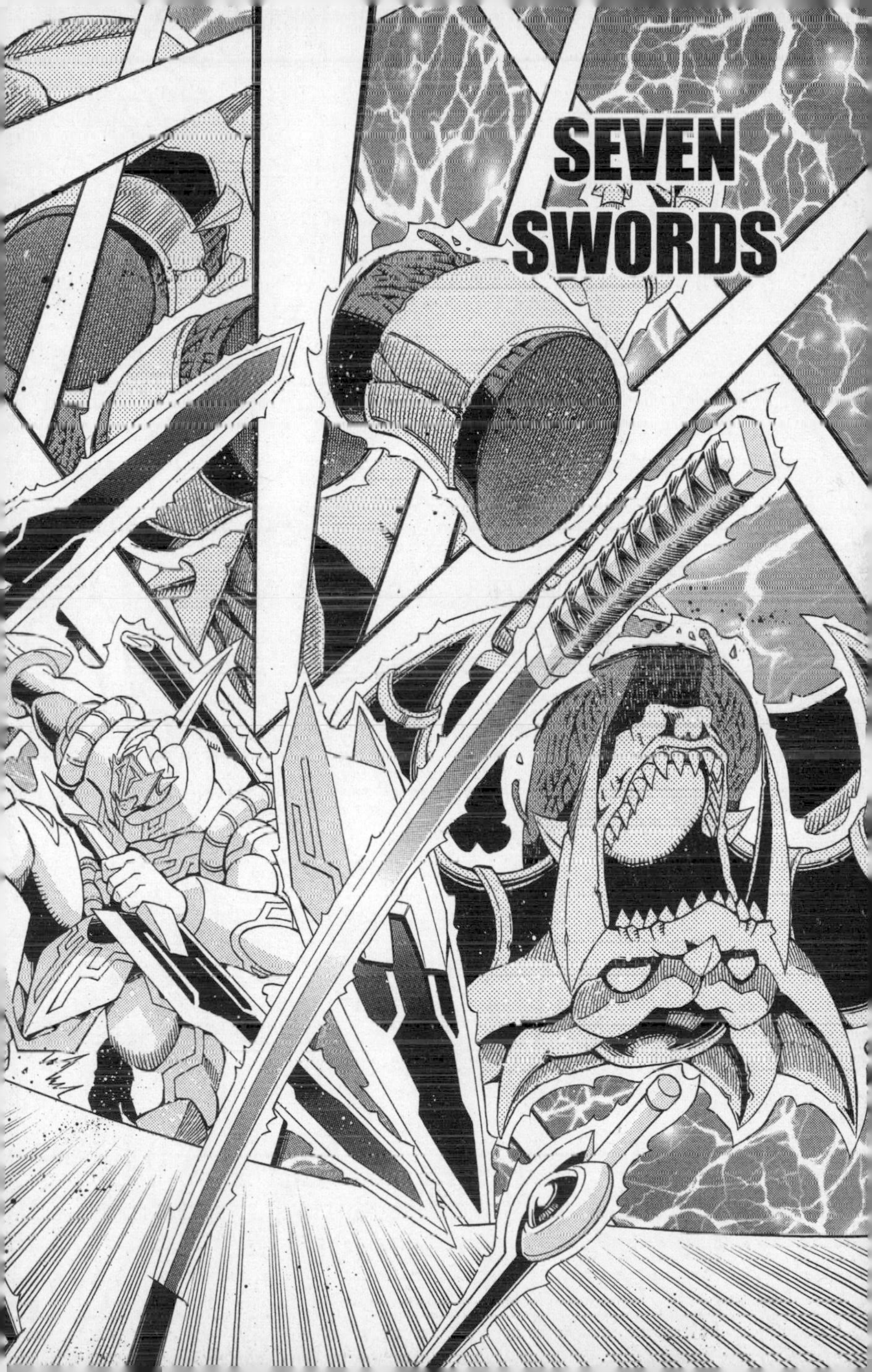
SEVEN
SWORDS

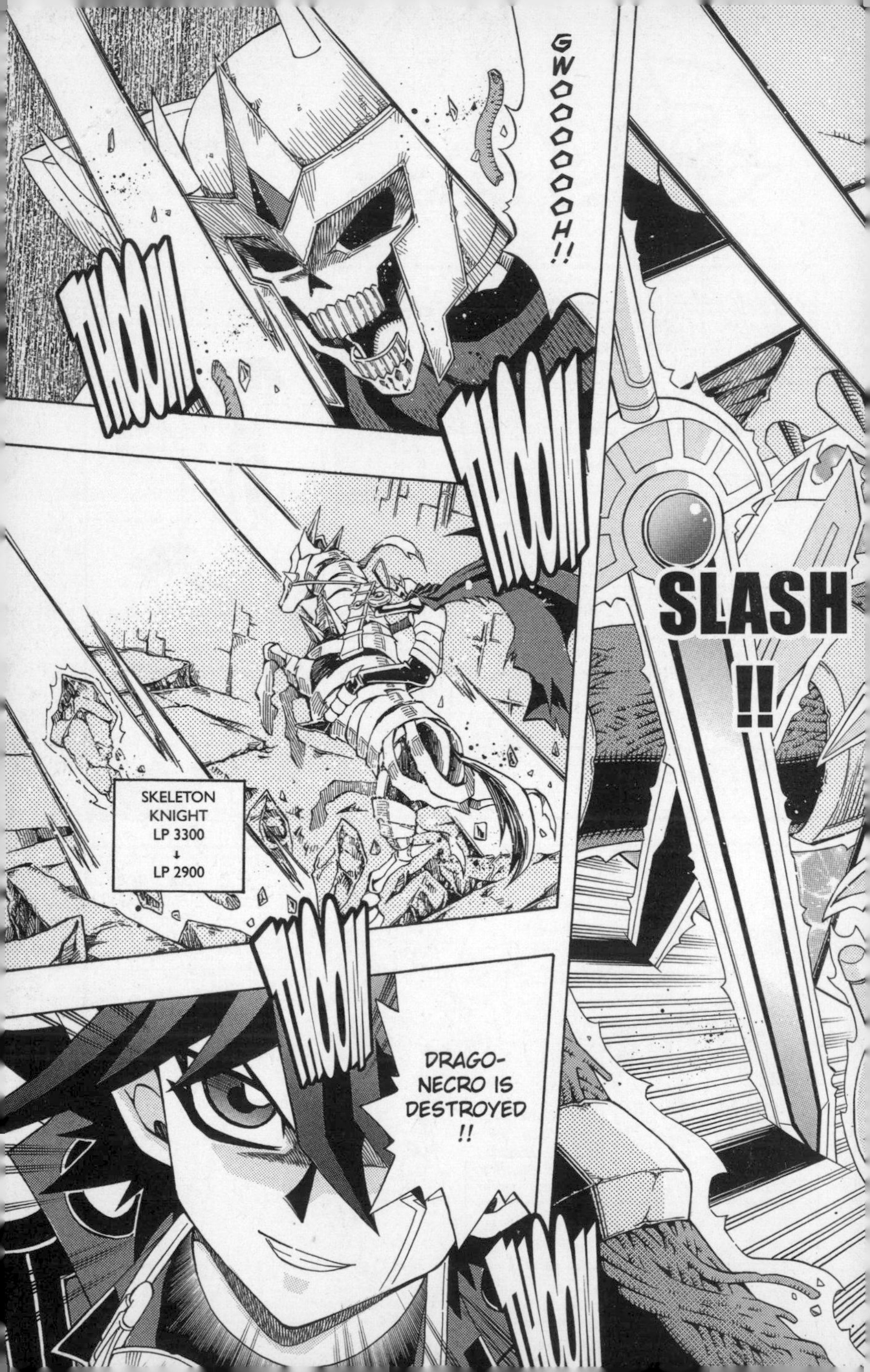
SLASH!!
GWOOOOOOOH!!
THOOM
THOOM
SKELETON KNIGHT LP 3300 ↓ LP 2900
THOOM
DRAGO-NECRO IS DESTROYED!!
THOOM

5D's TRACKS

THE 47TH

BY SATOMASA

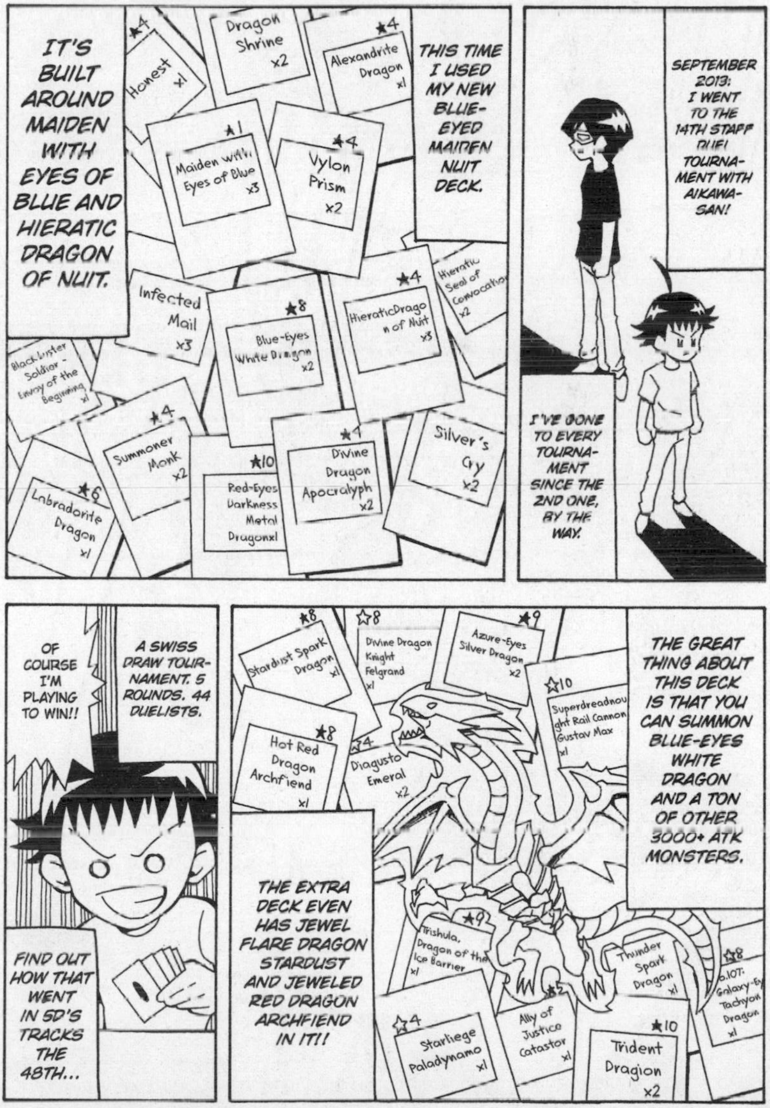

SEPTEMBER 2013: I WENT TO THE 14TH STAFF DUEL TOURNAMENT WITH AIKAWA-SAN!
I'VE GONE TO EVERY TOURNAMENT SINCE THE 2ND ONE, BY THE WAY.
THIS TIME I USED MY NEW BLUE-EYED MAIDEN NUIT DECK.
IT'S BUILT AROUND MAIDEN WITH EYES OF BLUE AND HIERATIC DRAGON OF NUIT.
★4 Honest x1
Dragon Shrine x2
★4 Alexandrite Dragon x1
★1 Maiden with Eyes of Blue x3
★4 Vylon Prism x2
Infected Mail x3
★8 Blue-Eyes White Dragon x2
★4 HieraticDragon of Nuit x3
Hieratic Seal of Convocation x2
Black Luster Soldier - Envoy of the Beginning x1
★4 Summoner Monk x2
★10 Red-Eyes Darkness Metal Dragon x1
★4 Divine Dragon Apocralyph x2
Silver's Cry x2
★6 Labradorite Dragon x1
THE GREAT THING ABOUT THIS DECK IS THAT YOU CAN SUMMON BLUE-EYES WHITE DRAGON AND A TON OF OTHER 3000+ ATK MONSTERS.
THE EXTRA DECK EVEN HAS JEWEL FLARE DRAGON STARDUST AND JEWELED RED DRAGON ARCHFIEND IN IT!!
★8 Stardust Spark Dragon x1
☆8 Divine Dragon Knight Felgrand x1
★9 Azure-Eyes Silver Dragon x2
☆10 Superdreadnought Rail Cannon Gustav Max x1
★8 Hot Red Dragon Archfiend x1
☆4 Diagusto Emeral x2
★9 Trishula, Dragon of the Ice Barrier x1
Thunder Spark Dragon x1
☆8 No.107: Galaxy-Eyes Tachyon Dragon x1
☆4 Starliege Paladynamo x1
Ally of Justice Catastor x1
★10 Trident Dragion x2
A SWISS DRAW TOURNAMENT. 5 ROUNDS. 44 DUELISTS.
OF COURSE I'M PLAYING TO WIN!!
FIND OUT HOW THAT WENT IN 5D'S TRACKS THE 48TH...

RIDE-49

NORTHERN CORRIDOR FURY!!

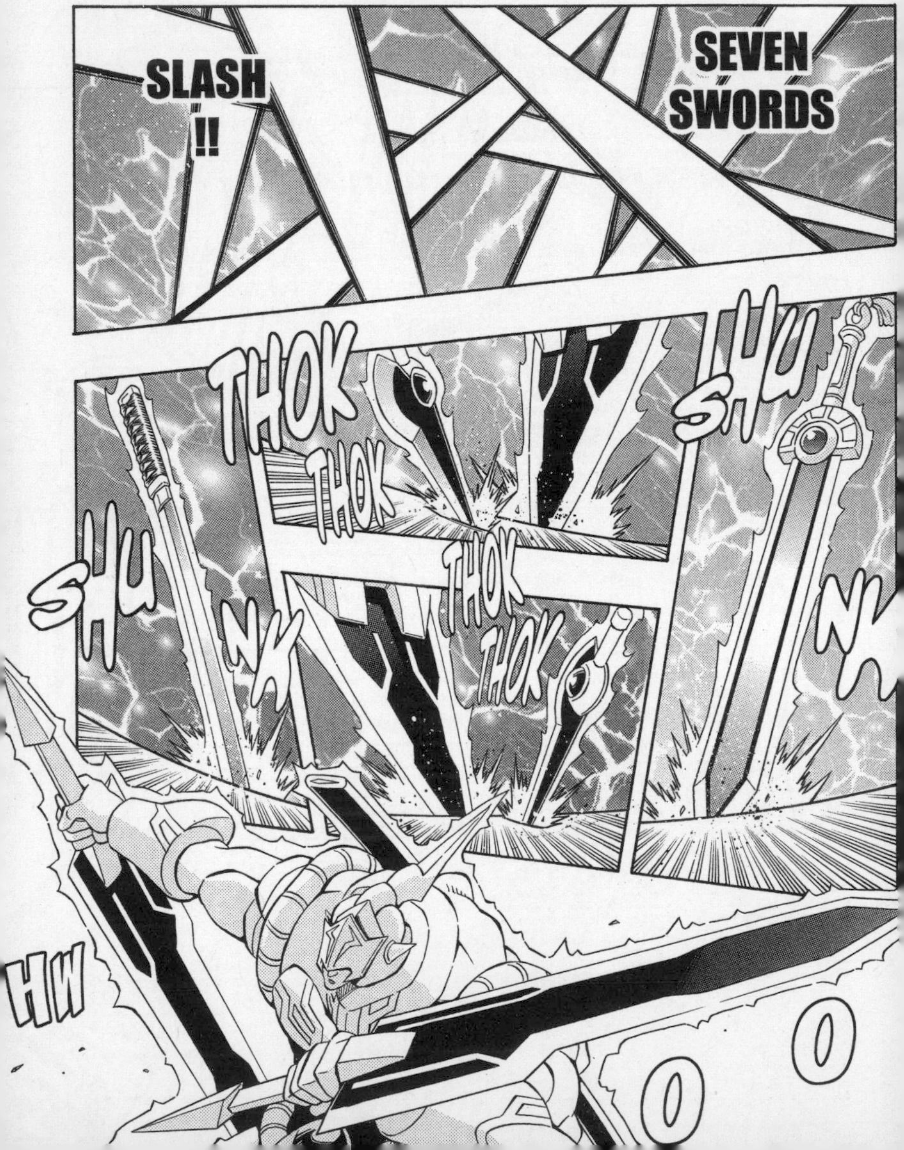
SEVEN SWORDS
SLASH !!
SHU
NK
THOK
THOK
THOK
THOK
SHU
NK
HW
OOO

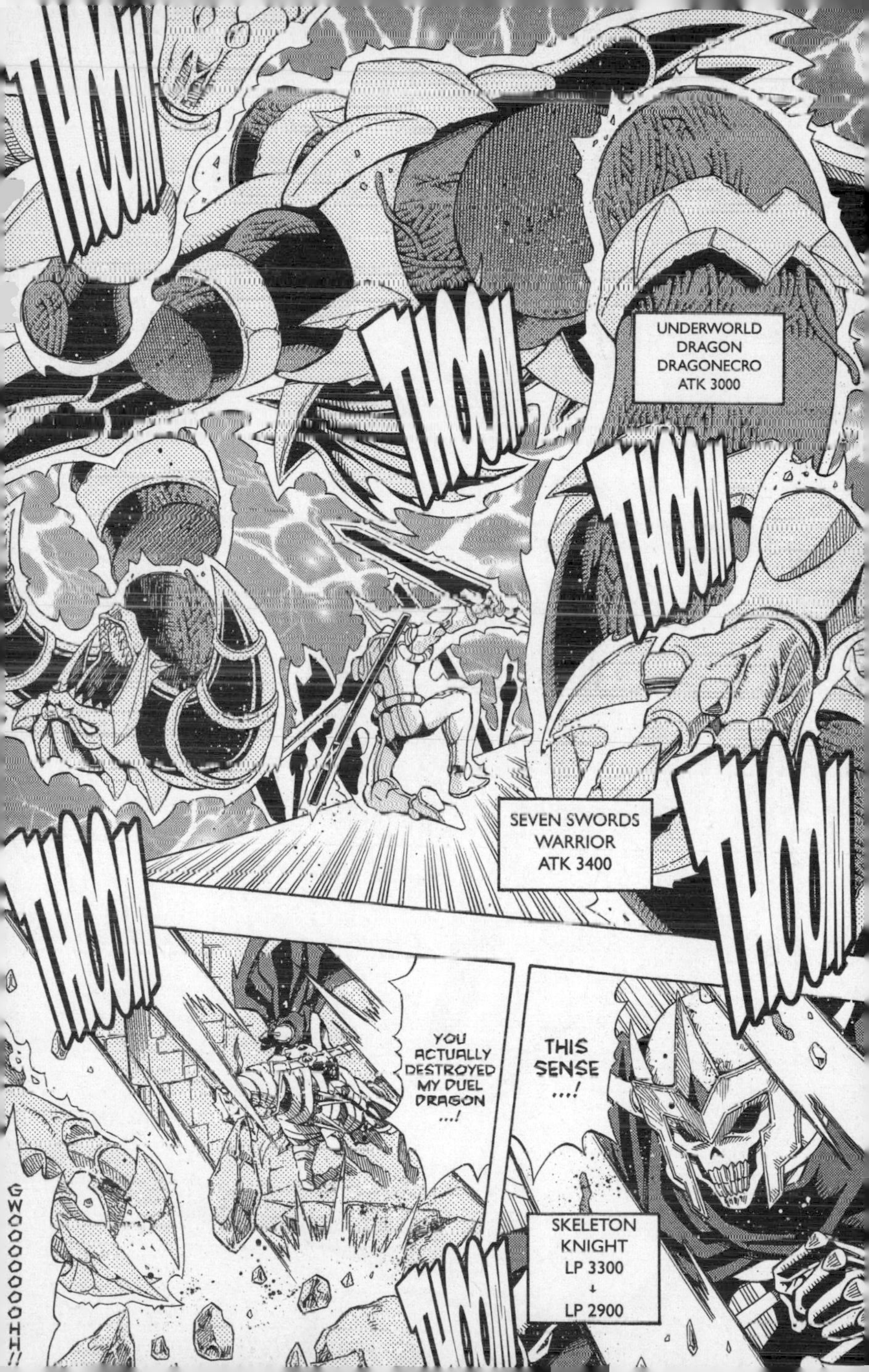
THOOM
UNDERWORLD DRAGON DRAGONECRO ATK 3000
THOOM
THOOM
THOOM
SEVEN SWORDS WARRIOR ATK 3400
THOOM
THIS SENSE ...!
SKELETON KNIGHT LP 3300 → LP 2900
THOOM
YOU ACTUALLY DESTROYED MY DUEL DRAGON ...!
GWOOOOOOOHH!!

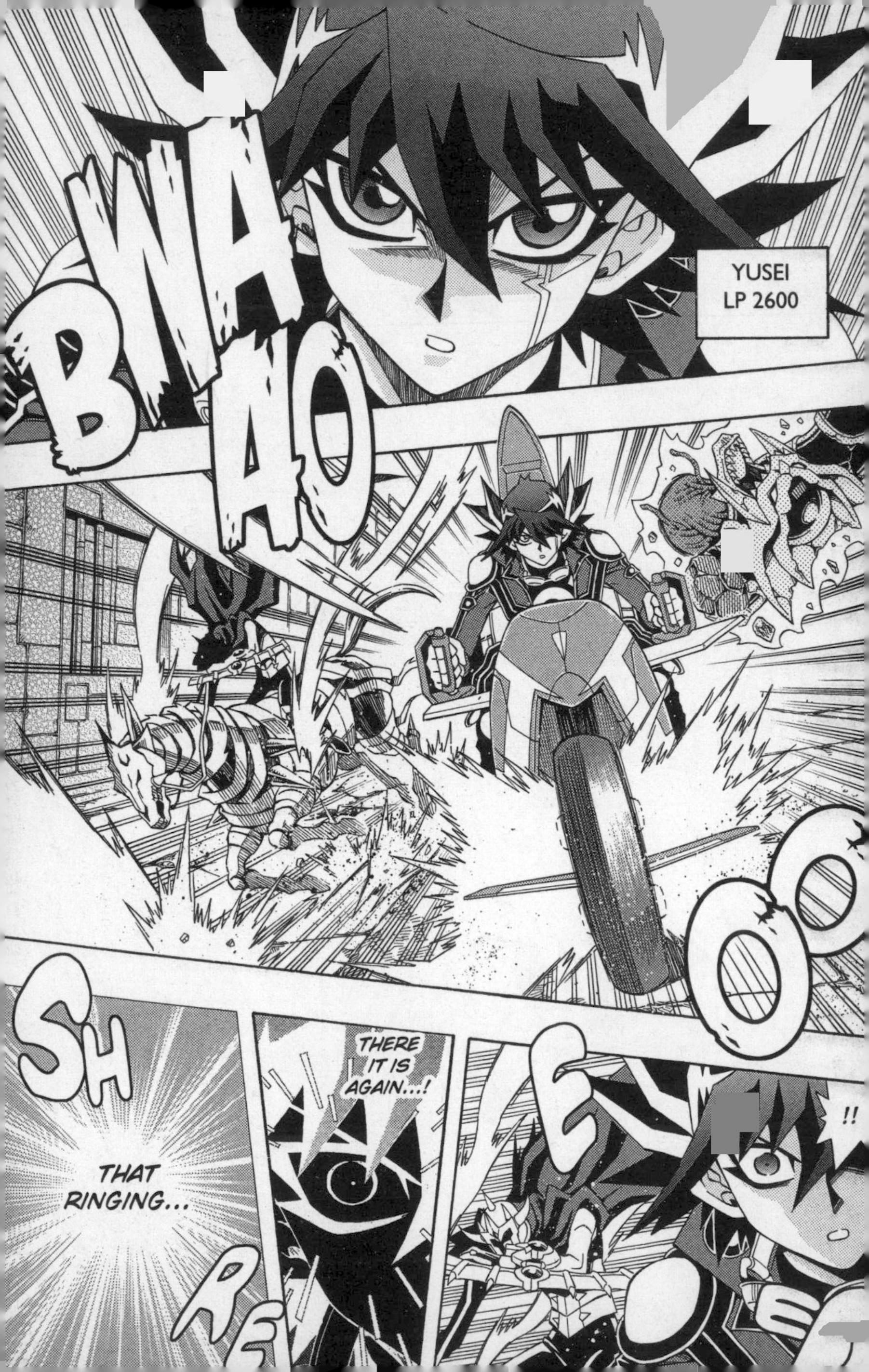
YUSEI
LP 2600
BWAAOOO
!!
THERE IT IS AGAIN...!
THAT RINGING...

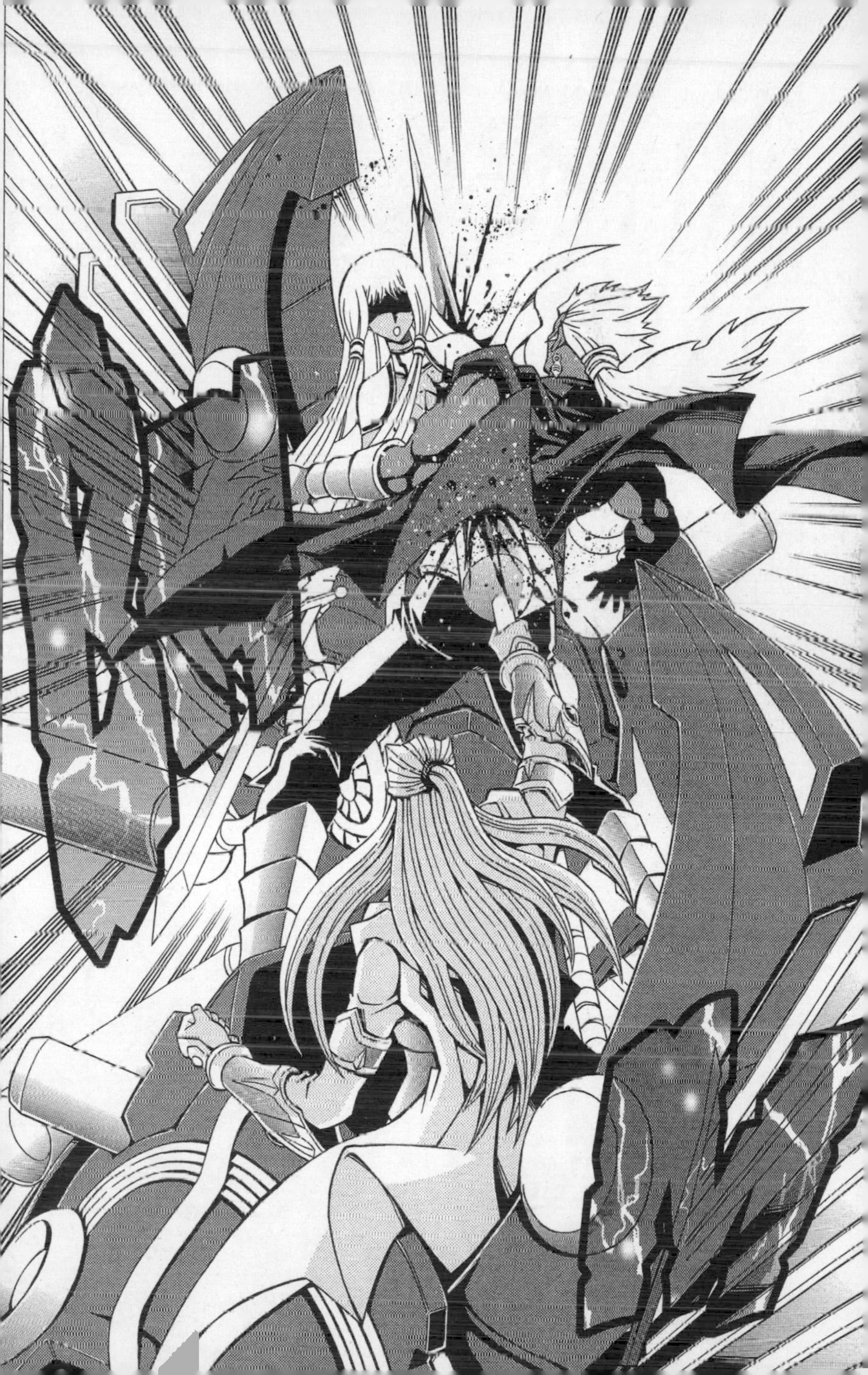

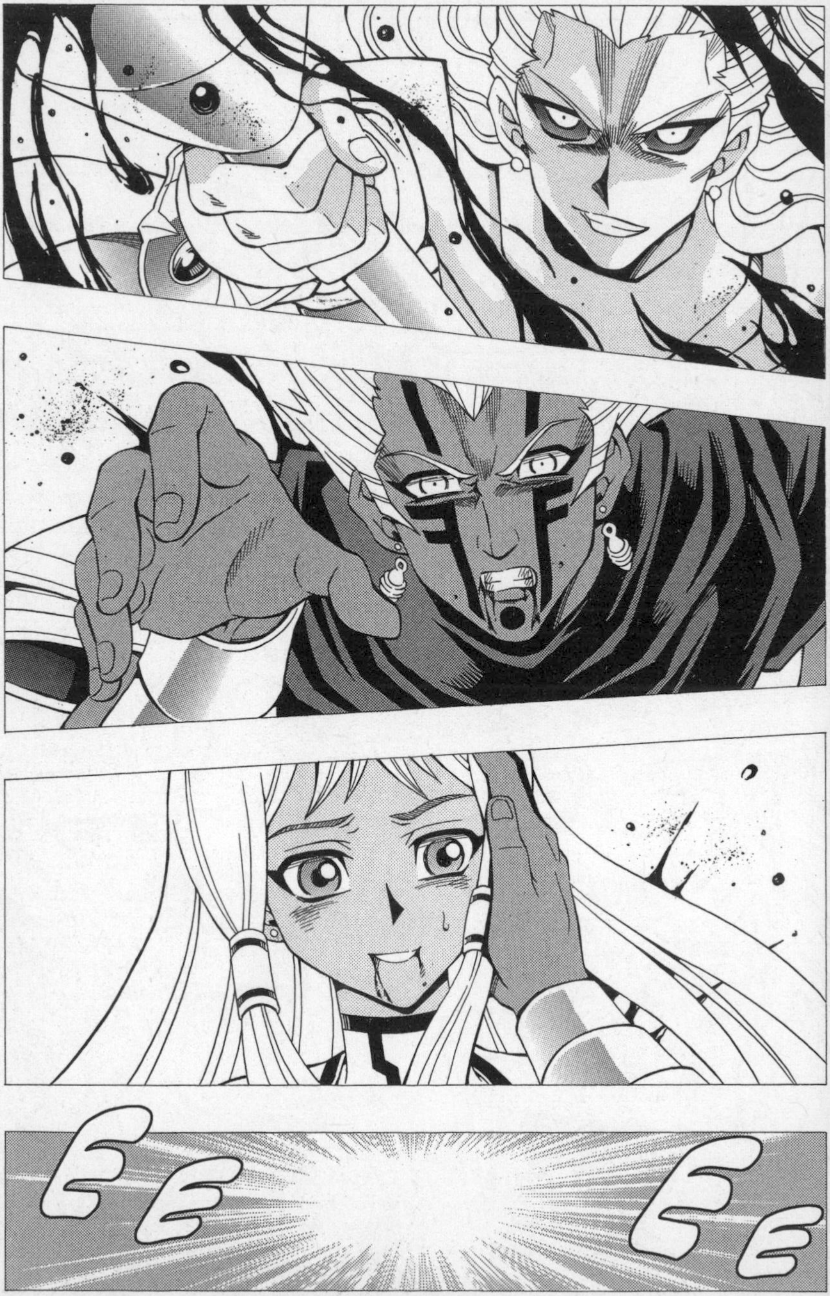
EEEEEE

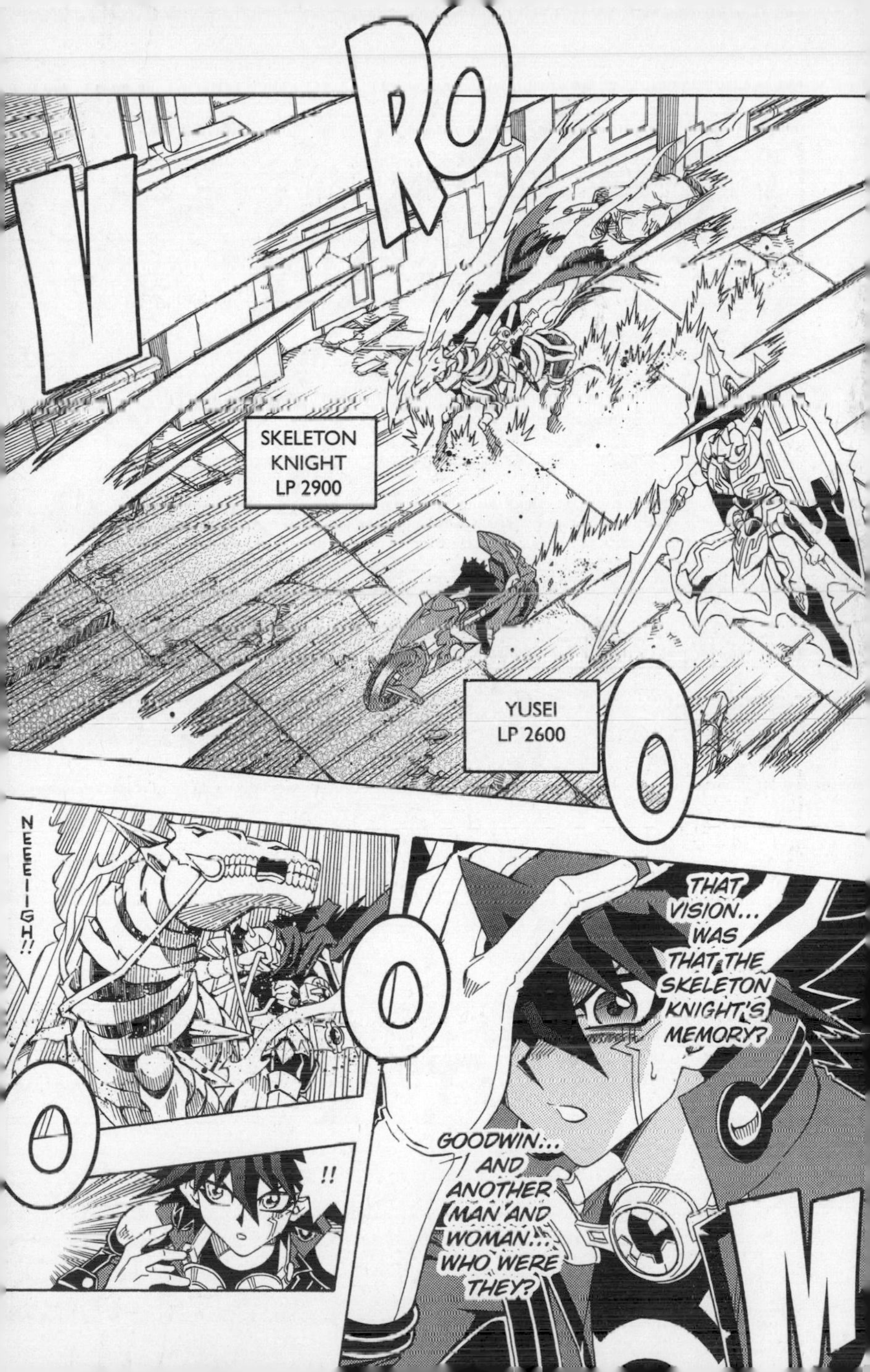
VROOOOM
SKELETON KNIGHT LP 2900
YUSEI LP 2600
THAT VISION... WAS THAT THE SKELETON KNIGHT'S MEMORY?
GOODWIN... AND ANOTHER MAN AND WOMAN... WHO WERE THEY?
NEEEIIGH!!
!!

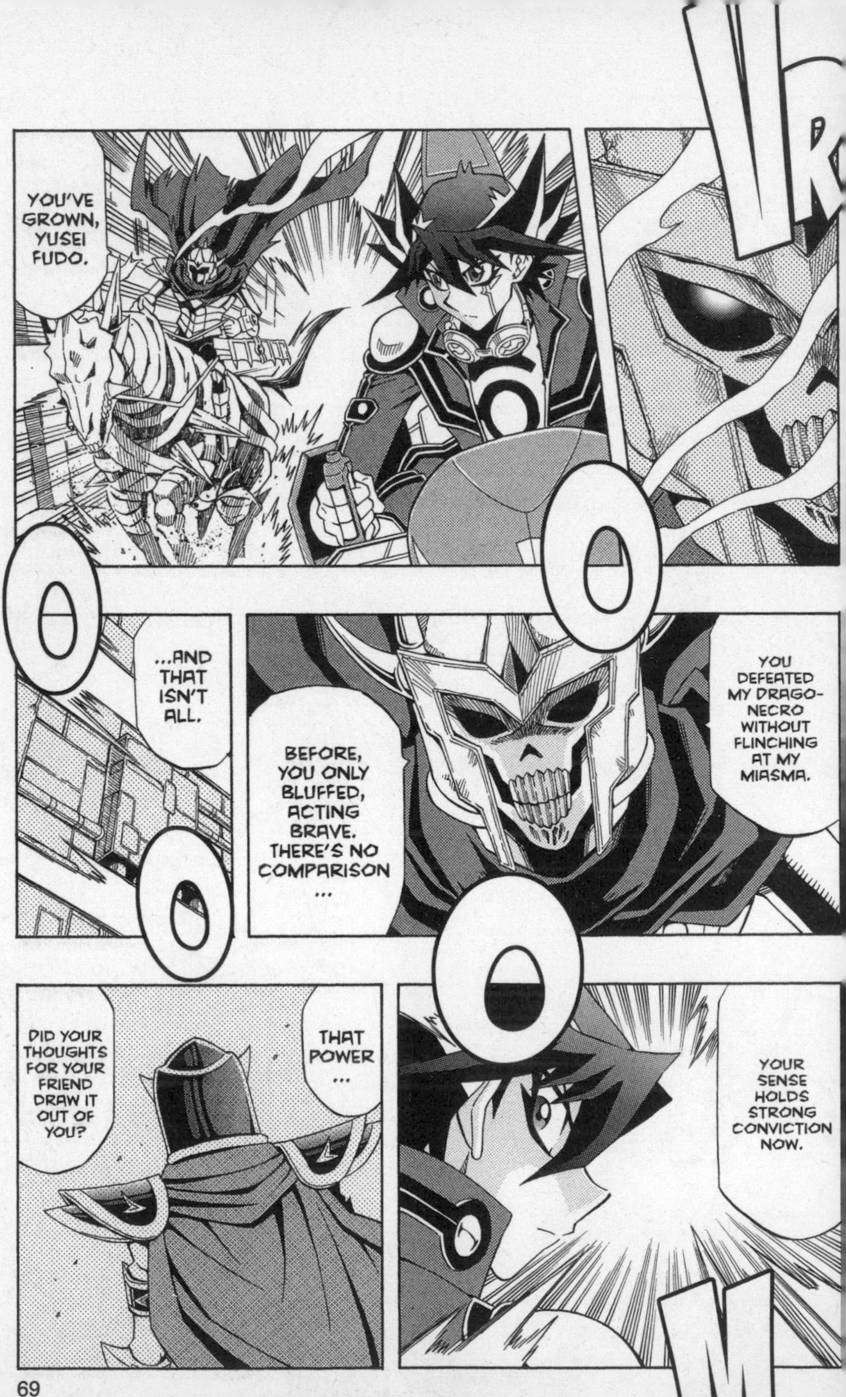
YOU'VE GROWN, YUSEI FUDO.
YOU DEFEATED MY DRAGO-NECRO WITHOUT FLINCHING AT MY MIASMA.
BEFORE, YOU ONLY BLUFFED, ACTING BRAVE. THERE'S NO COMPARISON ...
...AND THAT ISN'T ALL.
YOUR SENSE HOLDS STRONG CONVICTION NOW.
THAT POWER ...
DID YOUR THOUGHTS FOR YOUR FRIEND DRAW IT OUT OF YOU?

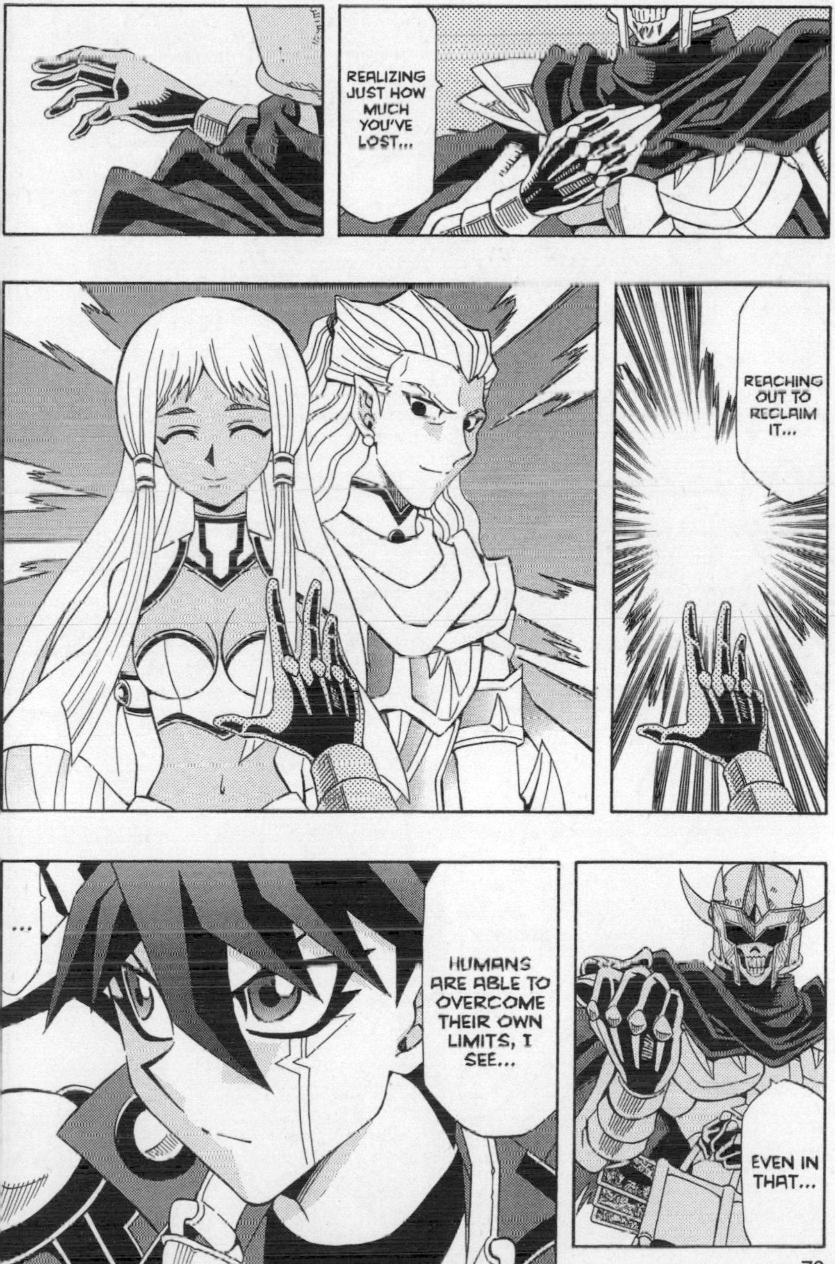
REALIZING JUST HOW MUCH YOU'VE LOST...
REACHING OUT TO RECLAIM IT...
EVEN IN THAT...
HUMANS ARE ABLE TO OVERCOME THEIR OWN LIMITS, I SEE...
...

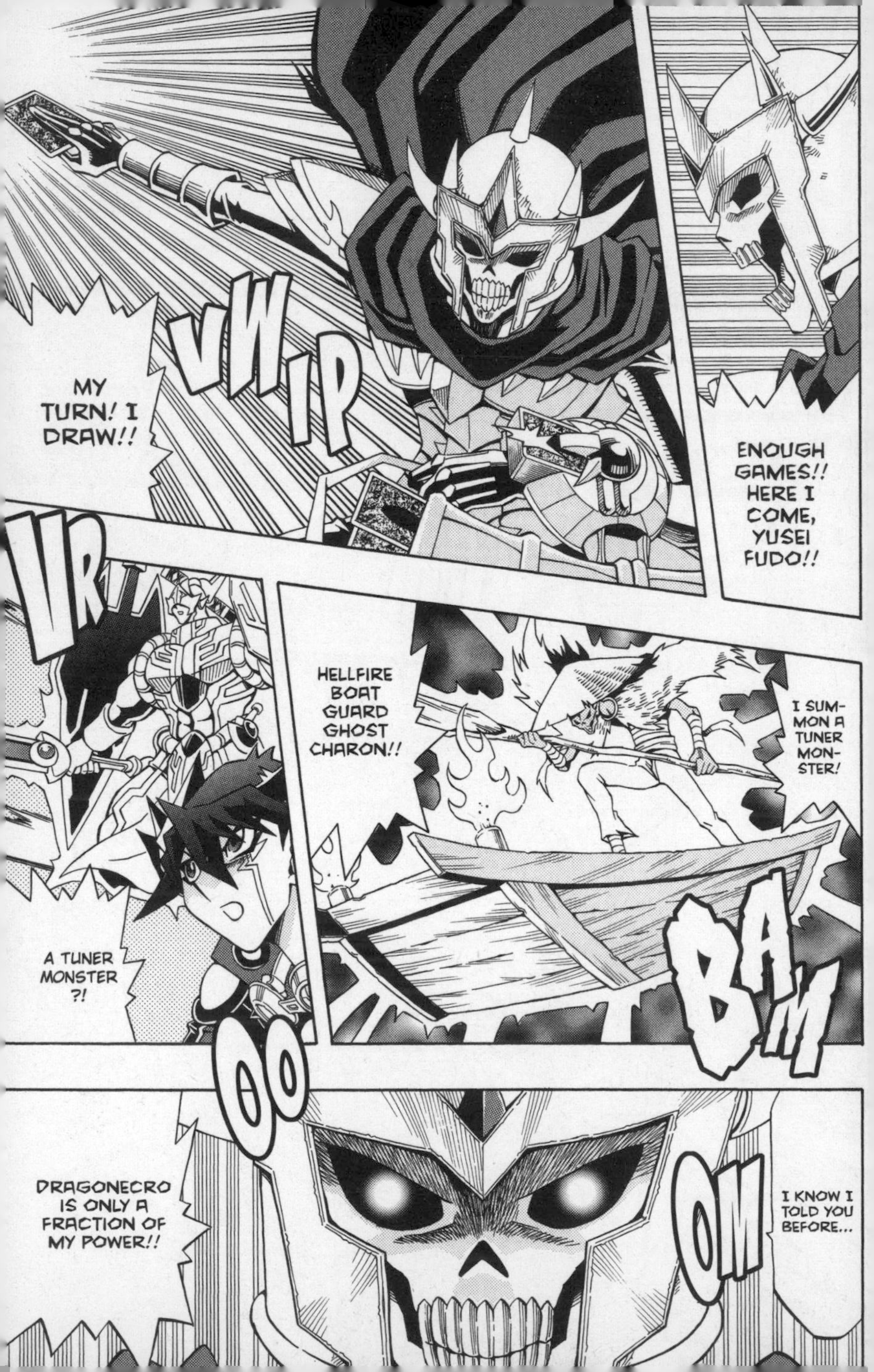
ENOUGH GAMES!! HERE I COME, YUSEI FUDO!!
VWIP
MY TURN! I DRAW!!
I SUM-MON A TUNER MON-STER!
HELLFIRE BOAT GUARD GHOST CHARON!!
BAM
A TUNER MONSTER ?!
I KNOW I TOLD YOU BEFORE...
OOOM
DRAGONECRO IS ONLY A FRACTION OF MY POWER!!

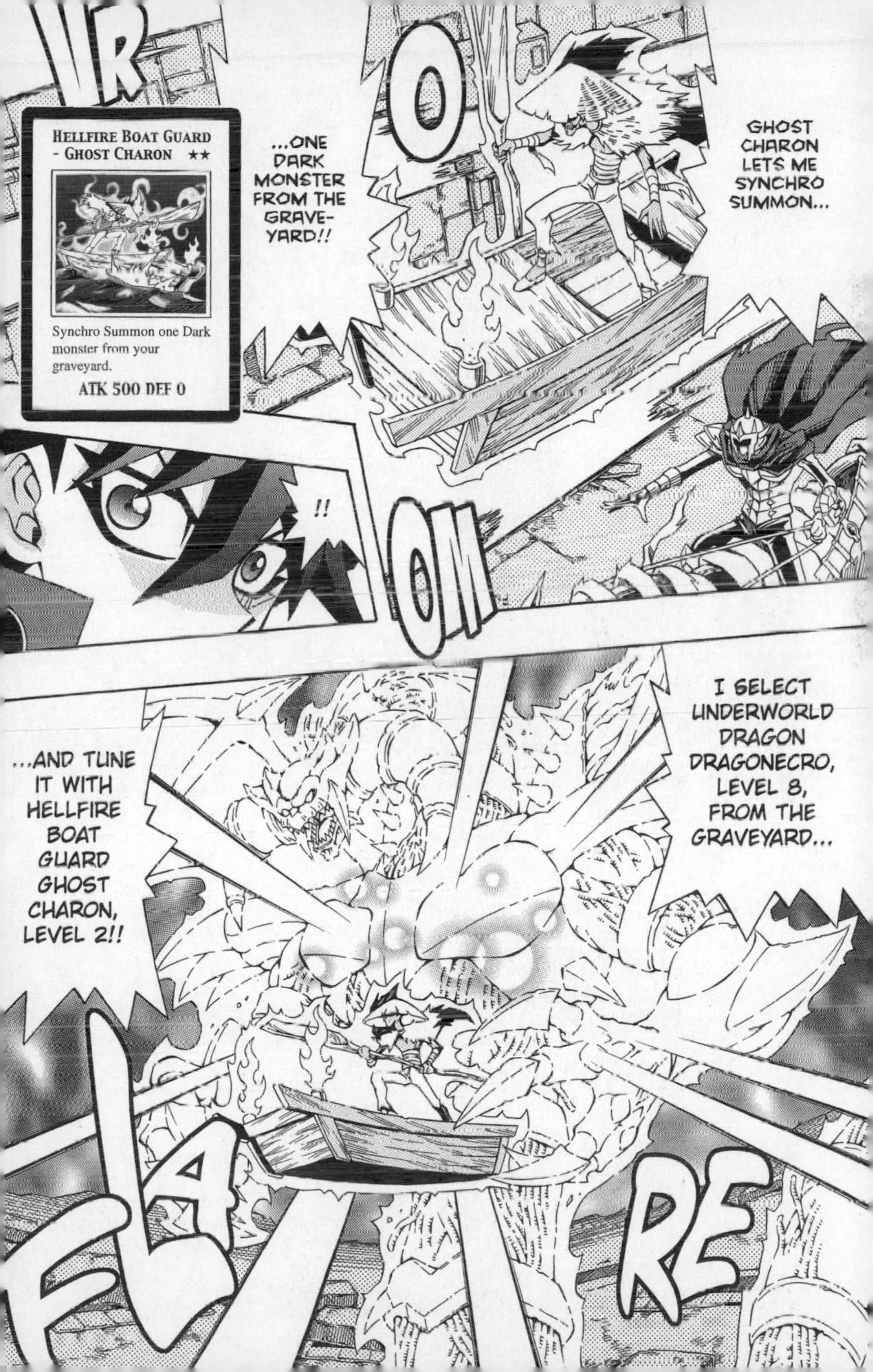
GHOST CHARON LETS ME SYNCHRO SUMMON...
...ONE DARK MONSTER FROM THE GRAVEYARD!!
HELLFIRE BOAT GUARD - GHOST CHARON ★★
Synchro Summon one Dark monster from your graveyard.
ATK 500 DEF 0
VR
O
OM
!!
I SELECT UNDERWORLD DRAGON DRAGONECRO, LEVEL 8, FROM THE GRAVEYARD...
...AND TUNE IT WITH HELLFIRE BOAT GUARD GHOST CHARON, LEVEL 2!!
FLA
RE

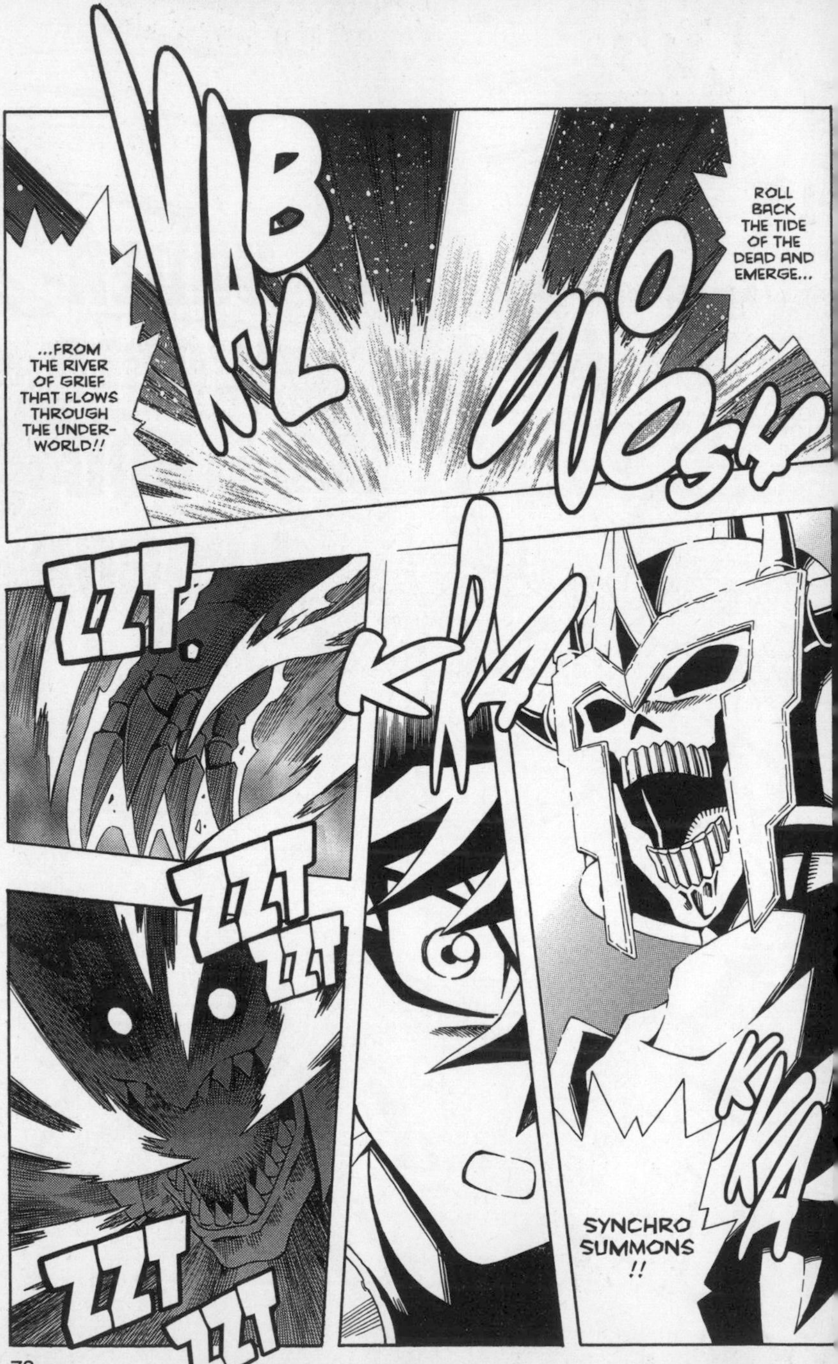
ROLL BACK THE TIDE OF THE DEAD AND EMERGE...
...FROM THE RIVER OF GRIEF THAT FLOWS THROUGH THE UNDER-WORLD!!
SYNCHRO SUMMONS!!
ZZT.
ZZT
ZZT
ZZT
ZZT

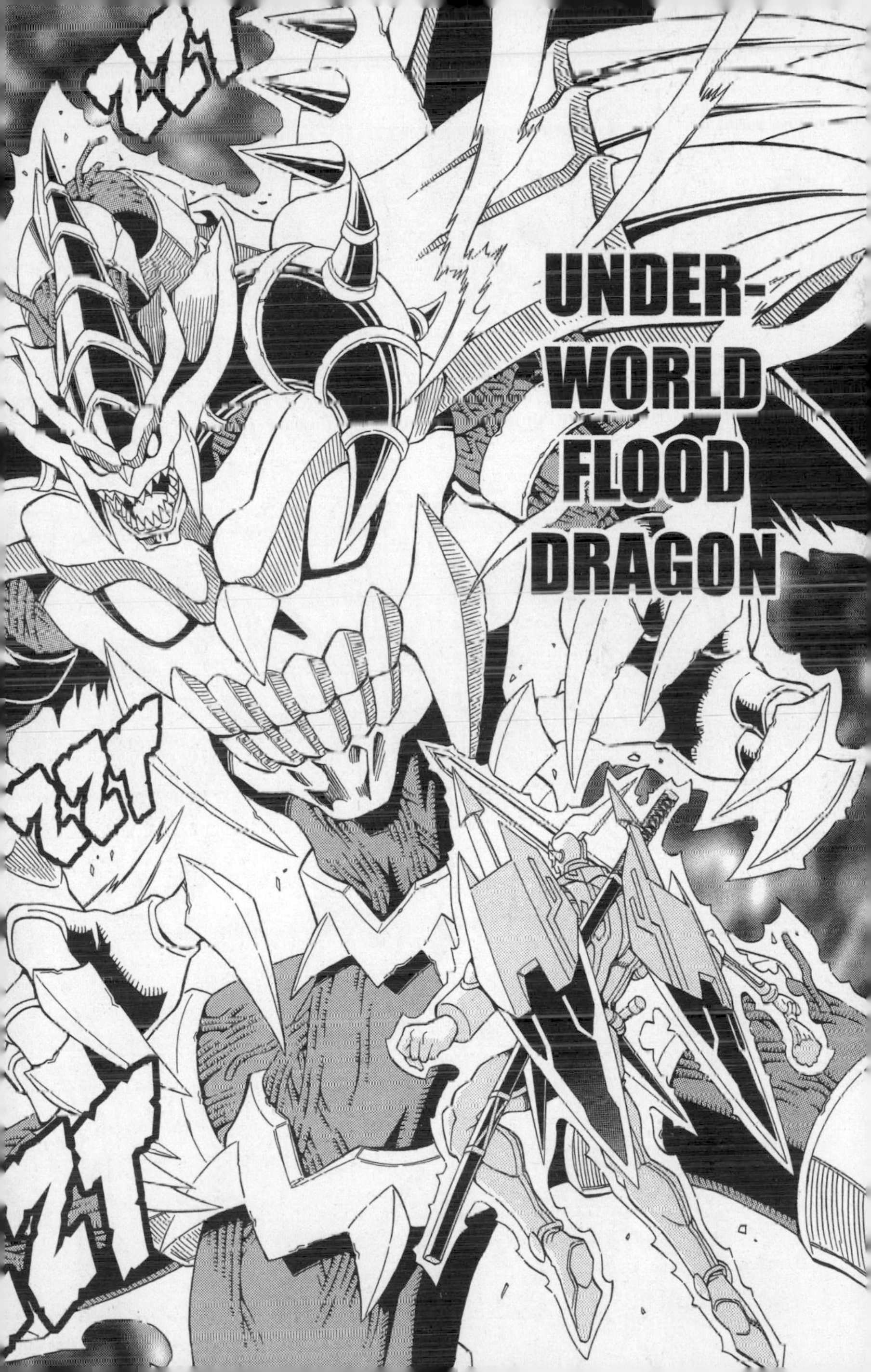
UNDER-WORLD FLOOD DRAGON

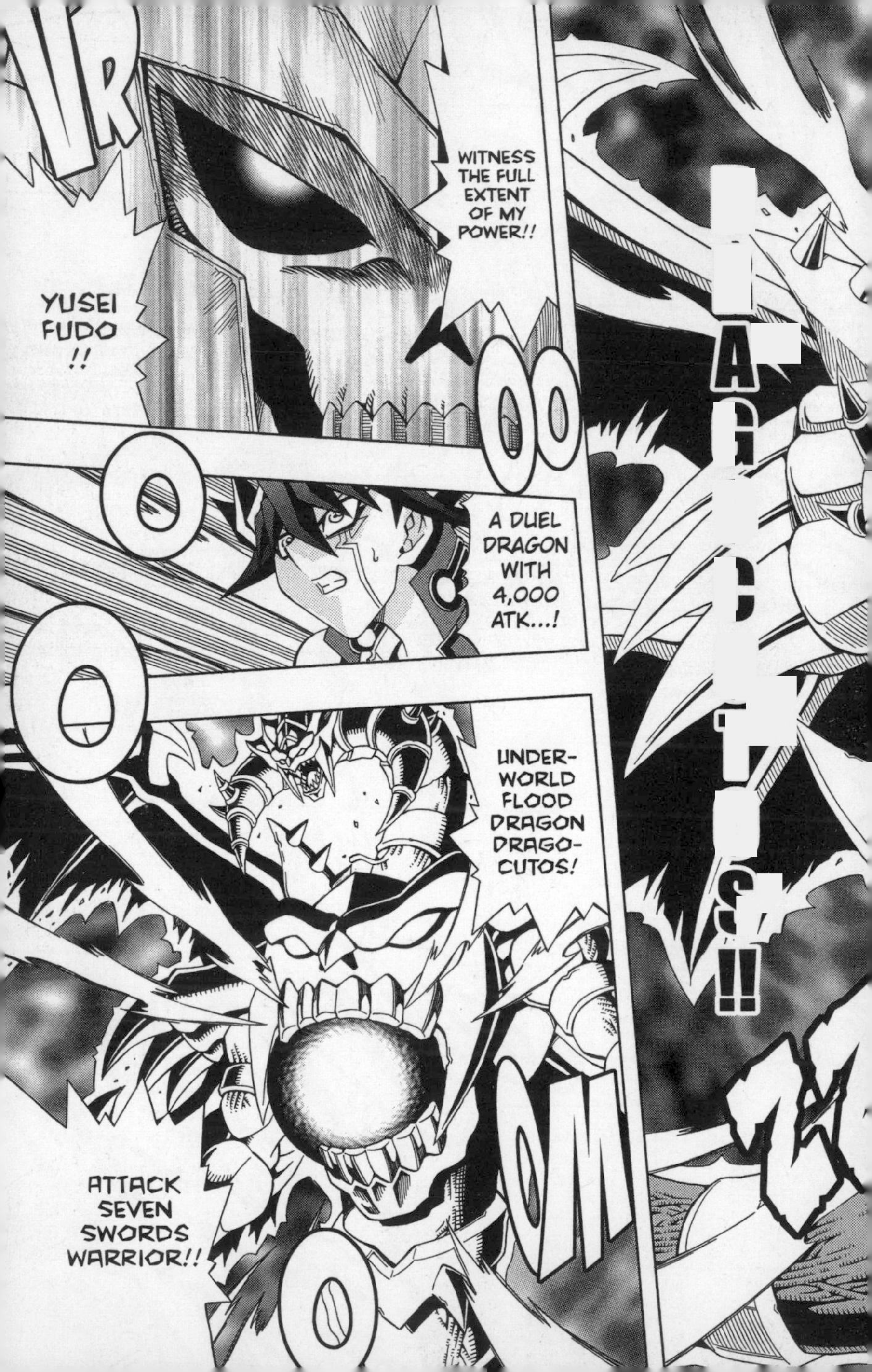
WITNESS THE FULL EXTENT OF MY POWER!!
YUSEI FUDO!!
A DUEL DRAGON WITH 4,000 ATK...!
UNDER-WORLD FLOOD DRAGON DRAGO-CUTOS!
ATTACK SEVEN SWORDS WARRIOR!!

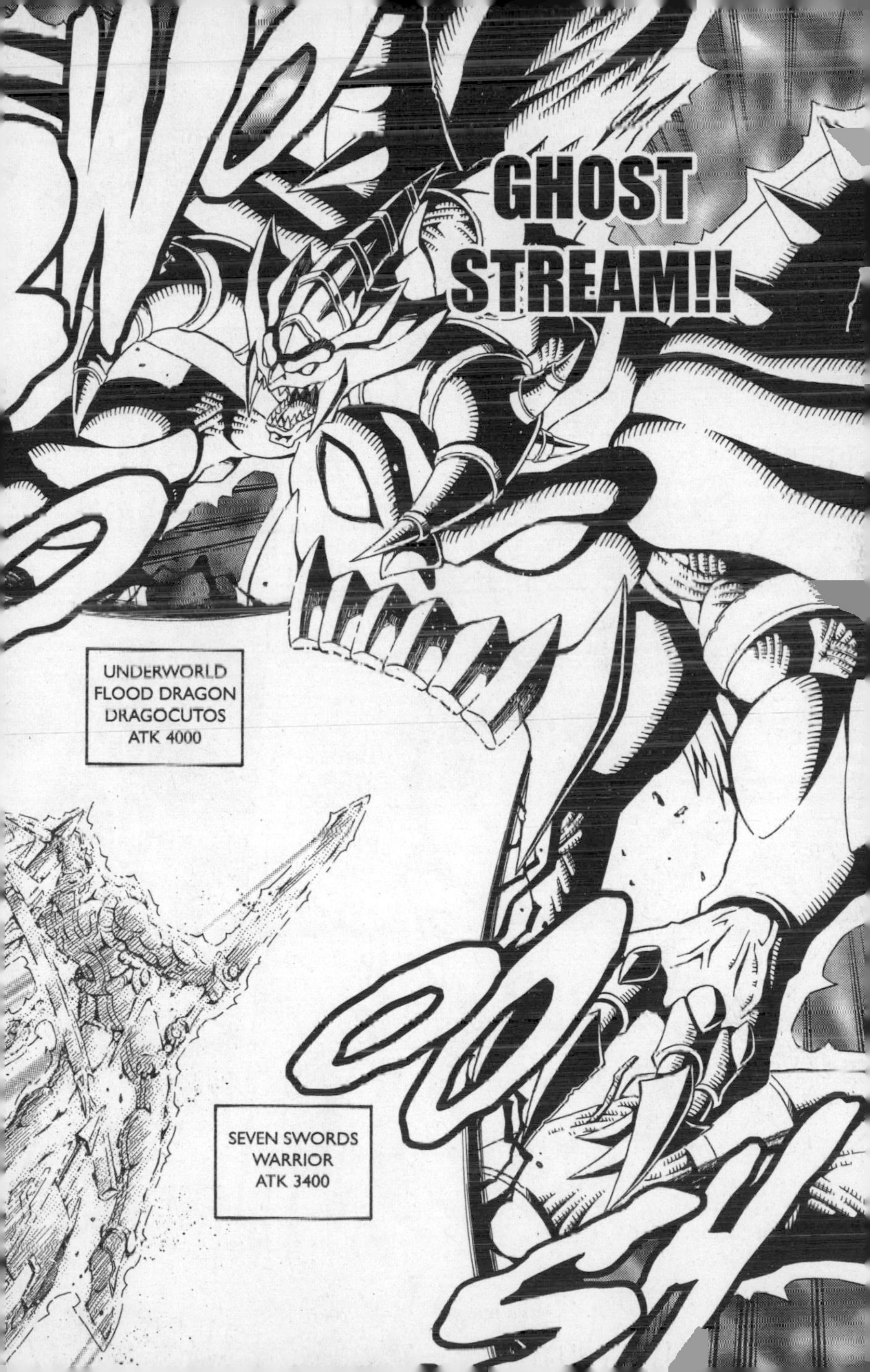
GHOST STREAM!!
UNDERWORLD FLOOD DRAGON DRAGOCUTOS ATK 4000
SEVEN SWORDS WARRIOR ATK 3400

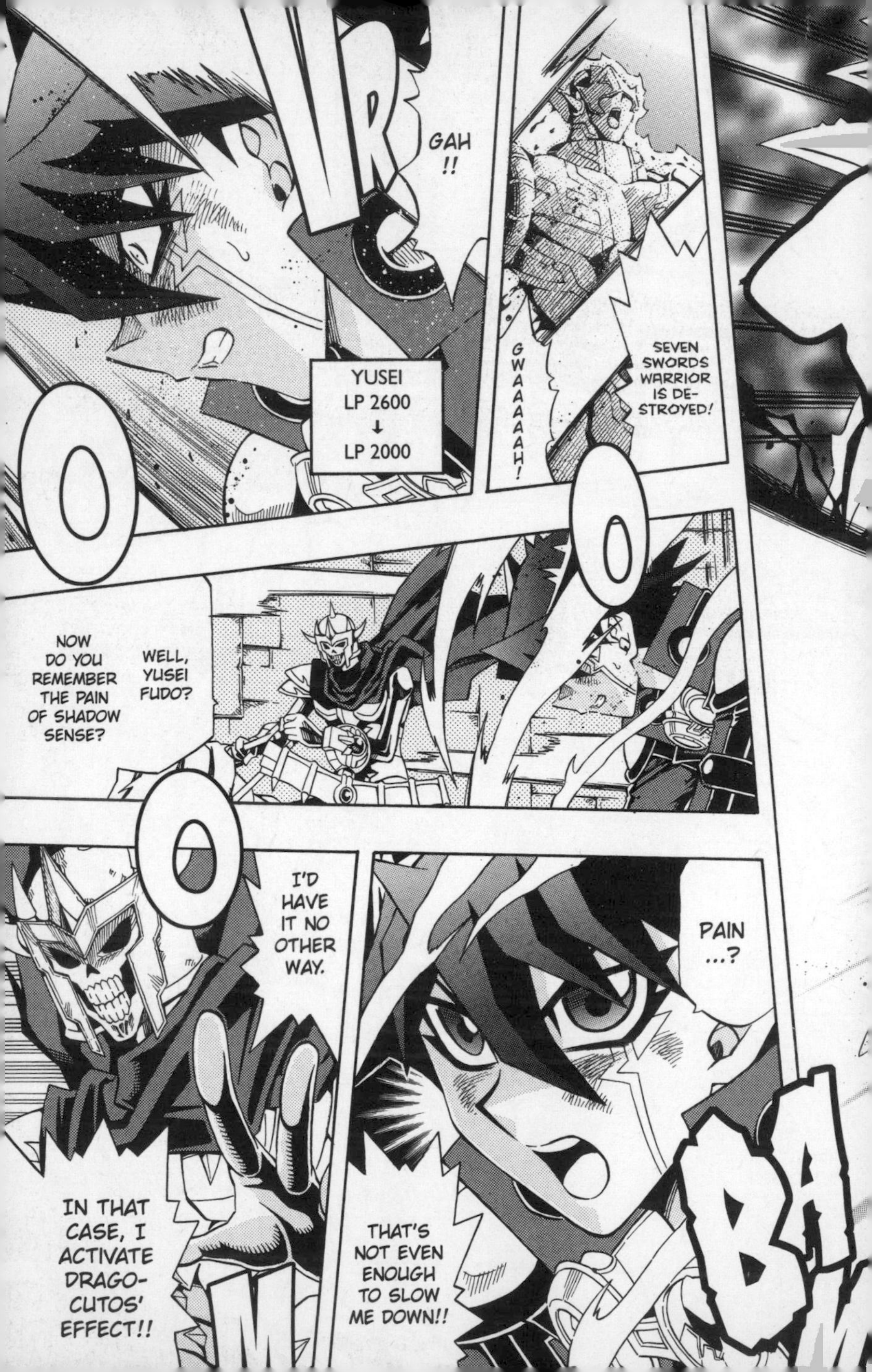
SEVEN SWORDS WARRIOR IS DE-STROYED!
GWAAAAAAAH!
GAH!!
YUSEI LP 2600 ↓ LP 2000
WELL, YUSEI FUDO?
NOW DO YOU REMEMBER THE PAIN OF SHADOW SENSE?
PAIN...?
THAT'S NOT EVEN ENOUGH TO SLOW ME DOWN!!
I'D HAVE IT NO OTHER WAY.
IN THAT CASE, I ACTIVATE DRAGO-CUTOS' EFFECT!!

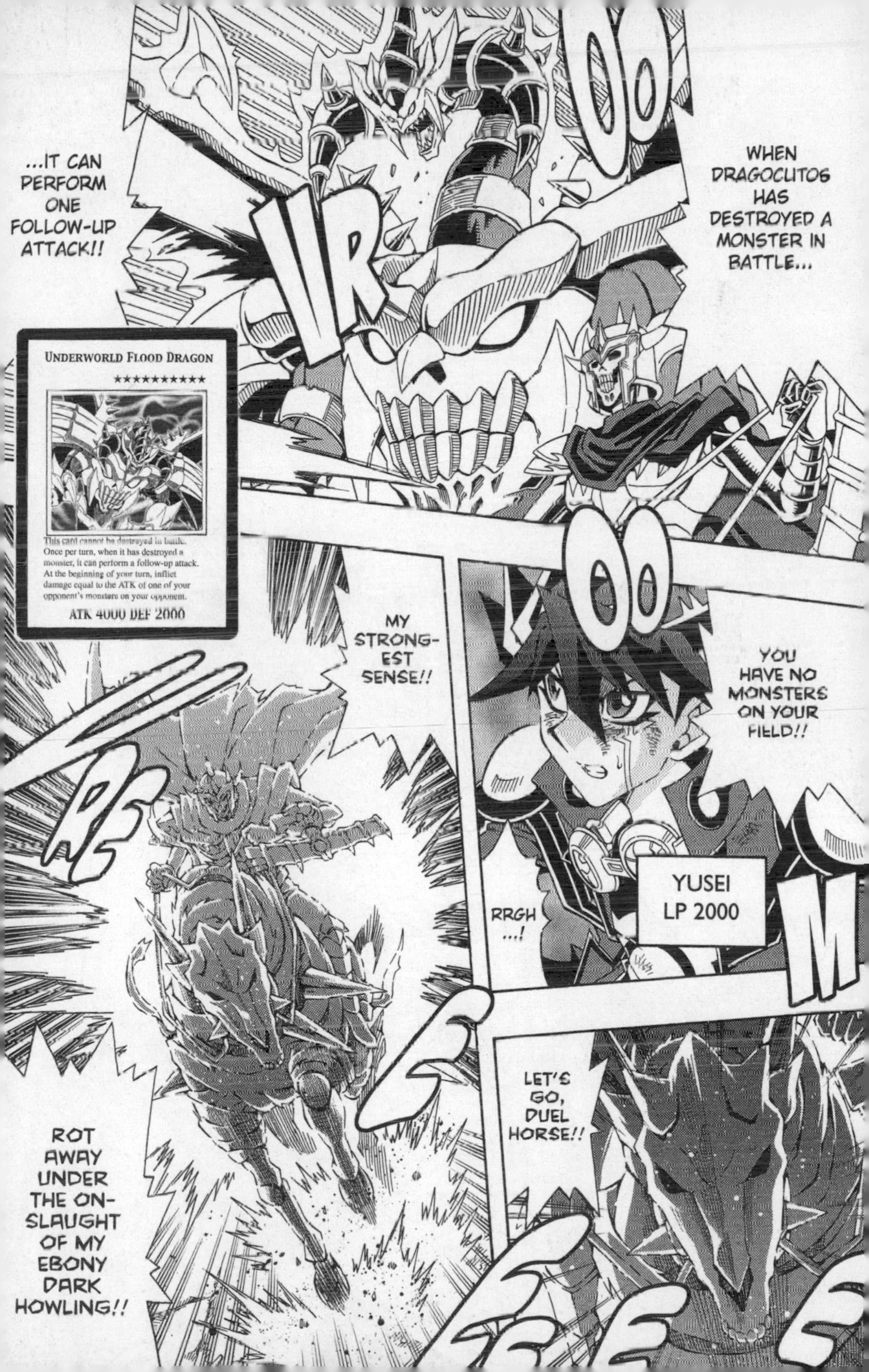
WHEN DRAGOCLITOS HAS DESTROYED A MONSTER IN BATTLE...
...IT CAN PERFORM ONE FOLLOW-UP ATTACK!!
UNDERWORLD FLOOD DRAGON
★★★★★★★★★★★
This card cannot be destroyed in battle. Once per turn, when it has destroyed a monster, it can perform a follow-up attack. At the beginning of your turn, inflict damage equal to the ATK of one of your opponent's monsters on your opponent.
ATK 4000 DEF 2000
YOU HAVE NO MONSTERS ON YOUR FIELD!!
YUSEI LP 2000
RRGH ...!
MY STRONG-EST SENSE!!
LET'S GO, DUEL HORSE!!
ROT AWAY UNDER THE ON-SLAUGHT OF MY EBONY DARK HOWLING!!

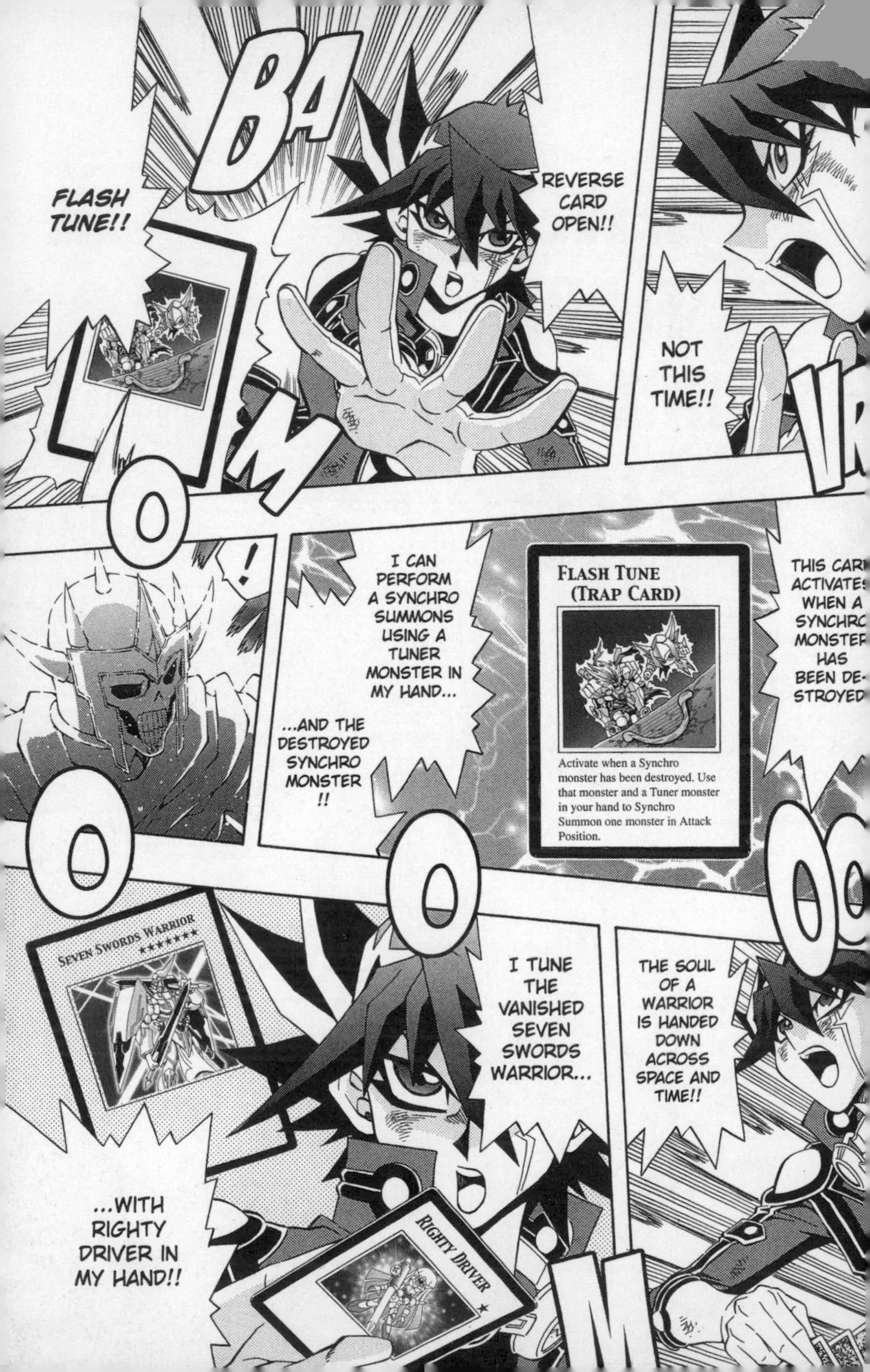
NOT THIS TIME!!
VR
REVERSE CARD OPEN!!
BA
FLASH TUNE!!
M
O
THIS CAR ACTIVATES WHEN A SYNCHRO MONSTER HAS BEEN DE-STROYED
FLASH TUNE (TRAP CARD)
Activate when a Synchro monster has been destroyed. Use that monster and a Tuner monster in your hand to Synchro Summon one monster in Attack Position.
I CAN PERFORM A SYNCHRO SUMMONS USING A TUNER MONSTER IN MY HAND...
...AND THE DESTROYED SYNCHRO MONSTER!!
!
O
O
O
THE SOUL OF A WARRIOR IS HANDED DOWN ACROSS SPACE AND TIME!!
I TUNE THE VANISHED SEVEN SWORDS WARRIOR...
SEVEN SWORDS WARRIOR
...WITH RIGHTY DRIVER IN MY HAND!!
RIGHTY DRIVER
M

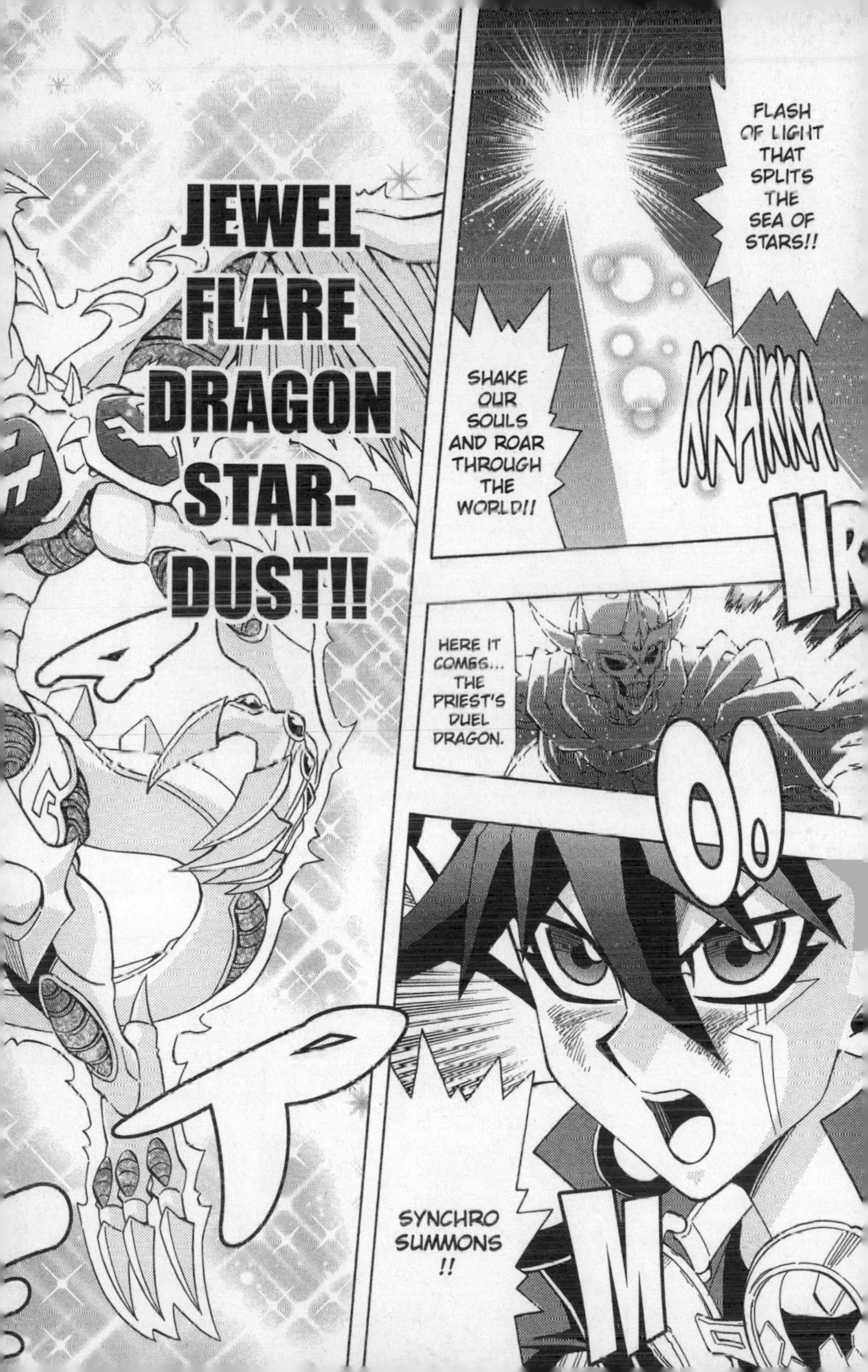
FLASH OF LIGHT THAT SPLITS THE SEA OF STARS!!
KRAKKA
SHAKE OUR SOULS AND ROAR THROUGH THE WORLD!!
VR
HERE IT COMES... THE PRIEST'S DUEL DRAGON.
OO
SYNCHRO SUMMONS !!
M
JEWEL FLARE DRAGON STAR-DUST!!

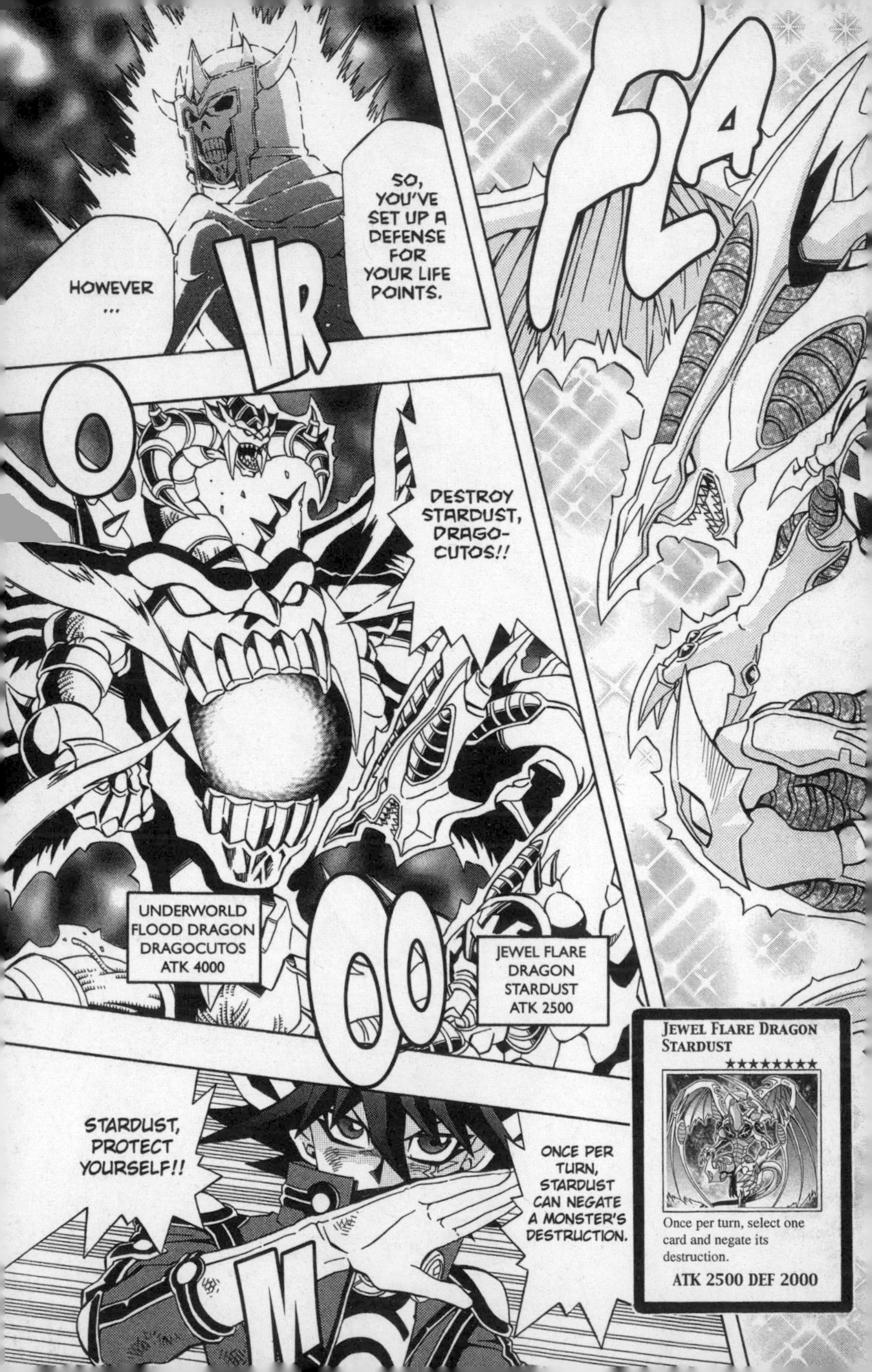
FLA
SO, YOU'VE SET UP A DEFENSE FOR YOUR LIFE POINTS.
HOWEVER ...
VR
DESTROY STARDUST, DRAGO-CUTOS!!
O
JEWEL FLARE DRAGON STARDUST ATK 2500
OO
UNDERWORLD FLOOD DRAGON DRAGOCUTOS ATK 4000
JEWEL FLARE DRAGON STARDUST
★★★★★★★★
Once per turn, select one card and negate its destruction.
ATK 2500 DEF 2000
ONCE PER TURN, STARDUST CAN NEGATE A MONSTER'S DESTRUCTION.
STARDUST, PROTECT YOURSELF!!
M

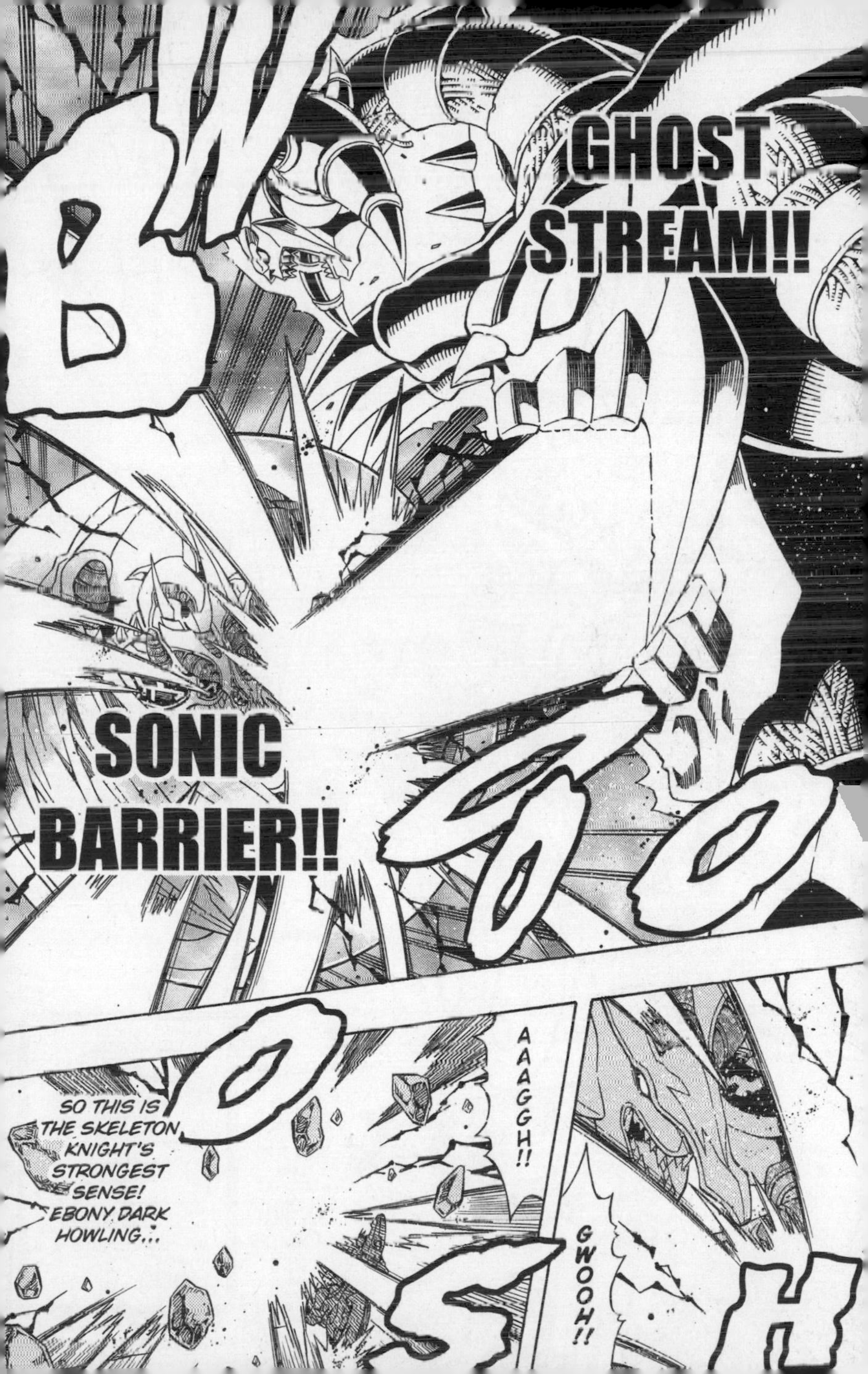
GHOST STREAM!!
SONIC BARRIER!!
AAAGGH!!
GWOOOH!!
SO THIS IS THE SKELETON KNIGHT'S STRONGEST SENSE! EBONY DARK HOWLING...

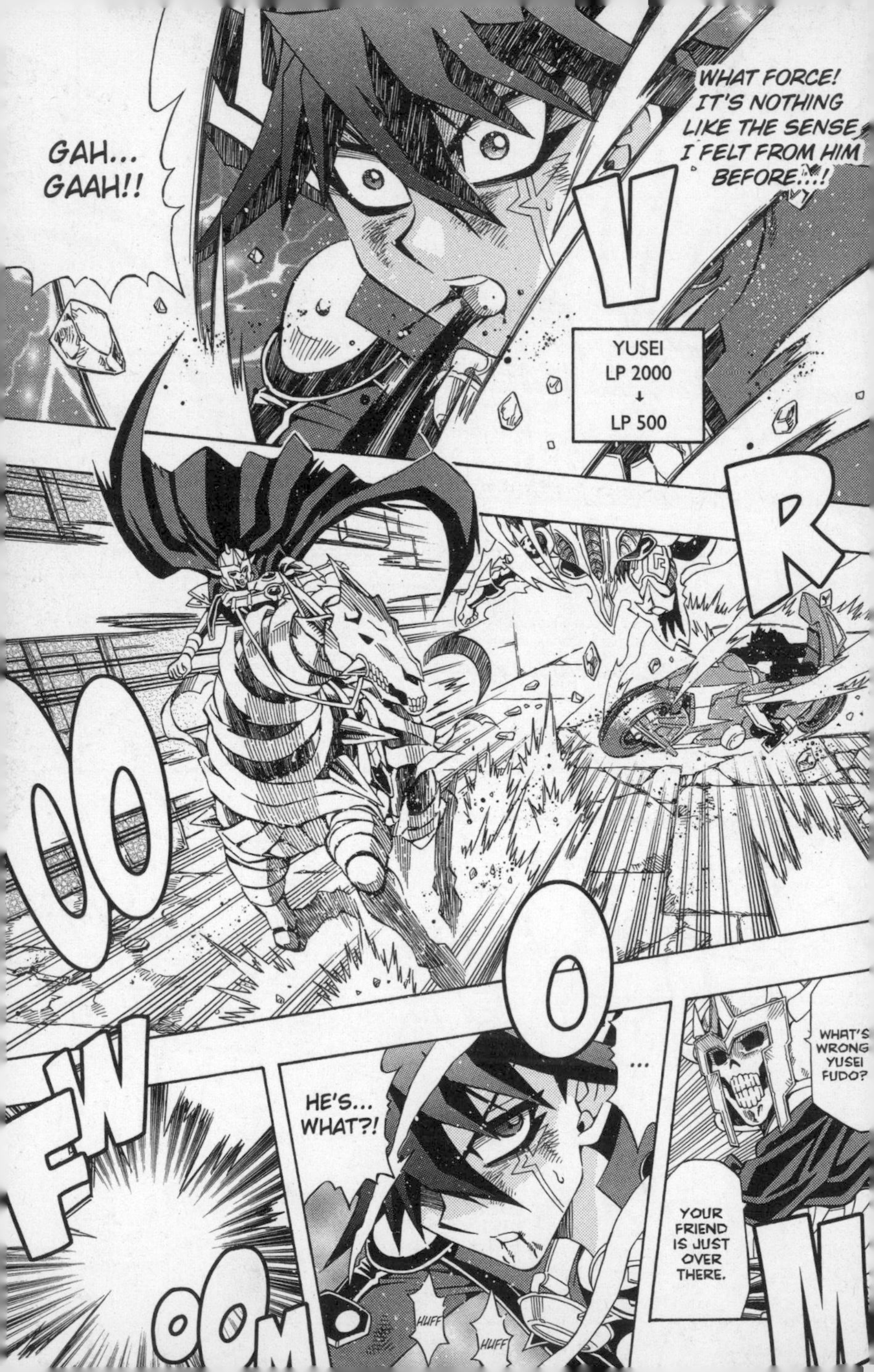

WHAT FORCE! IT'S NOTHING LIKE THE SENSE I FELT FROM HIM BEFORE...!
GAH... GAAH!!
V
YUSEI LP 2000 ↓ LP 500
R
OO
O
WHAT'S WRONG YUSEI FUDO?
YOUR FRIEND IS JUST OVER THERE.
M
...
HE'S... WHAT?!
HUFF
HUFF
FWN
OOM

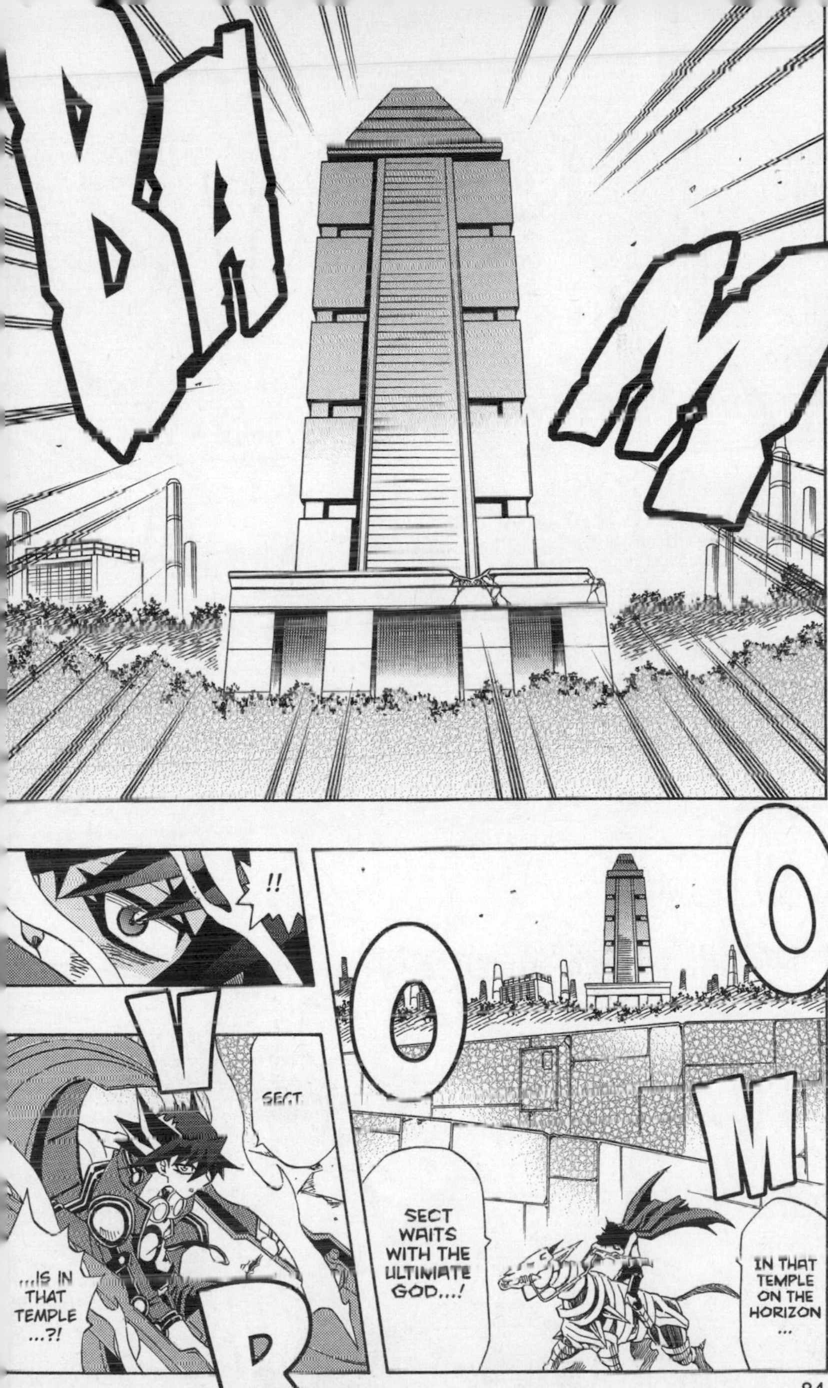
BAM
VROOM
IN THAT TEMPLE ON THE HORIZON ...
SECT WAITS WITH THE ULTIMATE GOD...!
!!
SECT
...IS IN THAT TEMPLE ...?!

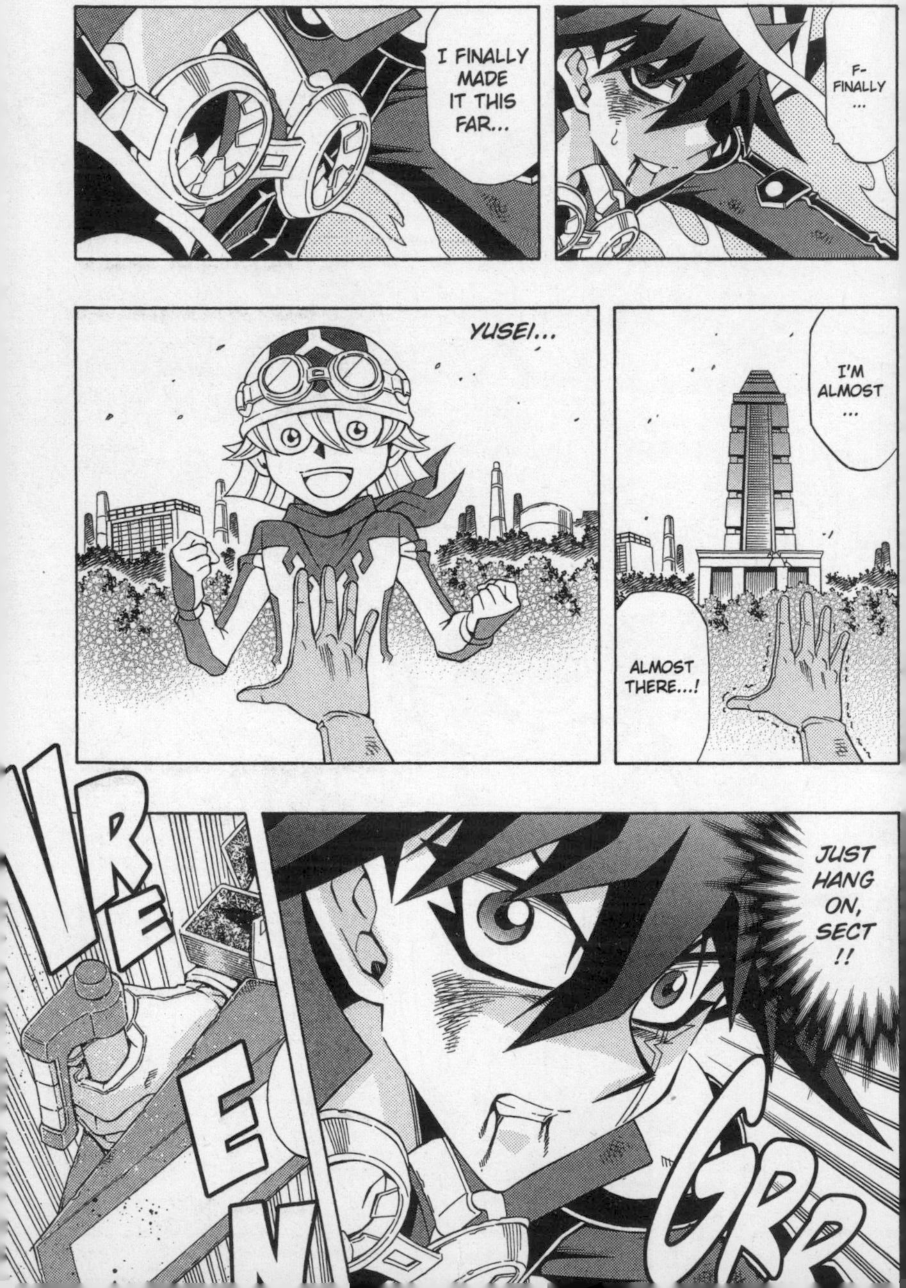
F-
FINALLY
...
I FINALLY MADE IT THIS FAR...
I'M ALMOST ...
ALMOST THERE...!
YUSEI...
VREEN
JUST HANG ON, SECT !!
GRR

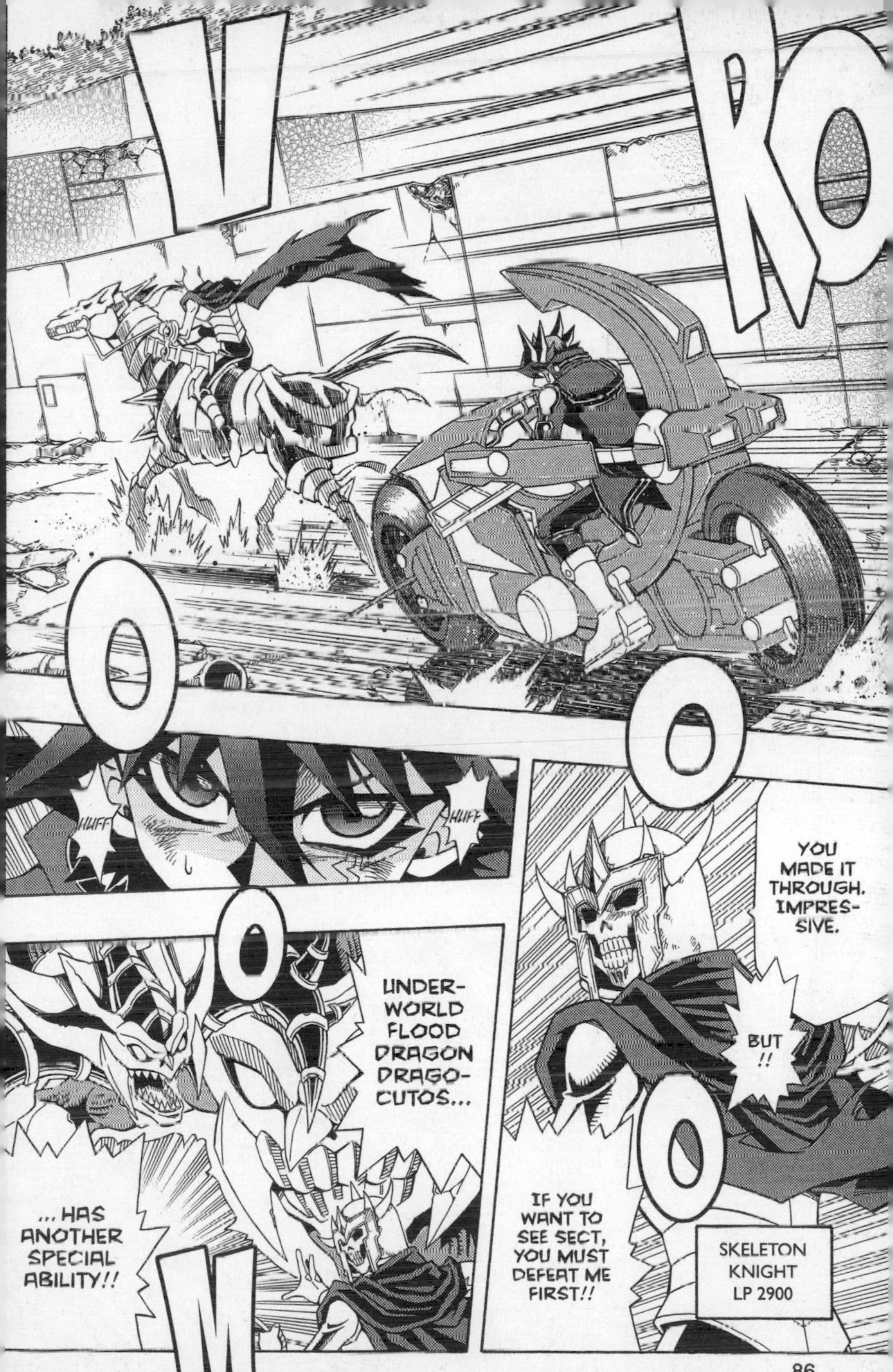
VROOOOOM
YOU MADE IT THROUGH. IMPRESSIVE.
BUT!!
IF YOU WANT TO SEE SECT, YOU MUST DEFEAT ME FIRST!!
SKELETON KNIGHT LP 2900
HUFF
HUFF
UNDERWORLD FLOOD DRAGON DRAGOCUTOS...
...HAS ANOTHER SPECIAL ABILITY!!

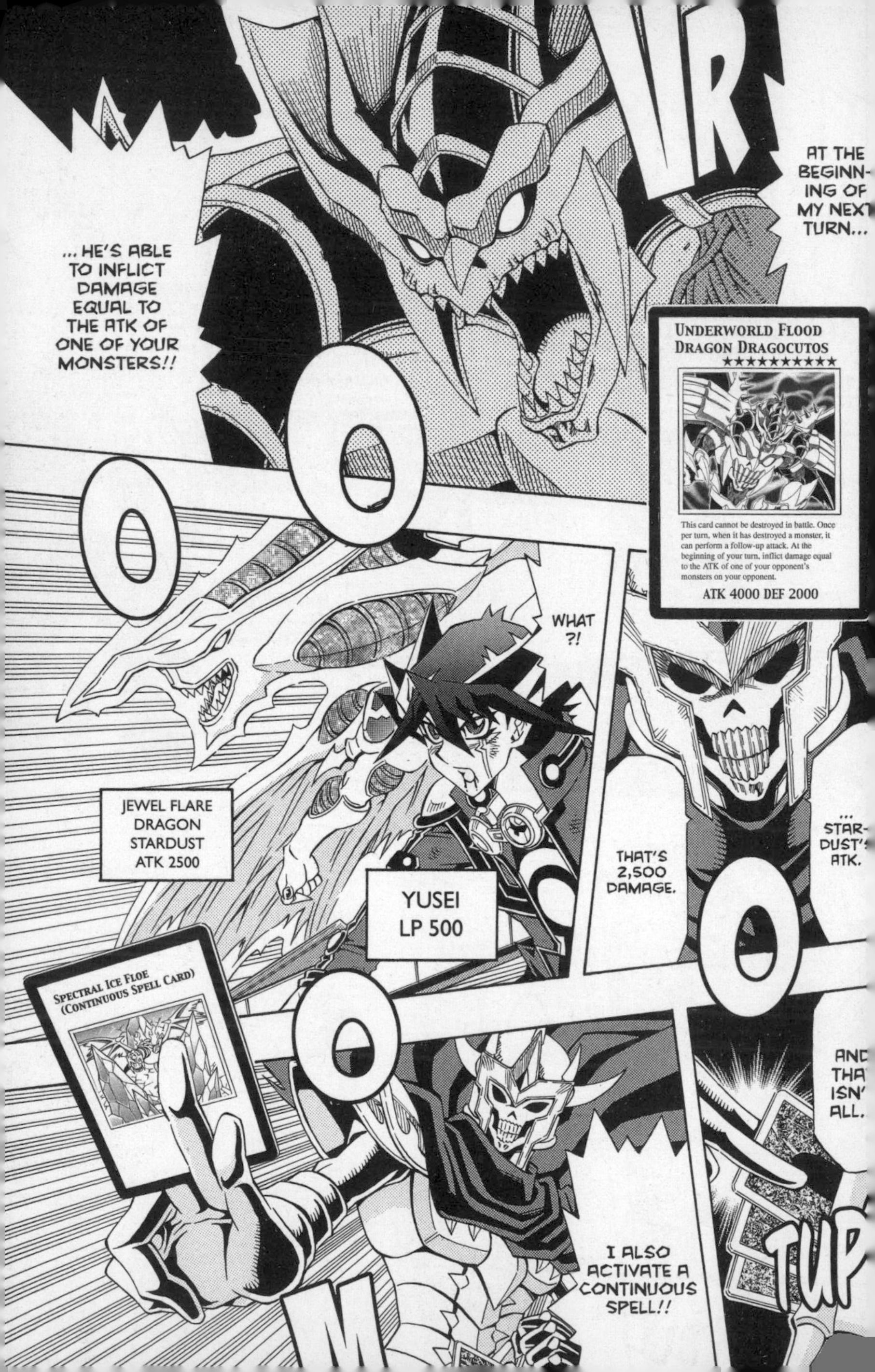
VR
AT THE BEGINN-ING OF MY NEXT TURN...
...HE'S ABLE TO INFLICT DAMAGE EQUAL TO THE ATK OF ONE OF YOUR MONSTERS!!
UNDERWORLD FLOOD DRAGON DRAGOCUTOS
★★★★★★★★★★
This card cannot be destroyed in battle. Once per turn, when it has destroyed a monster, it can perform a follow-up attack. At the beginning of your turn, inflict damage equal to the ATK of one of your opponent's monsters on your opponent.
ATK 4000 DEF 2000
OOO
... STAR-DUST'S ATK.
THAT'S 2,500 DAMAGE.
WHAT ?!
JEWEL FLARE DRAGON STARDUST ATK 2500
YUSEI LP 500
AND THA ISN' ALL.
TUP
I ALSO ACTIVATE A CONTINUOUS SPELL!!
SPECTRAL ICE FLOE (CONTINUOUS SPELL CARD)
OO
M

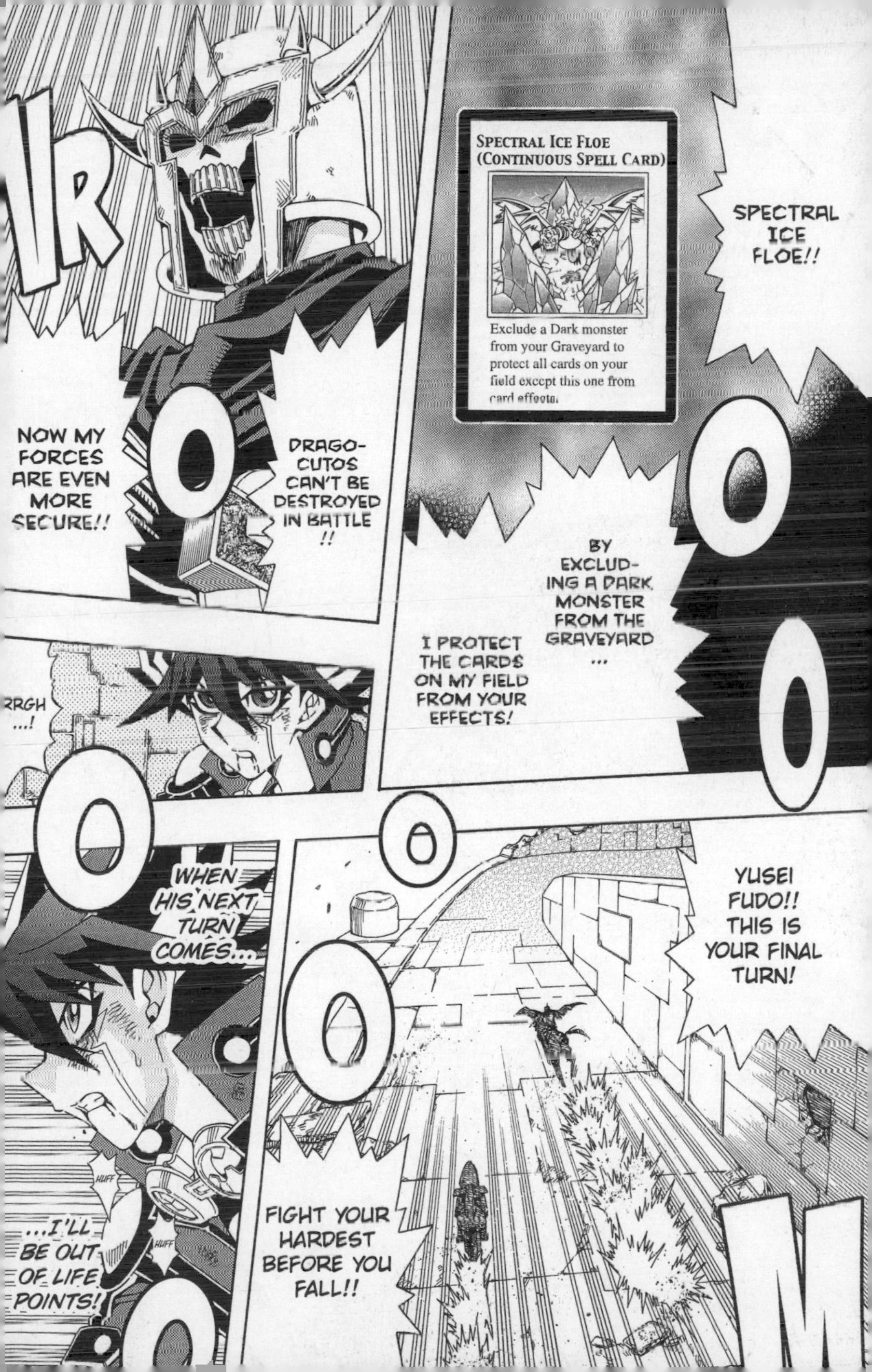

Spectral Ice Floe
(Continuous Spell Card)
Exclude a Dark monster from your Graveyard to protect all cards on your field except this one from card effects.
SPECTRAL ICE FLOE!!
BY EXCLUDING A DARK MONSTER FROM THE GRAVEYARD...
I PROTECT THE CARDS ON MY FIELD FROM YOUR EFFECTS!
DRAGO-CUTOS CAN'T BE DESTROYED IN BATTLE!!
NOW MY FORCES ARE EVEN MORE SECURE!!
RRGH...!
YUSEI FUDO!! THIS IS YOUR FINAL TURN!
FIGHT YOUR HARDEST BEFORE YOU FALL!!
WHEN HIS NEXT TURN COMES...
HUFF
HUFF
...I'LL BE OUT OF LIFE POINTS!

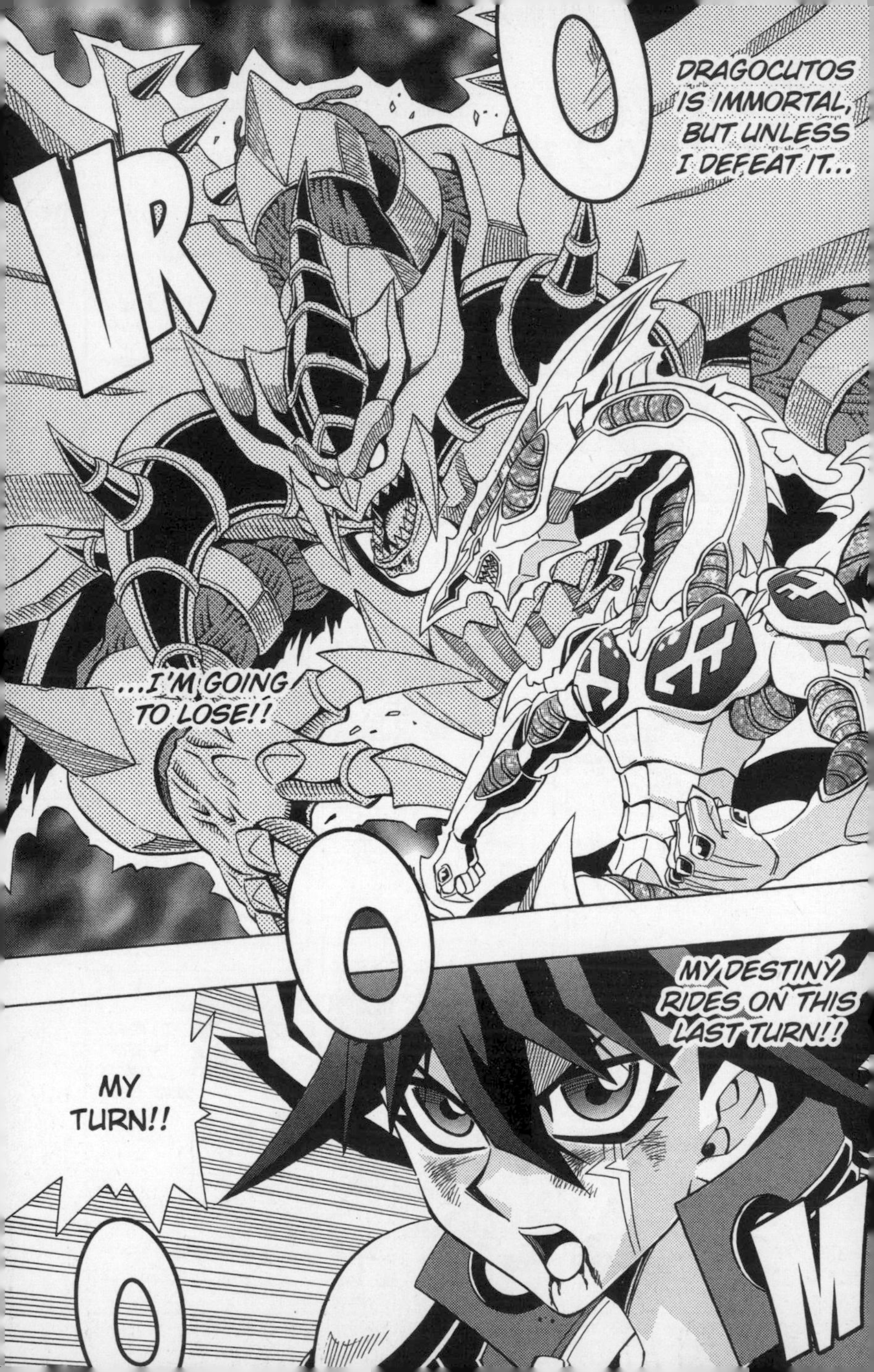
DRAGOCUTOS IS IMMORTAL, BUT UNLESS I DEFEAT IT...
...I'M GOING TO LOSE!!
VROOOOM
MY DESTINY RIDES ON THIS LAST TURN!!
MY TURN!!

5D's TRACKS

THE 48TH

BY SATOMASA

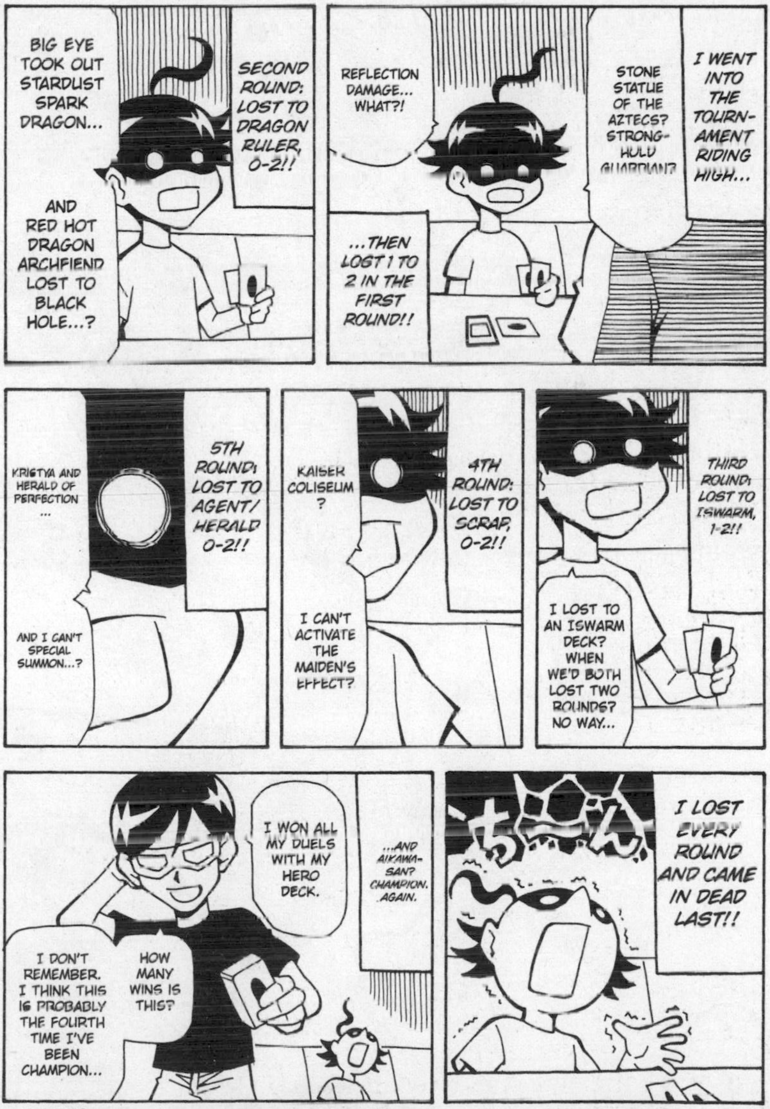
I WENT INTO THE TOURNAMENT RIDING HIGH...
STONE STATUE OF THE AZTECS? STRONG-HOLD GUARDIAN?
REFLECTION DAMAGE... WHAT?!
...THEN LOST 1 TO 2 IN THE FIRST ROUND!!
SECOND ROUND: LOST TO DRAGON RULER, 0-2!!
BIG EYE TOOK OUT STARDUST SPARK DRAGON...
AND RED HOT DRAGON ARCHFIEND LOST TO BLACK HOLE...?
THIRD ROUND: LOST TO ISWARM, 1-2!!
I LOST TO AN ISWARM DECK? WHEN WE'D BOTH LOST TWO ROUNDS? NO WAY...
4TH ROUND: LOST TO SCRAP, 0-2!!
KAISER COLISEUM?
I CAN'T ACTIVATE THE MAIDEN'S EFFECT?
5TH ROUND: LOST TO AGENT/HERALD 0-2!!
KRISTYA AND HERALD OF PERFECTION ...
AND I CAN'T SPECIAL SUMMON...?
I LOST EVERY ROUND AND CAME IN DEAD LAST!!
...AND AIKAWA-SAN? CHAMPION. AGAIN.
I WON ALL MY DUELS WITH MY HERO DECK.
HOW MANY WINS IS THIS?
I DON'T REMEMBER. I THINK THIS IS PROBABLY THE FOURTH TIME I'VE BEEN CHAMPION...

(AIKAWA) IT WAS A STRAIGHT-SET WIN THIS TIME, SATO-SAN. I DIDN'T LOSE A SINGLE MATCH!

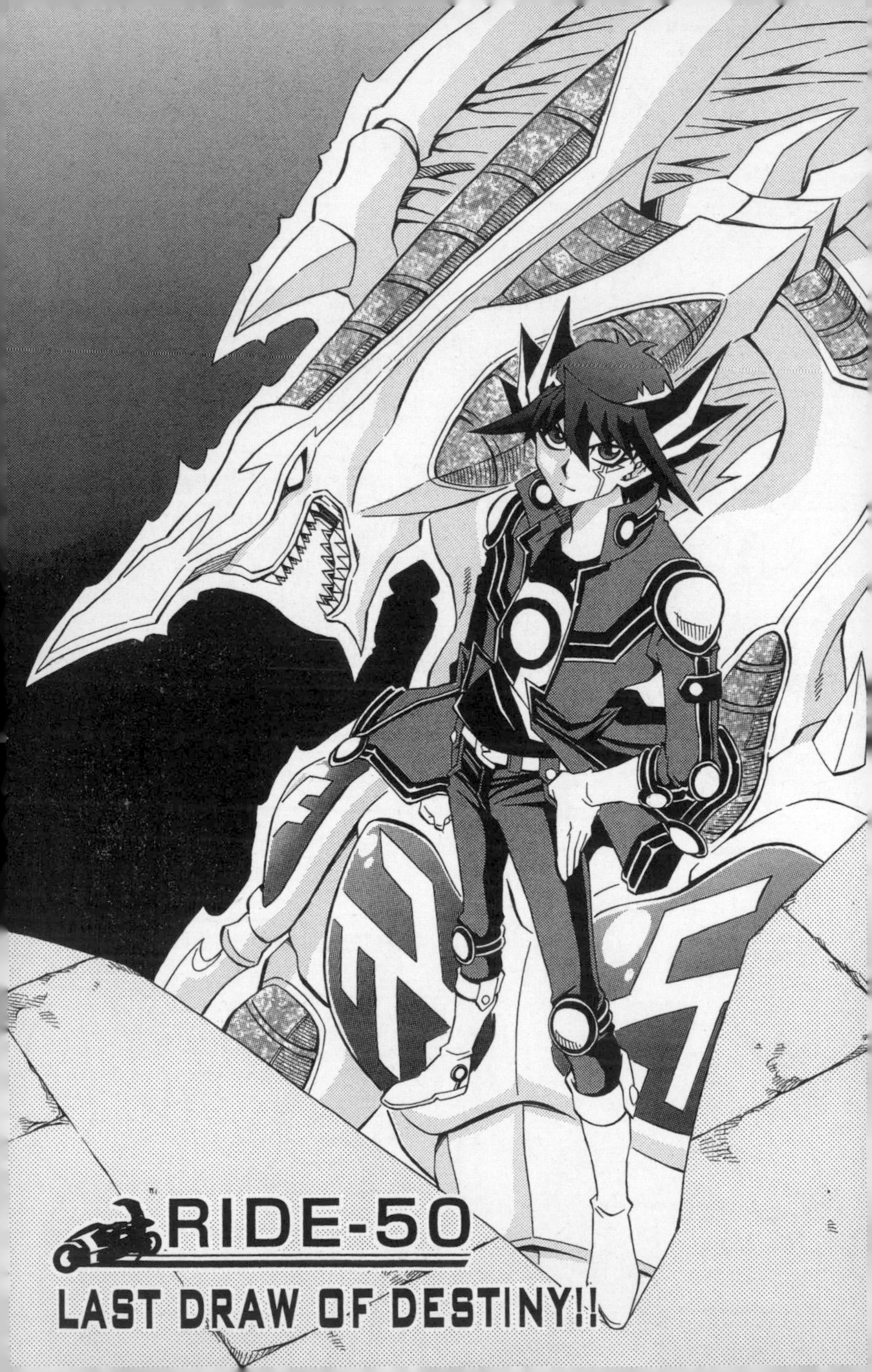
RIDE-50
LAST DRAW OF DESTINY!!

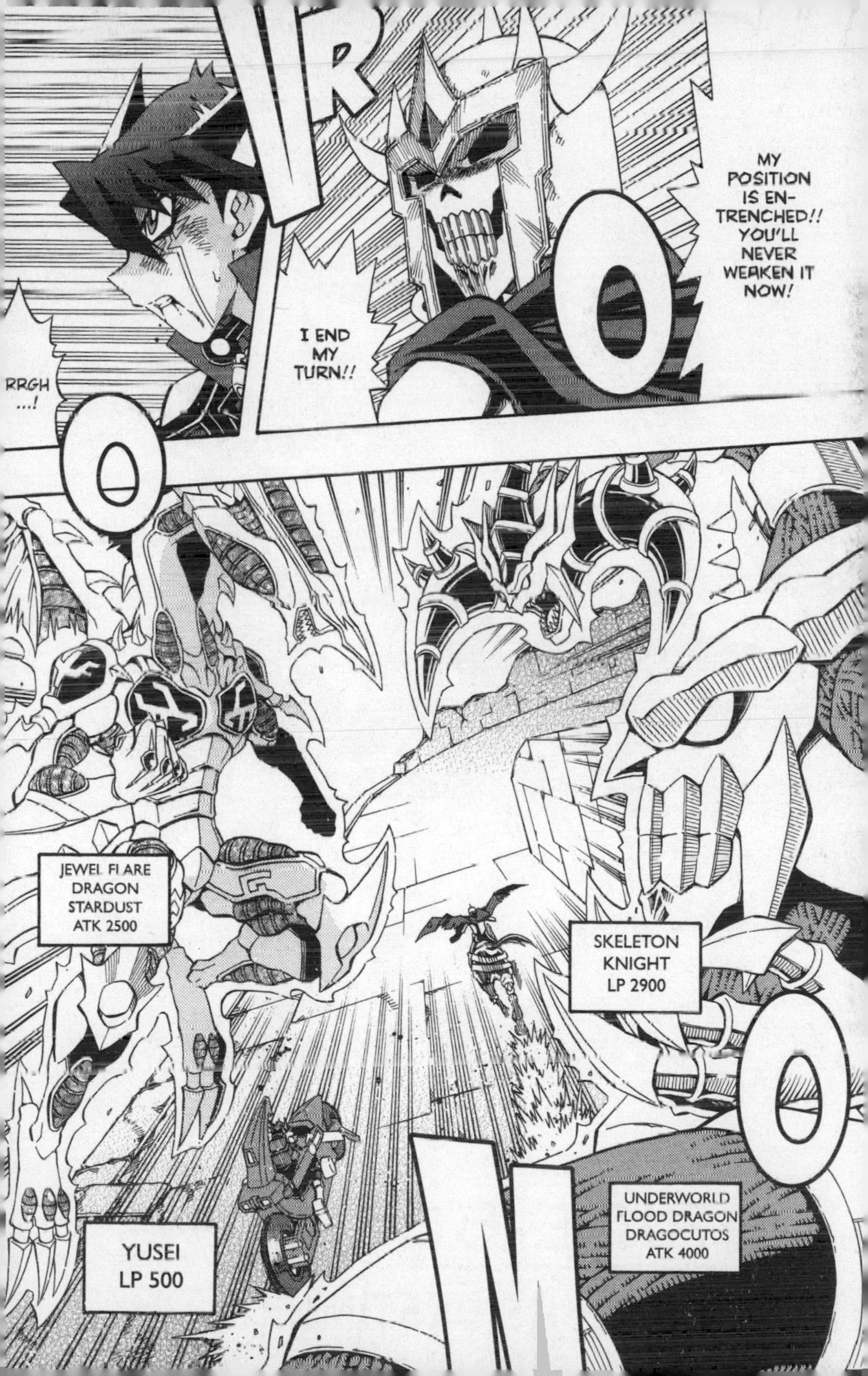
MY POSITION IS EN-TRENCHED!! YOU'LL NEVER WEAKEN IT NOW!
I END MY TURN!!
RRGH ...!
SKELETON KNIGHT LP 2900
JEWEL FLARE DRAGON STARDUST ATK 2500
UNDERWORLD FLOOD DRAGON DRAGOCUTOS ATK 4000
YUSEI LP 500

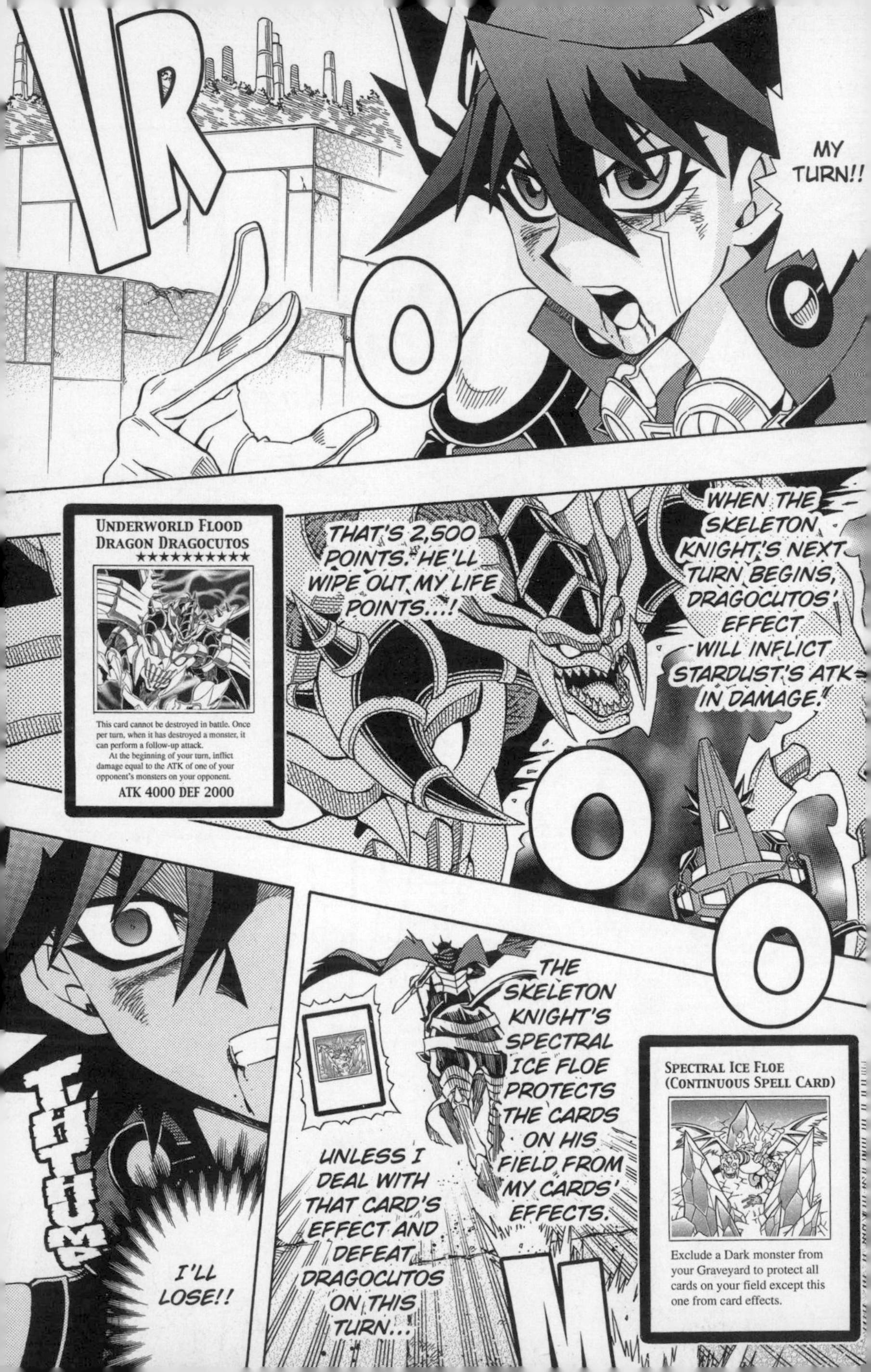
MY TURN!!
WHEN THE SKELETON KNIGHT'S NEXT TURN BEGINS, DRAGOCUTOS' EFFECT WILL INFLICT STARDUST'S ATK IN DAMAGE.
THAT'S 2,500 POINTS. HE'LL WIPE OUT MY LIFE POINTS...!
UNDERWORLD FLOOD DRAGON DRAGOCUTOS
★★★★★★★★★★
This card cannot be destroyed in battle. Once per turn, when it has destroyed a monster, it can perform a follow-up attack.
At the beginning of your turn, inflict damage equal to the ATK of one of your opponent's monsters on your opponent.
ATK 4000 DEF 2000
SPECTRAL ICE FLOE (CONTINUOUS SPELL CARD)
Exclude a Dark monster from your Graveyard to protect all cards on your field except this one from card effects.
THE SKELETON KNIGHT'S SPECTRAL ICE FLOE PROTECTS THE CARDS ON HIS FIELD FROM MY CARDS' EFFECTS.
UNLESS I DEAL WITH THAT CARD'S EFFECT AND DEFEAT DRAGOCUTOS ON THIS TURN...
I'LL LOSE!!

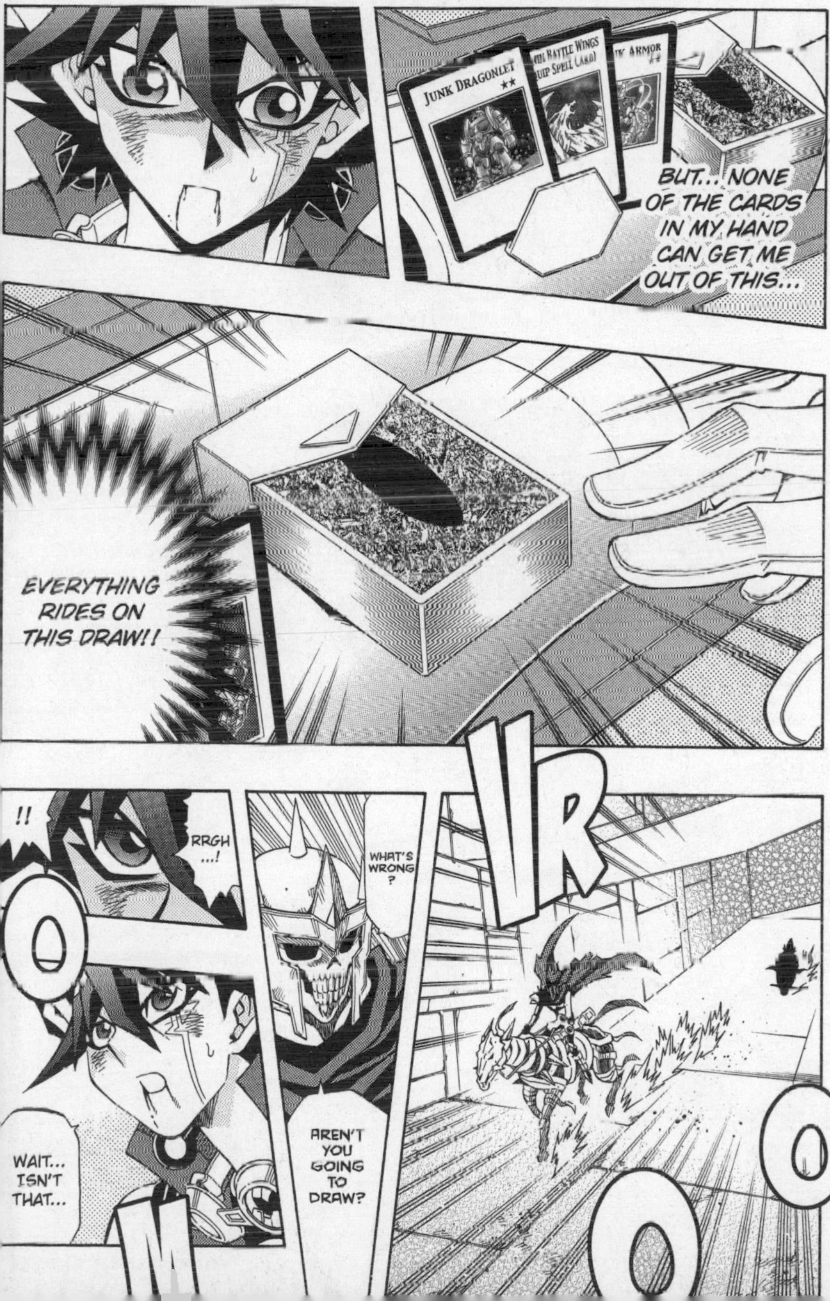
JUNK DRAGONLET
★★
BUT... NONE OF THE CARDS IN MY HAND CAN GET ME OUT OF THIS...
EVERYTHING RIDES ON THIS DRAW!!
VROOOM
WHAT'S WRONG?
AREN'T YOU GOING TO DRAW?
!!
RRGH...!
WAIT... ISN'T THAT...

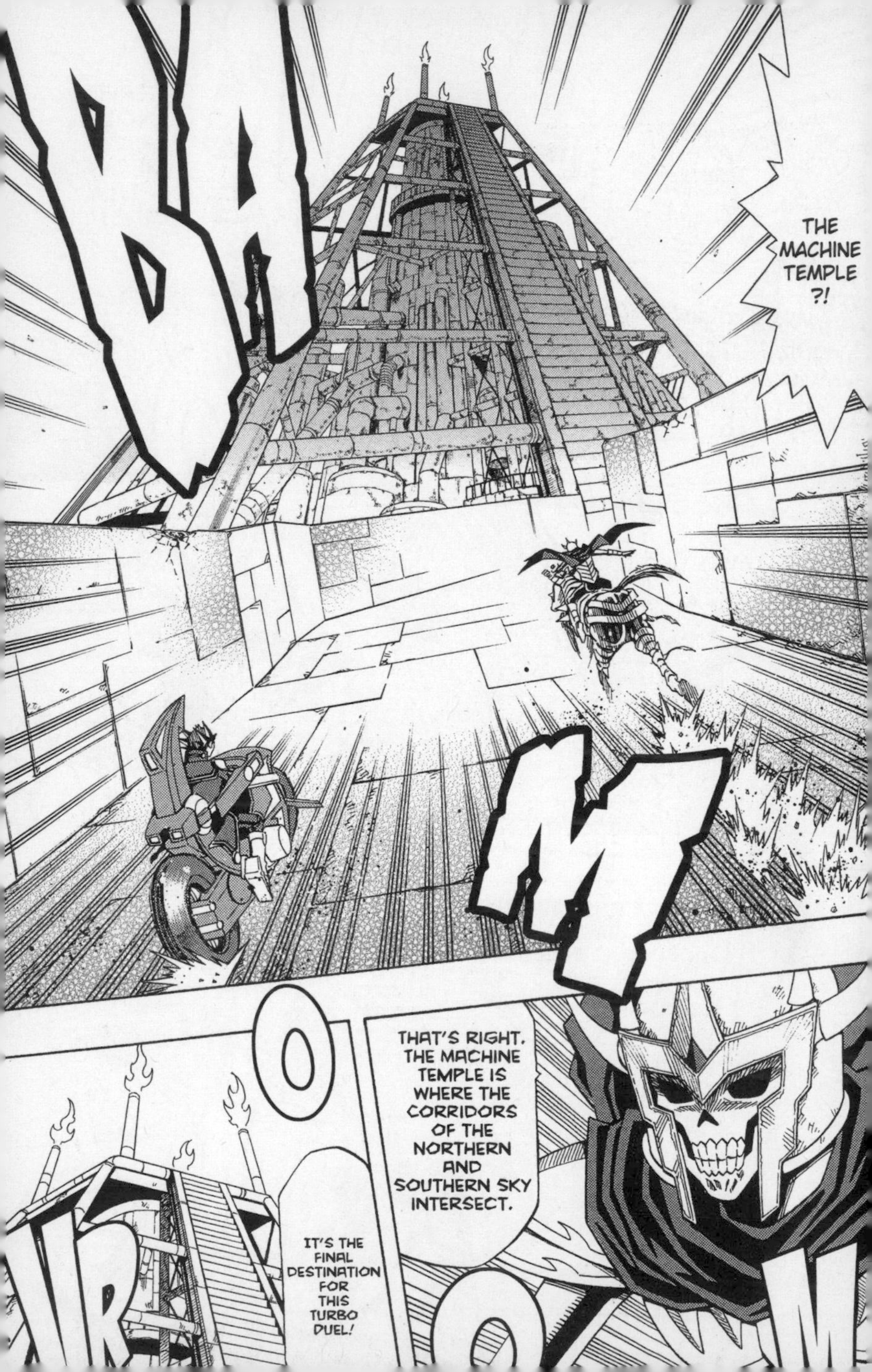
THE MACHINE TEMPLE ?!
THAT'S RIGHT. THE MACHINE TEMPLE IS WHERE THE CORRIDORS OF THE NORTHERN AND SOUTHERN SKY INTERSECT.
IT'S THE FINAL DESTINATION FOR THIS TURBO DUEL!

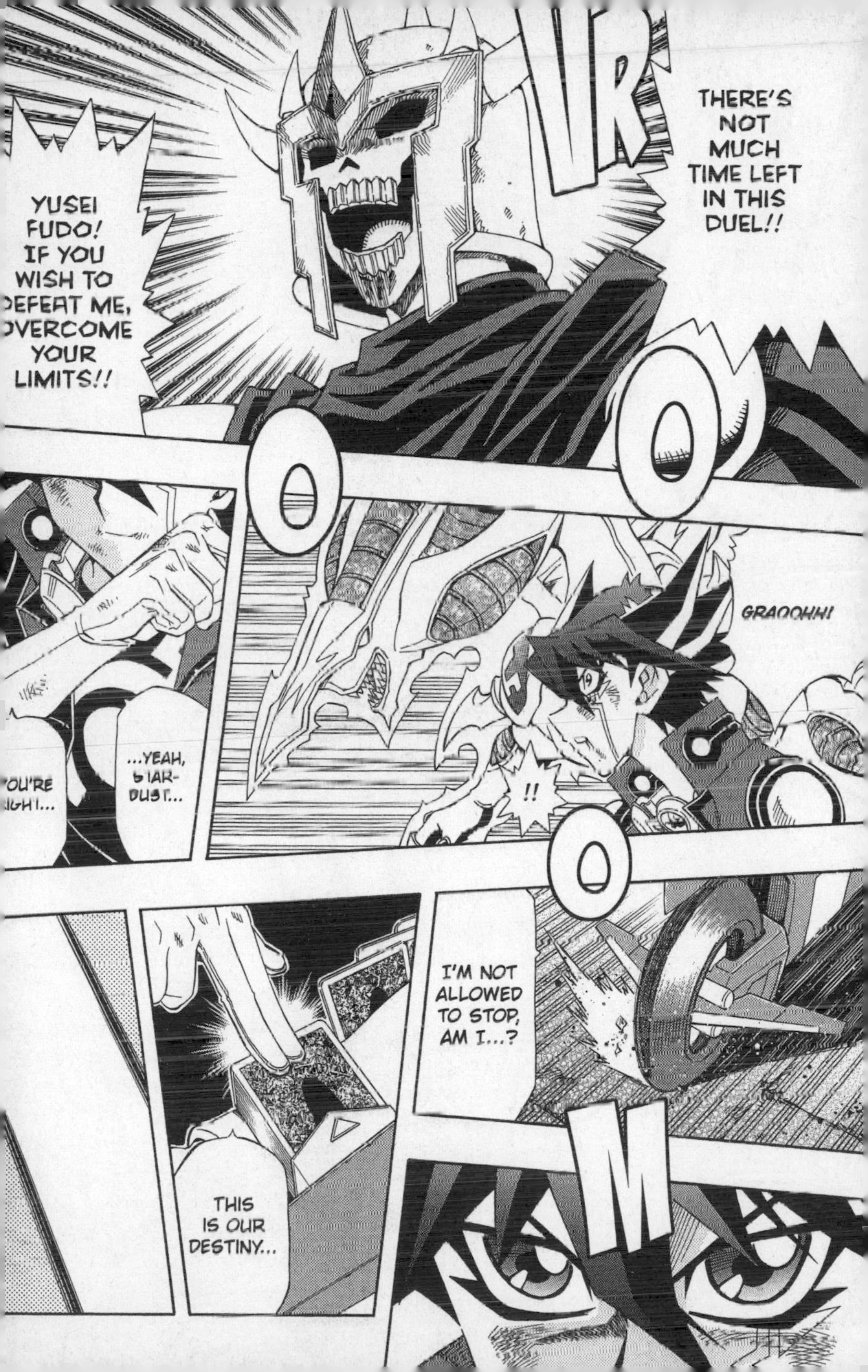
THERE'S NOT MUCH TIME LEFT IN THIS DUEL!!
YUSEI FUDO! IF YOU WISH TO DEFEAT ME, OVERCOME YOUR LIMITS!!
VR
GRAOOHH!
!!
...YEAH, STAR-DUST...
YOU'RE RIGHT...
I'M NOT ALLOWED TO STOP, AM I...?
THIS IS OUR DESTINY...
M

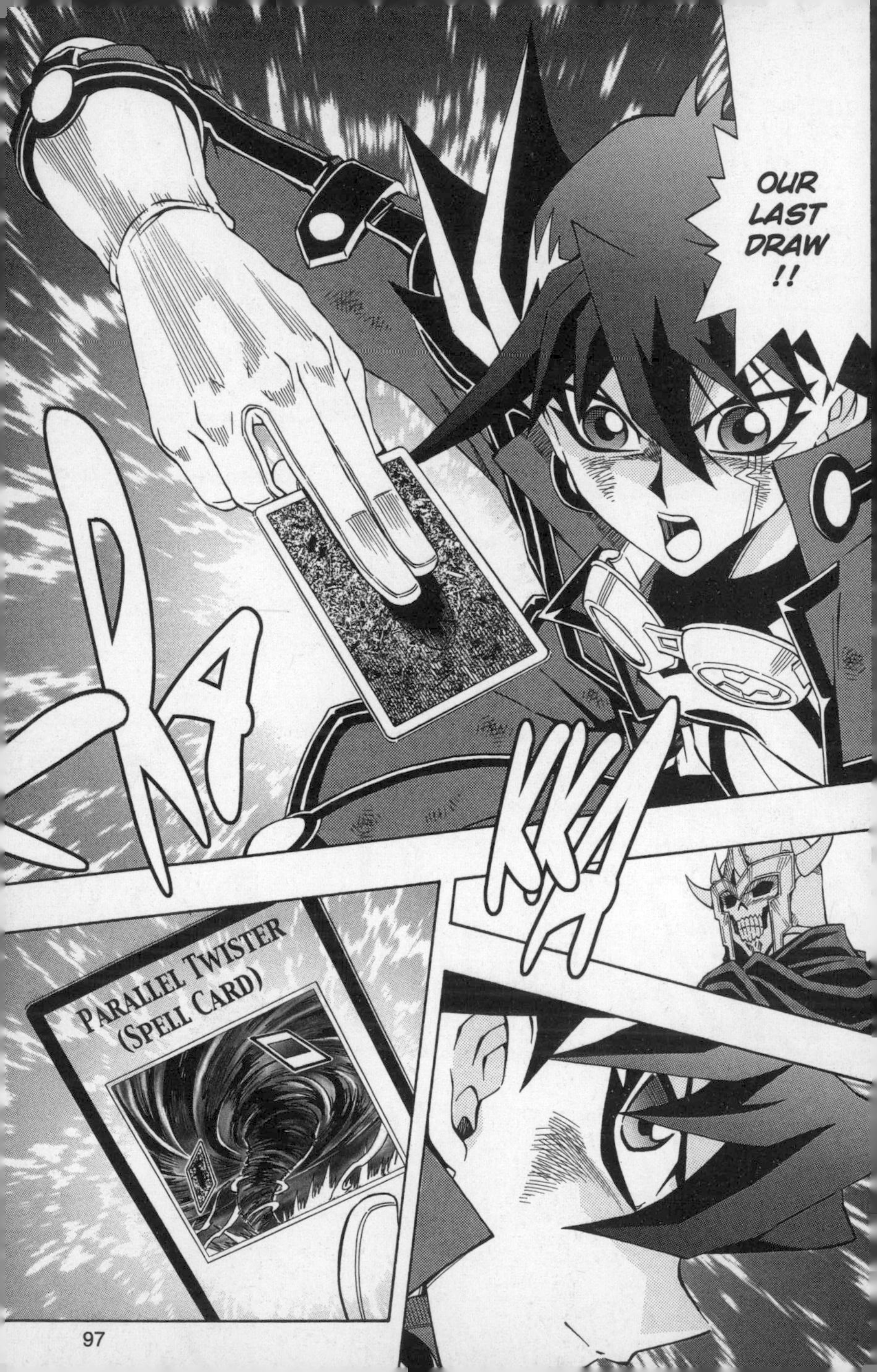
OUR LAST DRAW !!
DRA
KKA
PARALLEL TWISTER (SPELL CARD)

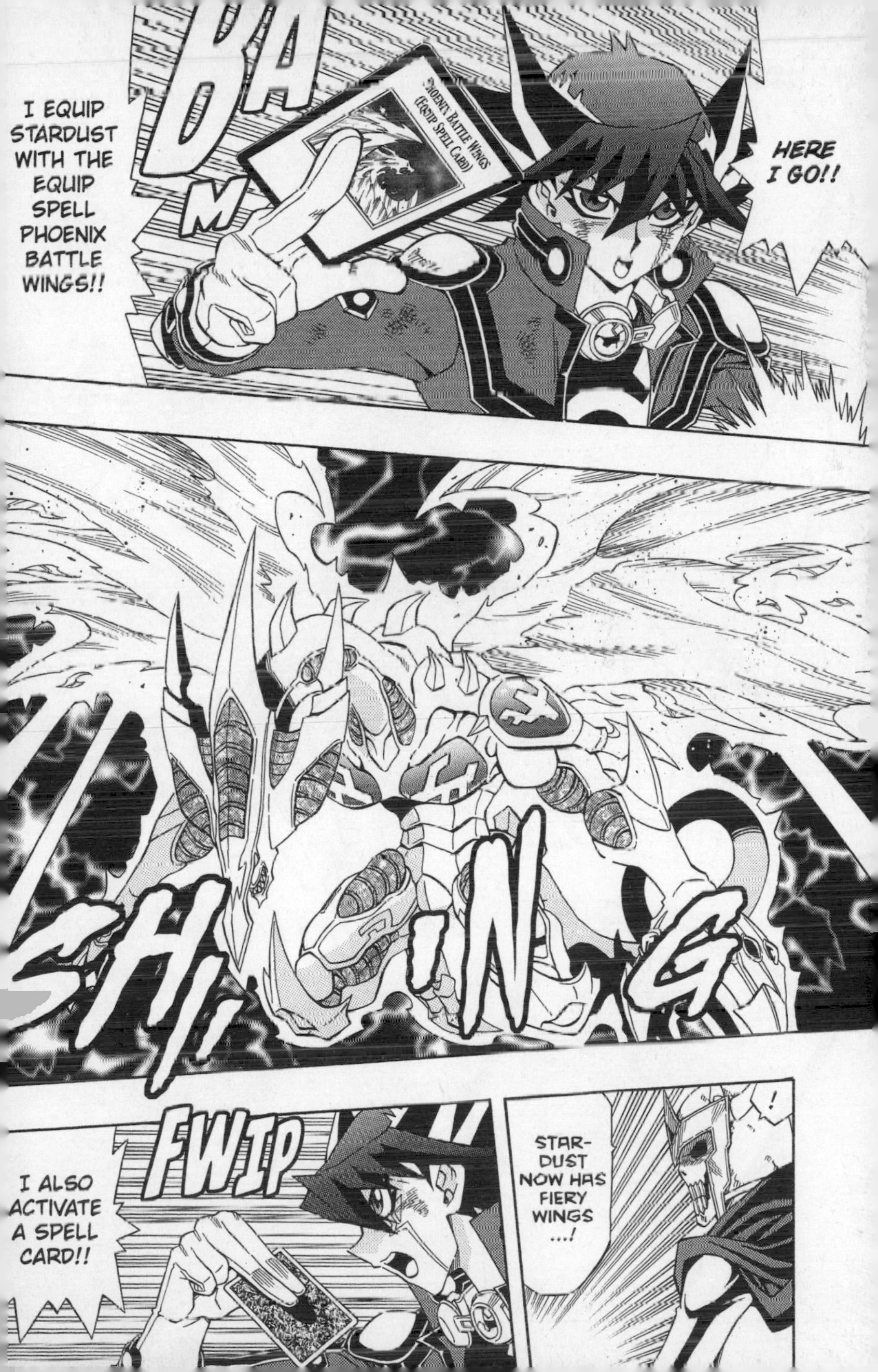
HERE I GO!!
PHOENIX BATTLE WINGS (EQUIP SPELL CARD)
BAM
I EQUIP STARDUST WITH THE EQUIP SPELL PHOENIX BATTLE WINGS!!
SHIING
!
STAR-DUST NOW HAS FIERY WINGS ...!
FWIP
I ALSO ACTIVATE A SPELL CARD!!

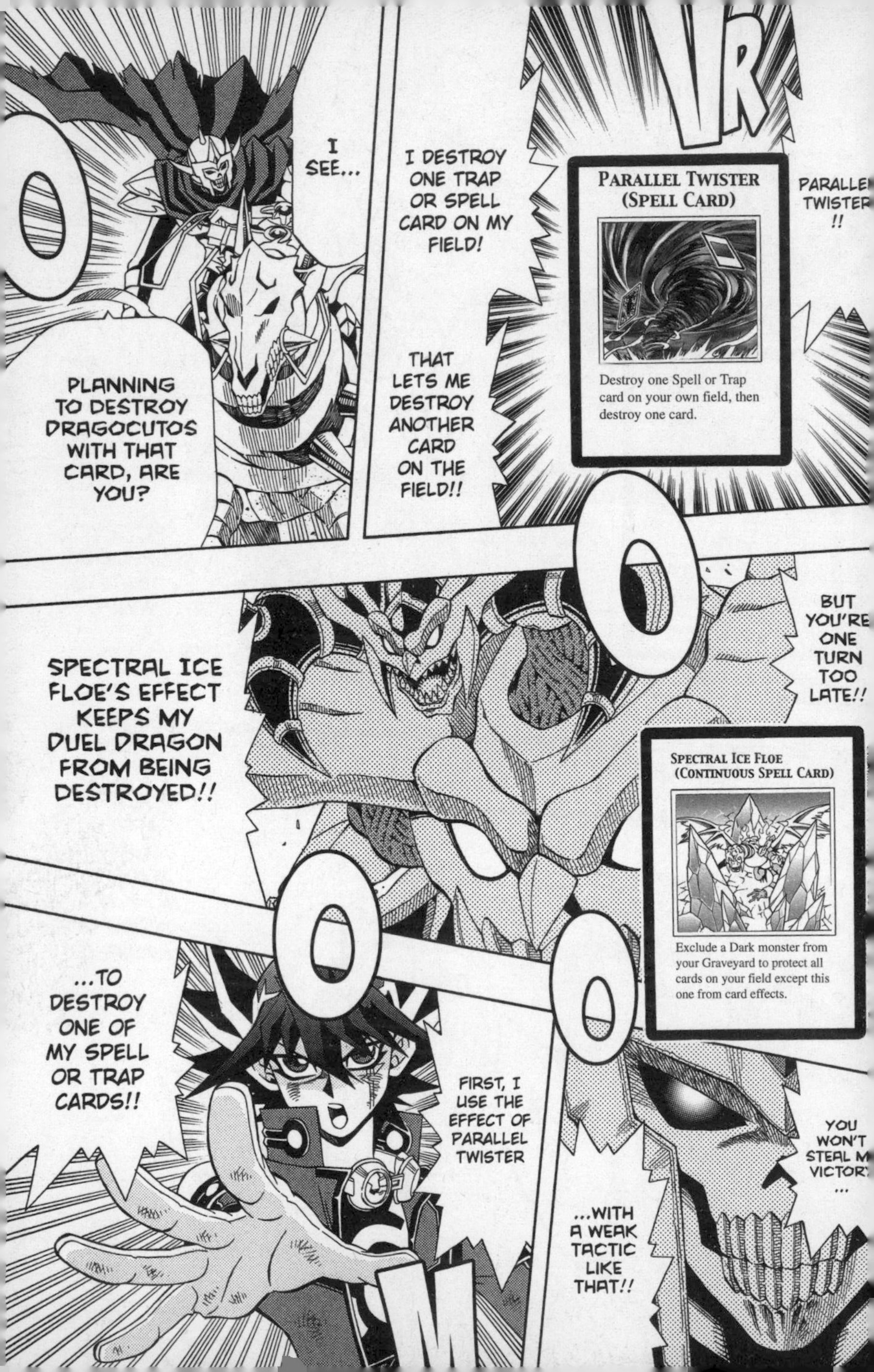

PARALLEL TWISTER!!
PARALLEL TWISTER (SPELL CARD)
Destroy one Spell or Trap card on your own field, then destroy one card.
I DESTROY ONE TRAP OR SPELL CARD ON MY FIELD!
THAT LETS ME DESTROY ANOTHER CARD ON THE FIELD!!
I SEE...
PLANNING TO DESTROY DRAGOCUTOS WITH THAT CARD, ARE YOU?
BUT YOU'RE ONE TURN TOO LATE!!
SPECTRAL ICE FLOE (CONTINUOUS SPELL CARD)
Exclude a Dark monster from your Graveyard to protect all cards on your field except this one from card effects.
SPECTRAL ICE FLOE'S EFFECT KEEPS MY DUEL DRAGON FROM BEING DESTROYED!!
YOU WON'T STEAL MY VICTORY...
...WITH A WEAK TACTIC LIKE THAT!!
FIRST, I USE THE EFFECT OF PARALLEL TWISTER
...TO DESTROY ONE OF MY SPELL OR TRAP CARDS!!

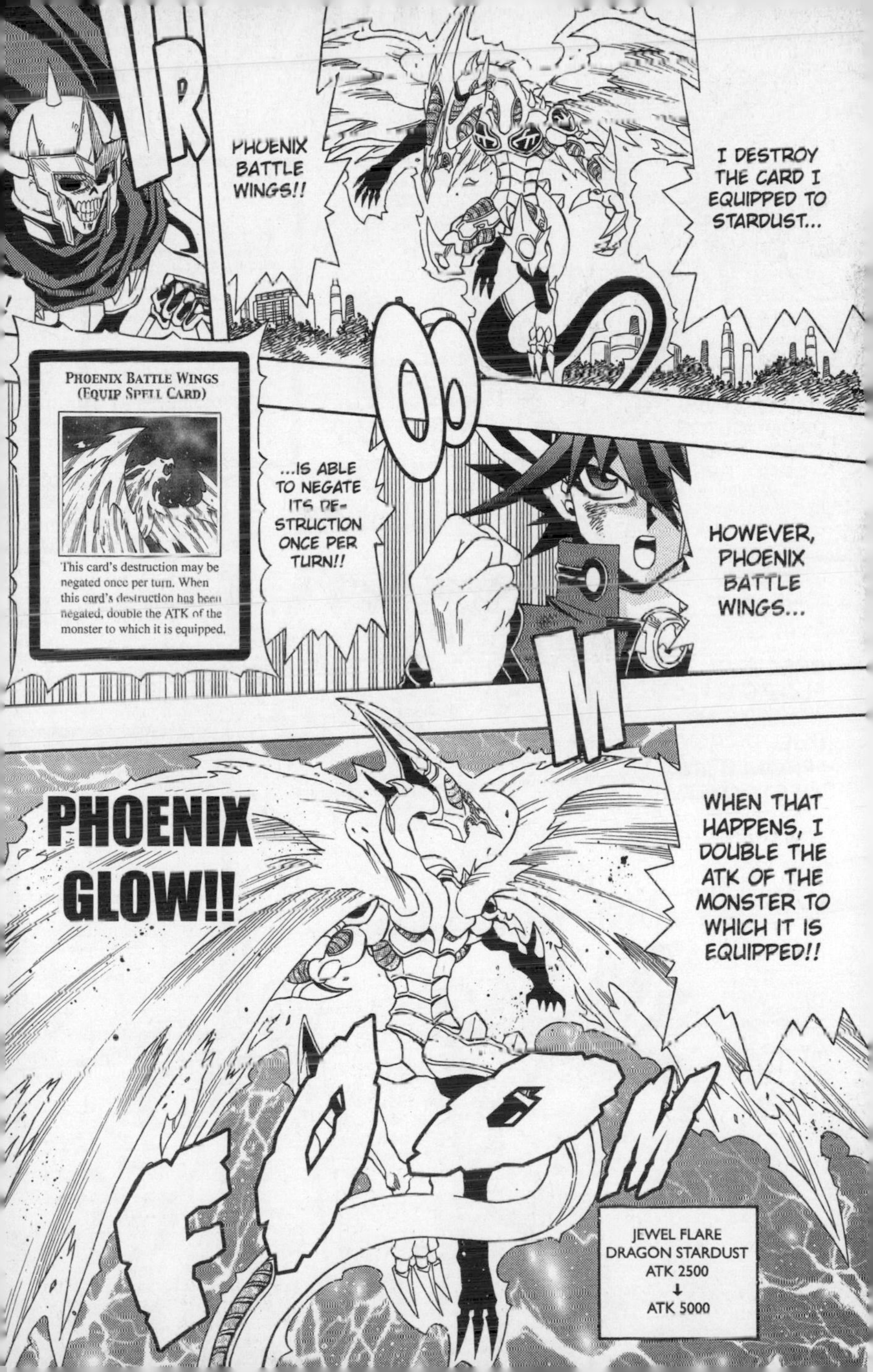
I DESTROY THE CARD I EQUIPPED TO STARDUST...
PHOENIX BATTLE WINGS!!
VR
OO
HOWEVER, PHOENIX BATTLE WINGS...
...IS ABLE TO NEGATE ITS DE-STRUCTION ONCE PER TURN!!
PHOENIX BATTLE WINGS (EQUIP SPELL CARD)
This card's destruction may be negated once per turn. When this card's destruction has been negated, double the ATK of the monster to which it is equipped.
M
WHEN THAT HAPPENS, I DOUBLE THE ATK OF THE MONSTER TO WHICH IT IS EQUIPPED!!
PHOENIX GLOW!!
FOOM
JEWEL FLARE DRAGON STARDUST ATK 2500 ↓ ATK 5000

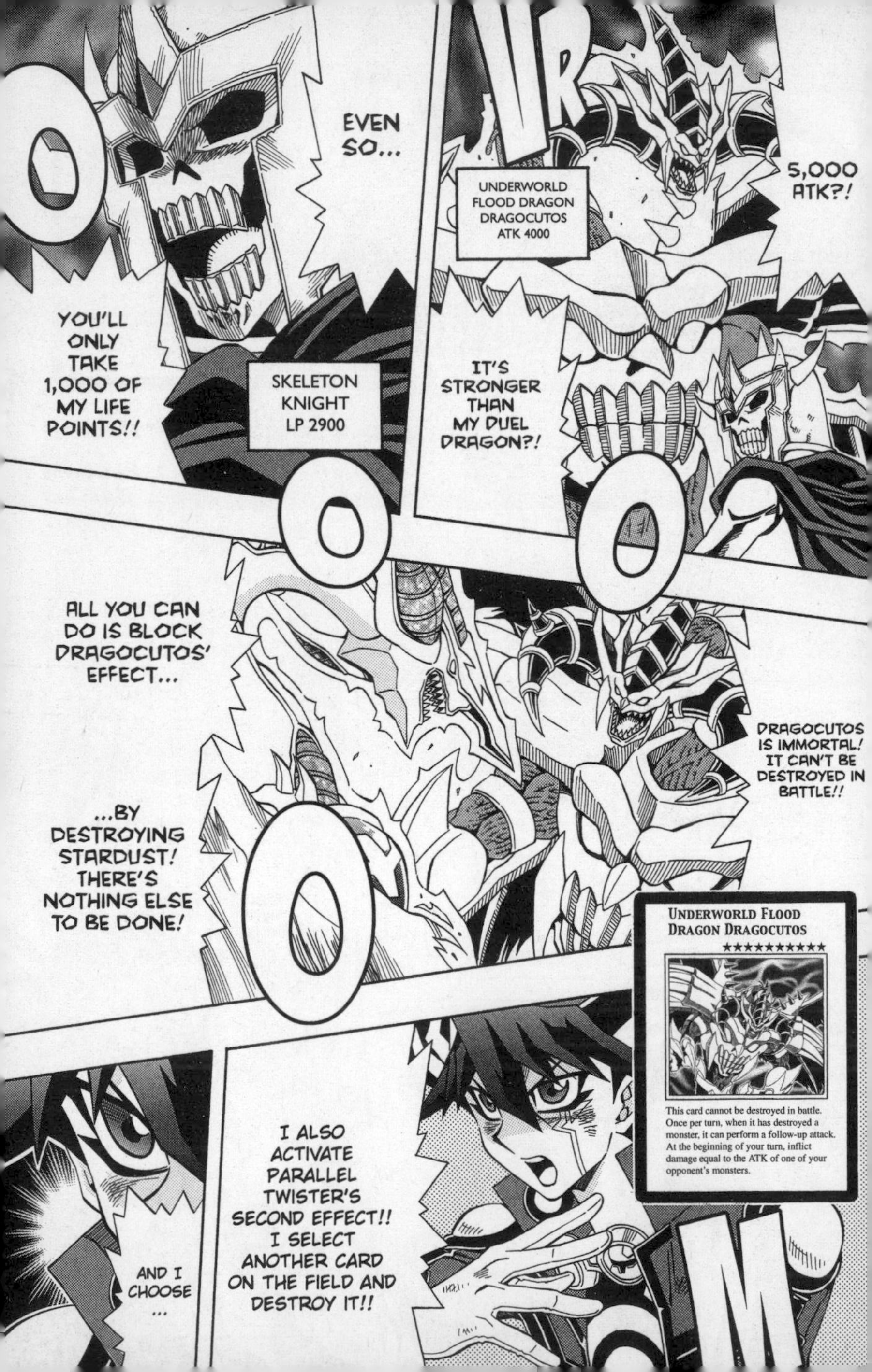

UNDERWORLD FLOOD DRAGON DRAGOCUTOS ATK 4000
5,000 ATK?!
IT'S STRONGER THAN MY DUEL DRAGON?!
EVEN SO...
YOU'LL ONLY TAKE 1,000 OF MY LIFE POINTS!!
SKELETON KNIGHT LP 2900
DRAGOCUTOS IS IMMORTAL! IT CAN'T BE DESTROYED IN BATTLE!!
ALL YOU CAN DO IS BLOCK DRAGOCUTOS' EFFECT...
...BY DESTROYING STARDUST! THERE'S NOTHING ELSE TO BE DONE!
UNDERWORLD FLOOD DRAGON DRAGOCUTOS
★★★★★★★★★★
This card cannot be destroyed in battle. Once per turn, when it has destroyed a monster, it can perform a follow-up attack. At the beginning of your turn, inflict damage equal to the ATK of one of your opponent's monsters.
I ALSO ACTIVATE PARALLEL TWISTER'S SECOND EFFECT!! I SELECT ANOTHER CARD ON THE FIELD AND DESTROY IT!!
AND I CHOOSE ...

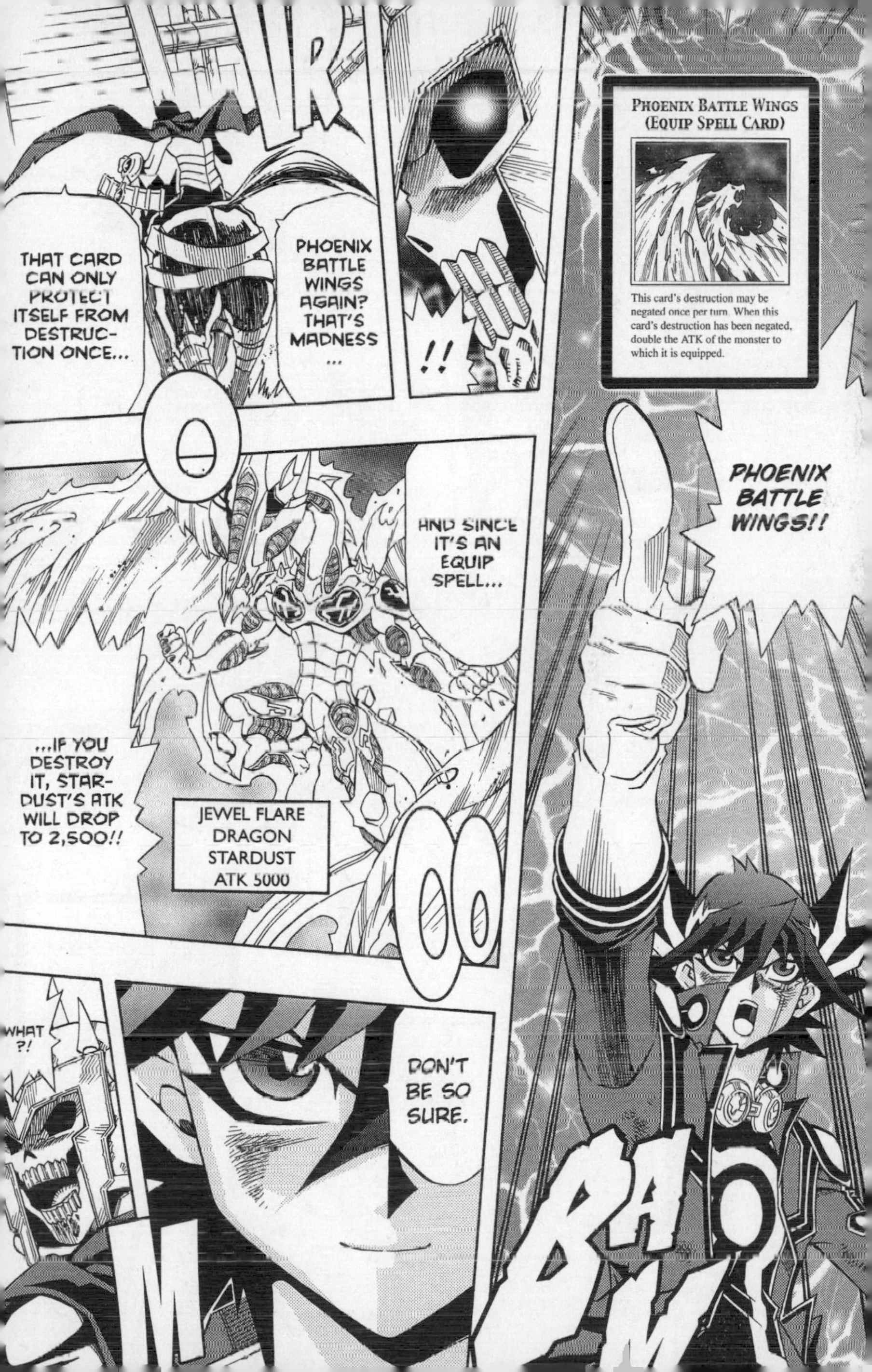
PHOENIX BATTLE WINGS
(EQUIP SPELL CARD)
This card's destruction may be negated once per turn. When this card's destruction has been negated, double the ATK of the monster to which it is equipped.
PHOENIX BATTLE WINGS!!
BAM
!!
PHOENIX BATTLE WINGS AGAIN? THAT'S MADNESS...
THAT CARD CAN ONLY PROTECT ITSELF FROM DESTRUCTION ONCE...
AND SINCE IT'S AN EQUIP SPELL...
...IF YOU DESTROY IT, STARDUST'S ATK WILL DROP TO 2,500!!
JEWEL FLARE DRAGON STARDUST ATK 5000
DON'T BE SO SURE.
WHAT?!

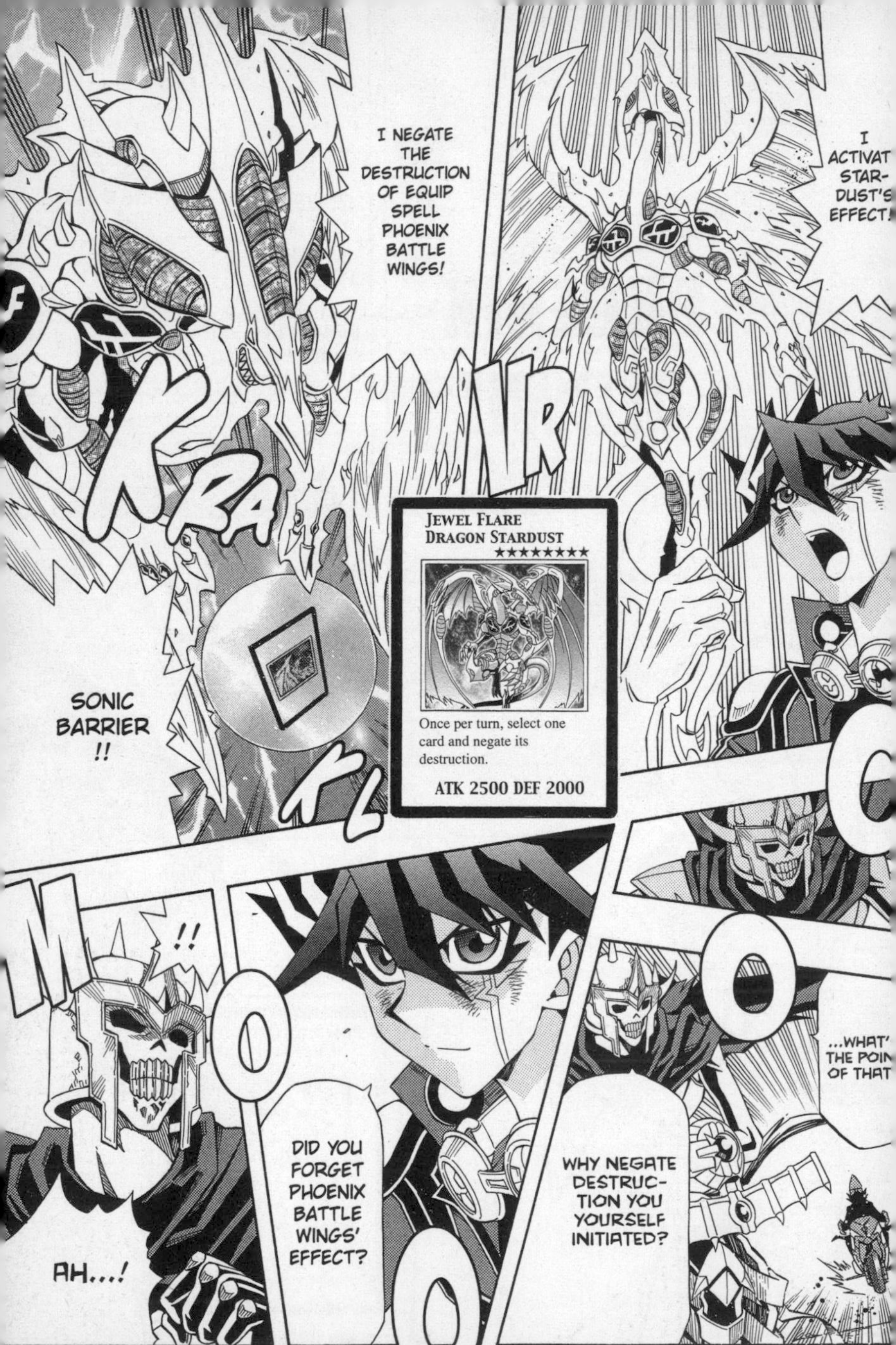

I ACTIVAT STAR-DUST'S EFFECT!
I NEGATE THE DESTRUCTION OF EQUIP SPELL PHOENIX BATTLE WINGS!
JEWEL FLARE DRAGON STARDUST
★★★★★★★★
Once per turn, select one card and negate its destruction.
ATK 2500 DEF 2000
SONIC BARRIER !!
...WHAT' THE POIN OF THAT
WHY NEGATE DESTRUC-TION YOU YOURSELF INITIATED?
DID YOU FORGET PHOENIX BATTLE WINGS' EFFECT?
!!
AH...!

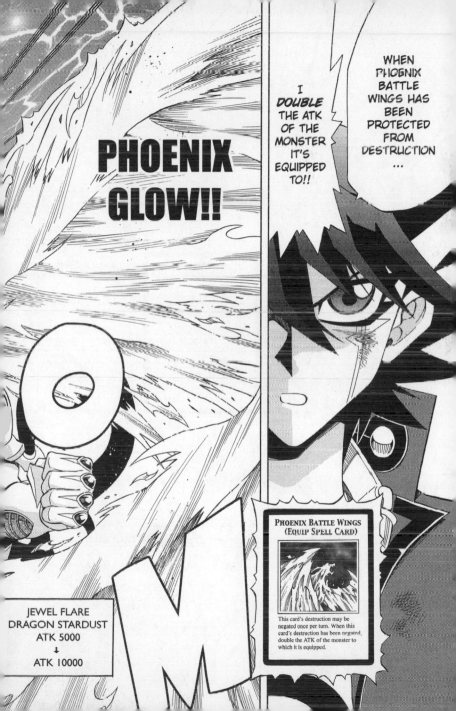

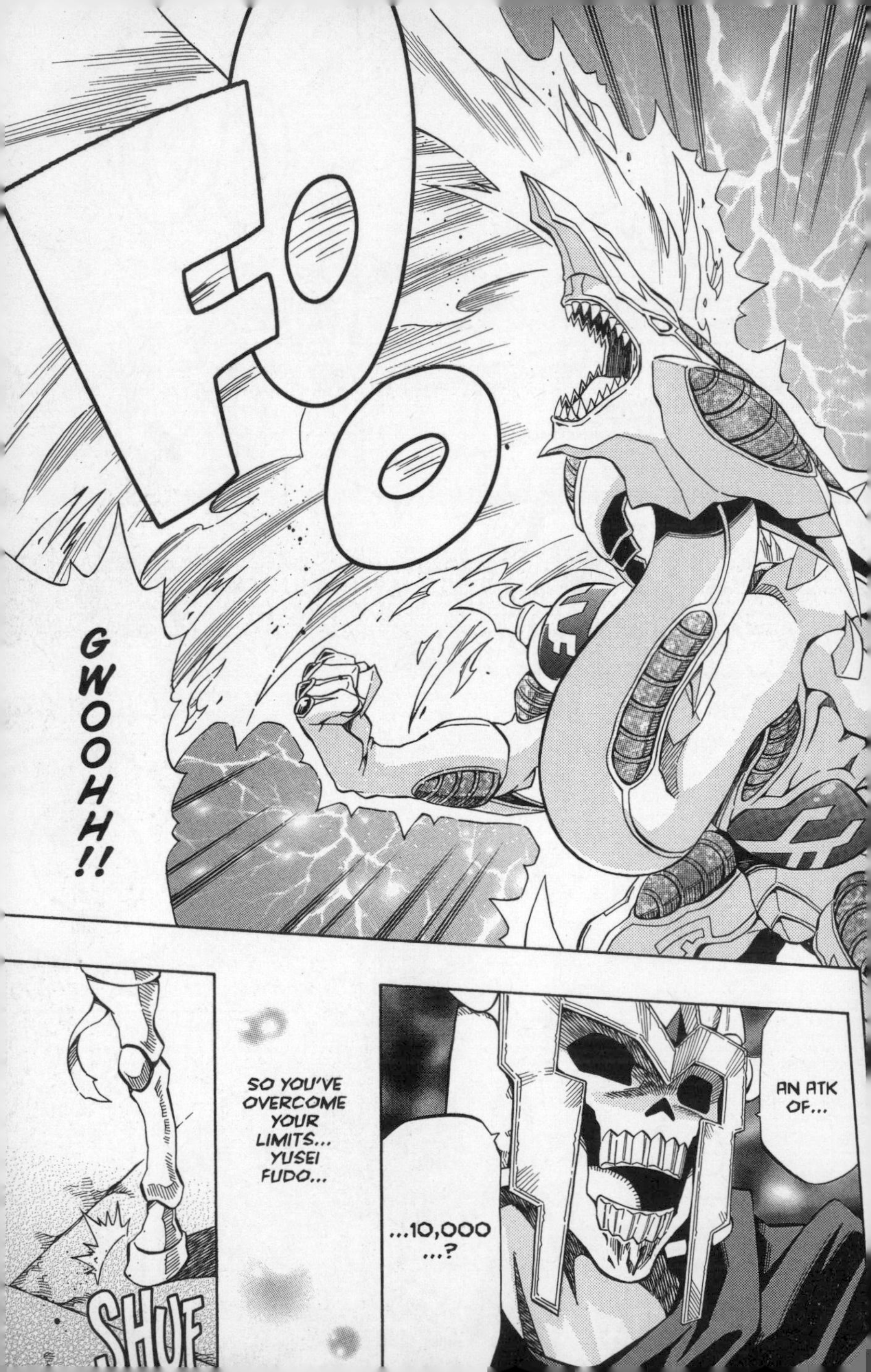
FOO
GWOOHHH!!
AN ATK OF...
...10,000 ...?
SO YOU'VE OVERCOME YOUR LIMITS... YUSEI FUDO...
SHUF

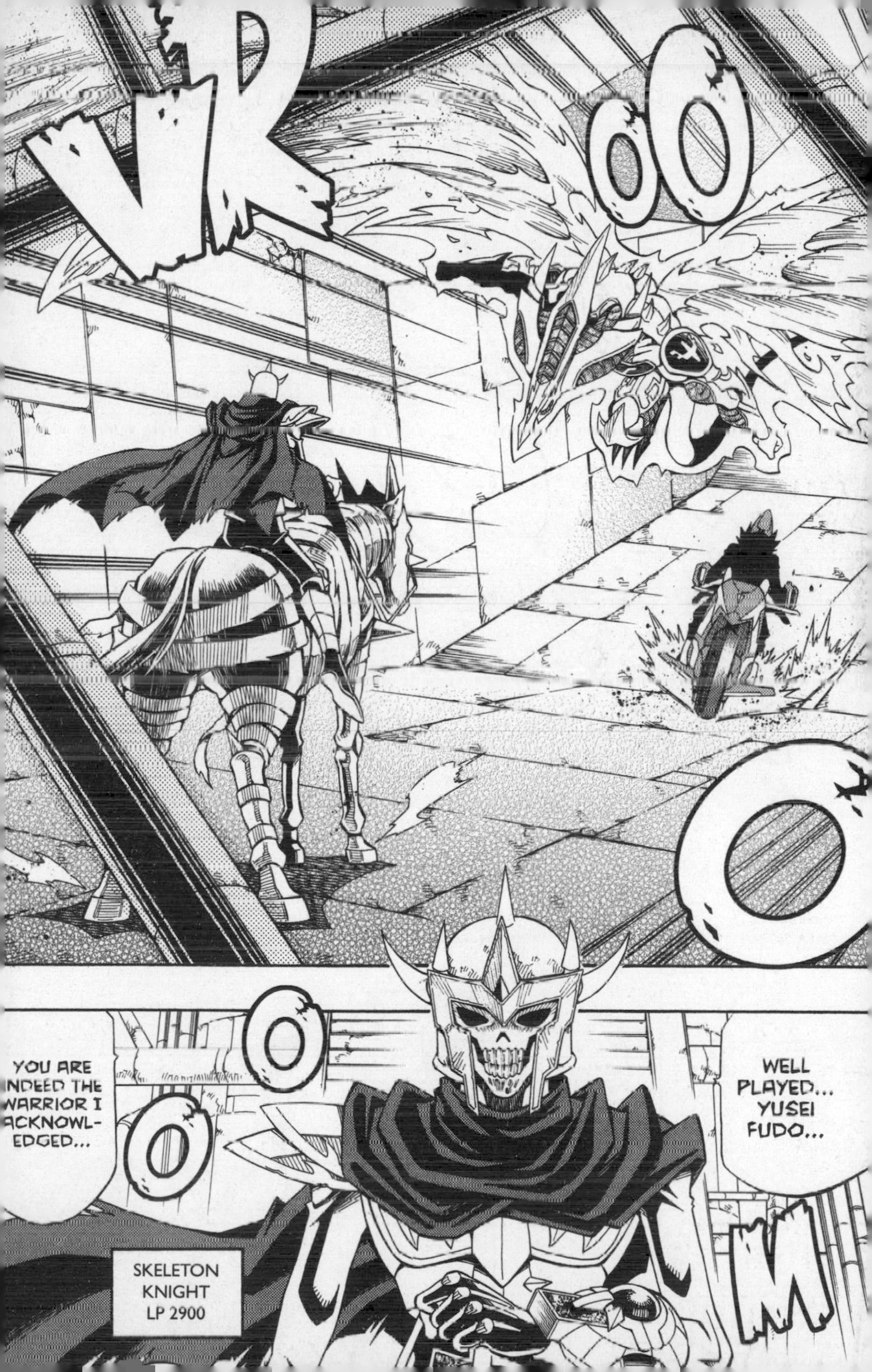
VROOOOOM
WELL PLAYED... YUSEI FUDO...
YOU ARE INDEED THE WARRIOR I ACKNOWL-EDGED...
SKELETON KNIGHT LP 2900

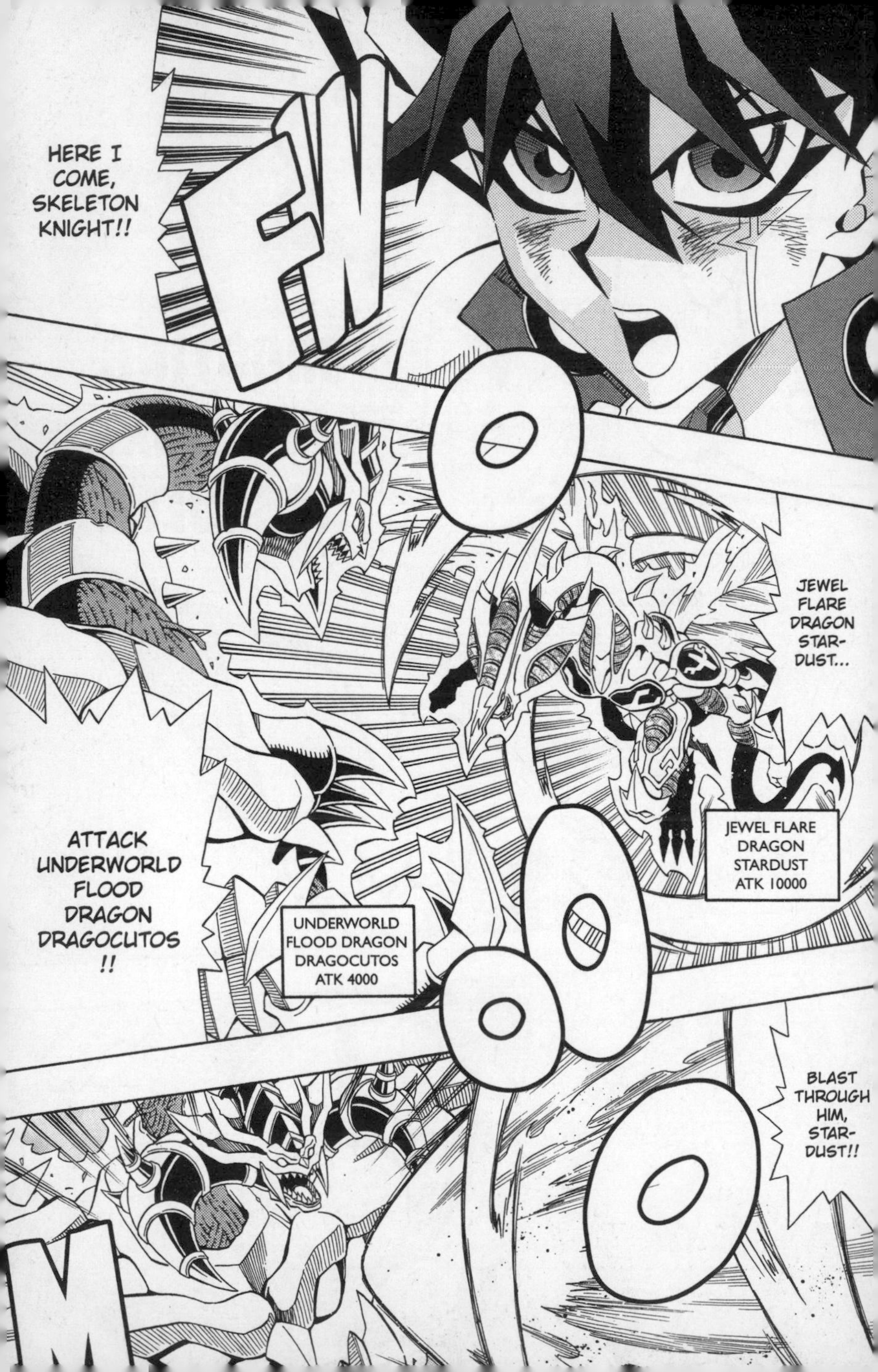
HERE I COME, SKELETON KNIGHT!!
FWOOOOOM
JEWEL FLARE DRAGON STAR-DUST...
JEWEL FLARE DRAGON STARDUST ATK 10000
ATTACK UNDERWORLD FLOOD DRAGON DRAGOCUTOS!!
UNDERWORLD FLOOD DRAGON DRAGOCUTOS ATK 4000
BLAST THROUGH HIM, STAR-DUST!!

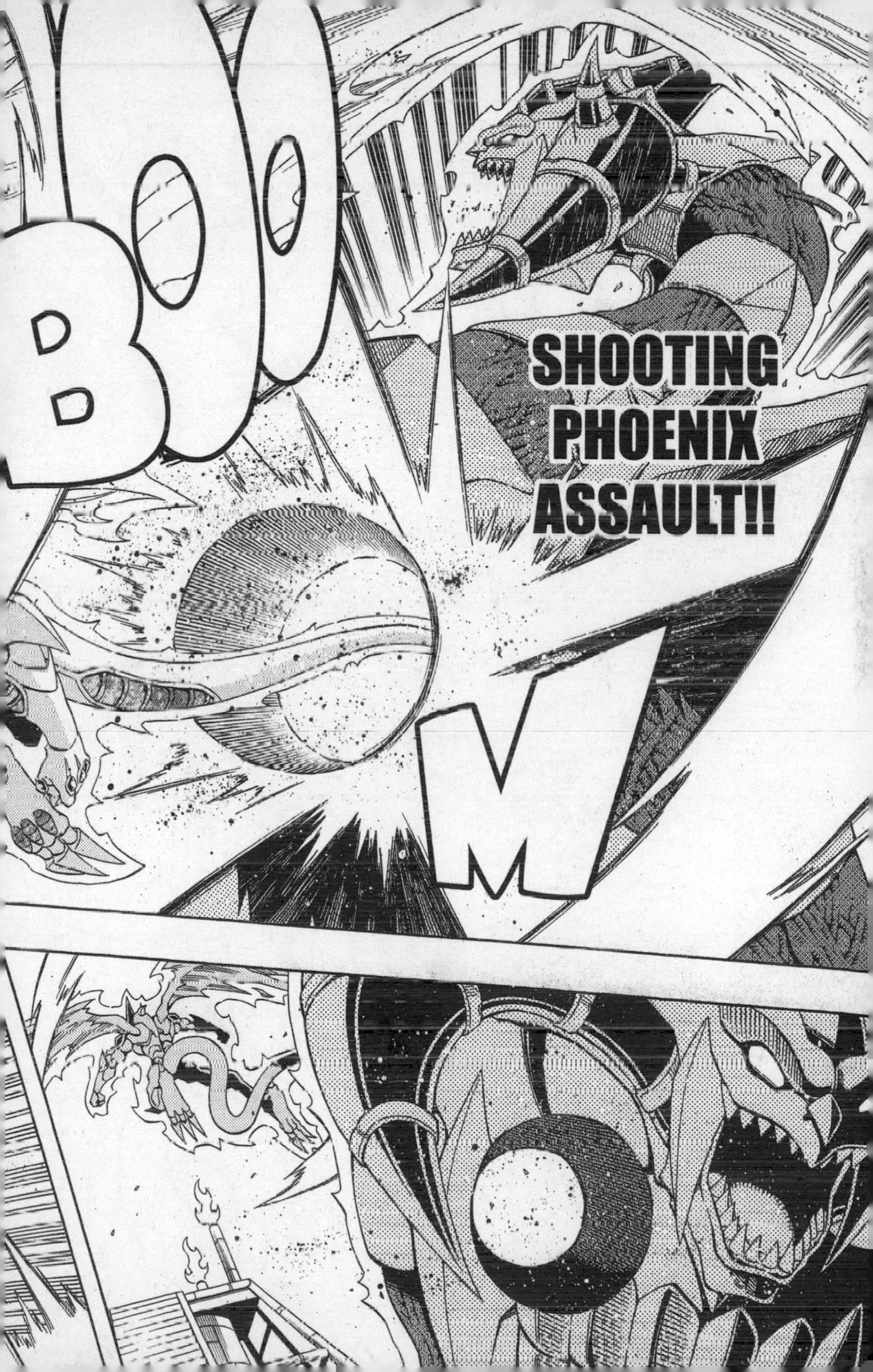
SHOOTING PHOENIX ASSAULT!!
BOOOM

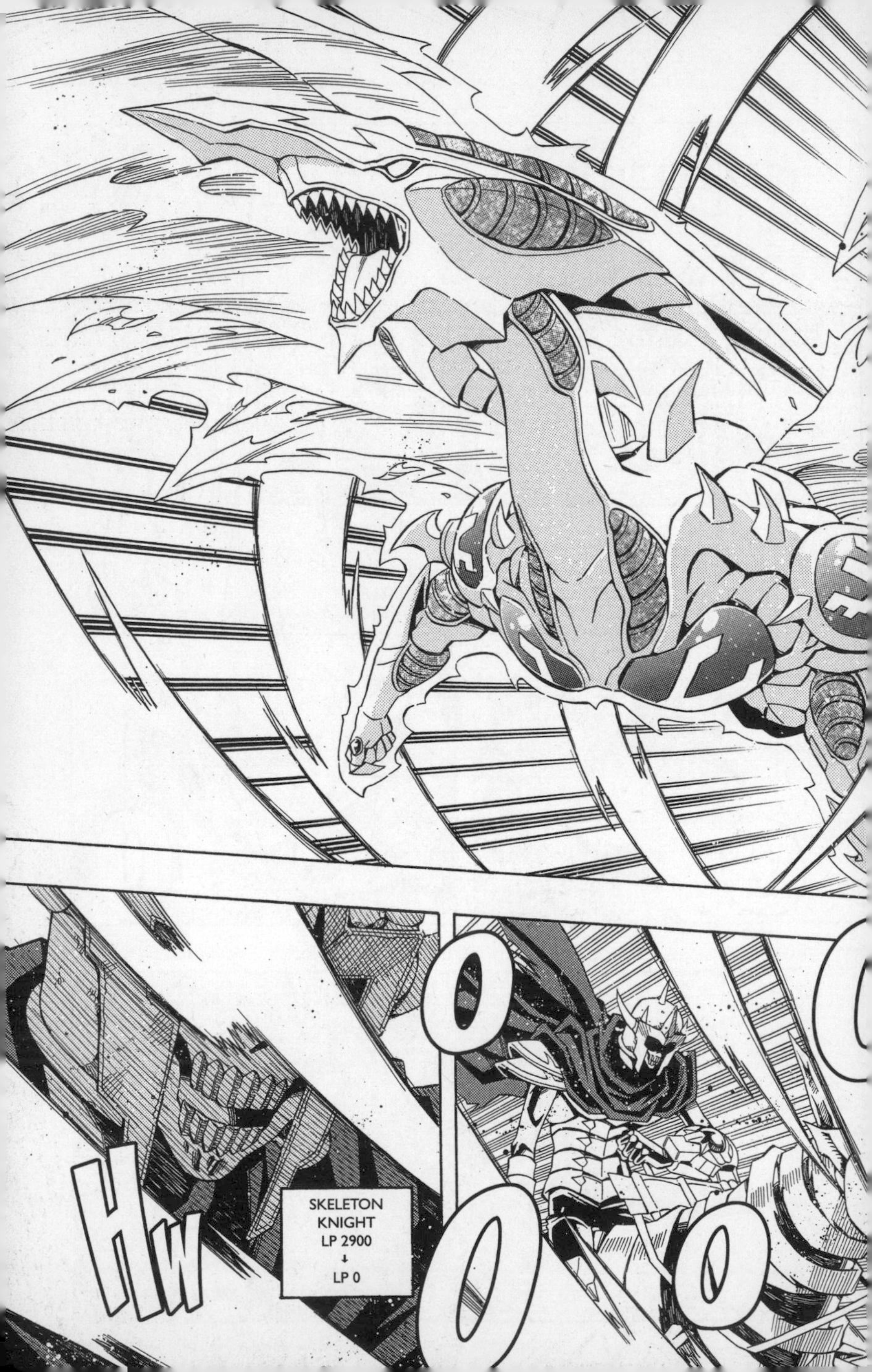

SKELETON KNIGHT LP 2900 ↓ LP 0
HWOOO

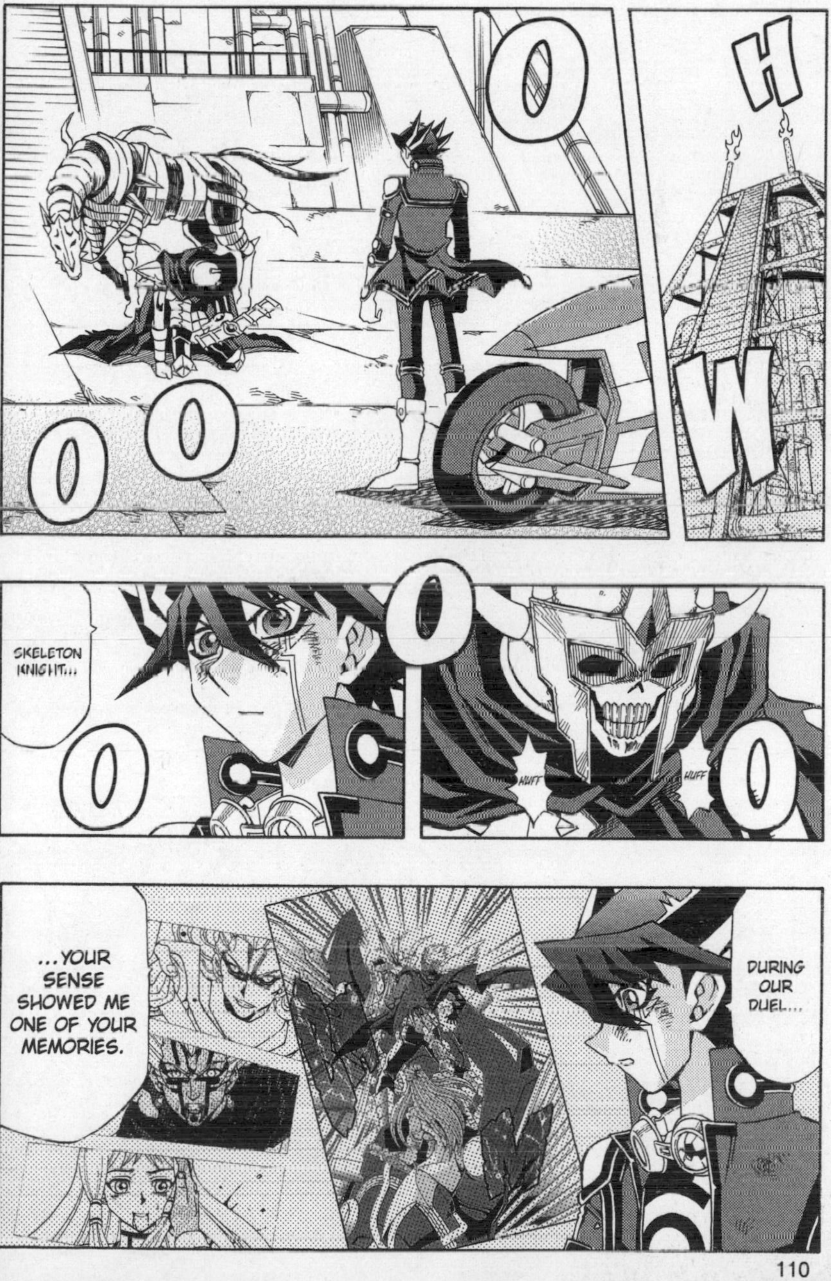
H
W
O
O
O
O
HUFF
HUFF
O
O
SKELETON KNIGHT...
DURING OUR DUEL...
...YOUR SENSE SHOWED ME ONE OF YOUR MEMORIES.

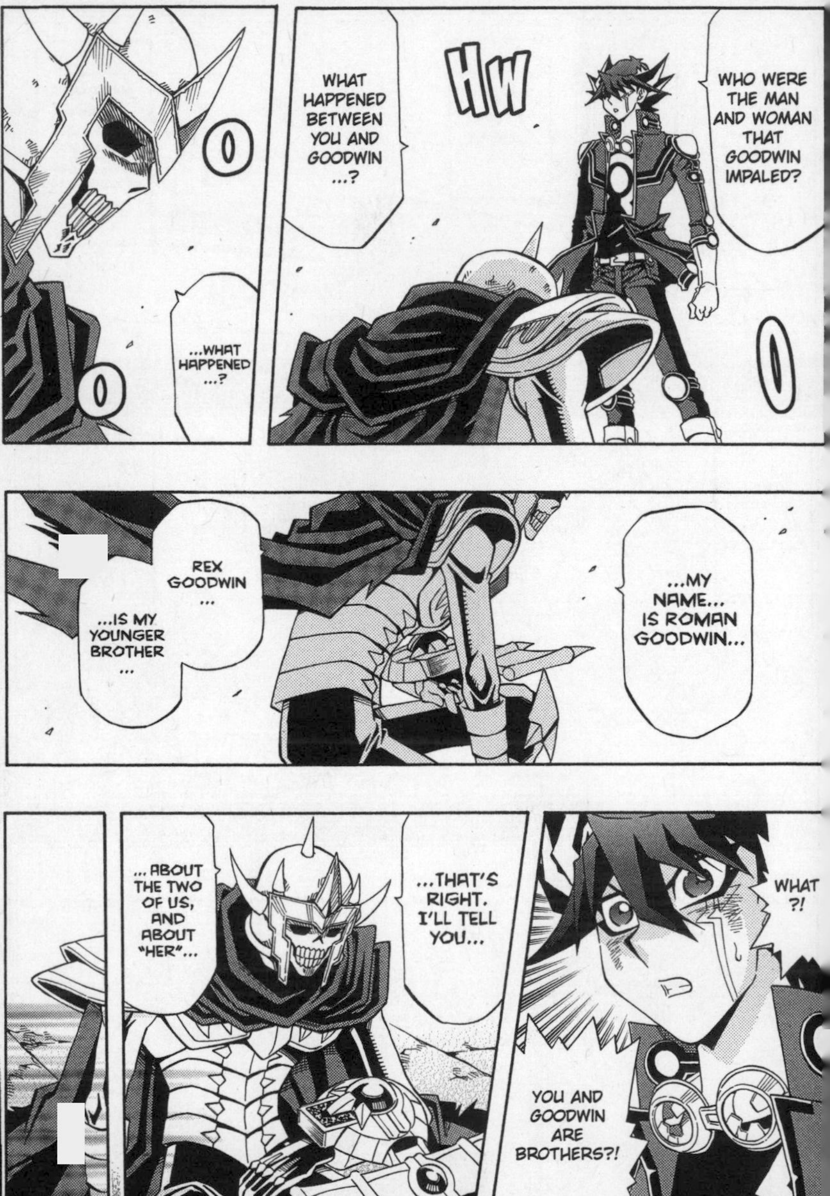
WHO WERE THE MAN AND WOMAN THAT GOODWIN IMPALED?
HW
WHAT HAPPENED BETWEEN YOU AND GOODWIN ...?
...WHAT HAPPENED ...?
...MY NAME... IS ROMAN GOODWIN...
REX GOODWIN ...
...IS MY YOUNGER BROTHER ...
WHAT ?!
YOU AND GOODWIN ARE BROTHERS?!
...THAT'S RIGHT. I'LL TELL YOU...
...ABOUT THE TWO OF US, AND ABOUT "HER"...

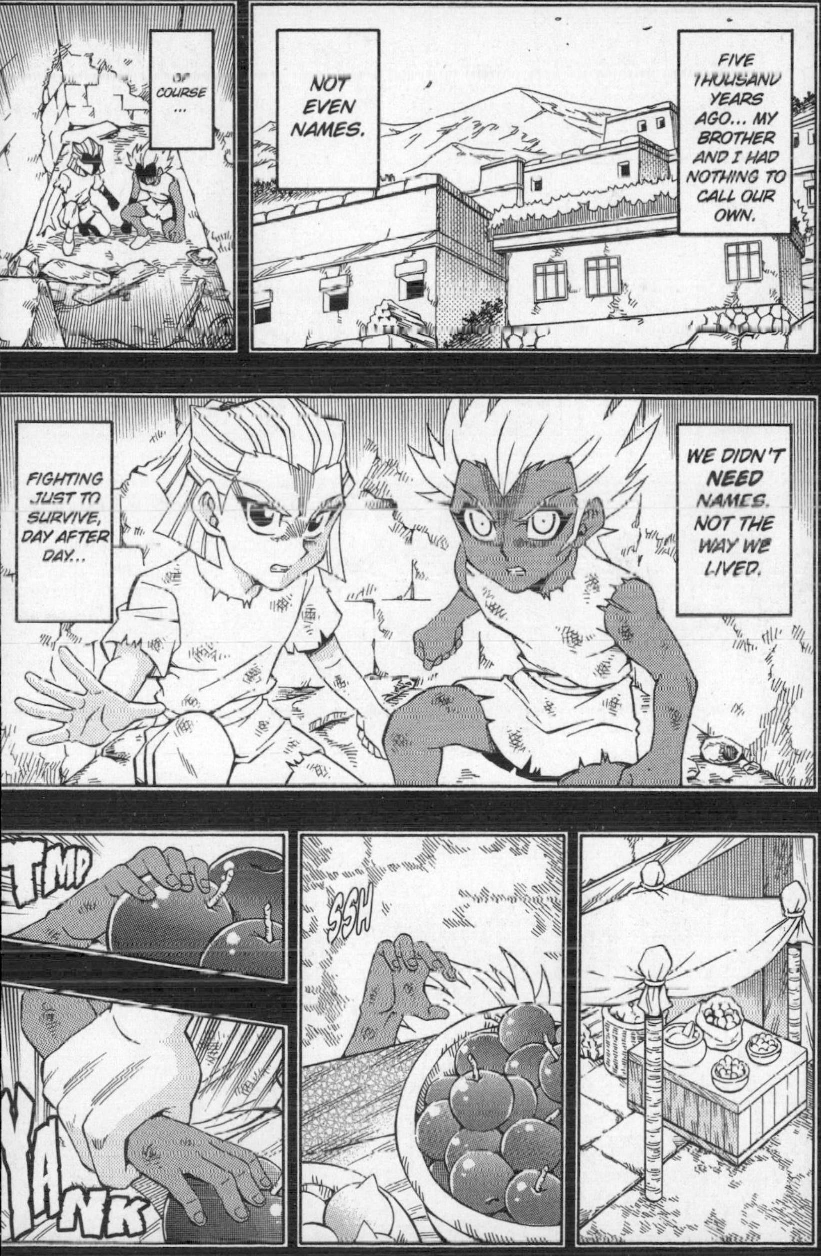
FIVE THOUSAND YEARS AGO... MY BROTHER AND I HAD NOTHING TO CALL OUR OWN.
NOT EVEN NAMES.
OF COURSE ...
WE DIDN'T NEED NAMES. NOT THE WAY WE LIVED.
FIGHTING JUST TO SURVIVE, DAY AFTER DAY...
SSH
TMP
YANK

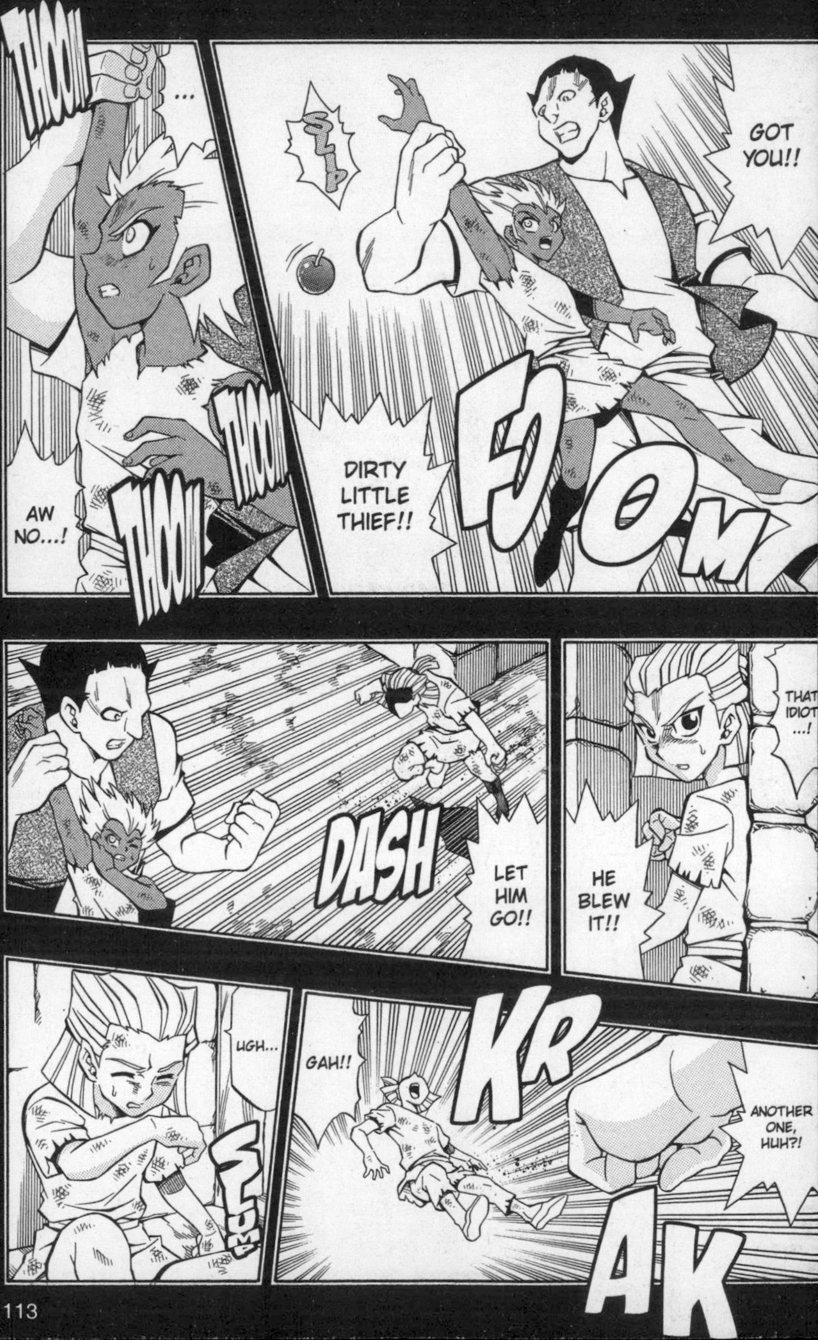
GOT YOU!!
DIRTY LITTLE THIEF!!
FWOOM
...
THOOM
THOOM
THOOM
AW NO...!
THAT IDIOT ...!
HE BLEW IT!!
LET HIM GO!!
DASH
ANOTHER ONE, HUH?!
KRAK
GAH!!
UGH...
SLUMP

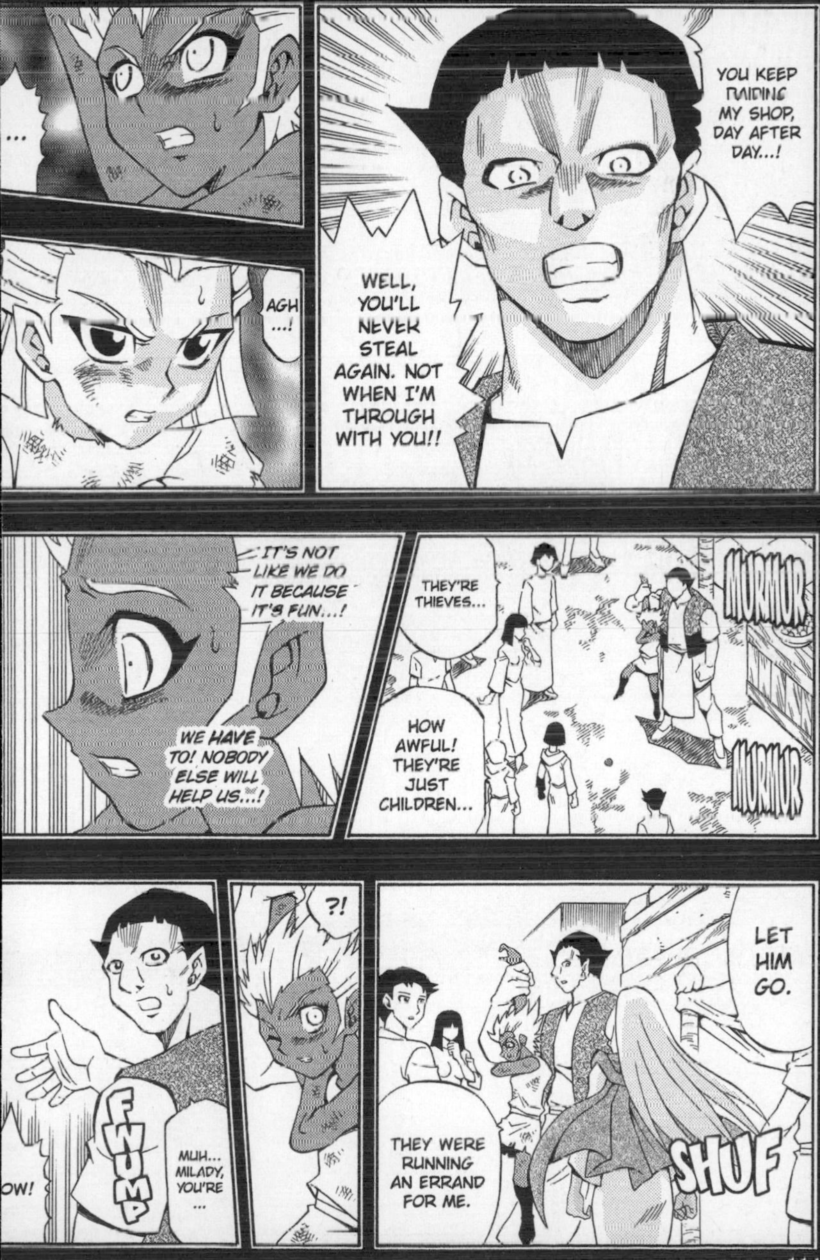
YOU KEEP RAIDING MY SHOP, DAY AFTER DAY...!
WELL, YOU'LL NEVER STEAL AGAIN. NOT WHEN I'M THROUGH WITH YOU!!
...
AGH ...!
MURMUR
THEY'RE THIEVES...
HOW AWFUL! THEY'RE JUST CHILDREN...
MURMUR
IT'S NOT LIKE WE DO IT BECAUSE IT'S FUN...!
WE HAVE TO! NOBODY ELSE WILL HELP US...!
LET HIM GO.
SHUF
THEY WERE RUNNING AN ERRAND FOR ME.
?!
MUH... MILADY, YOU'RE ...
FWUMP
OW!

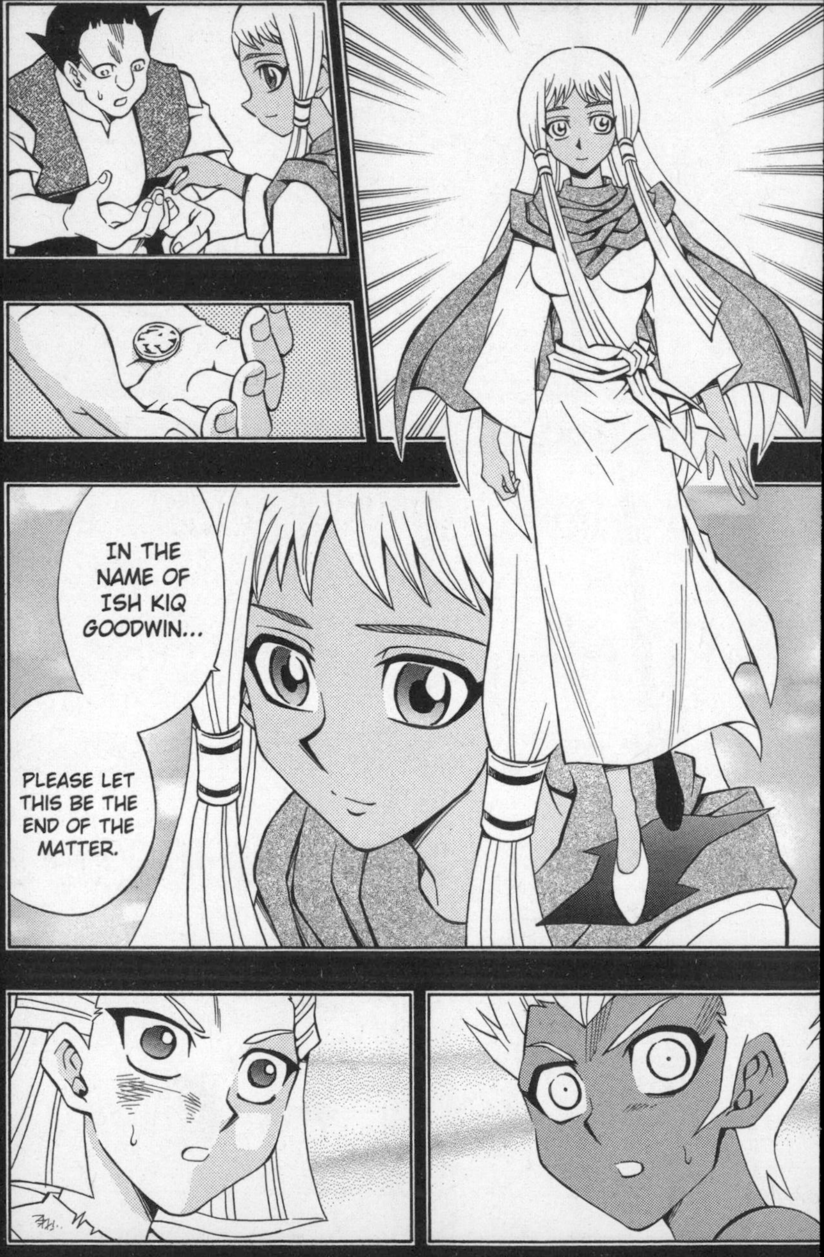
IN THE NAME OF ISH KIQ GOODWIN...
PLEASE LET THIS BE THE END OF THE MATTER.

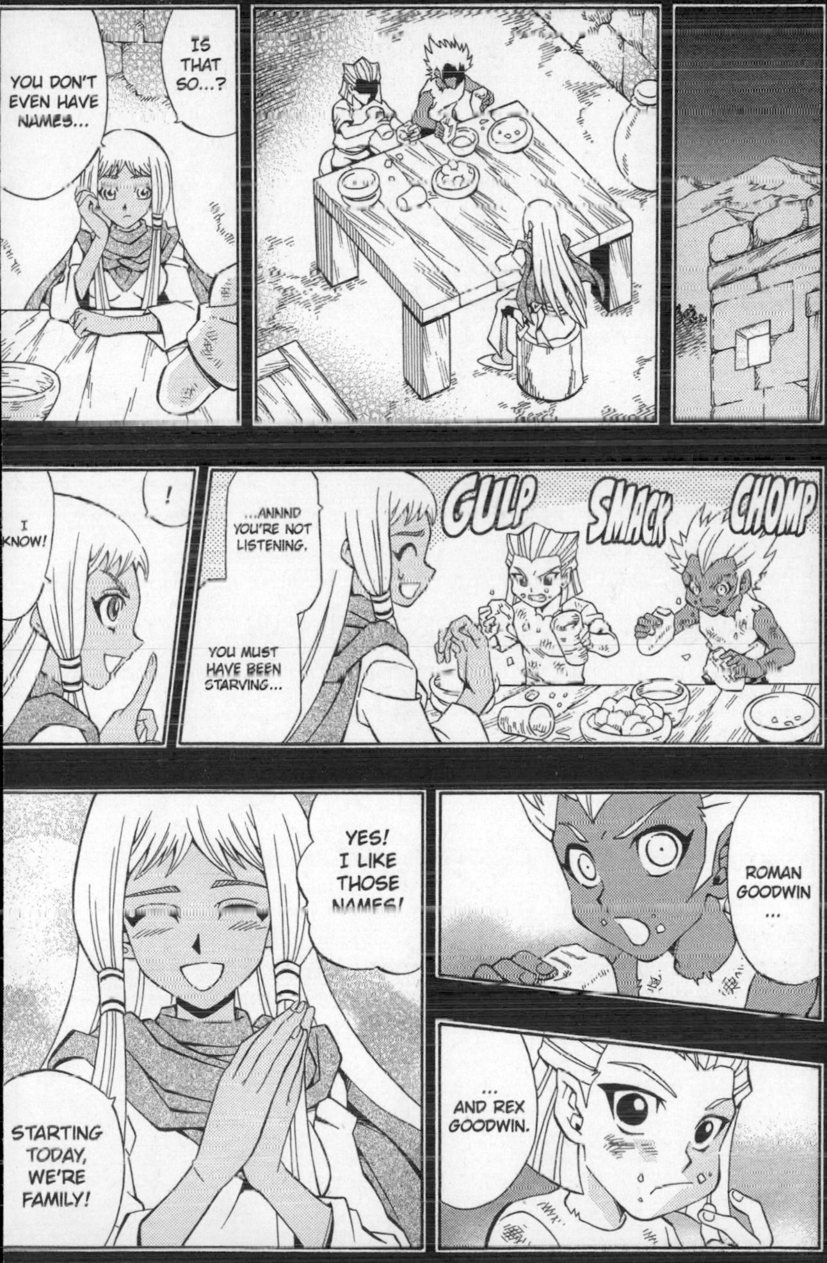
IS THAT SO...?
YOU DON'T EVEN HAVE NAMES...
CHOMP
SMACK
GULP
...ANNND YOU'RE NOT LISTENING.
YOU MUST HAVE BEEN STARVING...
!
I KNOW!
ROMAN GOODWIN ...
... AND REX GOODWIN.
YES! I LIKE THOSE NAMES!
STARTING TODAY, WE'RE FAMILY!

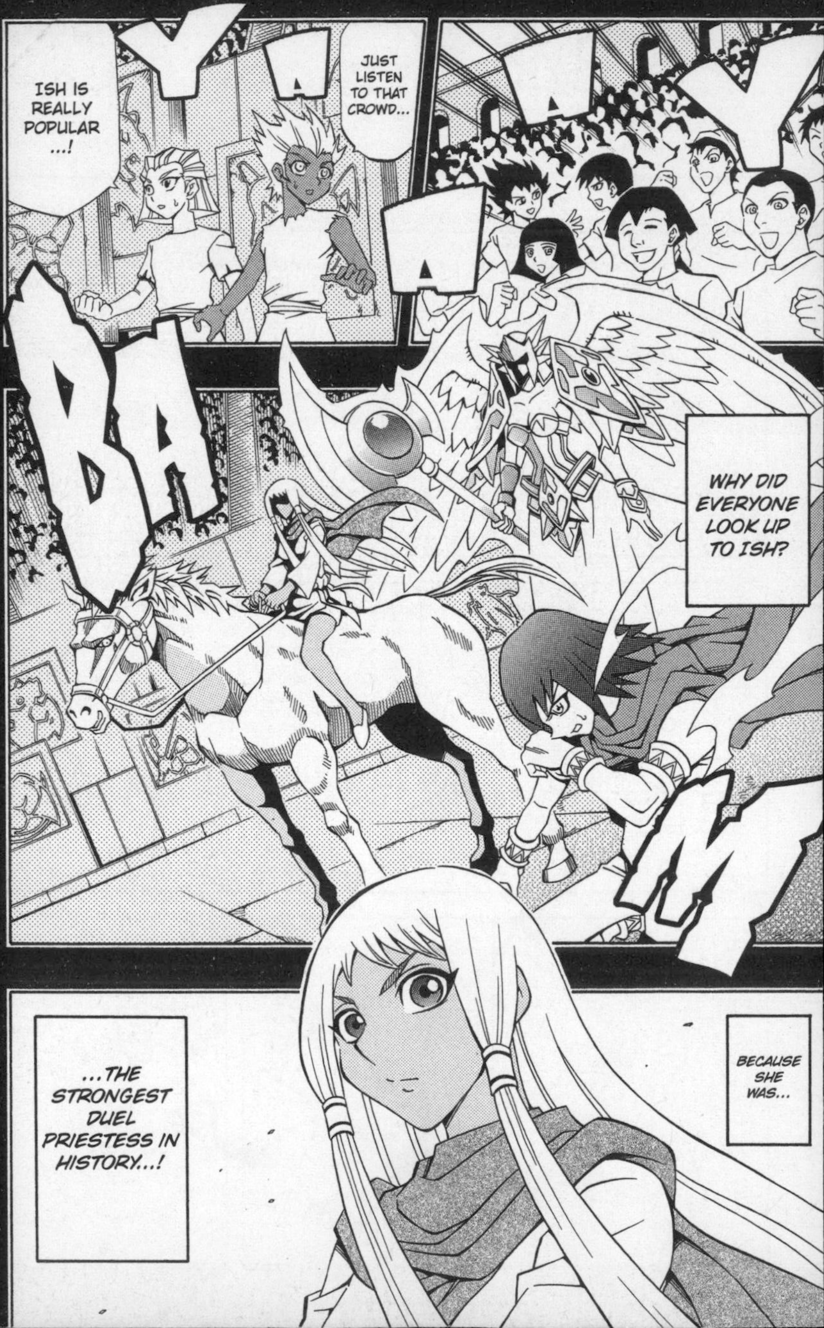
YAAAY
JUST LISTEN TO THAT CROWD...
ISH IS REALLY POPULAR ...!
WHY DID EVERYONE LOOK UP TO ISH?
BAM
BECAUSE SHE WAS...
...THE STRONGEST DUEL PRIESTESS IN HISTORY...!

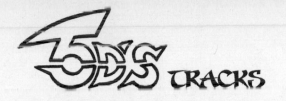

5D's Tracks

The 49th

By Satomasa

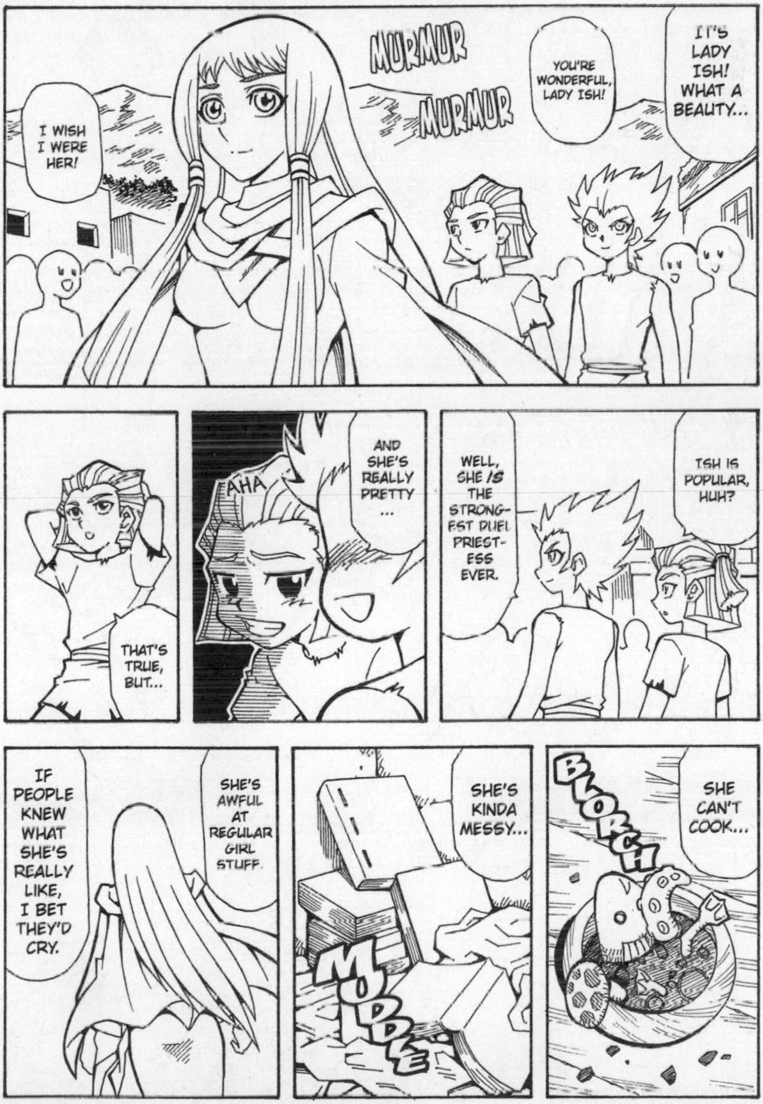
IT'S LADY ISH! WHAT A BEAUTY...
YOU'RE WONDERFUL, LADY ISH!
MURMUR
MURMUR
I WISH I WERE HER!
ISH IS POPULAR, HUH?
WELL, SHE IS THE STRONGEST DUEL PRIESTESS EVER.
AND SHE'S REALLY PRETTY...
AHA
THAT'S TRUE, BUT...
SHE CAN'T COOK...
BLORCH
SHE'S KINDA MESSY...
MUDDLE
SHE'S AWFUL AT REGULAR GIRL STUFF.
IF PEOPLE KNEW WHAT SHE'S REALLY LIKE, I BET THEY'D CRY.

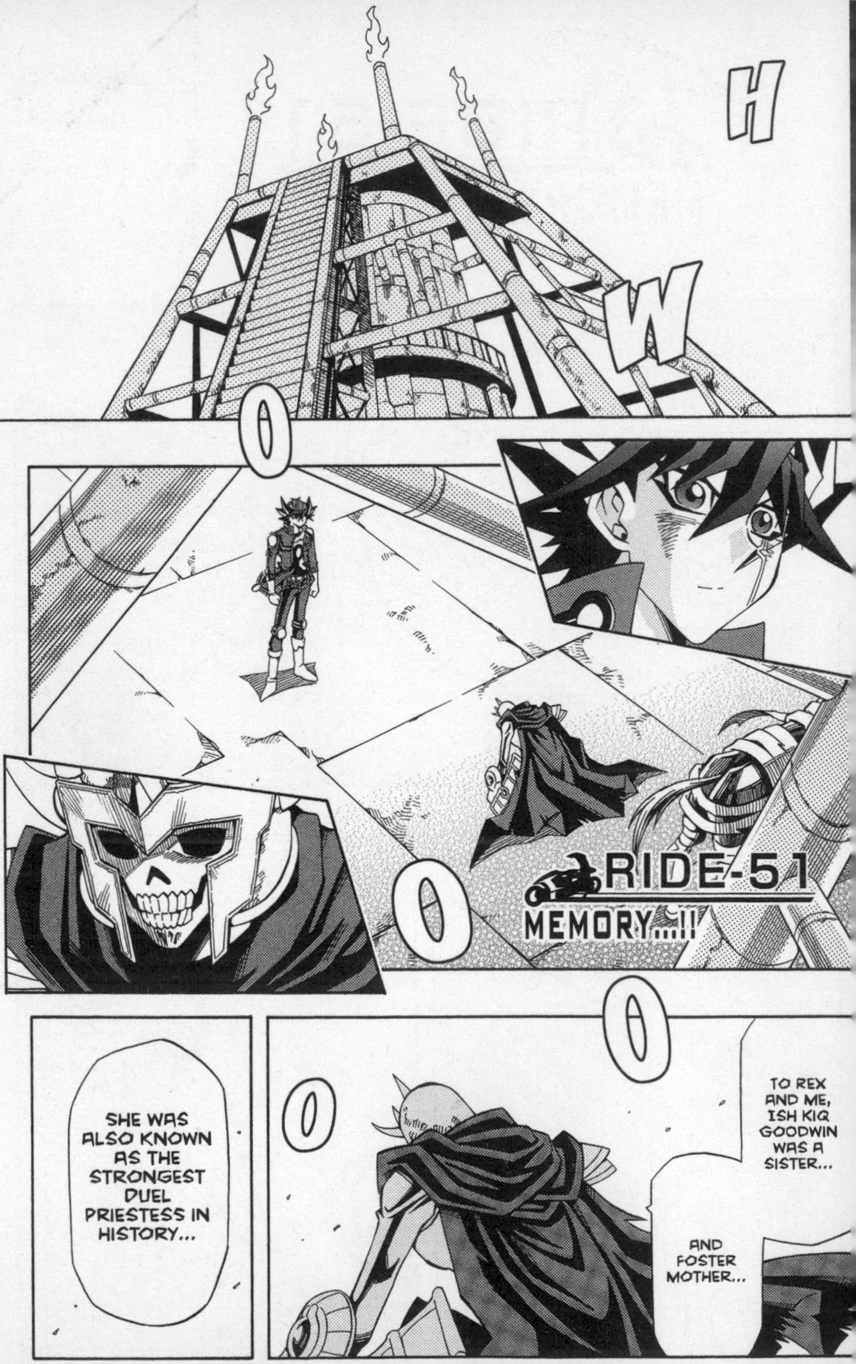
HWOOOO
RIDE-51
MEMORY...!!
TO REX AND ME, ISH KIQ GOODWIN WAS A SISTER...
AND FOSTER MOTHER...
SHE WAS ALSO KNOWN AS THE STRONGEST DUEL PRIESTESS IN HISTORY...

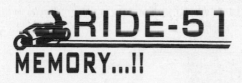

RIDE-51
MEMORY...!!

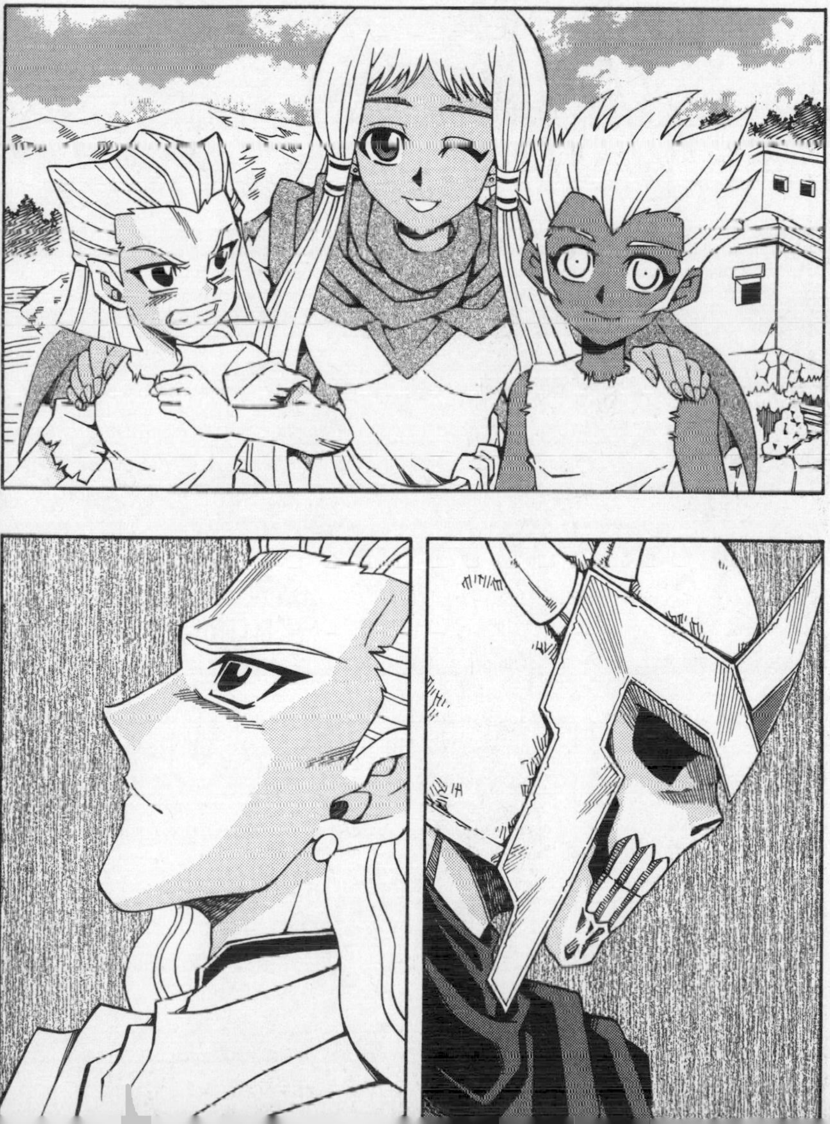

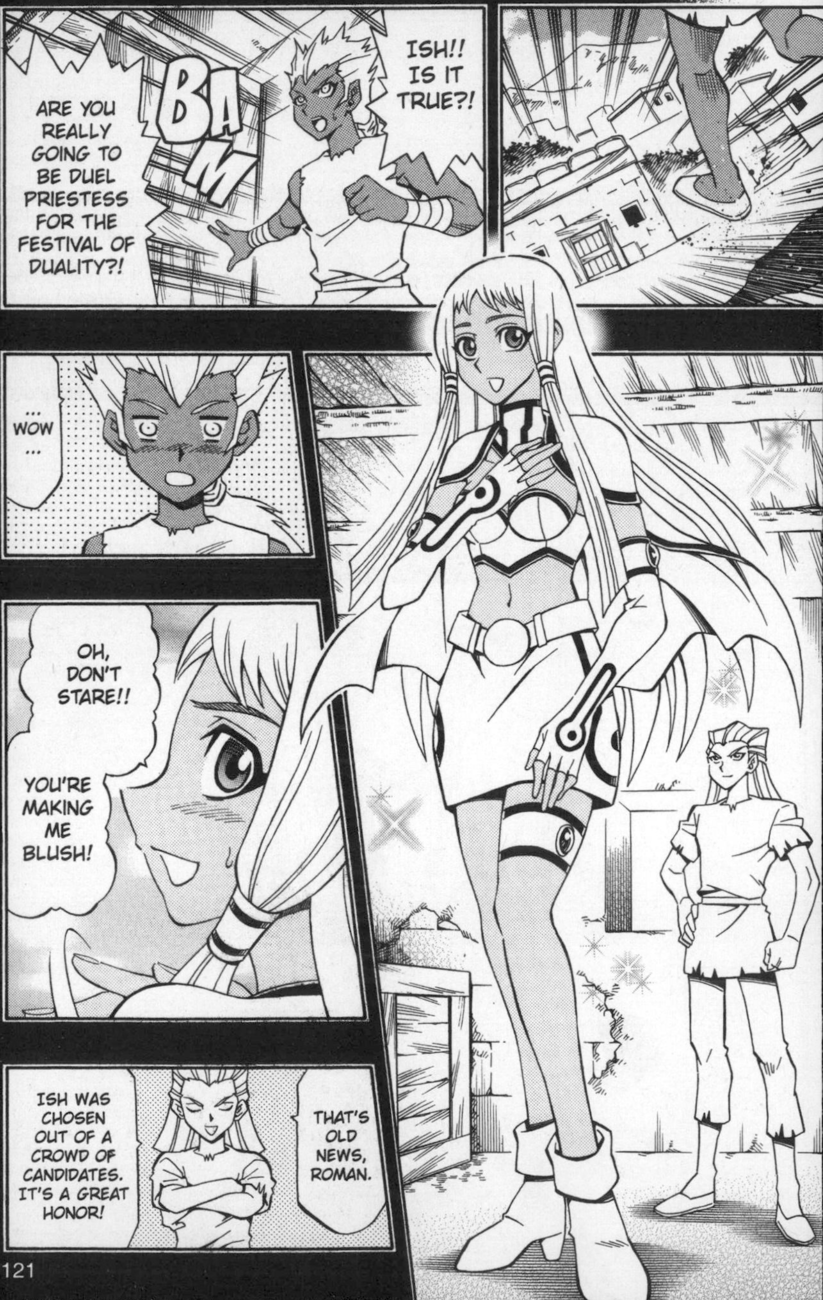
ISH!! IS IT TRUE?!
BAM
ARE YOU REALLY GOING TO BE DUEL PRIESTESS FOR THE FESTIVAL OF DUALITY?!
... WOW ...
OH, DON'T STARE!!
YOU'RE MAKING ME BLUSH!
THAT'S OLD NEWS, ROMAN.
ISH WAS CHOSEN OUT OF A CROWD OF CANDIDATES. IT'S A GREAT HONOR!

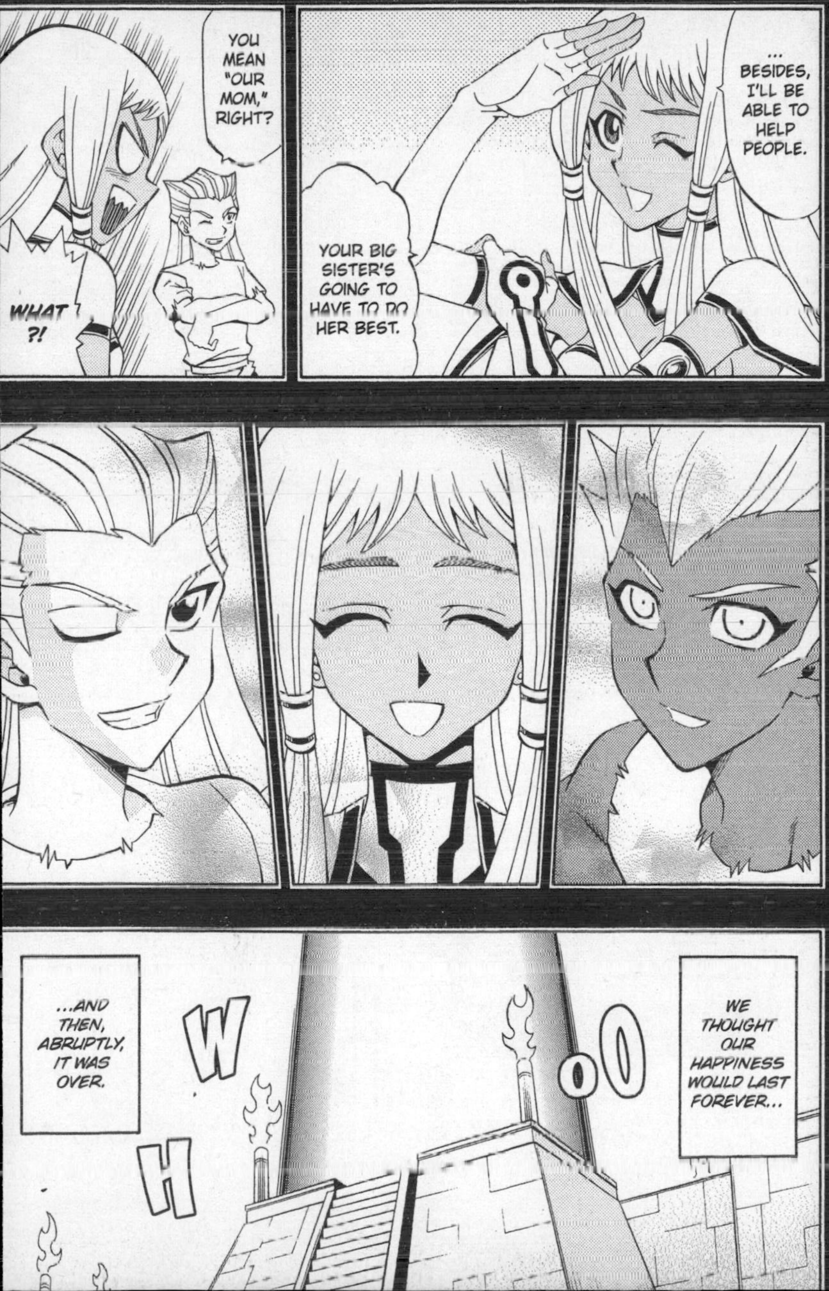
...BESIDES, I'LL BE ABLE TO HELP PEOPLE.
YOUR BIG SISTER'S GOING TO HAVE TO DO HER BEST.
YOU MEAN "OUR MOM," RIGHT?
WHAT?!
WE THOUGHT OUR HAPPINESS WOULD LAST FOREVER...
WHOO
...AND THEN, ABRUPTLY, IT WAS OVER.

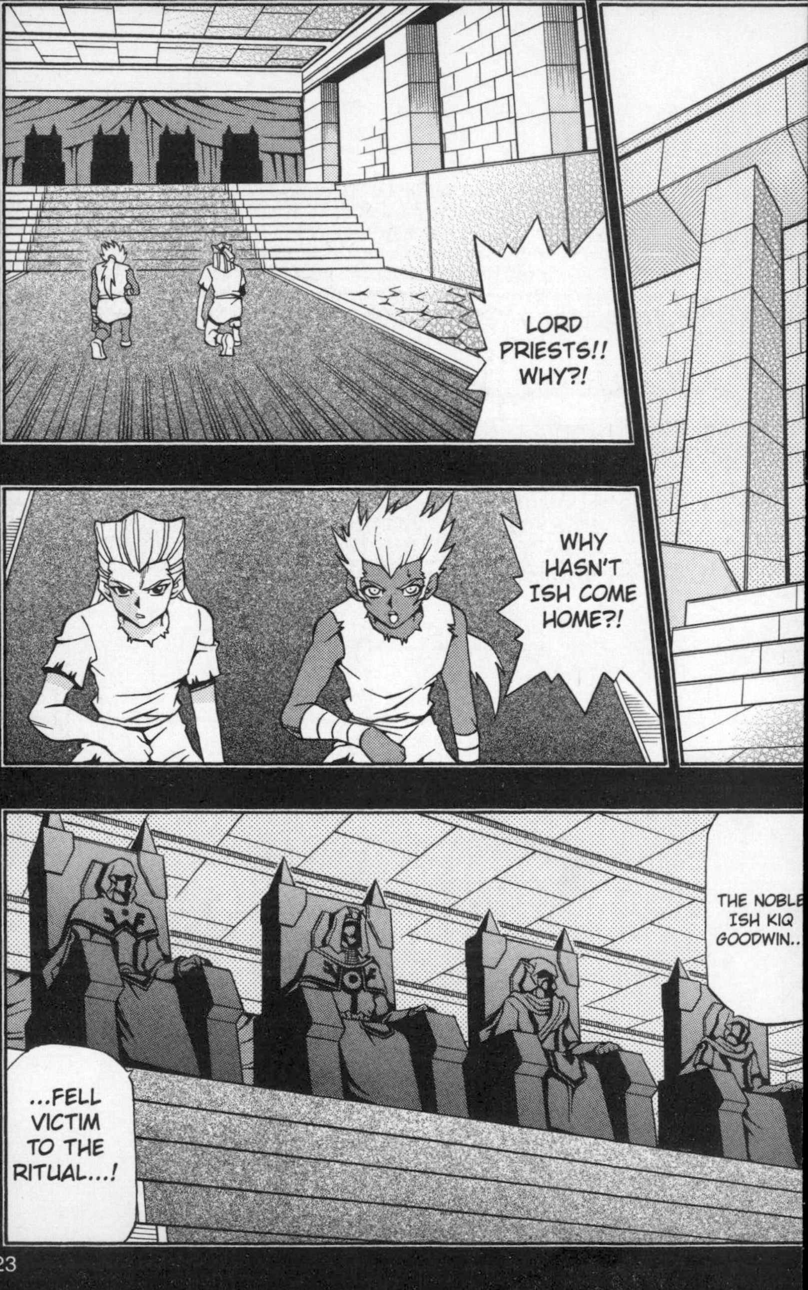
LORD PRIESTS!! WHY?!
WHY HASN'T ISH COME HOME?!
THE NOBLE ISH KIQ GOODWIN...
...FELL VICTIM TO THE RITUAL...!

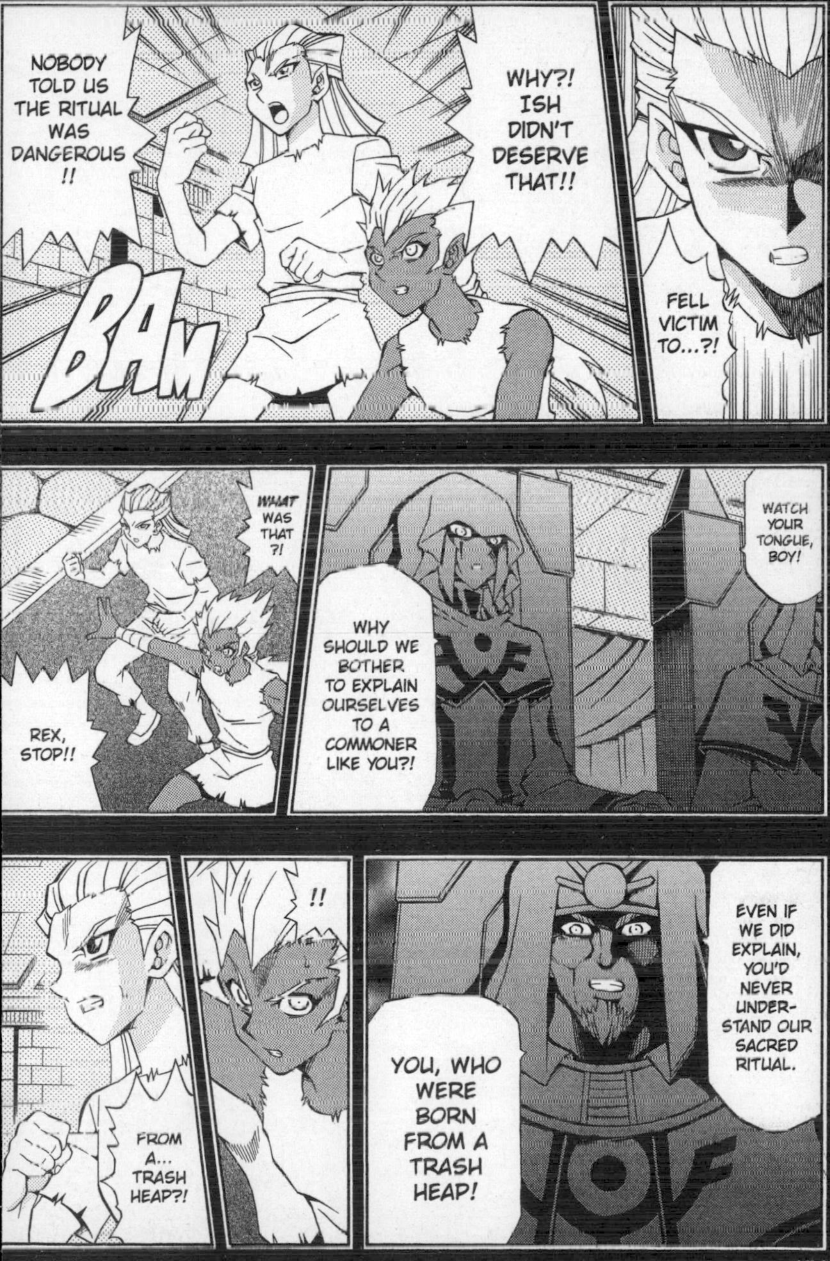
FELL VICTIM TO...?!
WHY?! ISH DIDN'T DESERVE THAT!!
NOBODY TOLD US THE RITUAL WAS DANGEROUS !!
BAM
WATCH YOUR TONGUE, BOY!
WHY SHOULD WE BOTHER TO EXPLAIN OURSELVES TO A COMMONER LIKE YOU?!
WHAT WAS THAT ?!
REX, STOP!!
EVEN IF WE DID EXPLAIN, YOU'D NEVER UNDER-STAND OUR SACRED RITUAL.
YOU, WHO WERE BORN FROM A TRASH HEAP!
!!
FROM A... TRASH HEAP?!

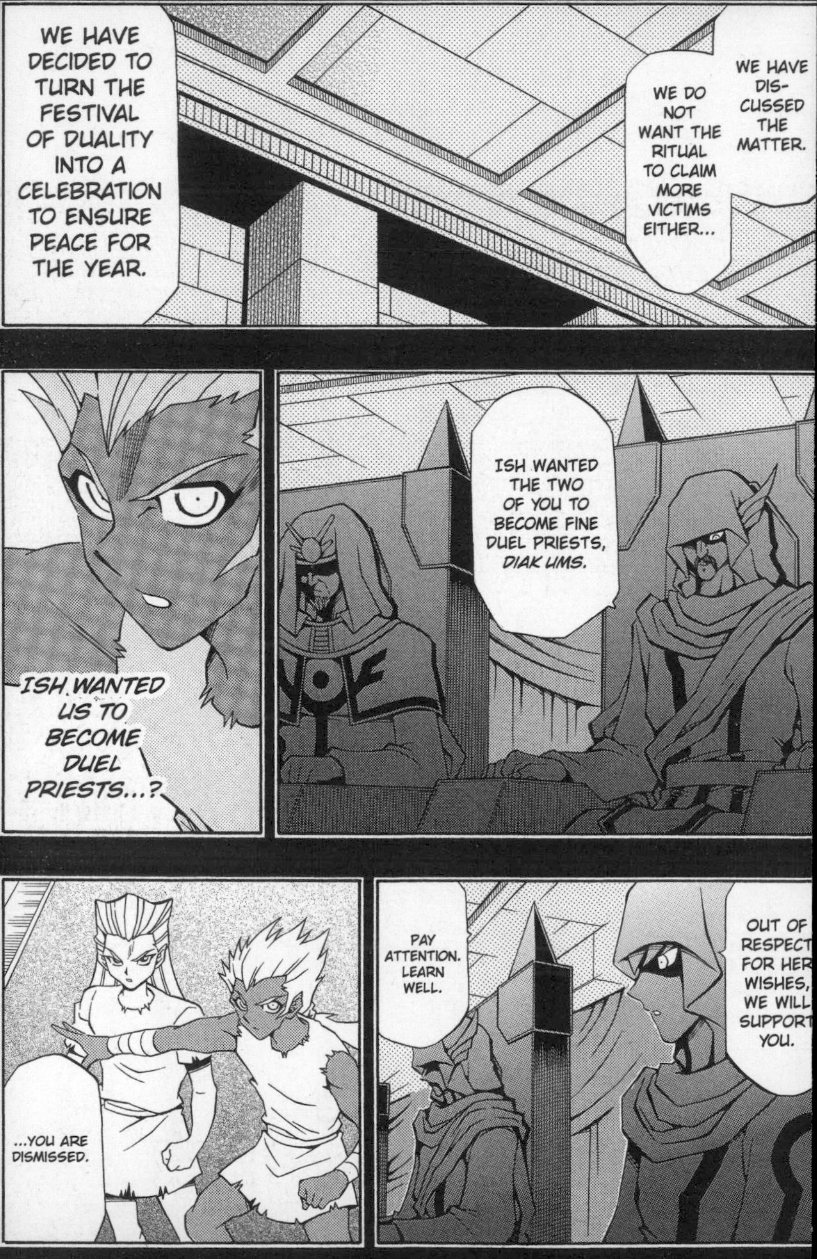
WE HAVE DIS-CUSSED THE MATTER.
WE DO NOT WANT THE RITUAL TO CLAIM MORE VICTIMS EITHER...
WE HAVE DECIDED TO TURN THE FESTIVAL OF DUALITY INTO A CELEBRATION TO ENSURE PEACE FOR THE YEAR.
ISH WANTED THE TWO OF YOU TO BECOME FINE DUEL PRIESTS, *DIAK UMS.*
ISH WANTED US TO BECOME DUEL PRIESTS...?
OUT OF RESPECT FOR HER WISHES, WE WILL SUPPORT YOU.
PAY ATTENTION. LEARN WELL.
...YOU ARE DISMISSED.

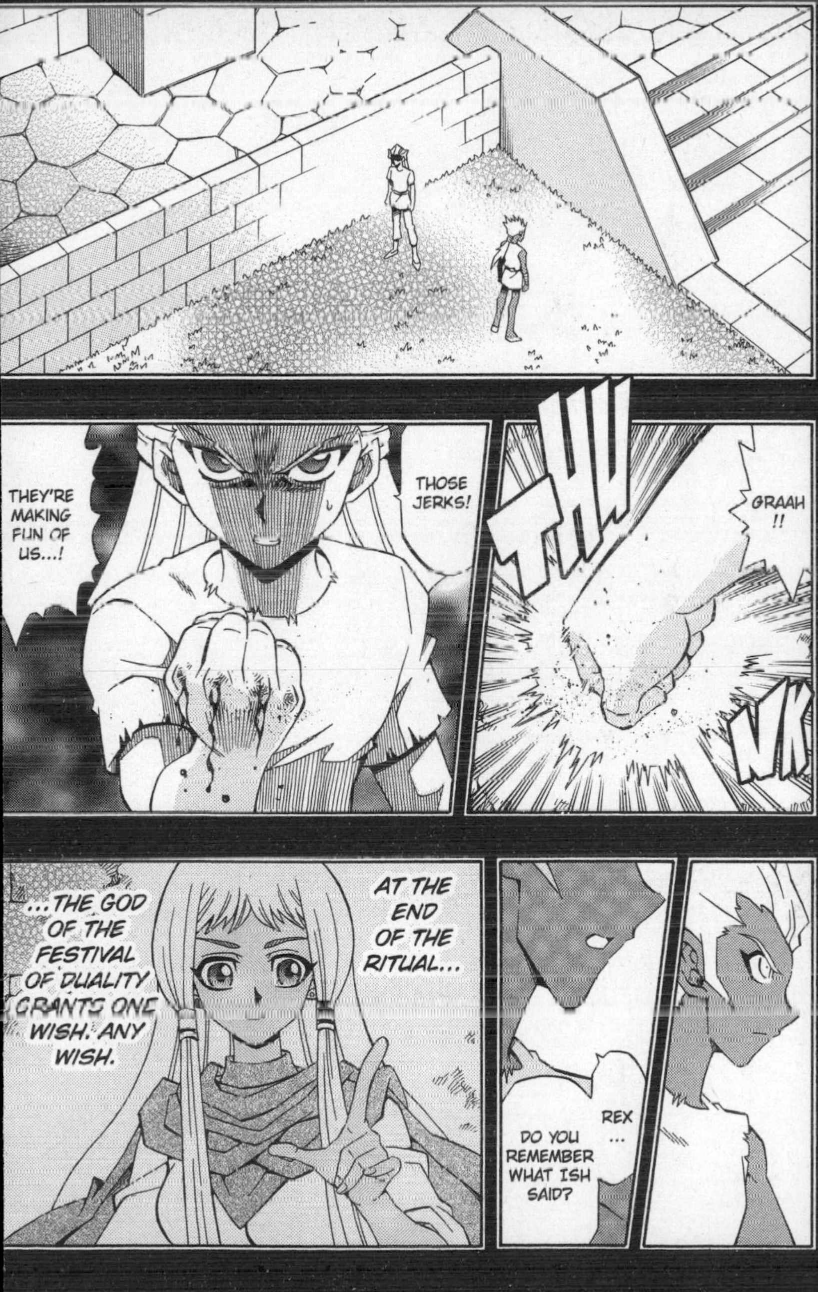
GRAAH !!
THU
NK
THOSE JERKS!
THEY'RE MAKING FUN OF US...!
REX ...
DO YOU REMEMBER WHAT ISH SAID?
AT THE END OF THE RITUAL...
...THE GOD OF THE FESTIVAL OF DUALITY GRANTS ONE WISH. ANY WISH.

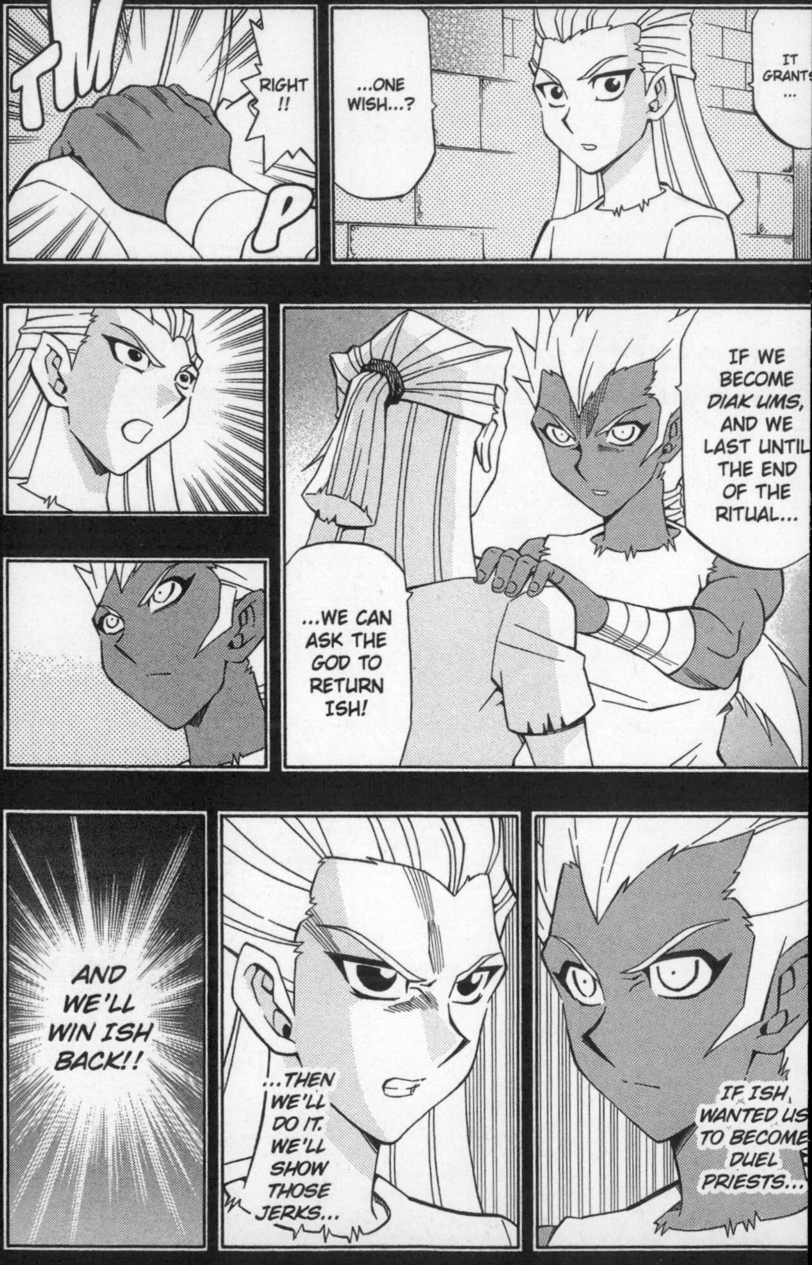
IT GRANTS ...
...ONE WISH...?
RIGHT !!
TMP
IF WE BECOME DIAK UMS, AND WE LAST UNTIL THE END OF THE RITUAL...
...WE CAN ASK THE GOD TO RETURN ISH!
IF ISH WANTED US TO BECOME DUEL PRIESTS...
...THEN WE'LL DO IT. WE'LL SHOW THOSE JERKS...
AND WE'LL WIN ISH BACK!!

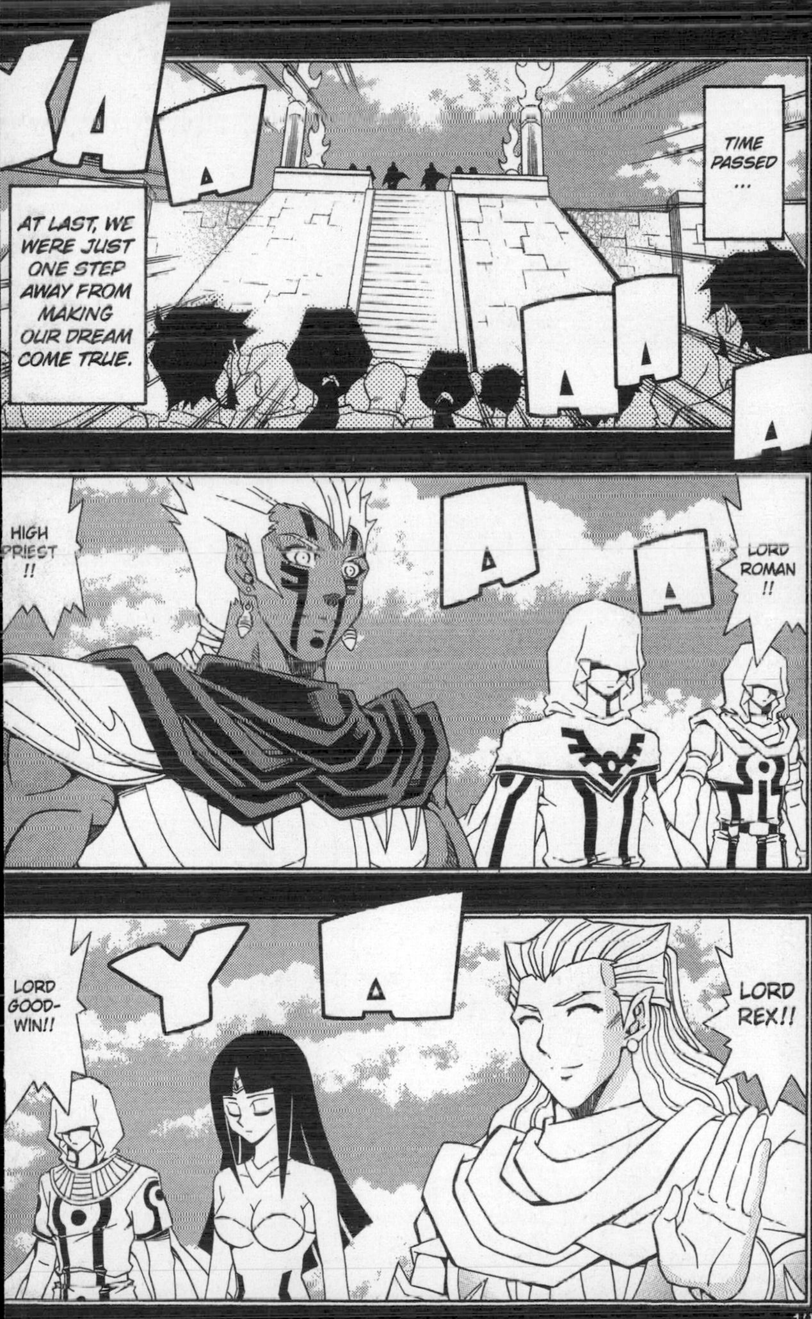
TIME PASSED ...
YA
A
AT LAST, WE WERE JUST ONE STEP AWAY FROM MAKING OUR DREAM COME TRUE.
A
A
A
A
LORD ROMAN !!
A
A
HIGH PRIEST !!
LORD REX!!
A
Y
LORD GOOD-WIN!!

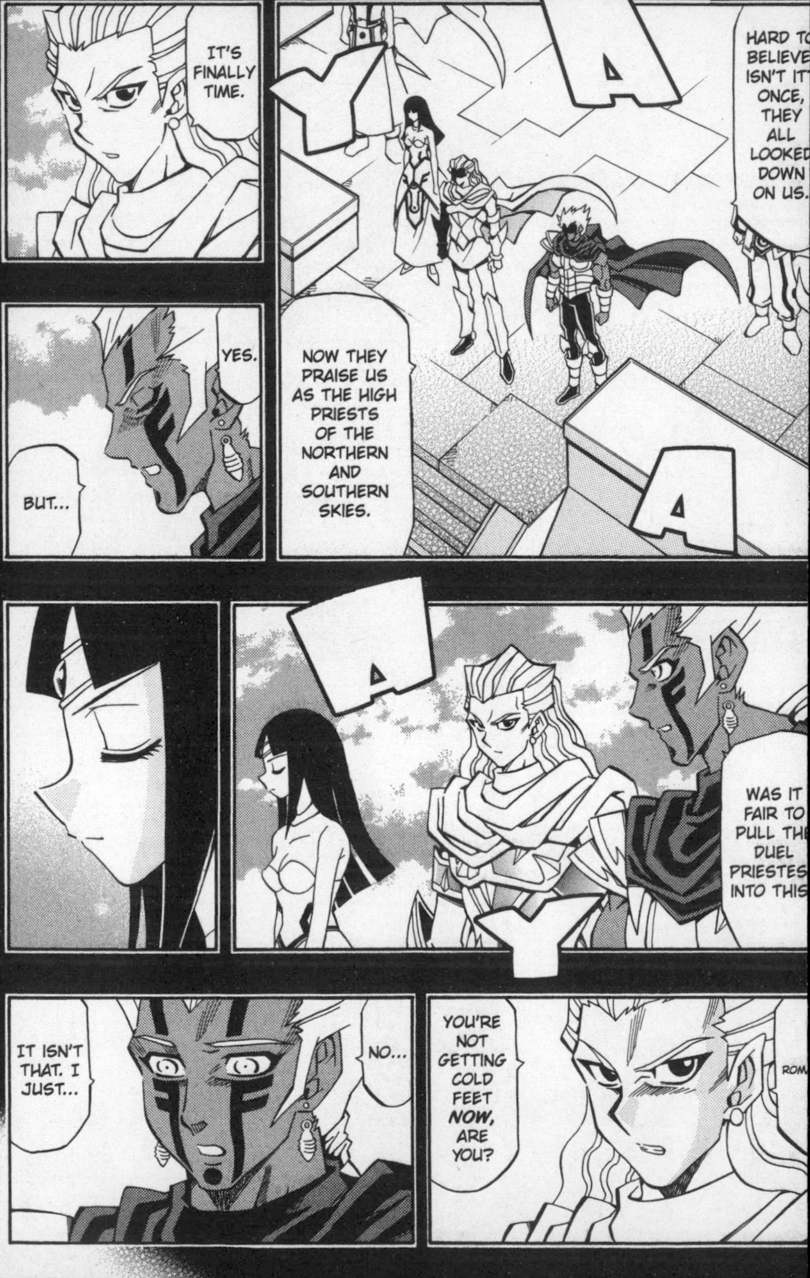
HARD TO BELIEVE ISN'T IT' ONCE, THEY ALL LOOKED DOWN ON US.
Y
A
NOW THEY PRAISE US AS THE HIGH PRIESTS OF THE NORTHERN AND SOUTHERN SKIES.
A
IT'S FINALLY TIME.
YES.
BUT...
WAS IT FAIR TO PULL TH DUEL PRIESTES INTO THIS
A
Y
ROM
YOU'RE NOT GETTING COLD FEET *NOW,* ARE YOU?
NO...
IT ISN'T THAT. I JUST...

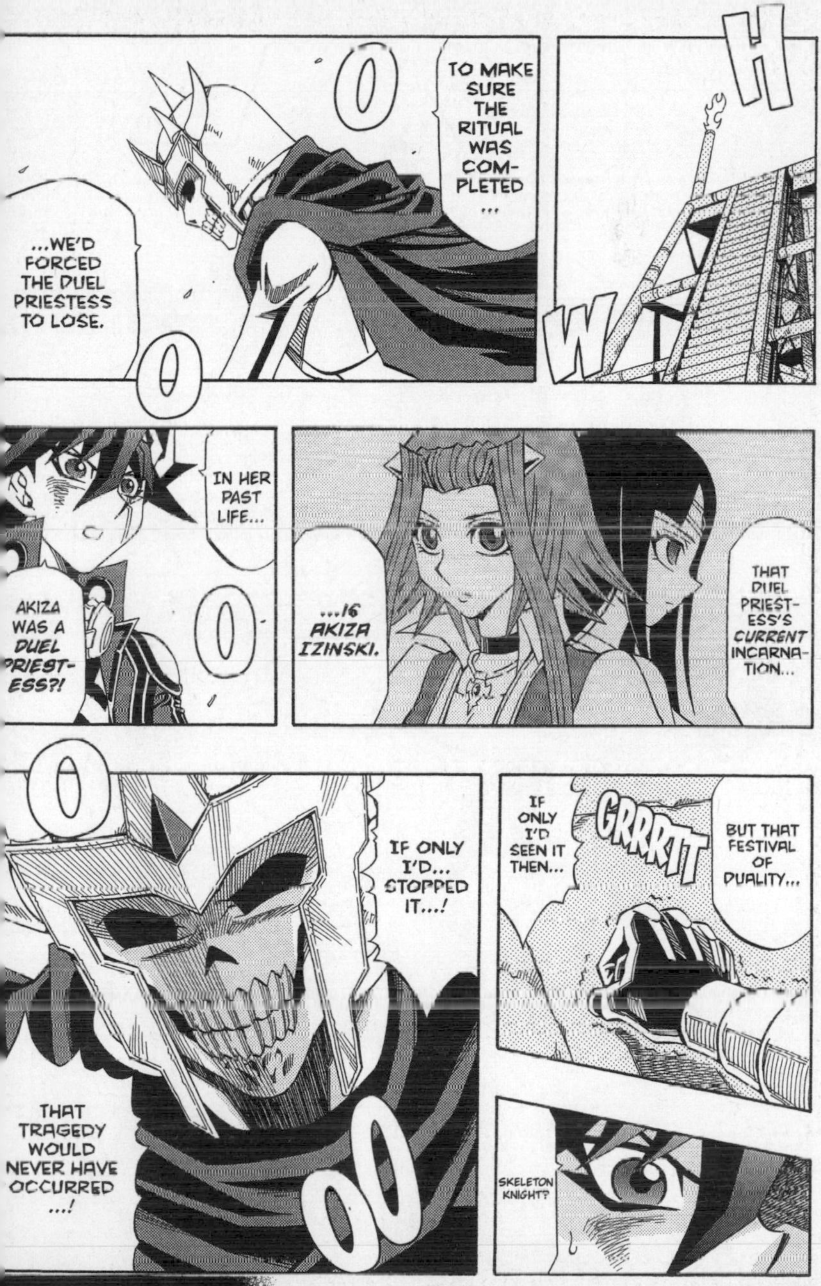
H
W
TO MAKE SURE THE RITUAL WAS COMPLETED...
...WE'D FORCED THE DUEL PRIESTESS TO LOSE.
O
O
THAT DUEL PRIESTESS'S CURRENT INCARNATION...
...IS AKIZA IZINSKI.
IN HER PAST LIFE...
AKIZA WAS A DUEL PRIESTESS?!
O
BUT THAT FESTIVAL OF DUALITY...
GRRRTT
IF ONLY I'D SEEN IT THEN...
SKELETON KNIGHT?
O
IF ONLY I'D... STOPPED IT...!
THAT TRAGEDY WOULD NEVER HAVE OCCURRED...!
OO

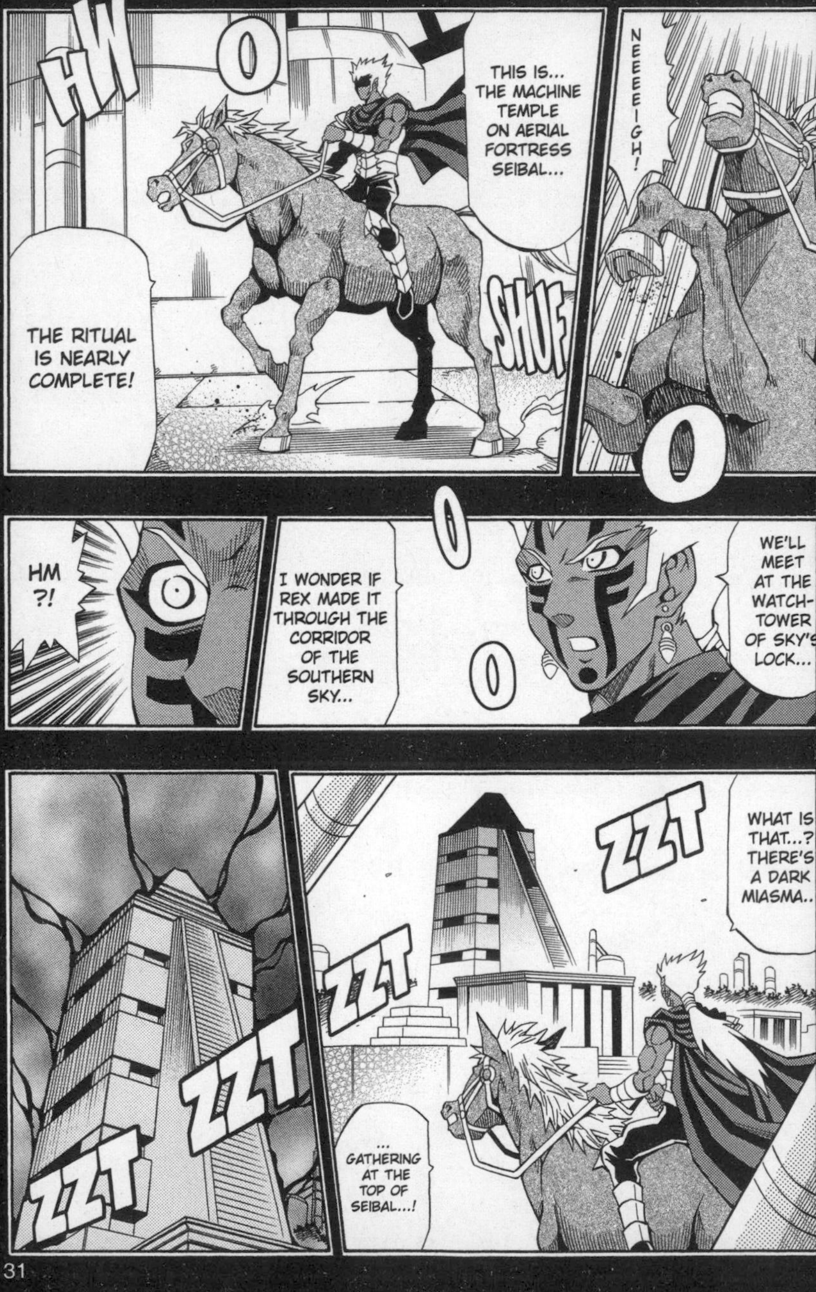
NEEEEEIGH!
O
HW O
THIS IS... THE MACHINE TEMPLE ON AERIAL FORTRESS SEIBAL...
SHUF
THE RITUAL IS NEARLY COMPLETE!
WE'LL MEET AT THE WATCH-TOWER OF SKY'S LOCK...
I WONDER IF REX MADE IT THROUGH THE CORRIDOR OF THE SOUTHERN SKY...
O
O
HM ?!
WHAT IS THAT...? THERE'S A DARK MIASMA...
ZZT
ZZT
...GATHERING AT THE TOP OF SEIBAL...!
ZZT
ZZT

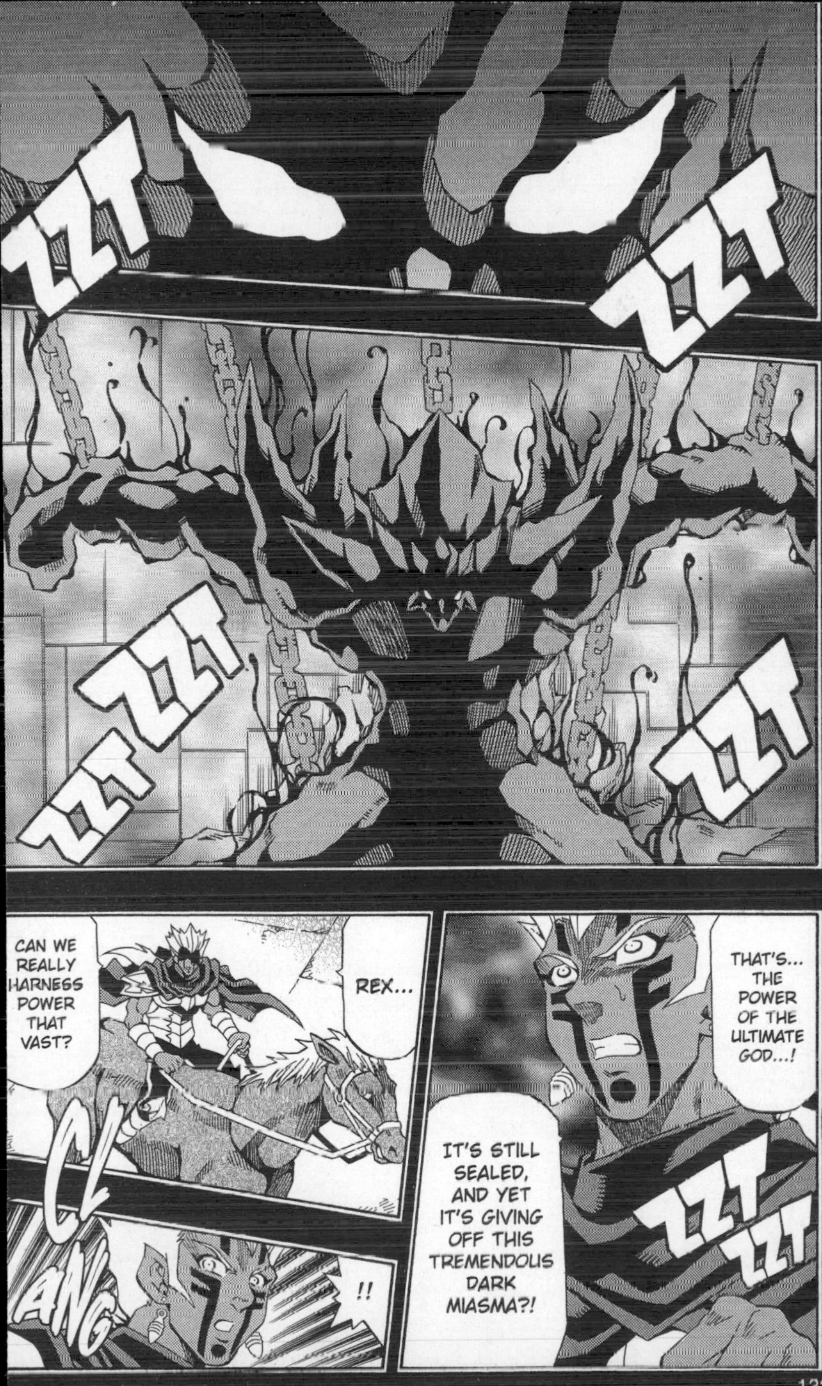
ZZZT
ZZZT
ZZZT
ZZZT
ZZZT
THAT'S... THE POWER OF THE ULTIMATE GOD...!
IT'S STILL SEALED, AND YET IT'S GIVING OFF THIS TREMENDOUS DARK MIASMA?!
ZZZT
ZZZT
REX...
CAN WE REALLY HARNESS POWER THAT VAST?
CLANG
!!

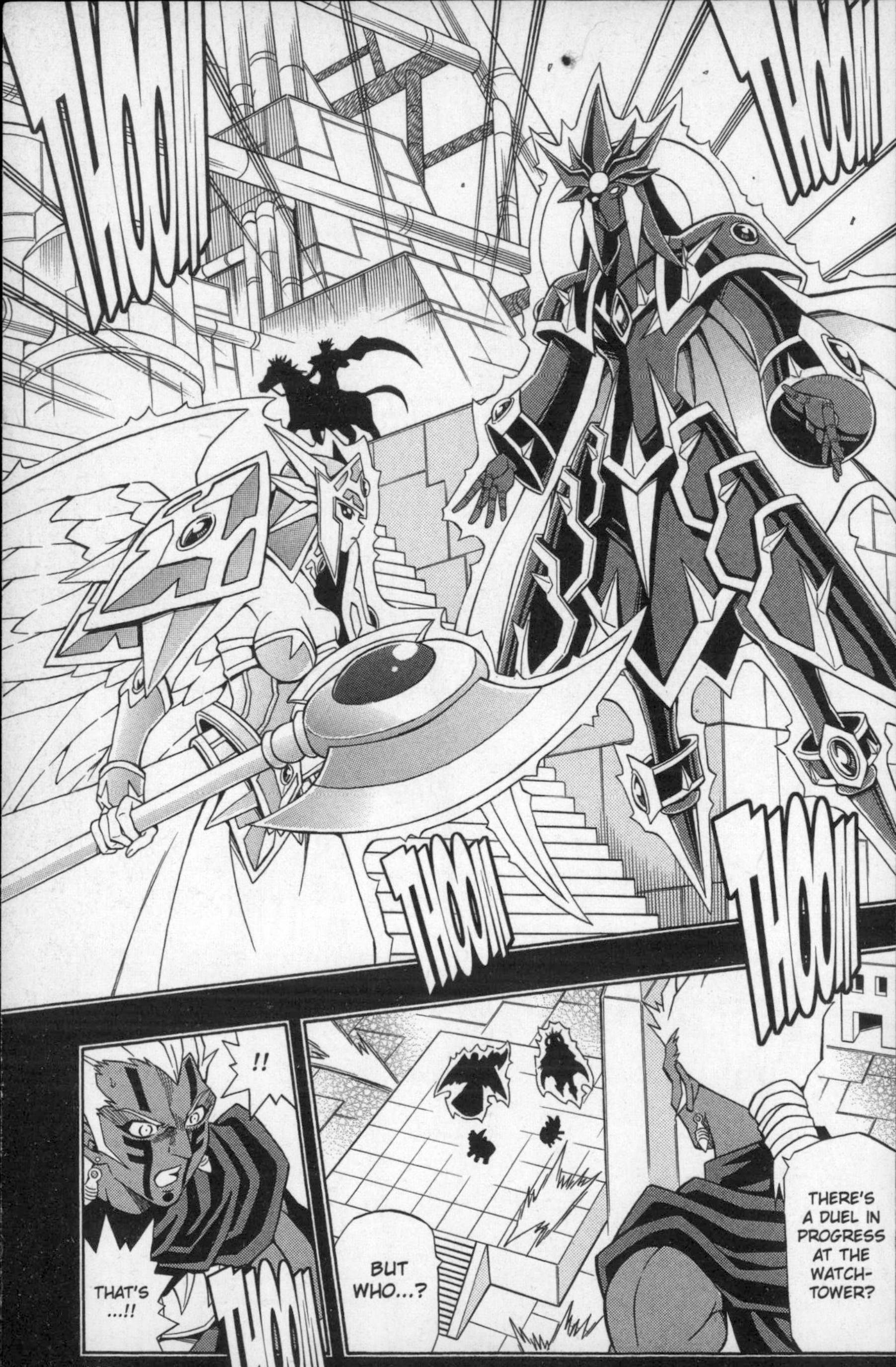
THOOM
THOOM
THOOM
THOOM
THERE'S A DUEL IN PROGRESS AT THE WATCH-TOWER?
BUT WHO...?
!!
THAT'S ...!!
THOOM

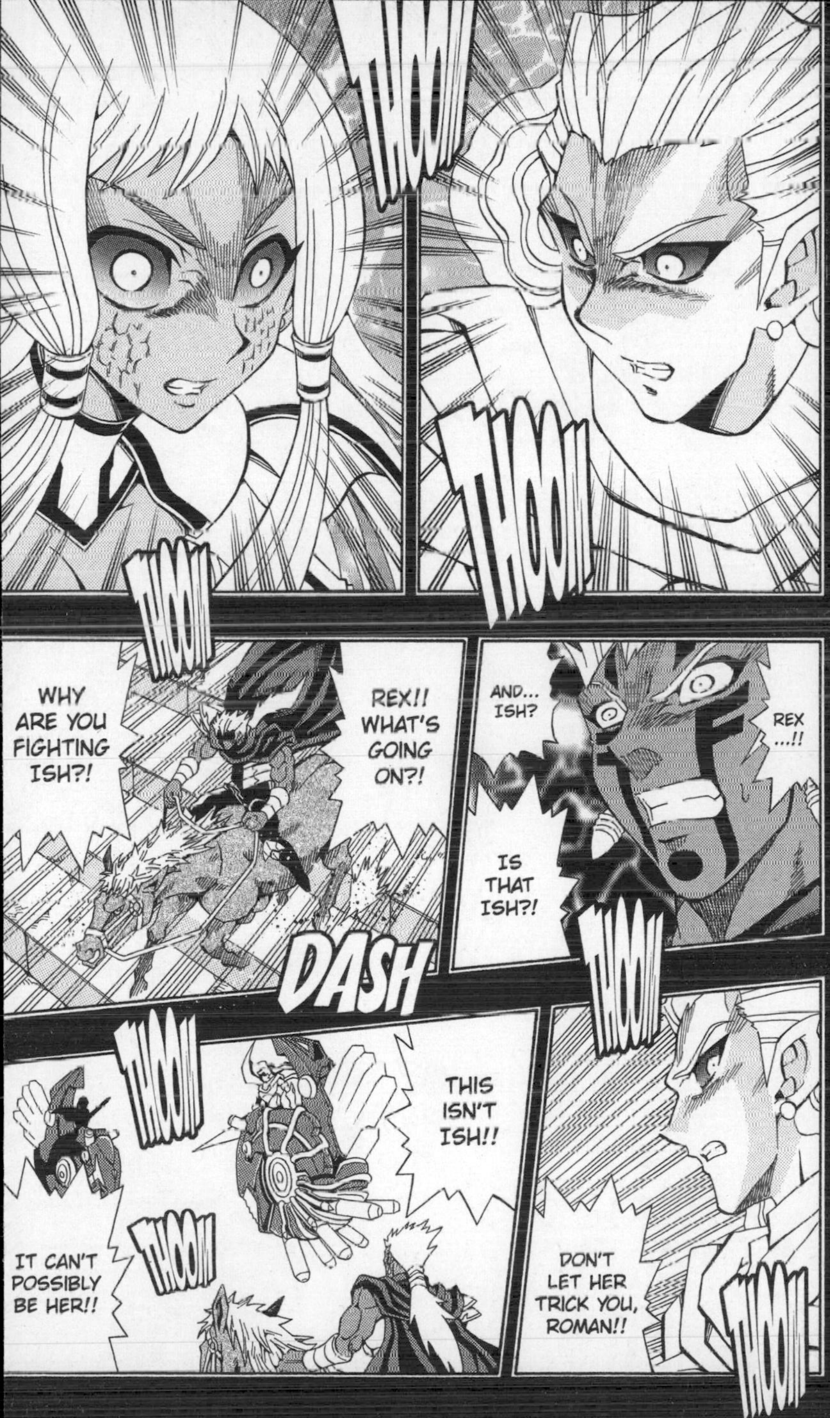
THOOM
THOOM
THOOM
REX ...!!
AND... ISH?
IS THAT ISH?!
THOOM
REX!! WHAT'S GOING ON?!
WHY ARE YOU FIGHTING ISH?!
THOOM
DASH
THOOM
DON'T LET HER TRICK YOU, ROMAN!!
THIS ISN'T ISH!!
THOOM
THOOM
IT CAN'T POSSIBLY BE HER!!

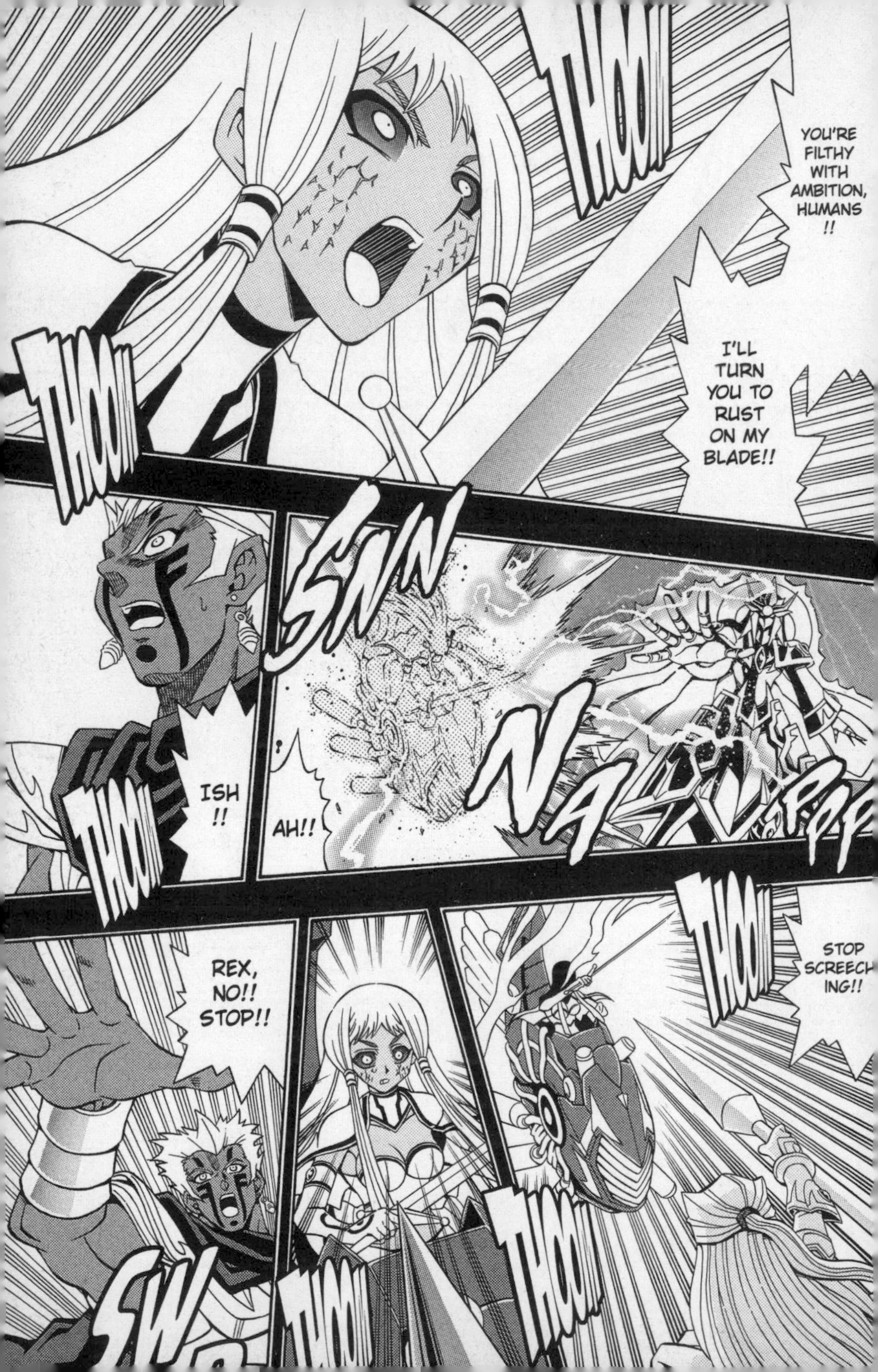
THOOM
YOU'RE FILTHY WITH AMBITION, HUMANS!!
I'LL TURN YOU TO RUST ON MY BLADE!!
THOOM
AH!!
ISH!!
THOOM
THOOM
STOP SCREECH ING!!
THOOM
REX, NO!! STOP!!

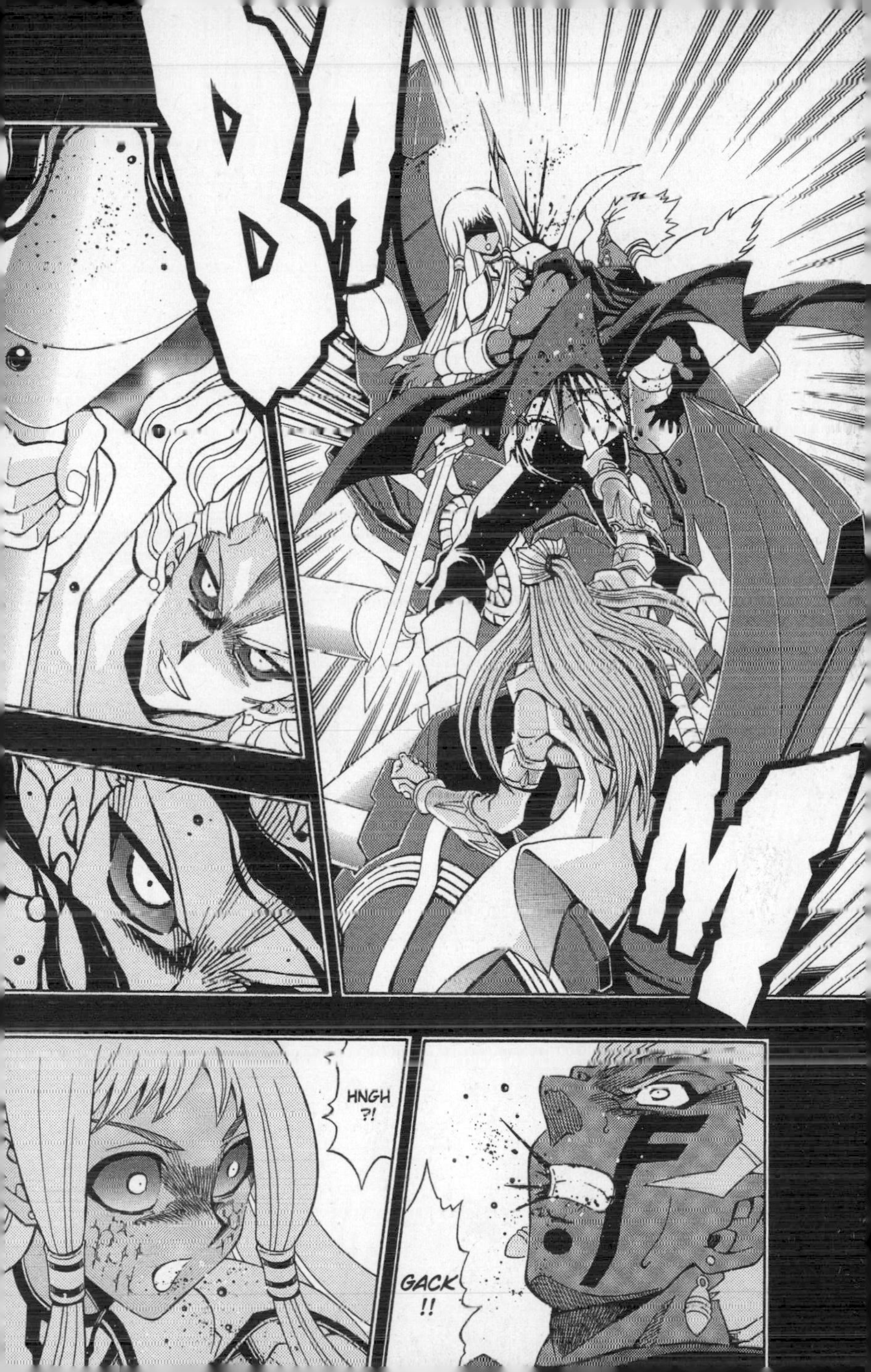
BAM
GACK !!
HNGH ?!

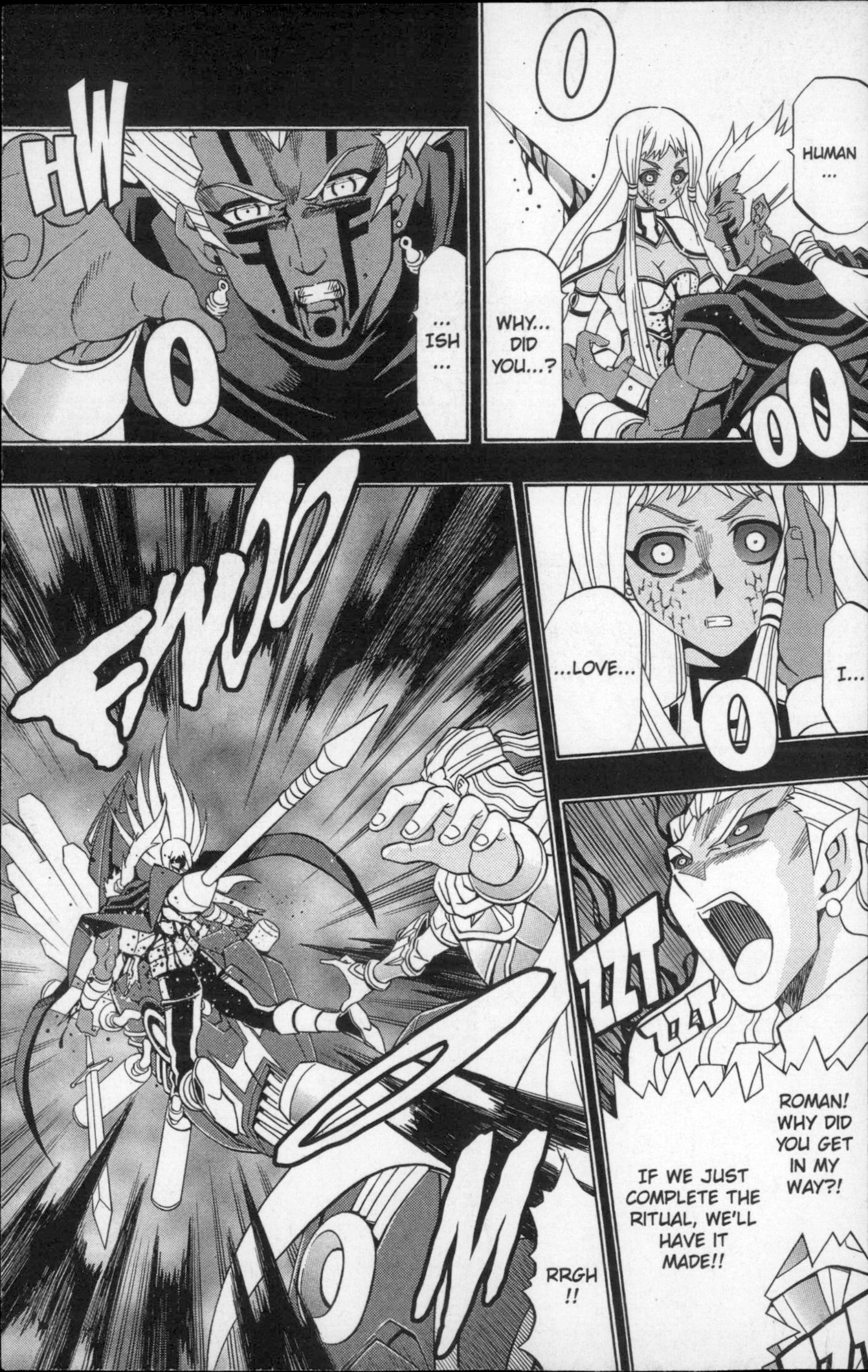
O
HUMAN ...
WHY... DID YOU...?
OO
HW
... ISH ...
O
I...
...LOVE...
O
ZZT
ZZT
ROMAN! WHY DID YOU GET IN MY WAY?!
IF WE JUST COMPLETE THE RITUAL, WE'LL HAVE IT MADE!!
RRGH !!
FWOO
OM

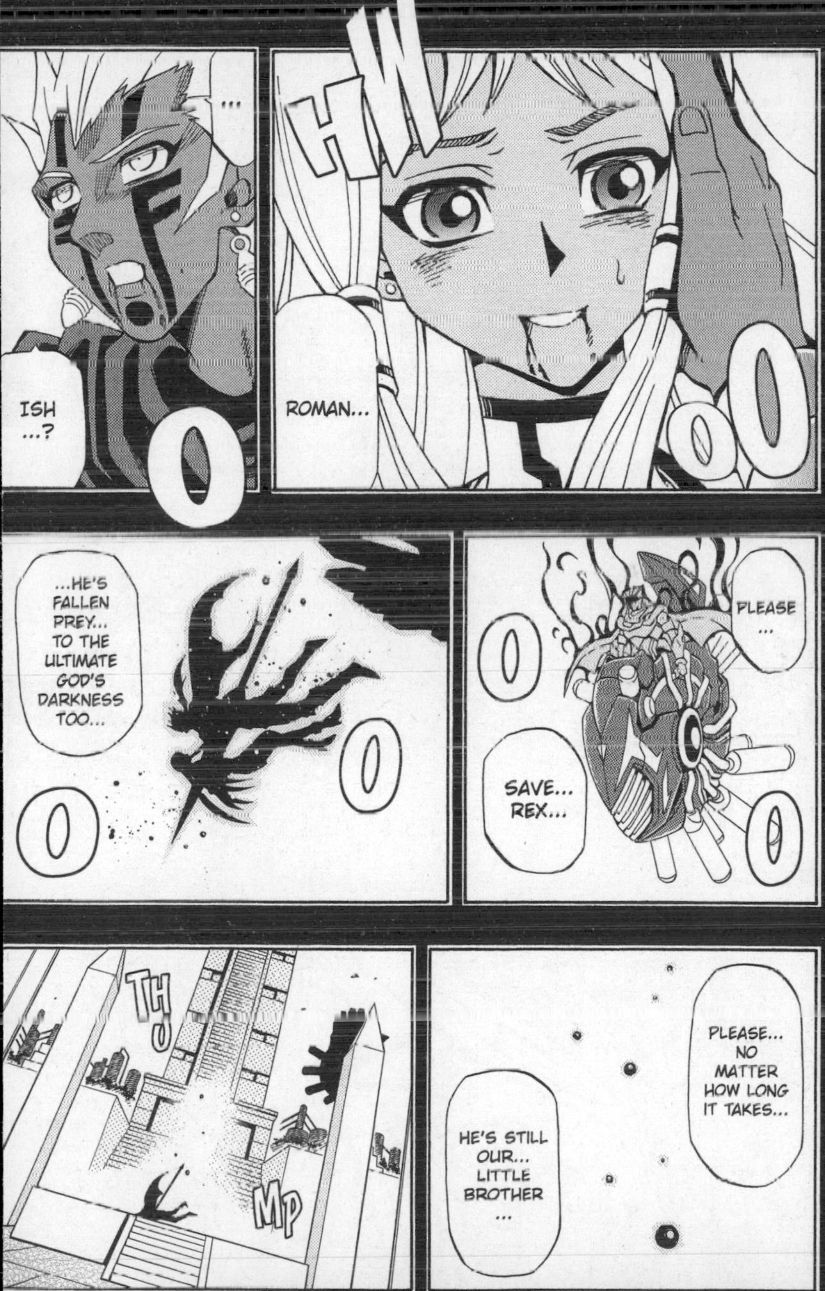
ROMAN...
...
ISH ...?
PLEASE ...
SAVE... REX...
...HE'S FALLEN PREY... TO THE ULTIMATE GOD'S DARKNESS TOO...
PLEASE... NO MATTER HOW LONG IT TAKES...
HE'S STILL OUR... LITTLE BROTHER ...
TH
MP

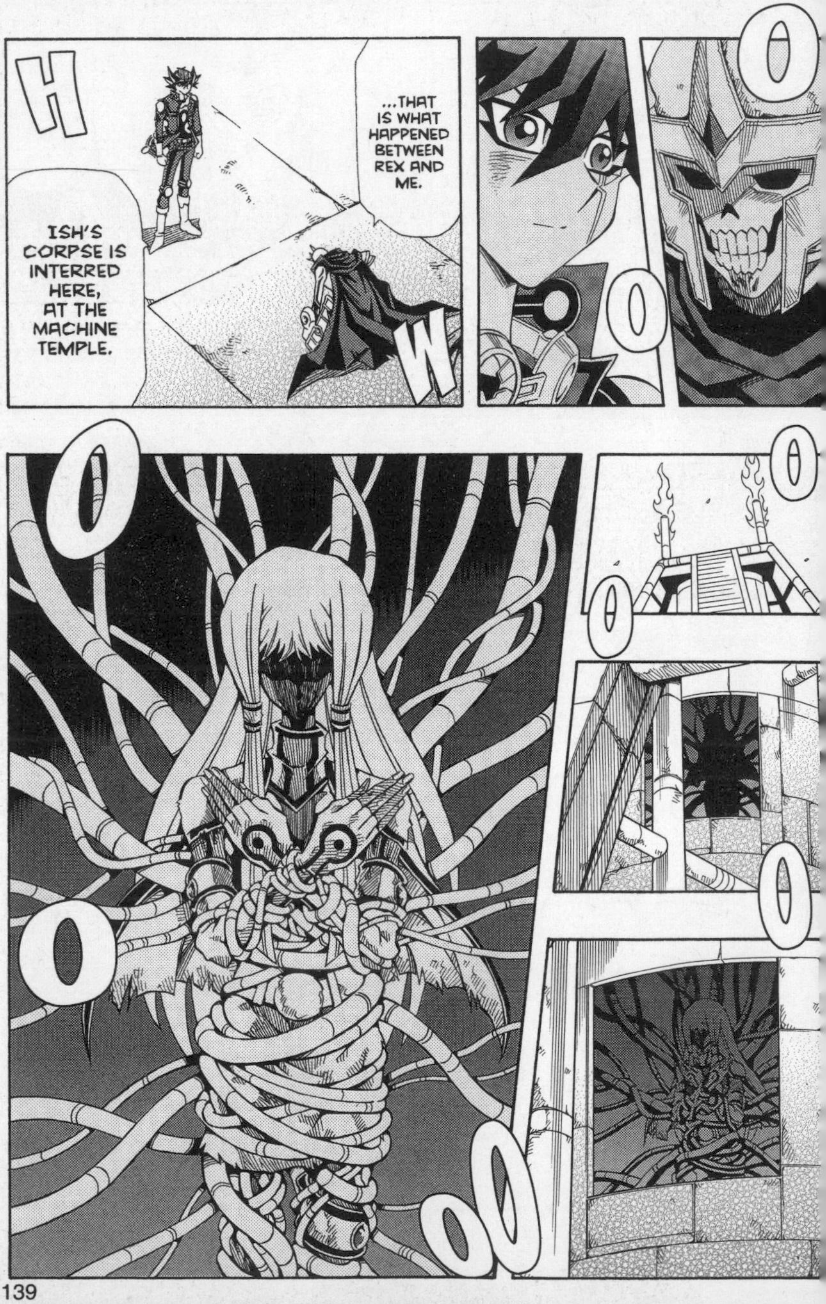

...THAT IS WHAT HAPPENED BETWEEN REX AND ME.
ISH'S CORPSE IS INTERRED HERE, AT THE MACHINE TEMPLE.
HWOOOOOOOOOO

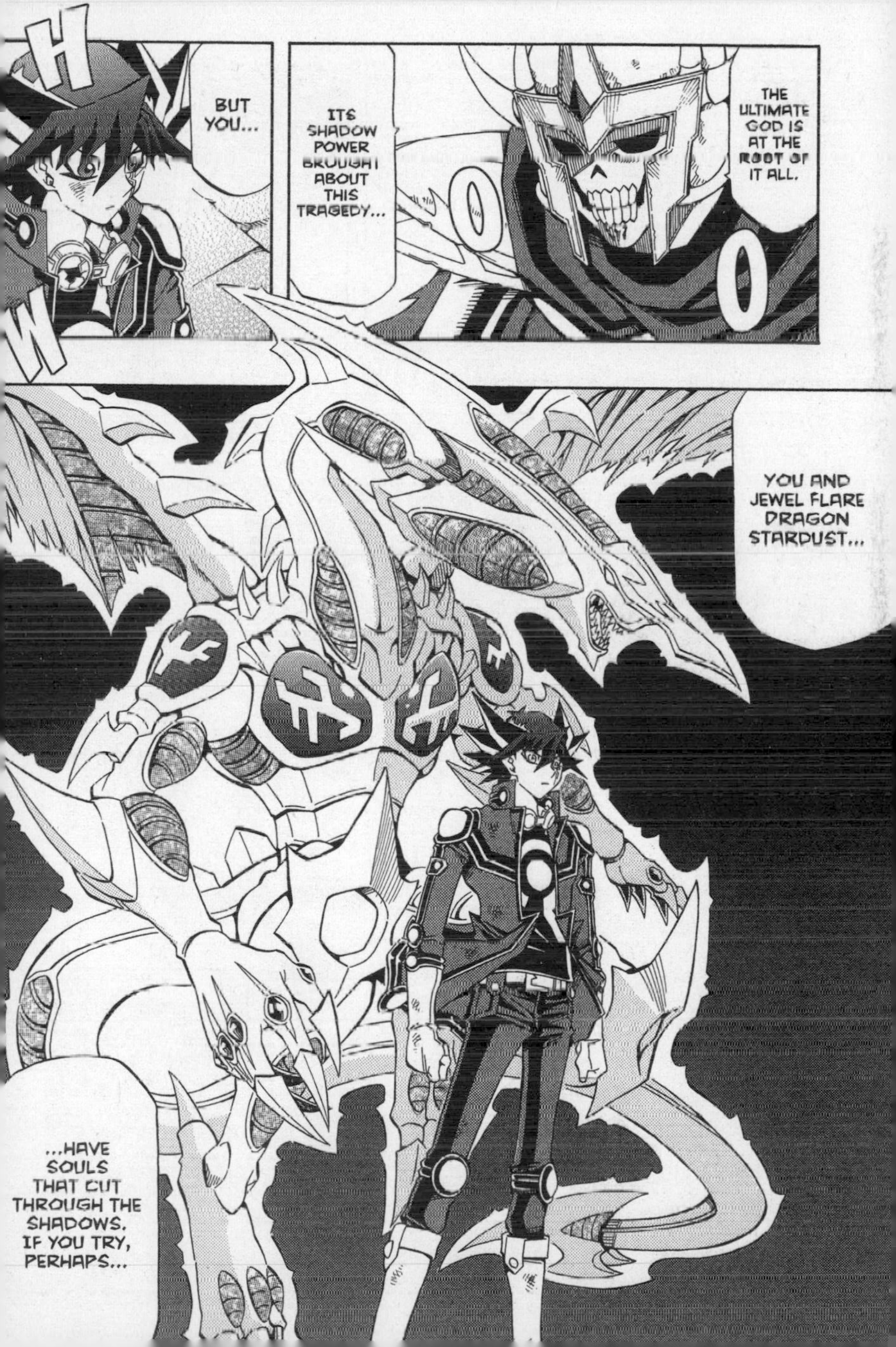
THE ULTIMATE GOD IS AT THE ROOT OF IT ALL.
ITS SHADOW POWER BROUGHT ABOUT THIS TRAGEDY...
BUT YOU...
YOU AND JEWEL FLARE DRAGON STARDUST...
...HAVE SOULS THAT CUT THROUGH THE SHADOWS. IF YOU TRY, PERHAPS...

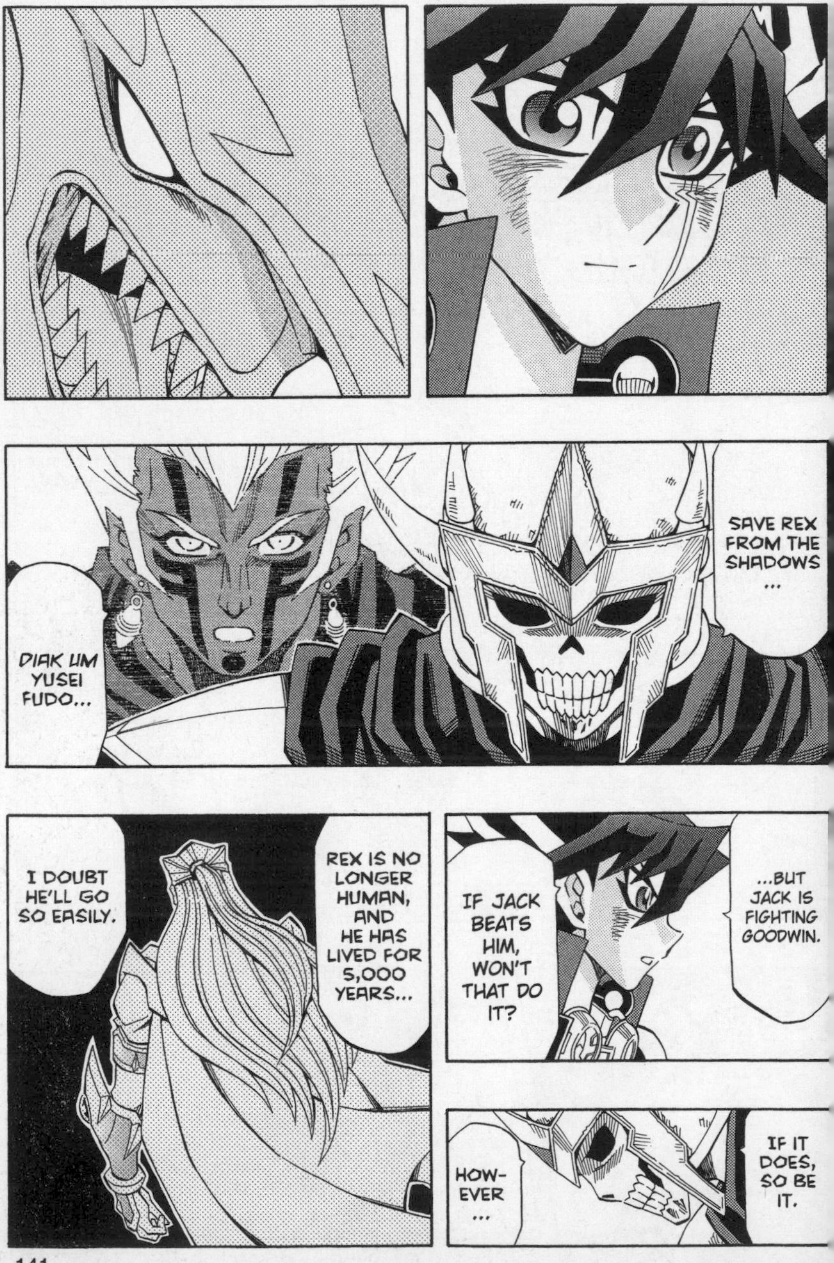
SAVE REX FROM THE SHADOWS...
DIAK UM YUSEI FUDO...
...BUT JACK IS FIGHTING GOODWIN.
IF JACK BEATS HIM, WON'T THAT DO IT?
IF IT DOES, SO BE IT.
HOW-EVER...
REX IS NO LONGER HUMAN, AND HE HAS LIVED FOR 5,000 YEARS...
I DOUBT HE'LL GO SO EASILY.

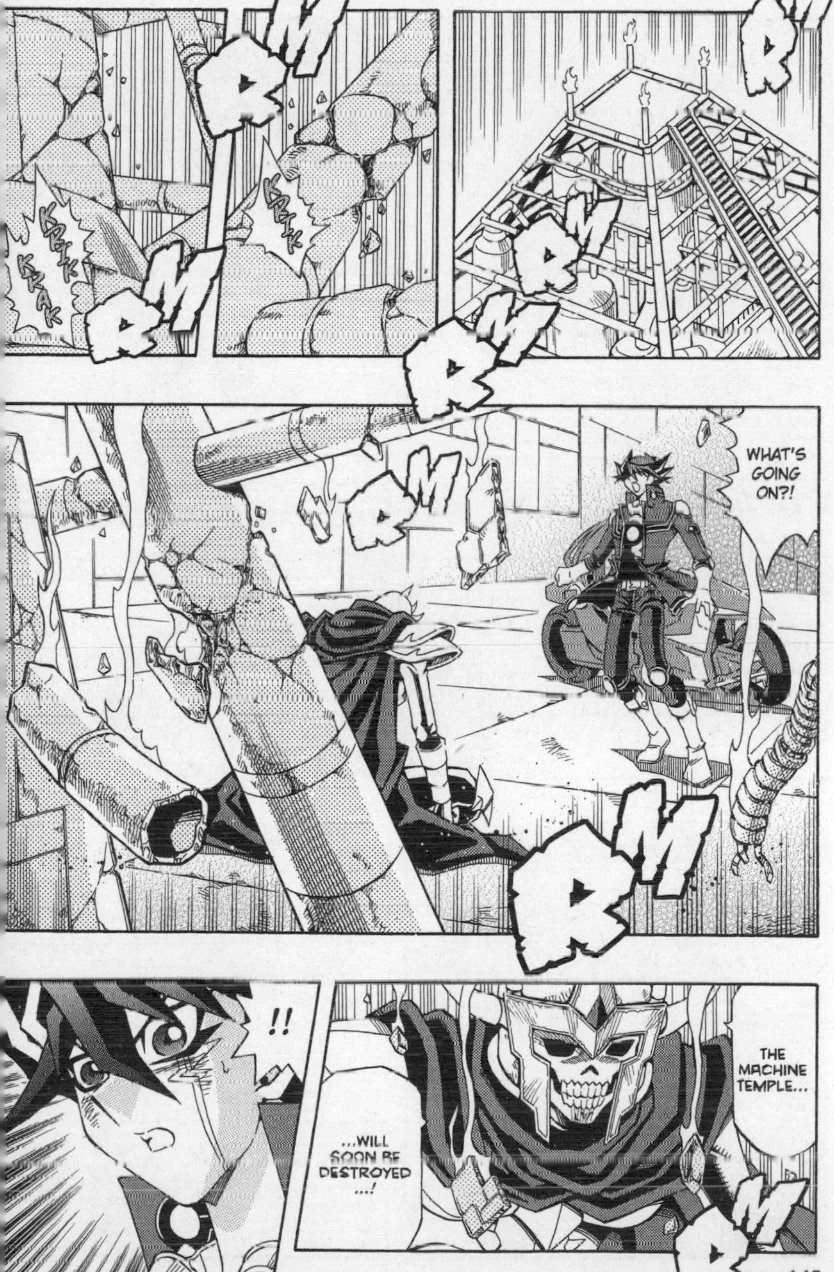
RM
RM
RM
RM
KRAK
KRAK
KRAK
RM
RM
WHAT'S GOING ON?!
RM
RM
THE MACHINE TEMPLE...
...WILL SOON BE DESTROYED ...!
RM
!!

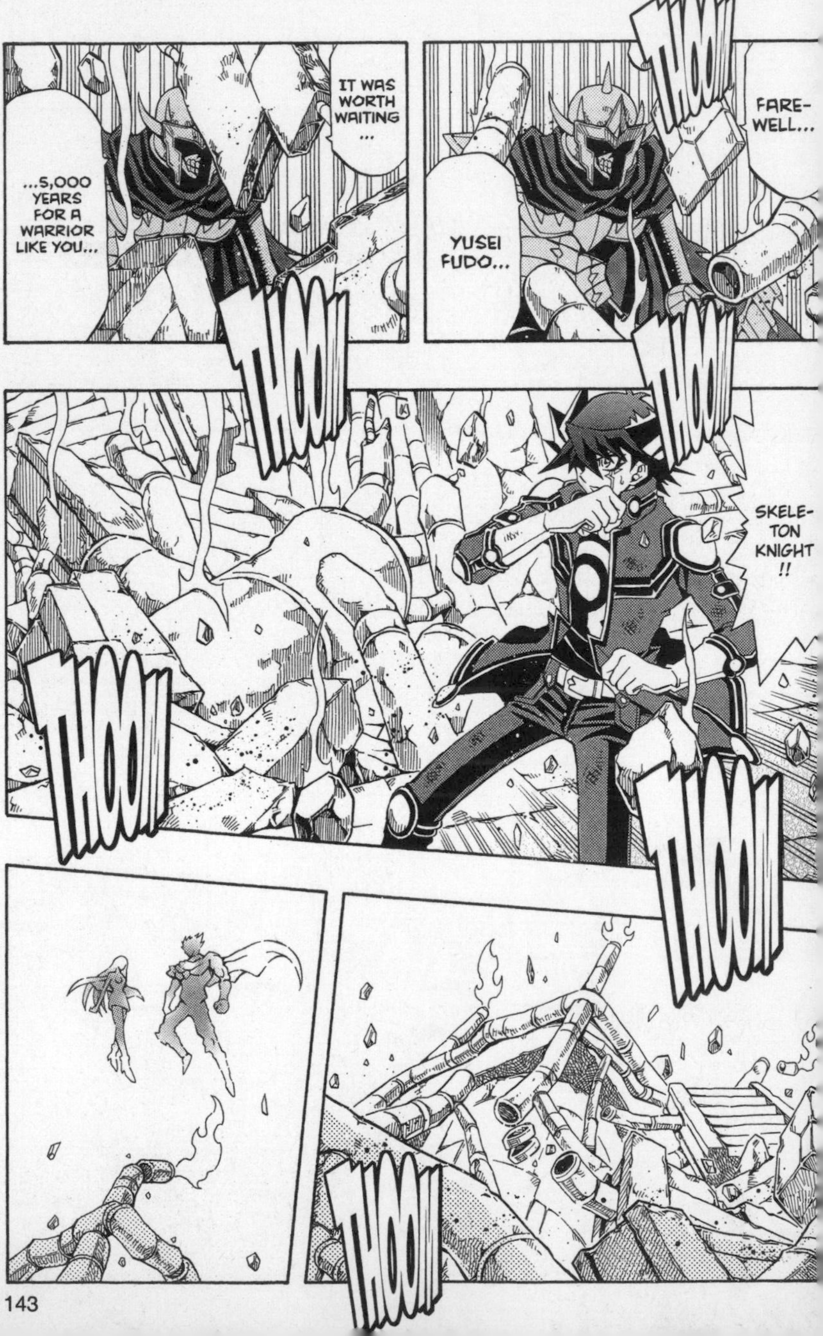
THOOM
FARE-WELL...
YUSEI FUDO...
IT WAS WORTH WAITING...
...5,000 YEARS FOR A WARRIOR LIKE YOU...
THOOM
THOOM
SKELETON KNIGHT!!
THOOM
THOOM
THOOM

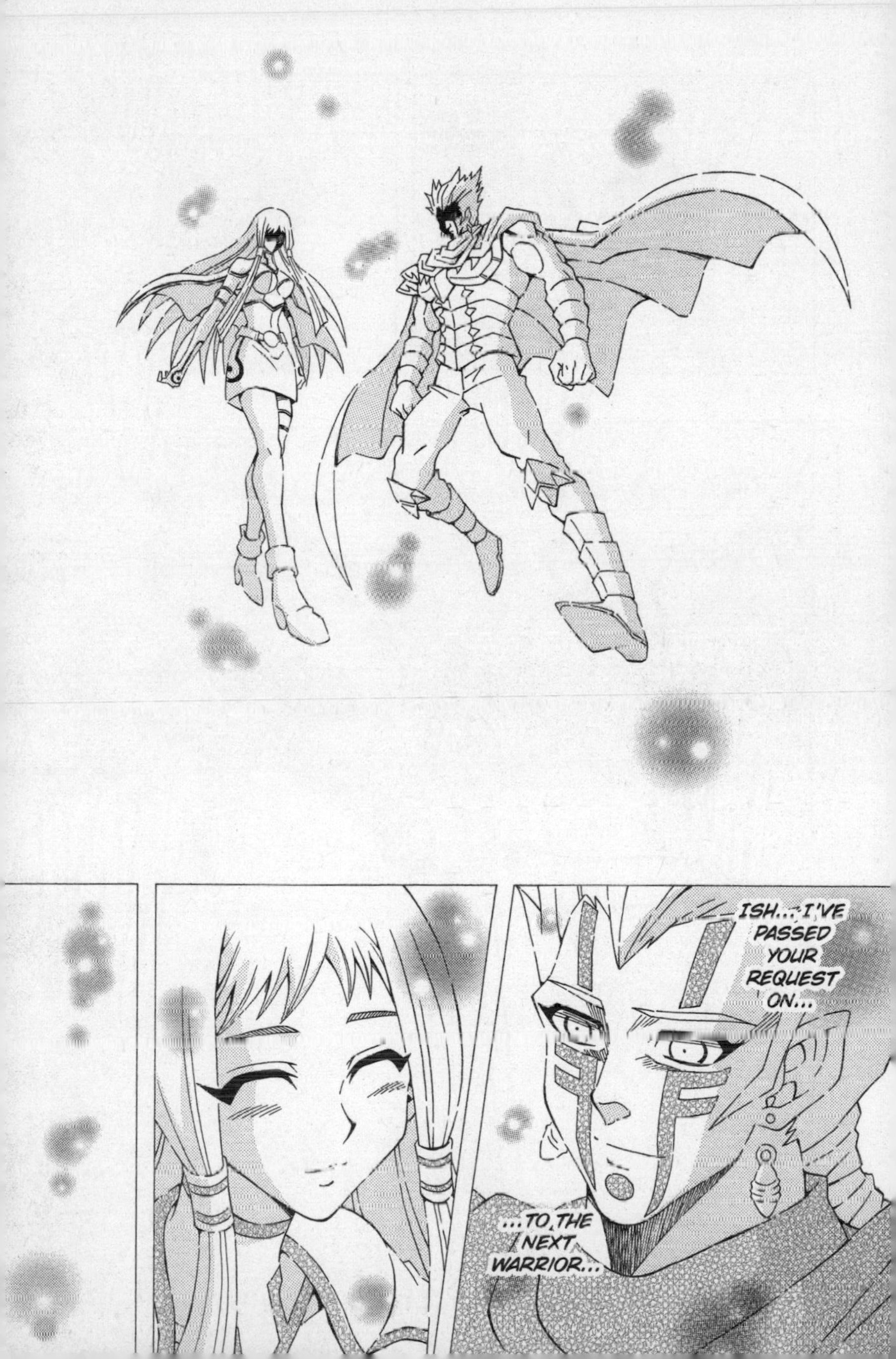
ISH... I'VE PASSED YOUR REQUEST ON...
...TO THE NEXT WARRIOR...

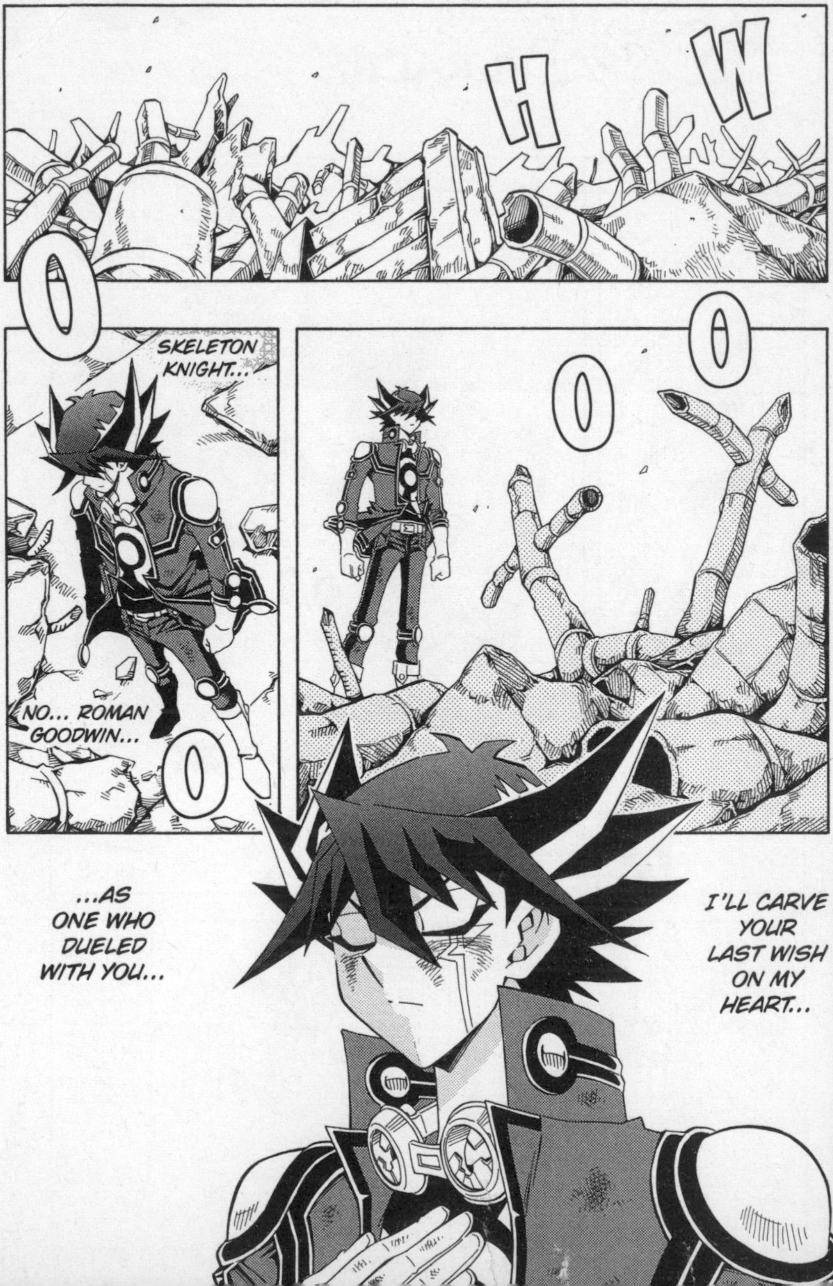
WHOOOO
SKELETON KNIGHT...
NO... ROMAN GOODWIN...
I'LL CARVE YOUR LAST WISH ON MY HEART...
...AS ONE WHO DUELED WITH YOU...

5D's TRACKS

THE 50TH

BY SATOMASA

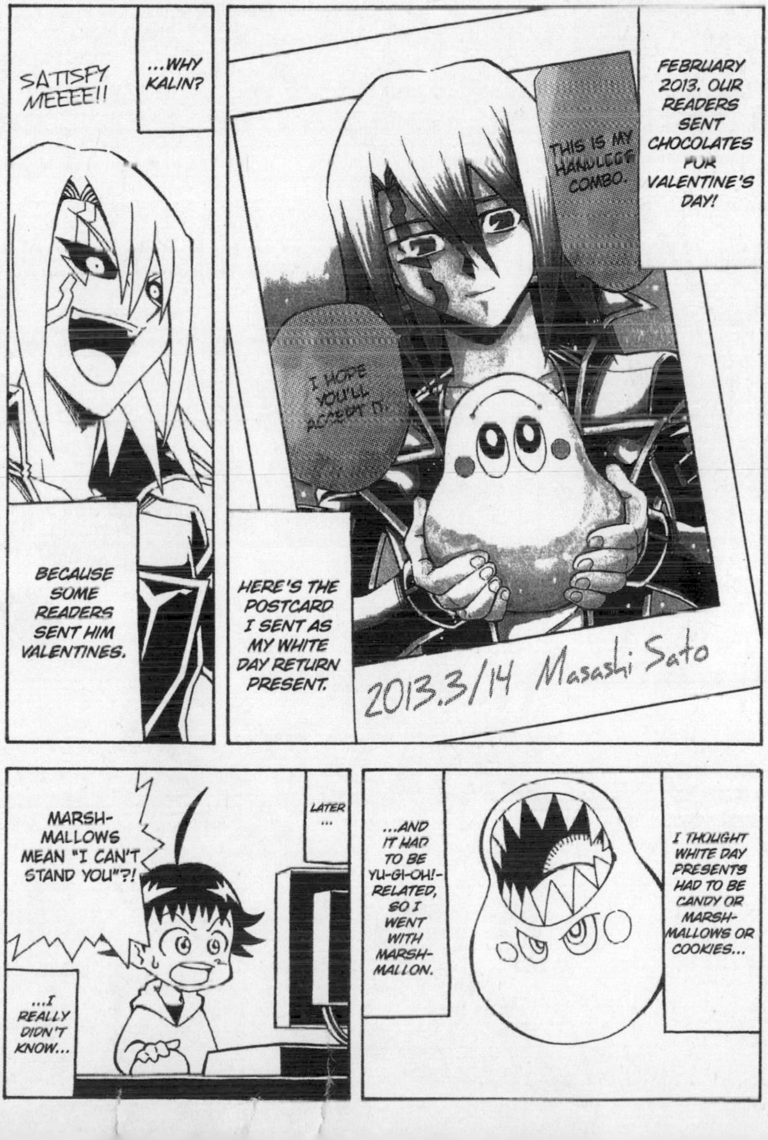
FEBRUARY 2013. OUR READERS SENT CHOCOLATES FOR VALENTINE'S DAY!
THIS IS MY HANDLOOP COMBO.
I HOPE YOU'LL ACCEPT IT.
HERE'S THE POSTCARD I SENT AS MY WHITE DAY RETURN PRESENT.
2013.3/14 Masashi Sato
...WHY KALIN?
SATISFY MEEEE!!
BECAUSE SOME READERS SENT HIM VALENTINES.
I THOUGHT WHITE DAY PRESENTS HAD TO BE CANDY OR MARSHMALLOWS OR COOKIES...
...AND IT HAD TO BE YU-GI-OH!-RELATED, SO I WENT WITH MARSHMALLON.
LATER...
MARSHMALLOWS MEAN "I CAN'T STAND YOU"?!
...I REALLY DIDN'T KNOW...

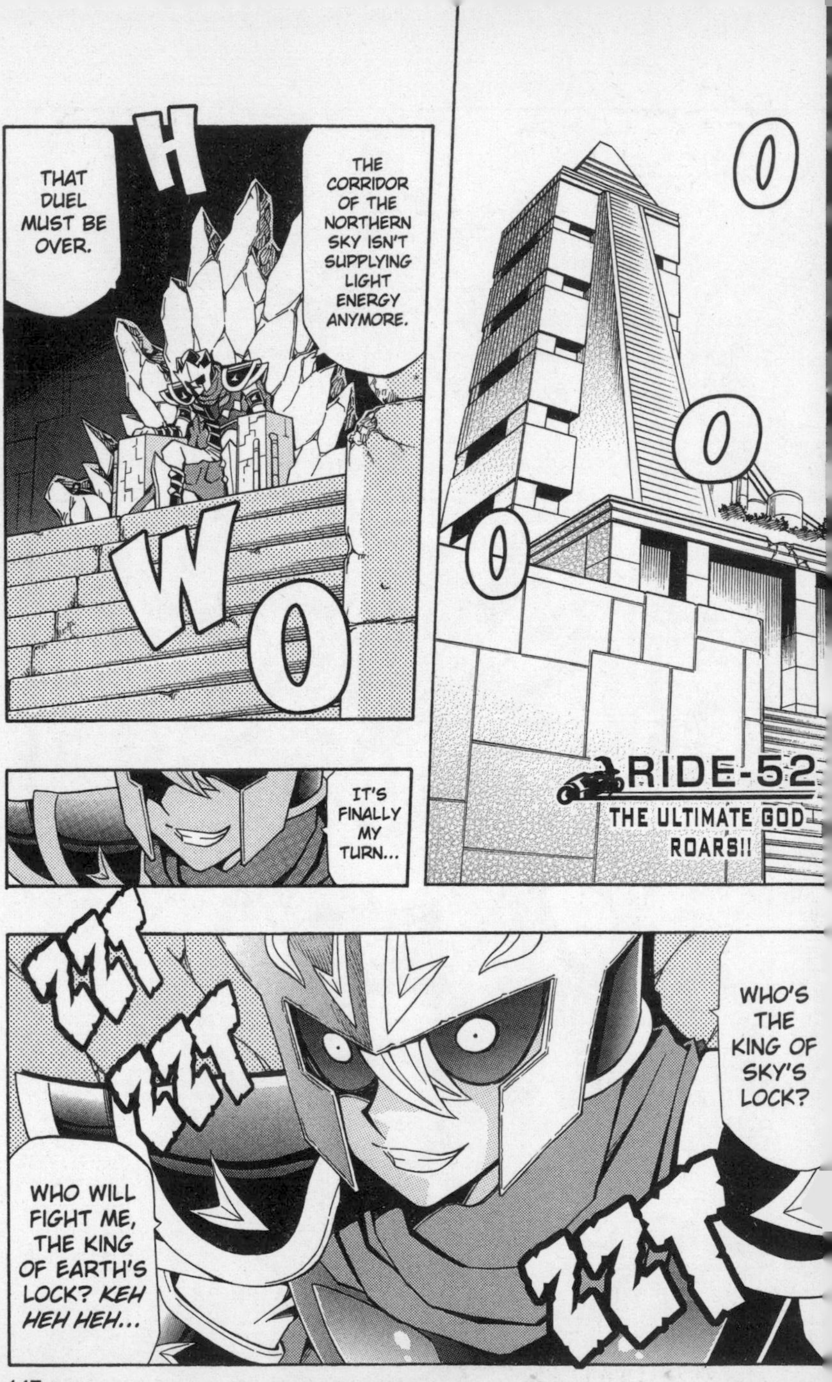
O
O
O
RIDE-52
THE ULTIMATE GOD ROARS!!
H
THE CORRIDOR OF THE NORTHERN SKY ISN'T SUPPLYING LIGHT ENERGY ANYMORE.
THAT DUEL MUST BE OVER.
W
O
IT'S FINALLY MY TURN...
WHO'S THE KING OF SKY'S LOCK?
ZZZT
ZZZT
WHO WILL FIGHT ME, THE KING OF EARTH'S LOCK? KEH HEH HEH...
ZZZT

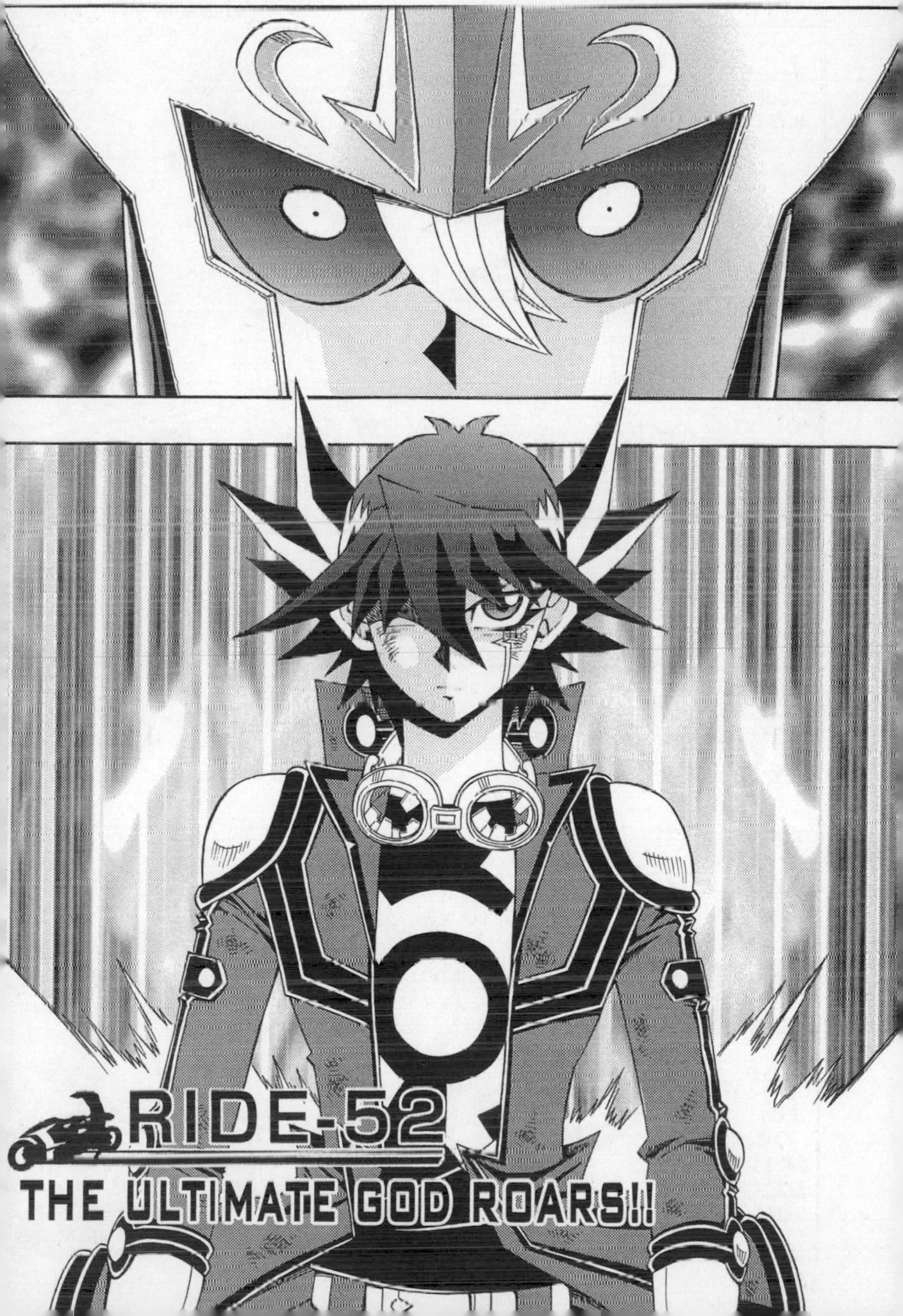
RIDE-52
THE ULTIMATE GOD ROARS!!

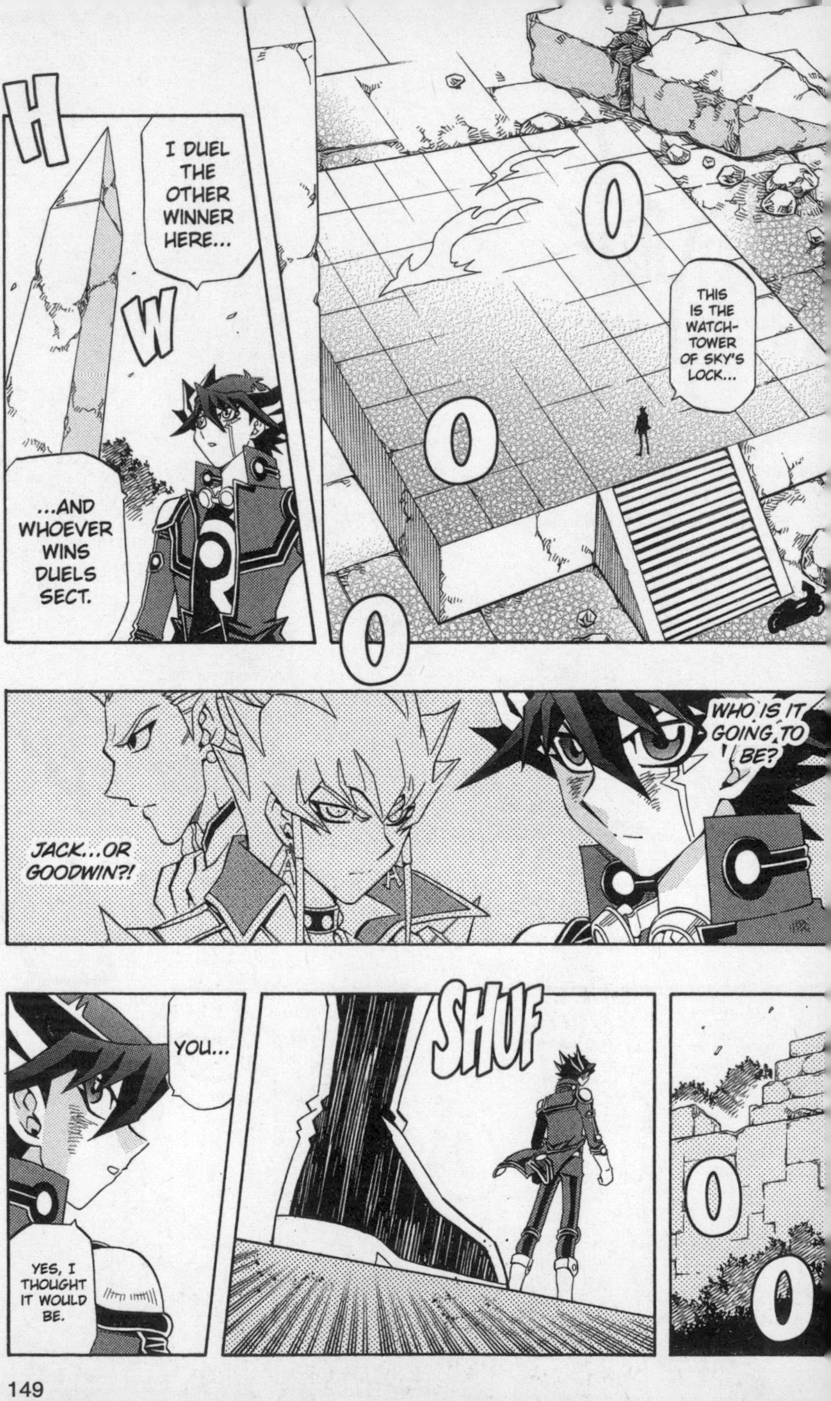
THIS IS THE WATCH-TOWER OF SKY'S LOCK...
HWOOOO
I DUEL THE OTHER WINNER HERE...
...AND WHOEVER WINS DUELS SECT.
WHO IS IT GOING TO BE?
JACK...OR GOODWIN?!
OO
SHUF
YOU...
YES, I THOUGHT IT WOULD BE.

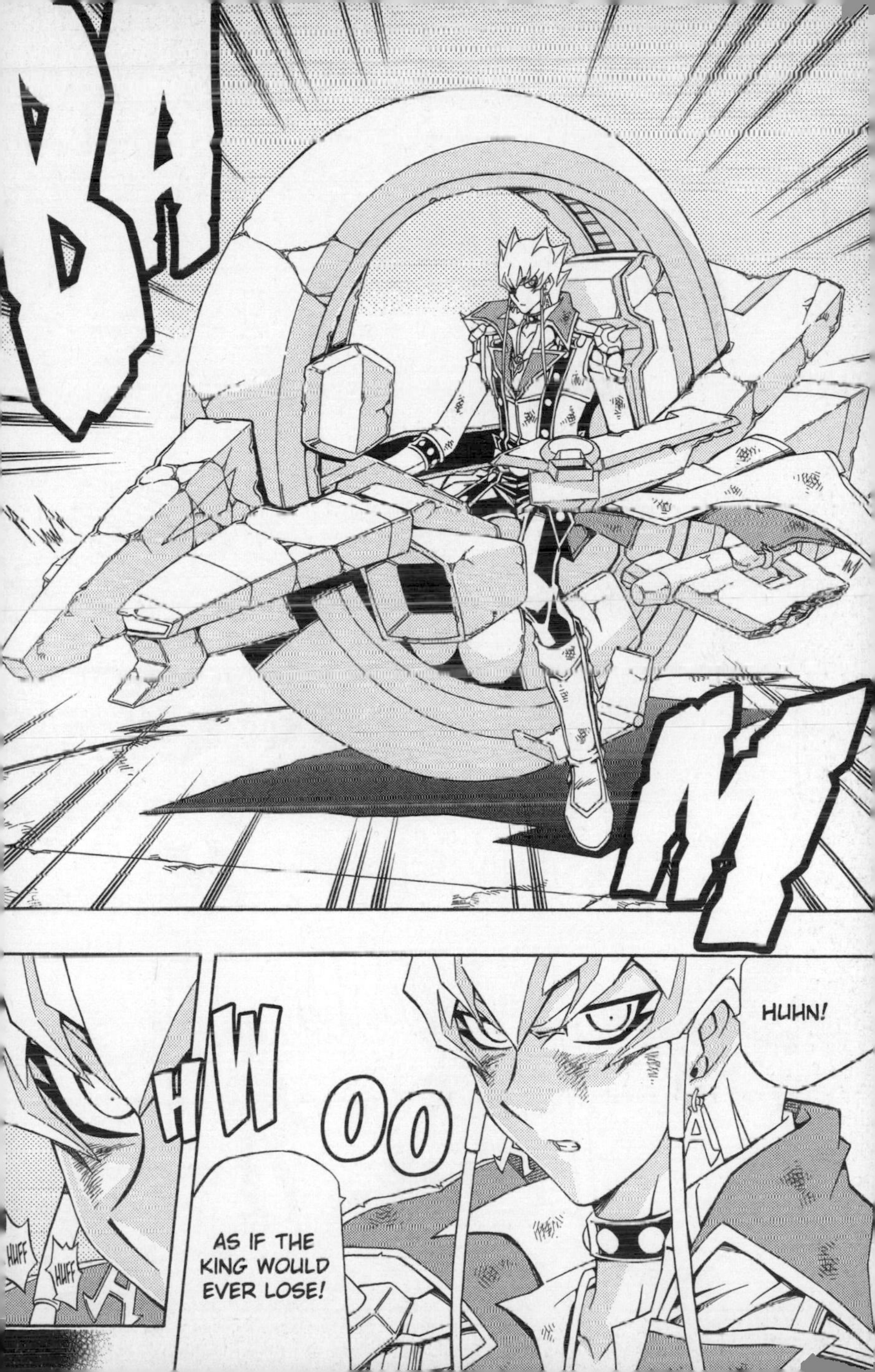
BAM
HUHN!
HWOO
AS IF THE KING WOULD EVER LOSE!
HUFF
HUFF

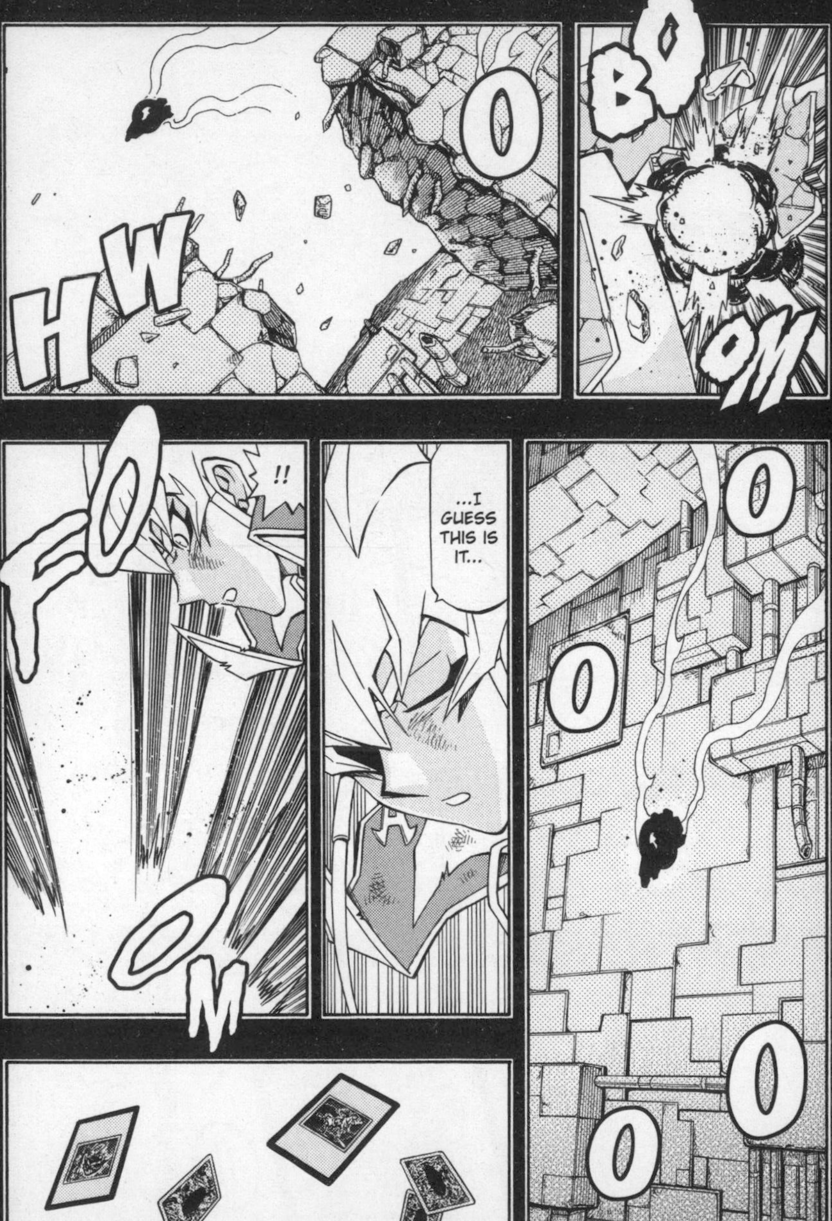
BOOM
HWO
OOOOO
...I GUESS THIS IS IT...
!!
FOOM

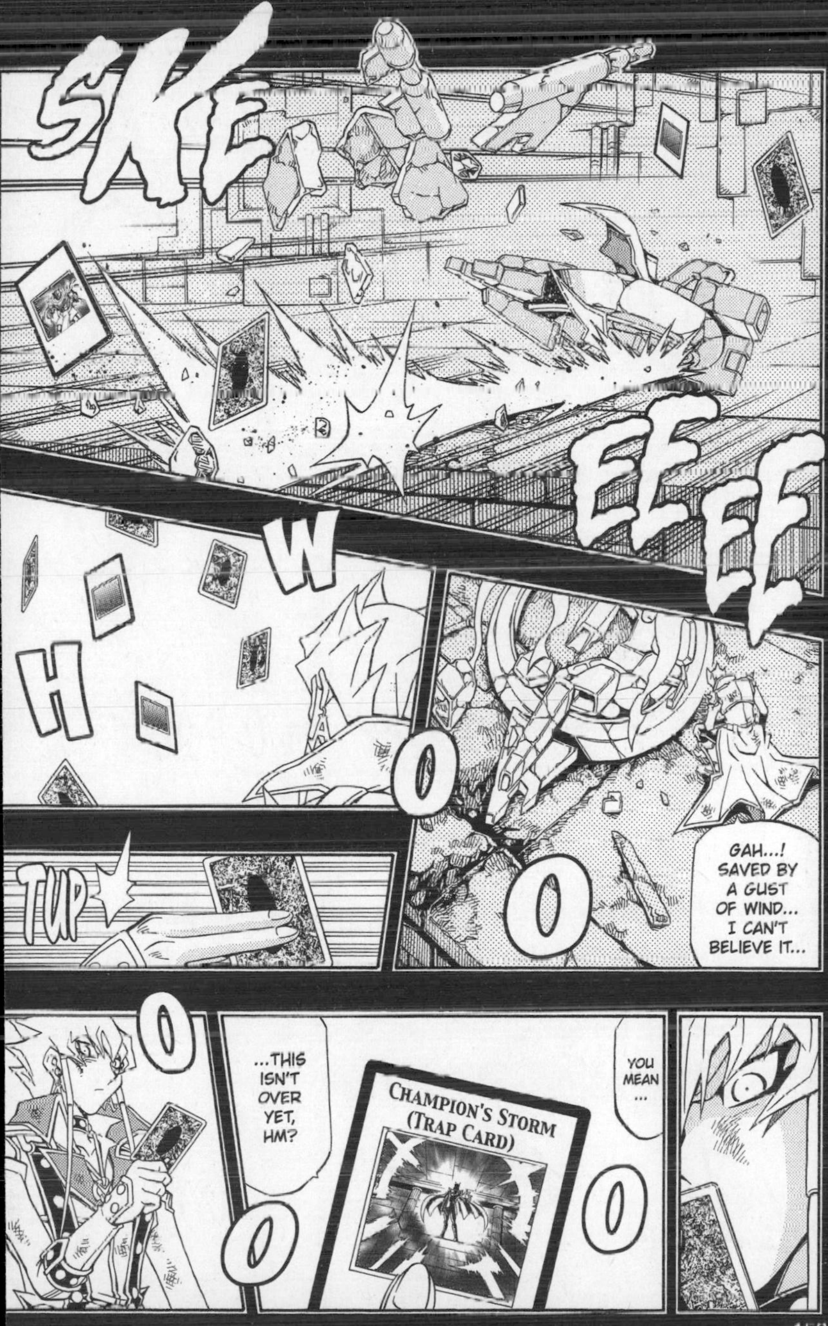
SKE
EEEEEE
GAH...! SAVED BY A GUST OF WIND... I CAN'T BELIEVE IT...
WHOOOO
TUP
YOU MEAN ...
...THIS ISN'T OVER YET, HM?
CHAMPION'S STORM (TRAP CARD)
OOO

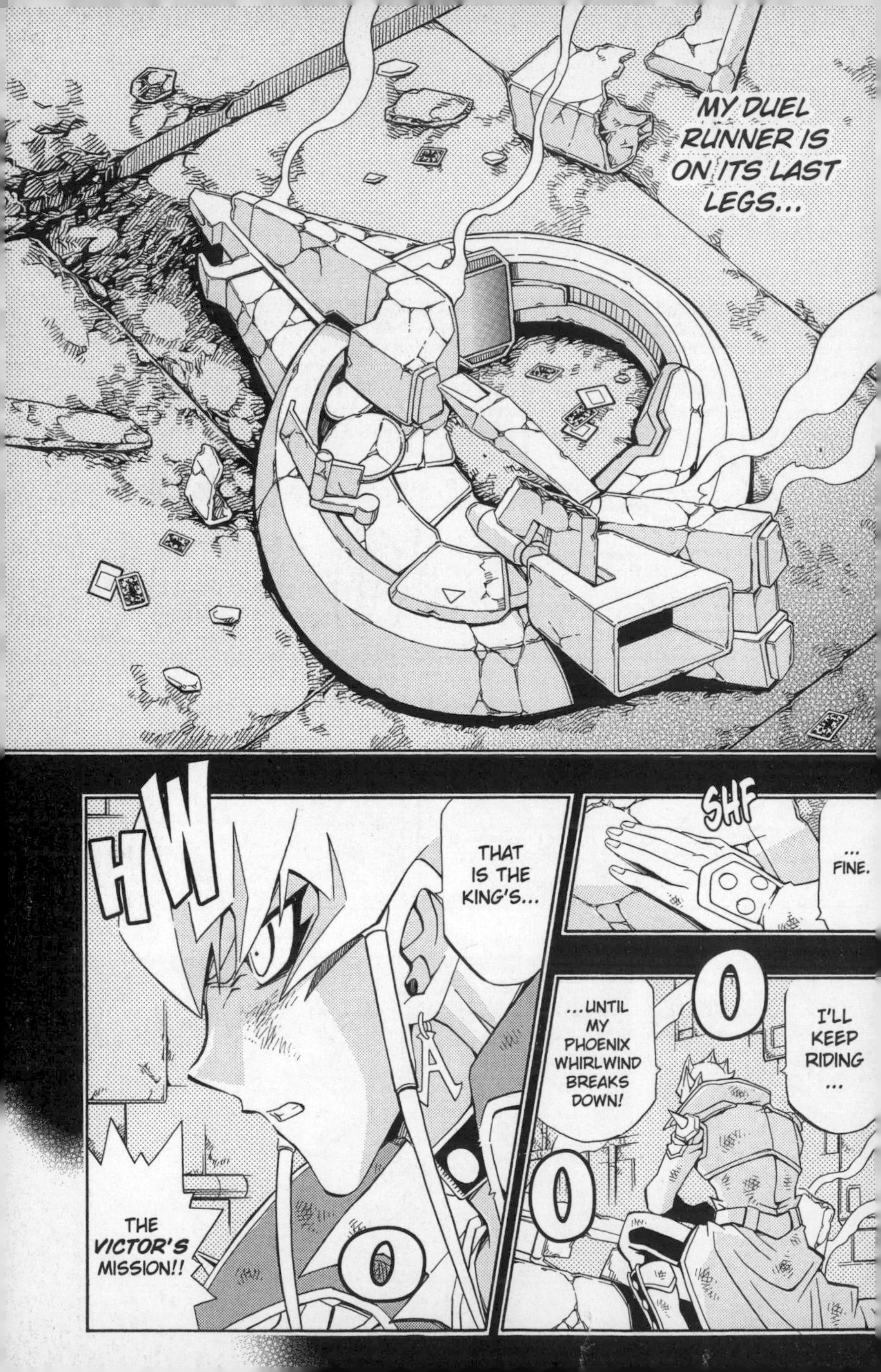
MY DUEL RUNNER IS ON ITS LAST LEGS...
SHF
...FINE.
I'LL KEEP RIDING...
...UNTIL MY PHOENIX WHIRLWIND BREAKS DOWN!
O
O
HW
THAT IS THE KING'S...
THE VICTOR'S MISSION!!
O

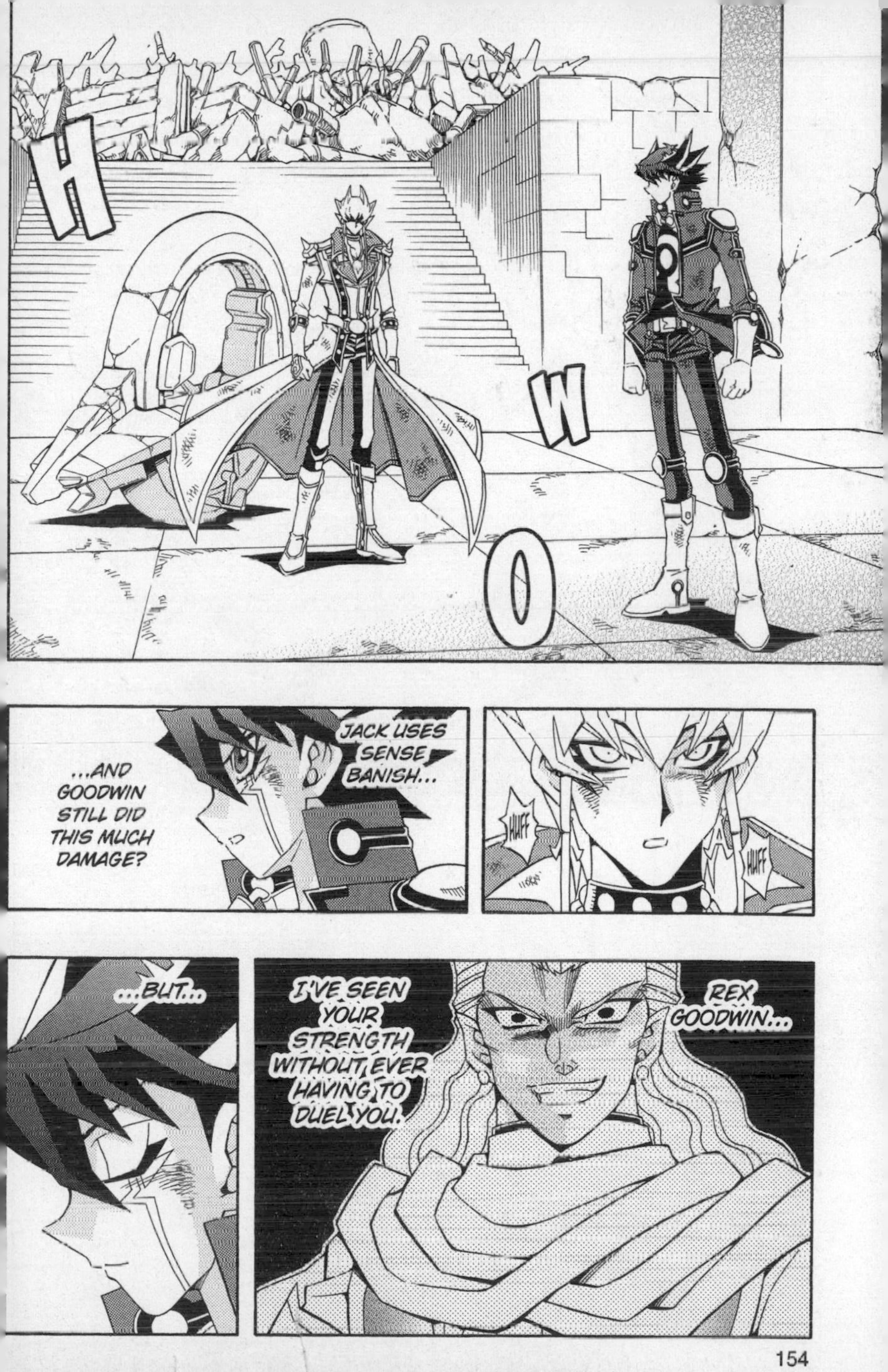
H
W
O
HUFF
HUFF
JACK USES SENSE BANISH...
...AND GOODWIN STILL DID THIS MUCH DAMAGE?
REX GOODWIN...
I'VE SEEN YOUR STRENGTH WITHOUT EVER HAVING TO DUEL YOU.
...BUT...

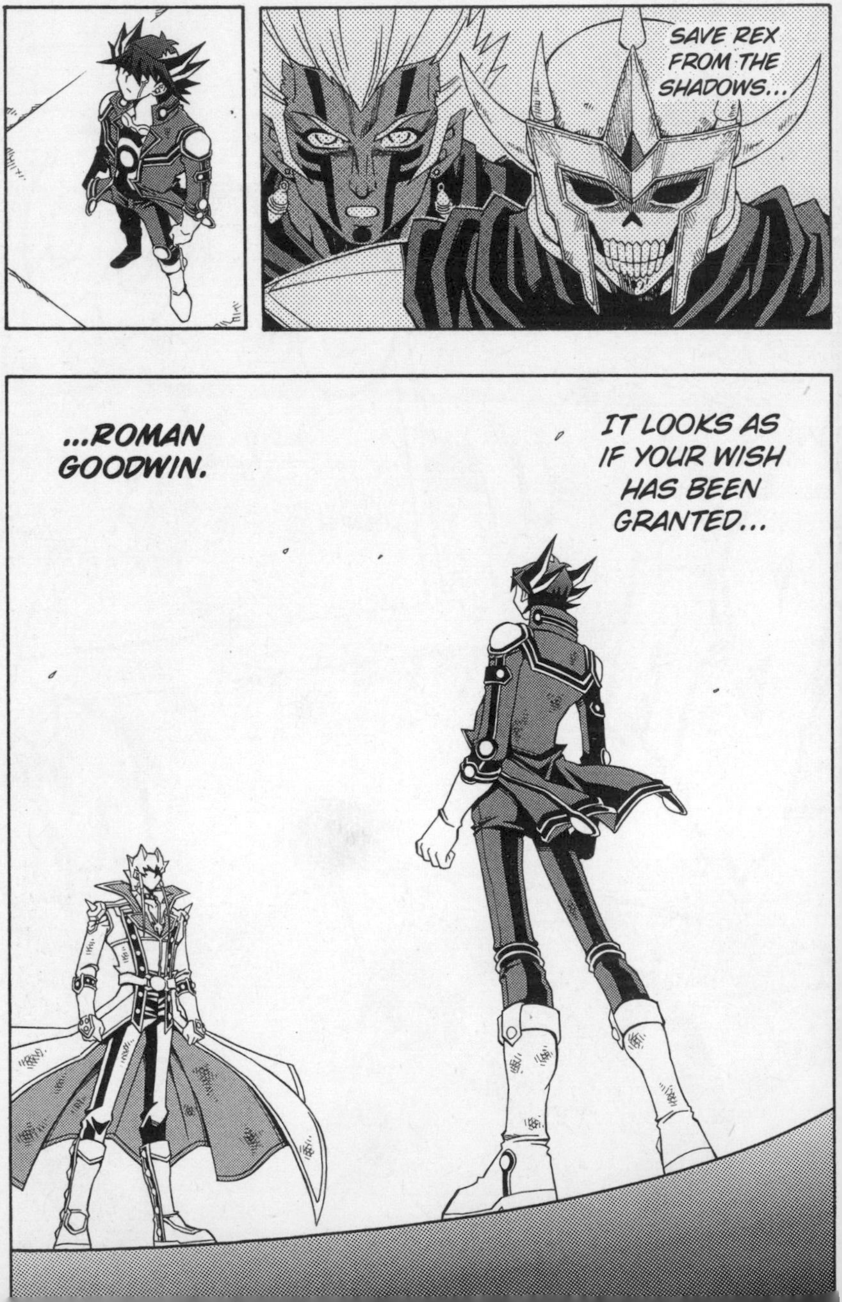
SAVE REX FROM THE SHADOWS...
IT LOOKS AS IF YOUR WISH HAS BEEN GRANTED...
...ROMAN GOODWIN.

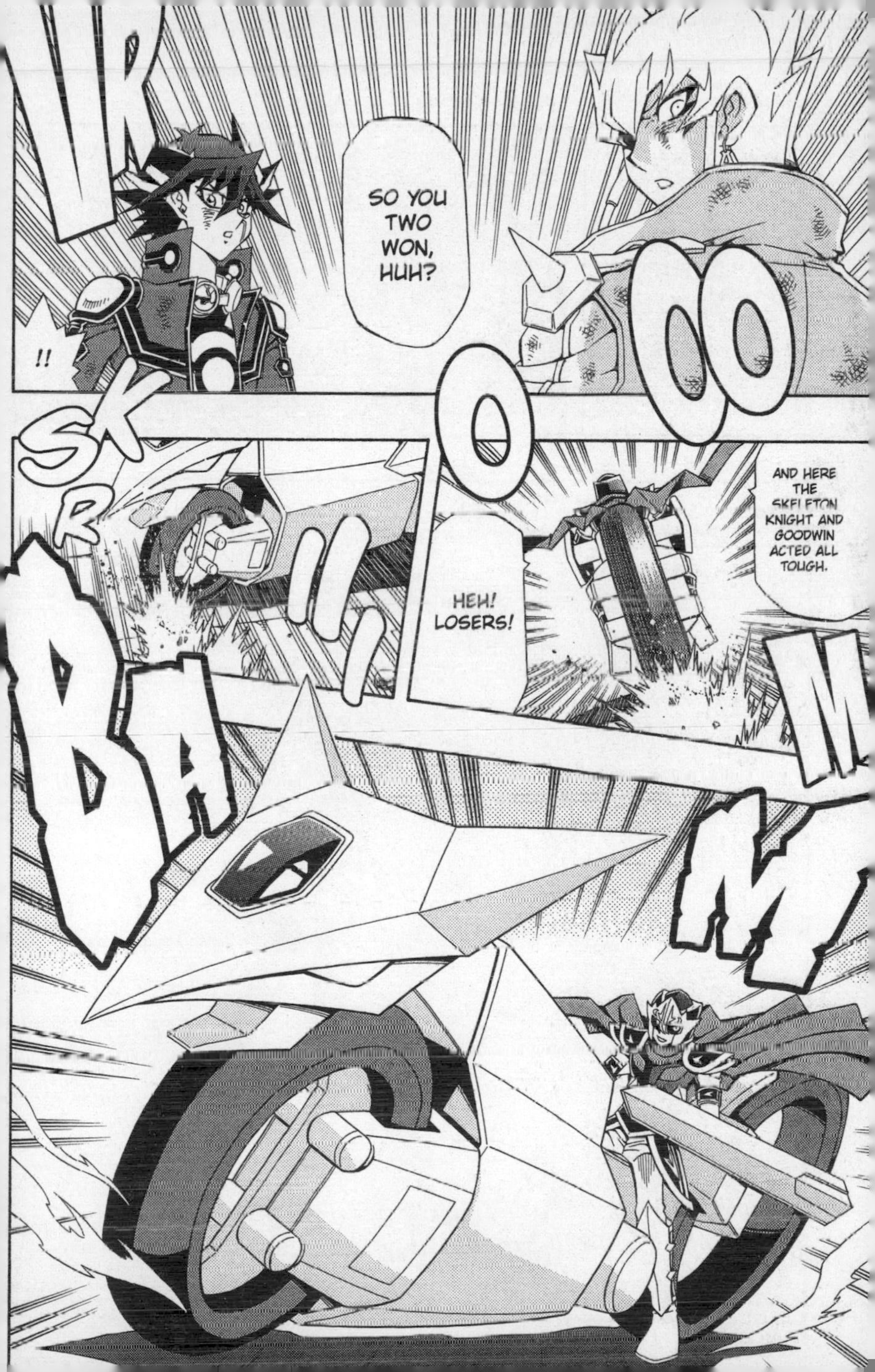
SO YOU TWO WON, HUH?
!!
VR
OOOO
AND HERE THE SKELETON KNIGHT AND GOODWIN ACTED ALL TOUGH.
HEH! LOSERS!
SK
R
BA
MM

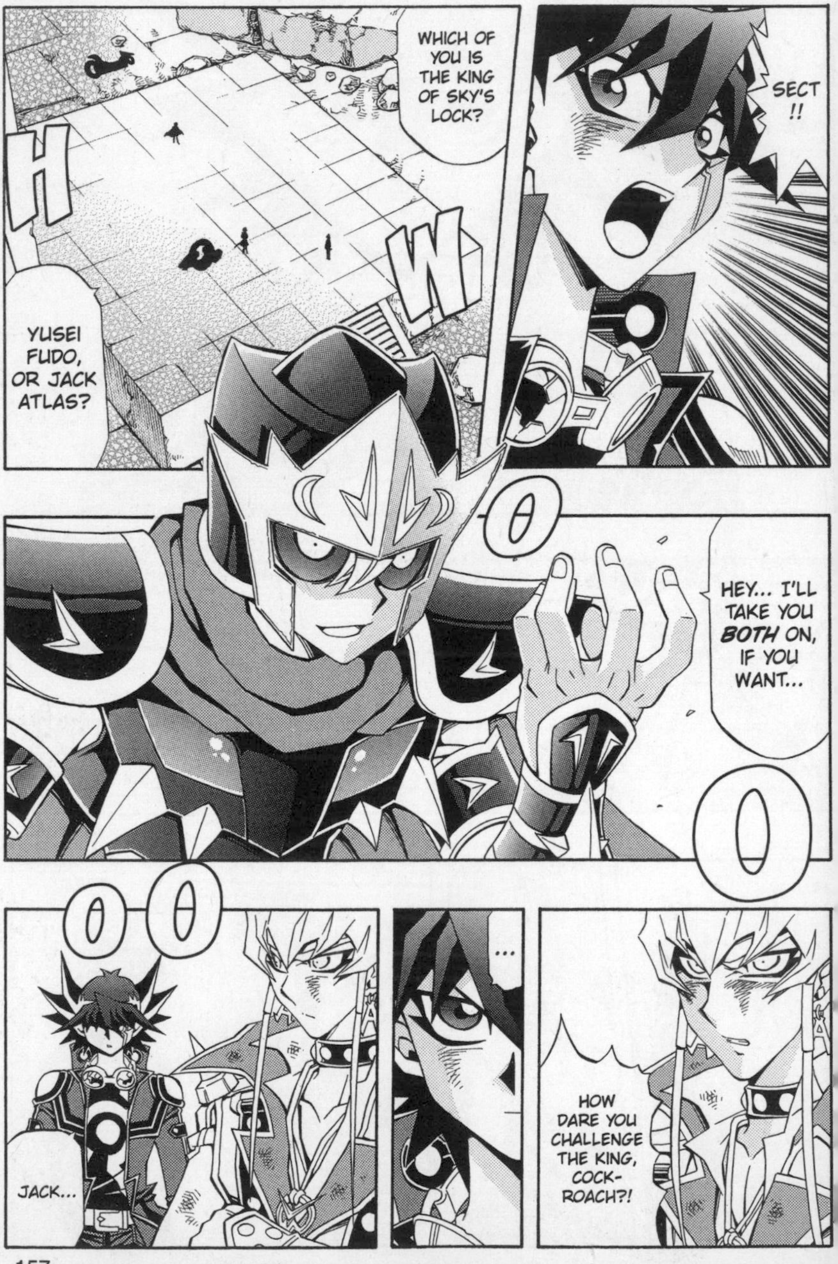
SECT !!
WHICH OF YOU IS THE KING OF SKY'S LOCK?
YUSEI FUDO, OR JACK ATLAS?
HWOOOO
HEY... I'LL TAKE YOU *BOTH* ON, IF YOU WANT...
HOW DARE YOU CHALLENGE THE KING, COCK-ROACH?!
...
JACK...

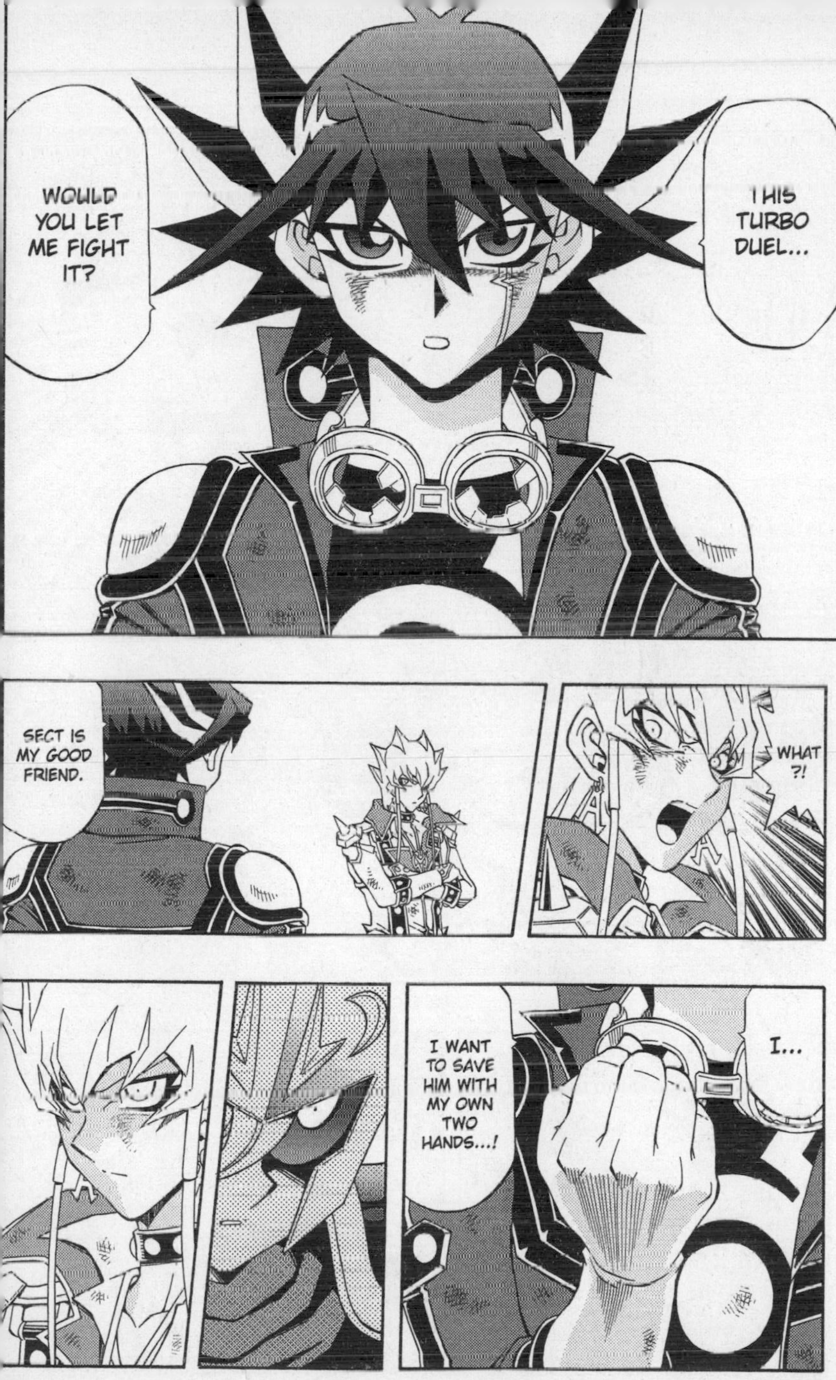
THIS TURBO DUEL...
WOULD YOU LET ME FIGHT IT?
WHAT ?!
SECT IS MY GOOD FRIEND.
I...
I WANT TO SAVE HIM WITH MY OWN TWO HANDS...!

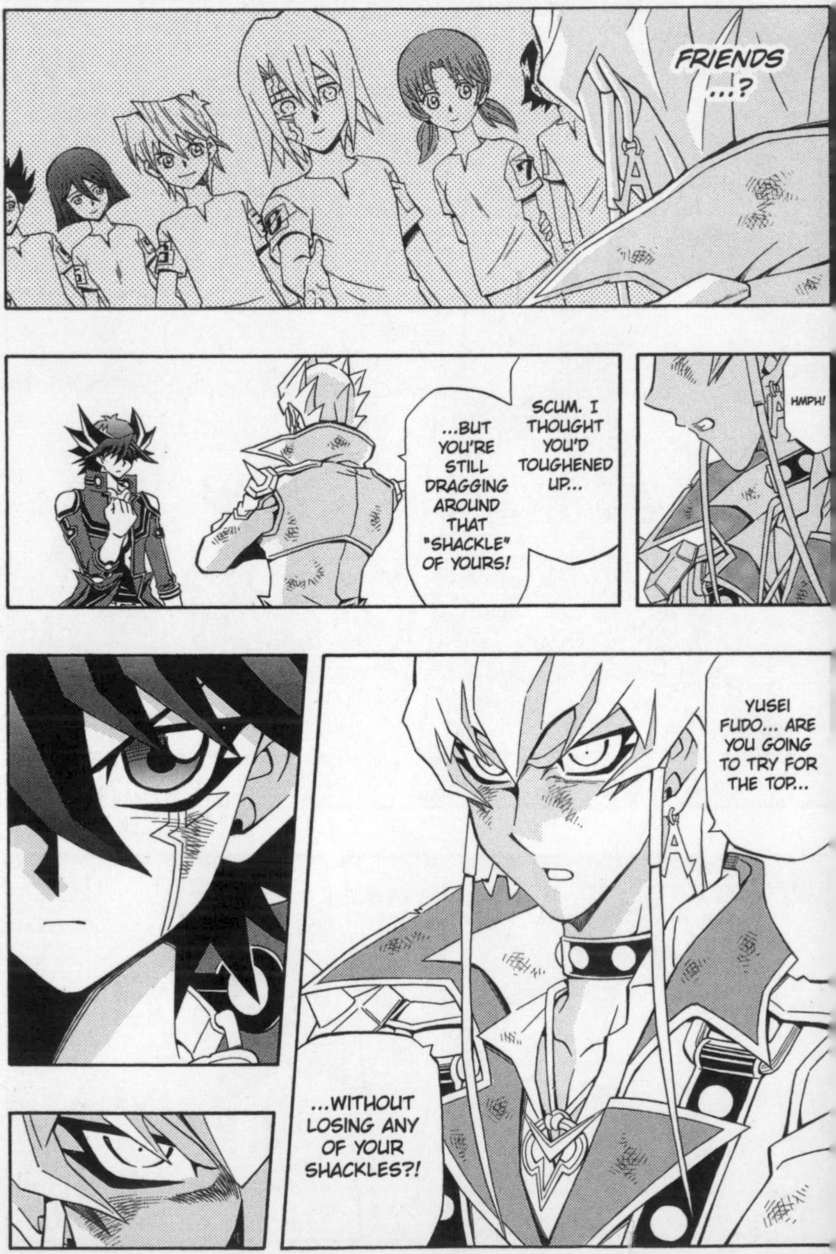
FRIENDS ...?
HMPH!
SCUM. I THOUGHT YOU'D TOUGHENED UP...
...BUT YOU'RE STILL DRAGGING AROUND THAT "SHACKLE" OF YOURS!
YUSEI FUDO... ARE YOU GOING TO TRY FOR THE TOP...
...WITHOUT LOSING ANY OF YOUR SHACKLES?!

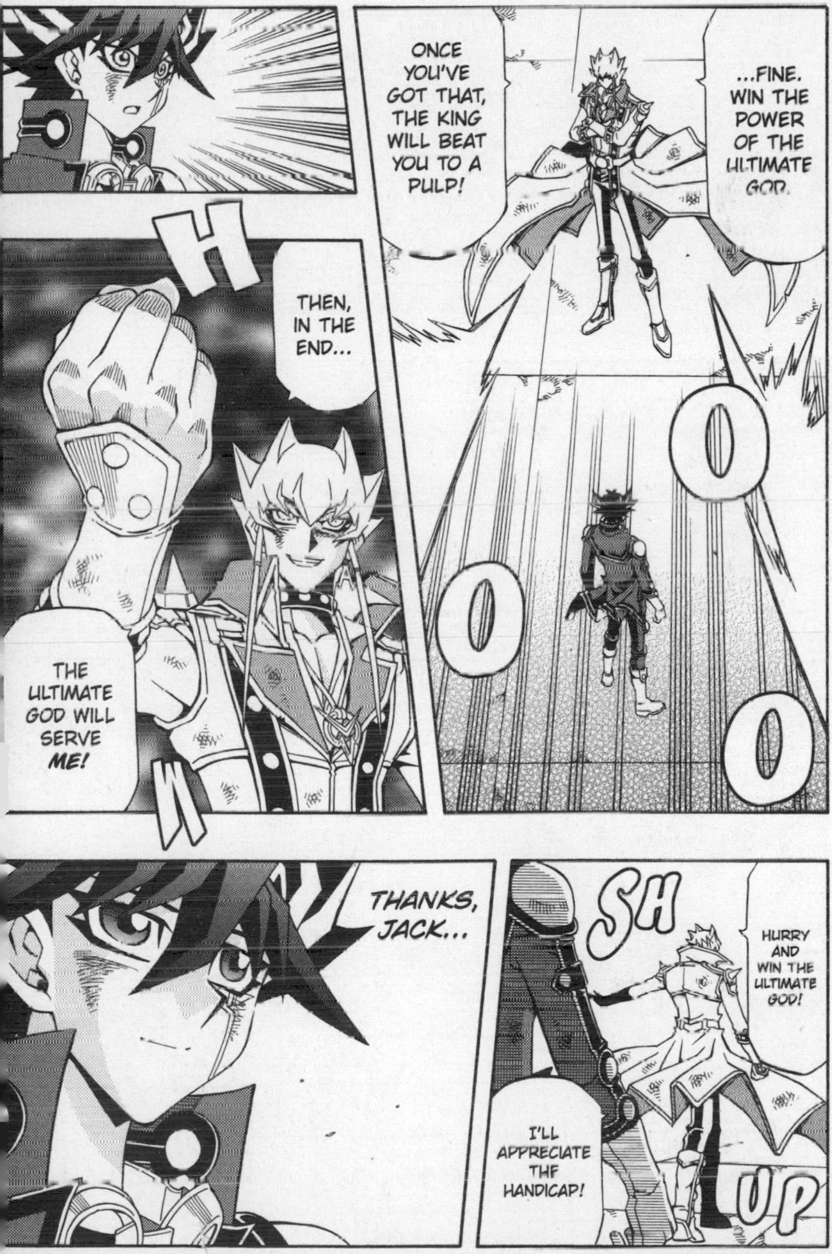
...FINE. WIN THE POWER OF THE ULTIMATE GOD.
ONCE YOU'VE GOT THAT, THE KING WILL BEAT YOU TO A PULP!
O
O
O
H
THEN, IN THE END...
THE ULTIMATE GOD WILL SERVE *ME!*
W
SH
HURRY AND WIN THE ULTIMATE GOD!
I'LL APPRECIATE THE HANDICAP!
UP
THANKS, JACK...

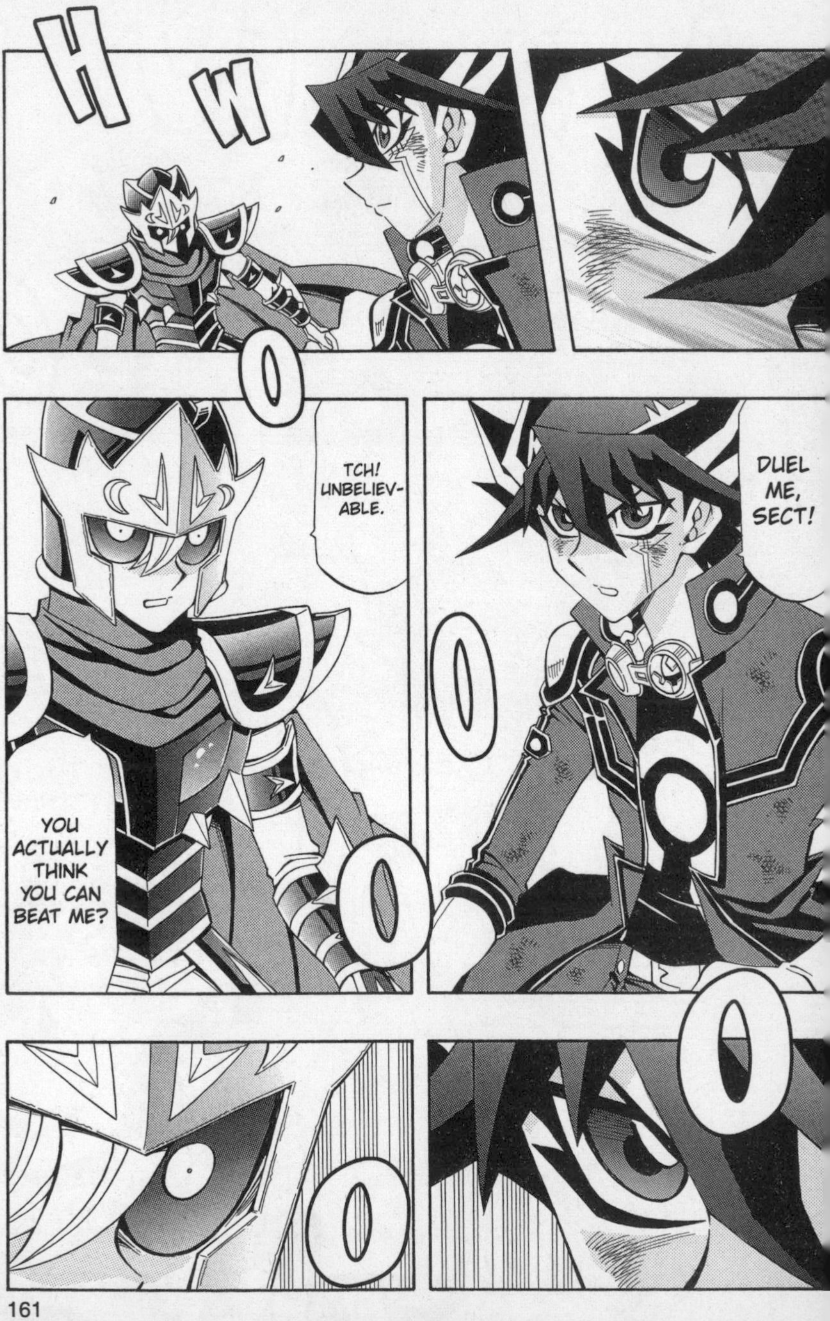
HWOOOOO
DUEL ME, SECT!
TCH! UNBELIEVABLE.
YOU ACTUALLY THINK YOU CAN BEAT ME?

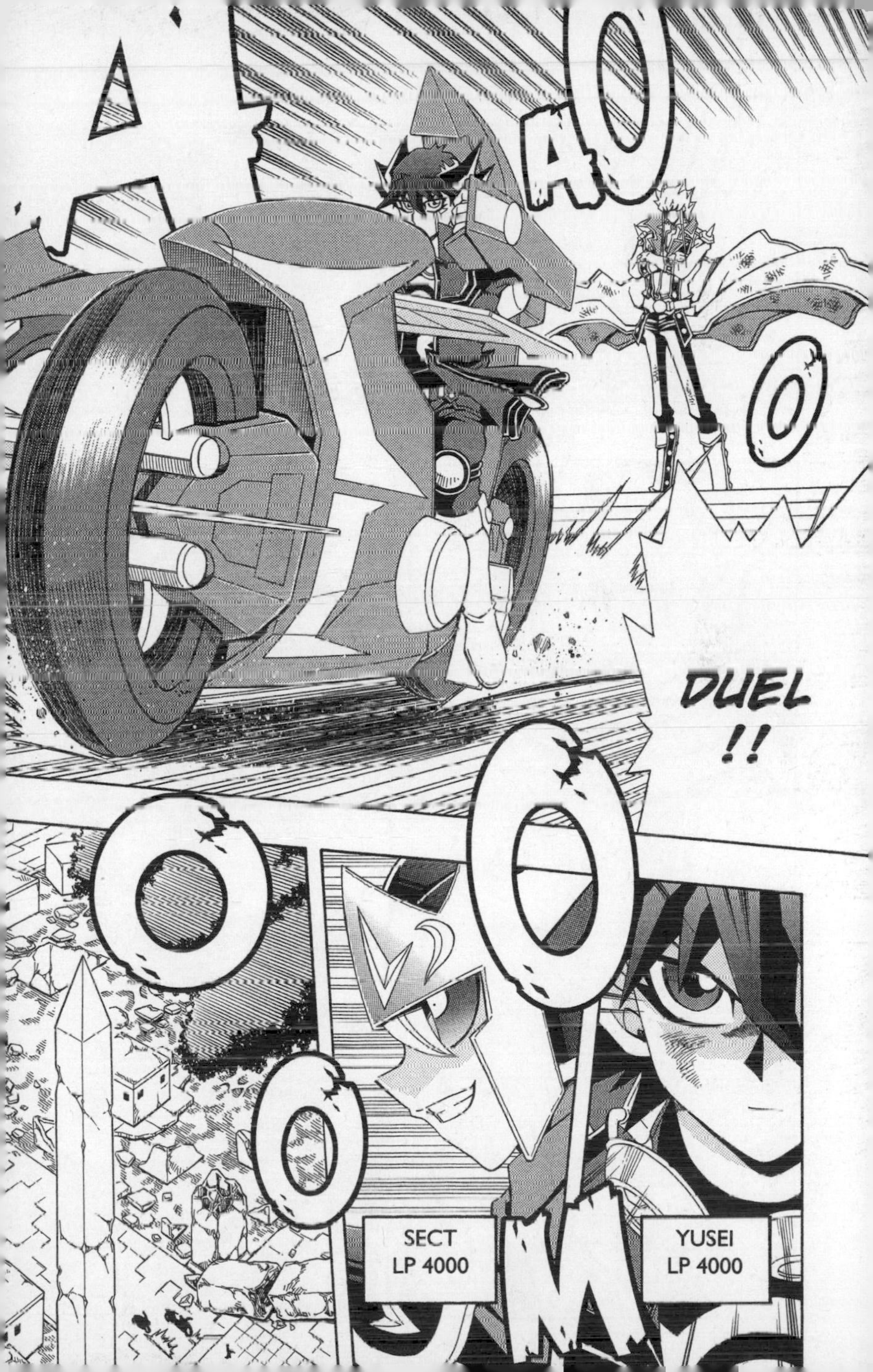
AAOOOOOM
DUEL !!
YUSEI LP 4000
SECT LP 4000

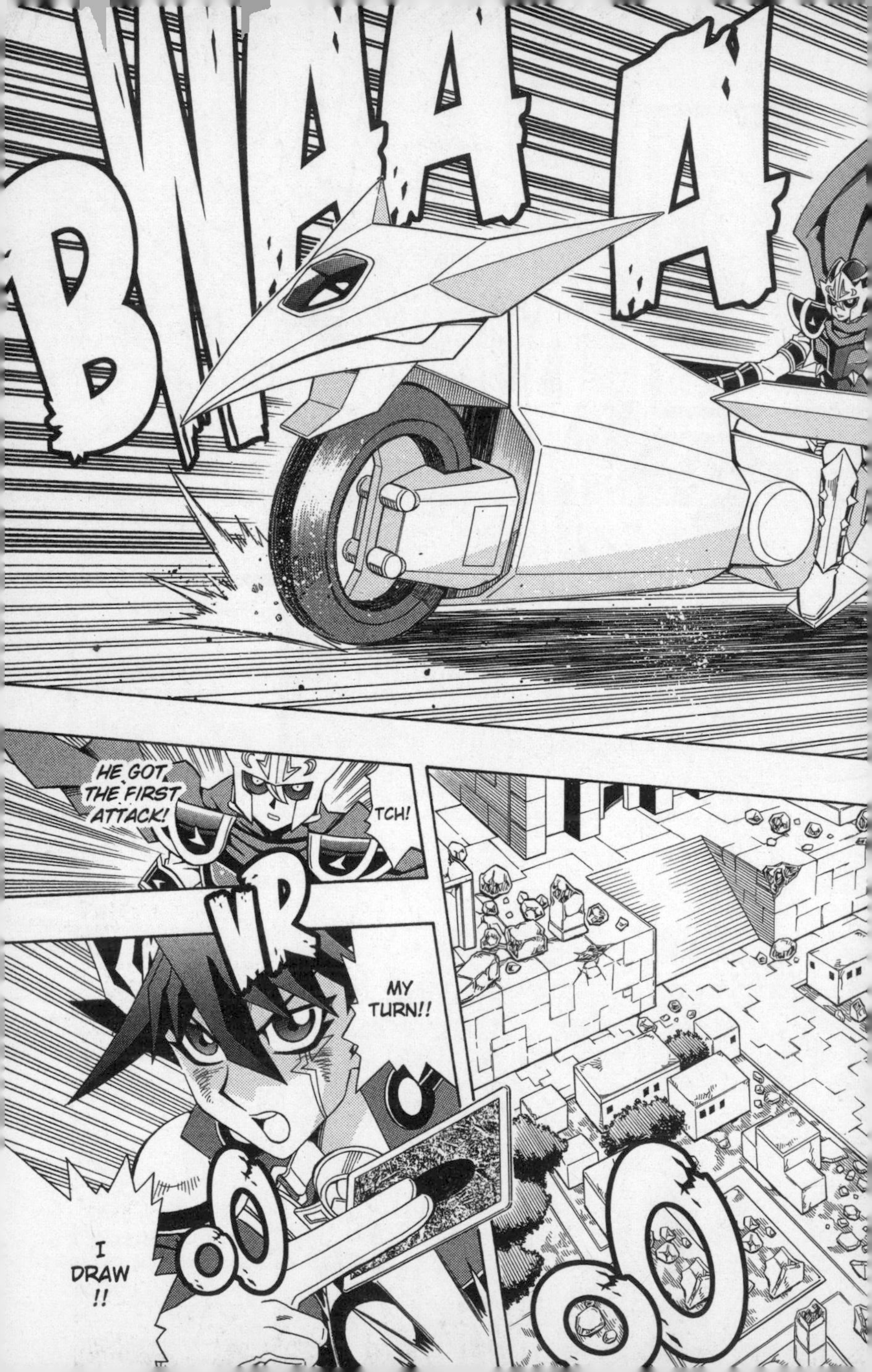
BWAAA
HE GOT THE FIRST ATTACK!
TCH!
VROOOO
MY TURN!!
I DRAW!!

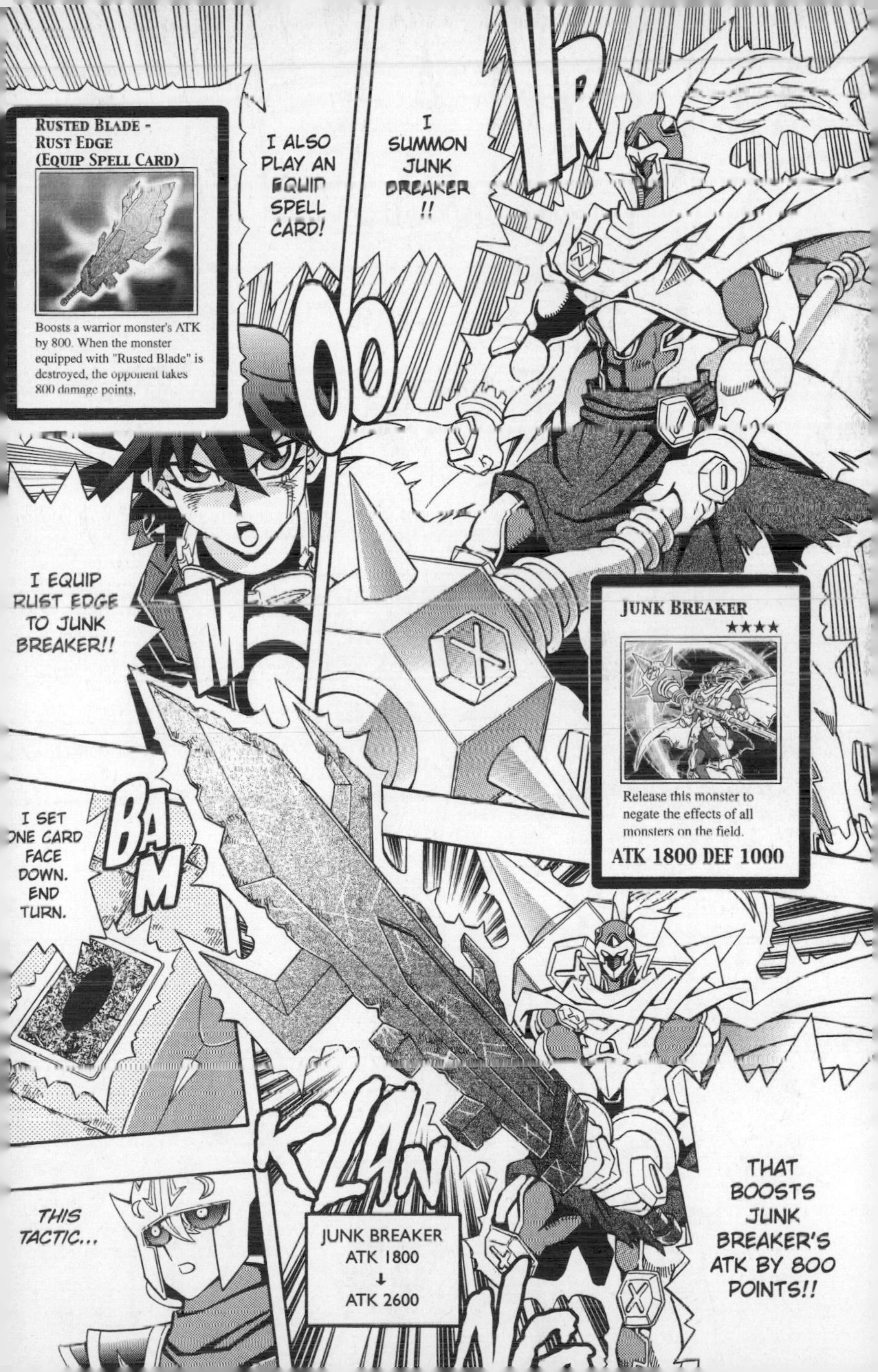
VR
I SUMMON JUNK BREAKER!!
I ALSO PLAY AN EQUIP SPELL CARD!
RUSTED BLADE - RUST EDGE (EQUIP SPELL CARD)
Boosts a warrior monster's ATK by 800. When the monster equipped with "Rusted Blade" is destroyed, the opponent takes 800 damage points.
JUNK BREAKER ★★★★
Release this monster to negate the effects of all monsters on the field.
ATK 1800 DEF 1000
I EQUIP RUST EDGE TO JUNK BREAKER!!
BAM
I SET ONE CARD FACE DOWN. END TURN.
THAT BOOSTS JUNK BREAKER'S ATK BY 800 POINTS!!
KLAN
JUNK BREAKER ATK 1800 ↓ ATK 2600
THIS TACTIC...

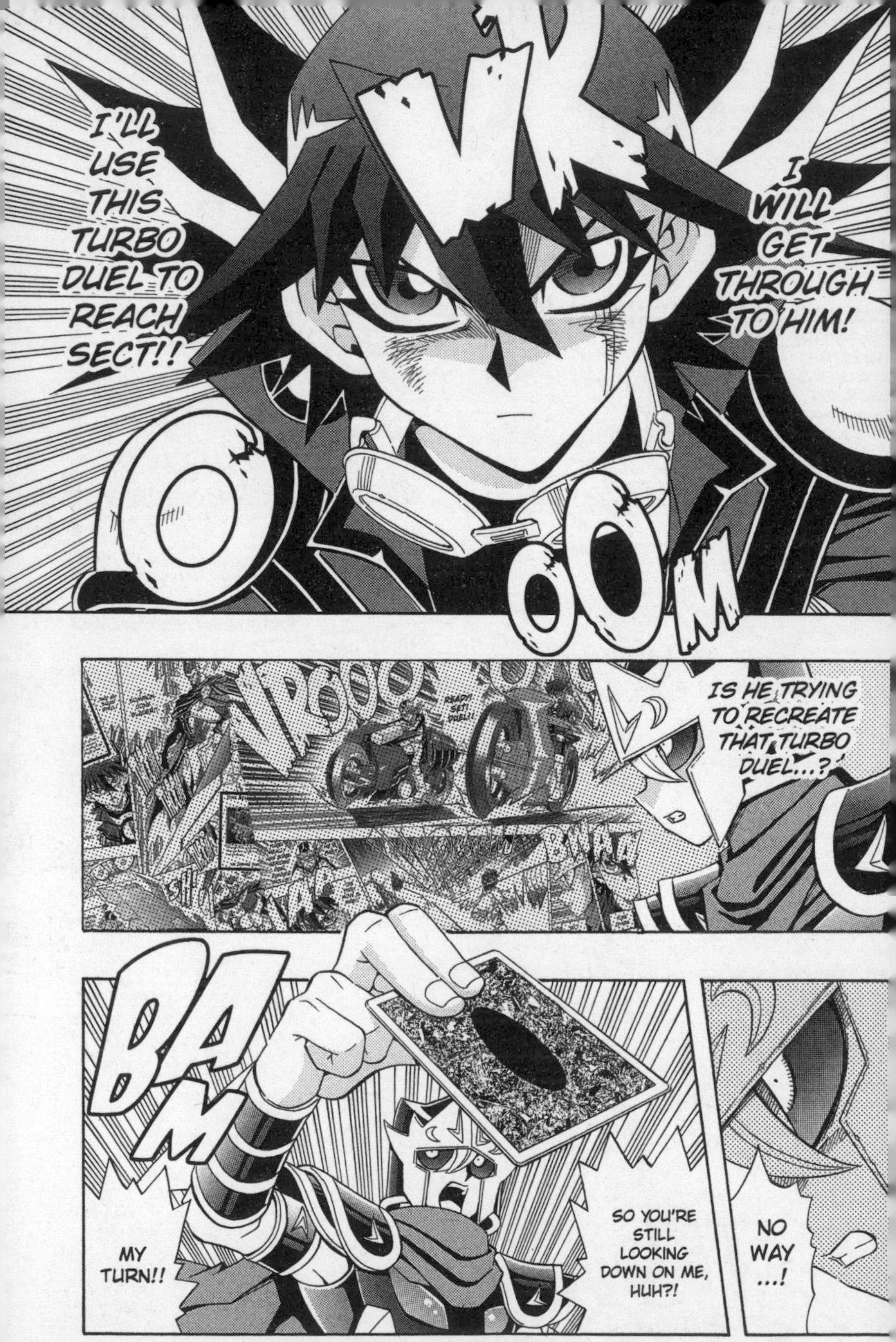
I WILL GET THROUGH TO HIM!
I'LL USE THIS TURBO DUEL TO REACH SECT!!
IS HE TRYING TO RECREATE THAT TURBO DUEL...?
NO WAY ...!
SO YOU'RE STILL LOOKING DOWN ON ME, HUH?!
MY TURN!!
BAM

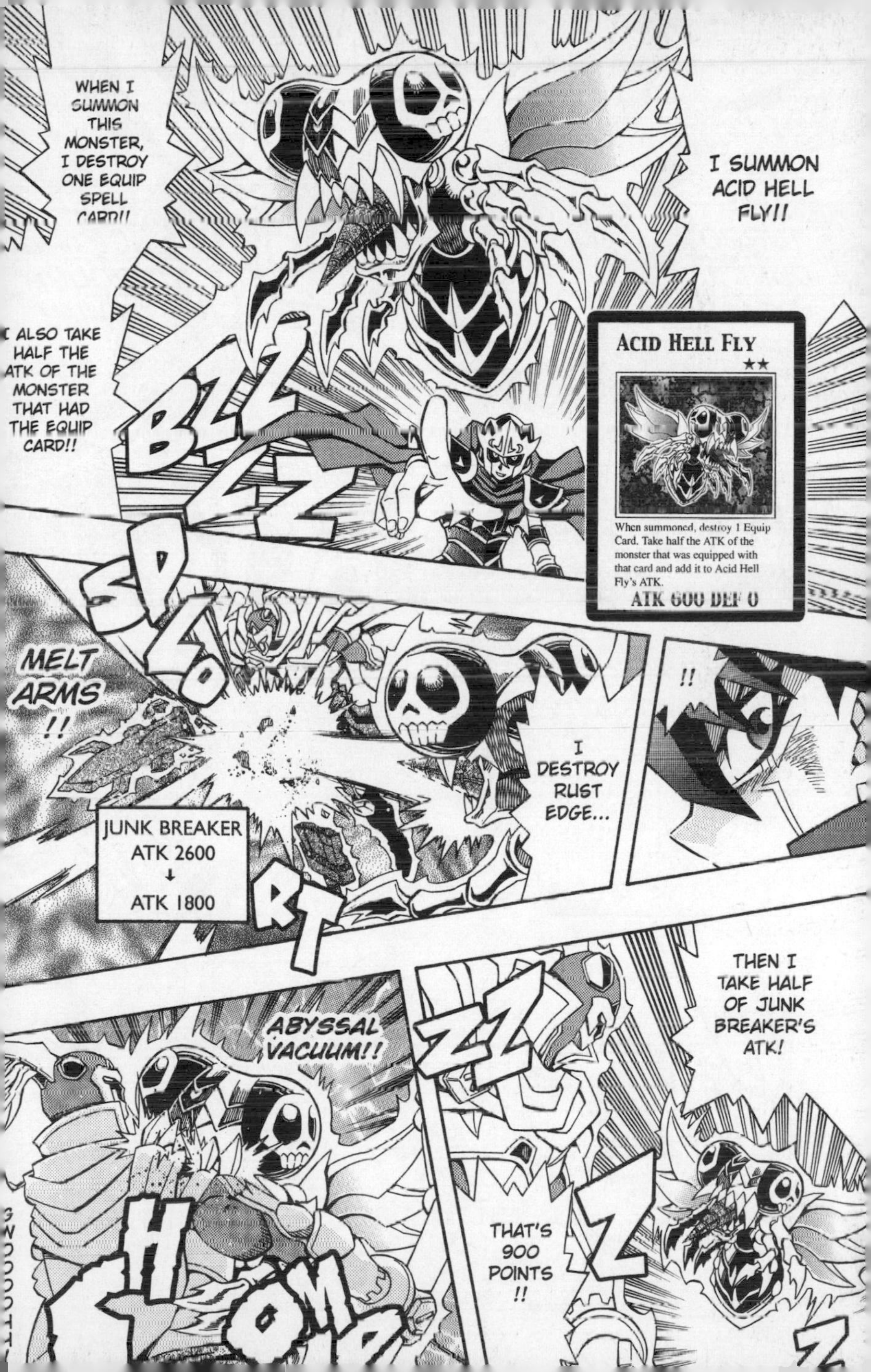
I SUMMON ACID HELL FLY!!
WHEN I SUMMON THIS MONSTER, I DESTROY ONE EQUIP SPELL CARD!!
I ALSO TAKE HALF THE ATK OF THE MONSTER THAT HAD THE EQUIP CARD!!
BZZ
ZZ
ACID HELL FLY
★★
When summoned, destroy 1 Equip Card. Take half the ATK of the monster that was equipped with that card and add it to Acid Hell Fly's ATK.
ATK 600 DEF 0
!!
I DESTROY RUST EDGE...
MELT ARMS !!
SPLORT
JUNK BREAKER ATK 2600 ↓ ATK 1800
THEN I TAKE HALF OF JUNK BREAKER'S ATK!
ZZ
THAT'S 900 POINTS !!
Z
ABYSSAL VACUUM!!

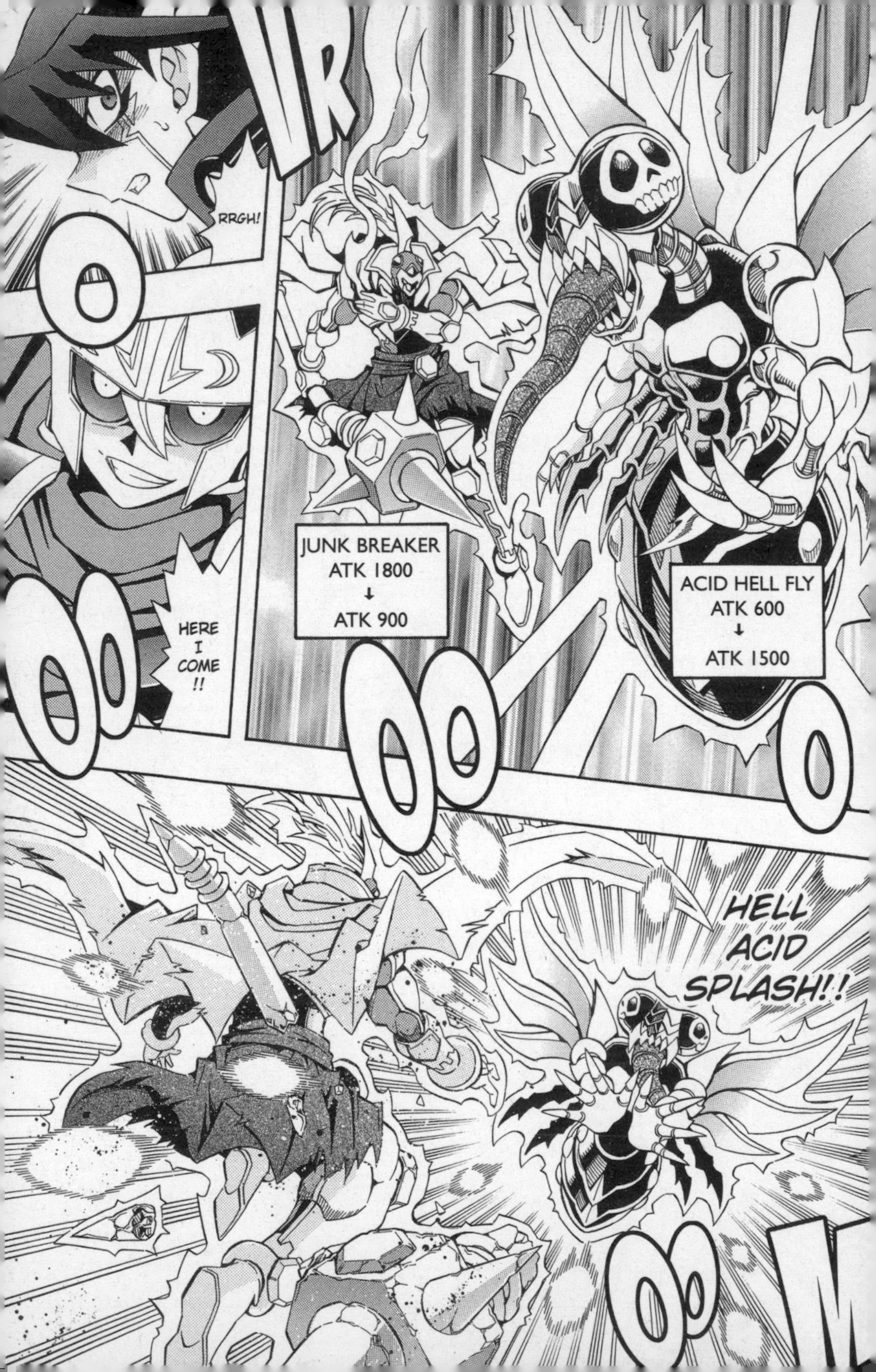
ACID HELL FLY ATK 600 ↓ ATK 1500
JUNK BREAKER ATK 1800 ↓ ATK 900
RRGH!
HERE I COME!!
HELL ACID SPLASH!!

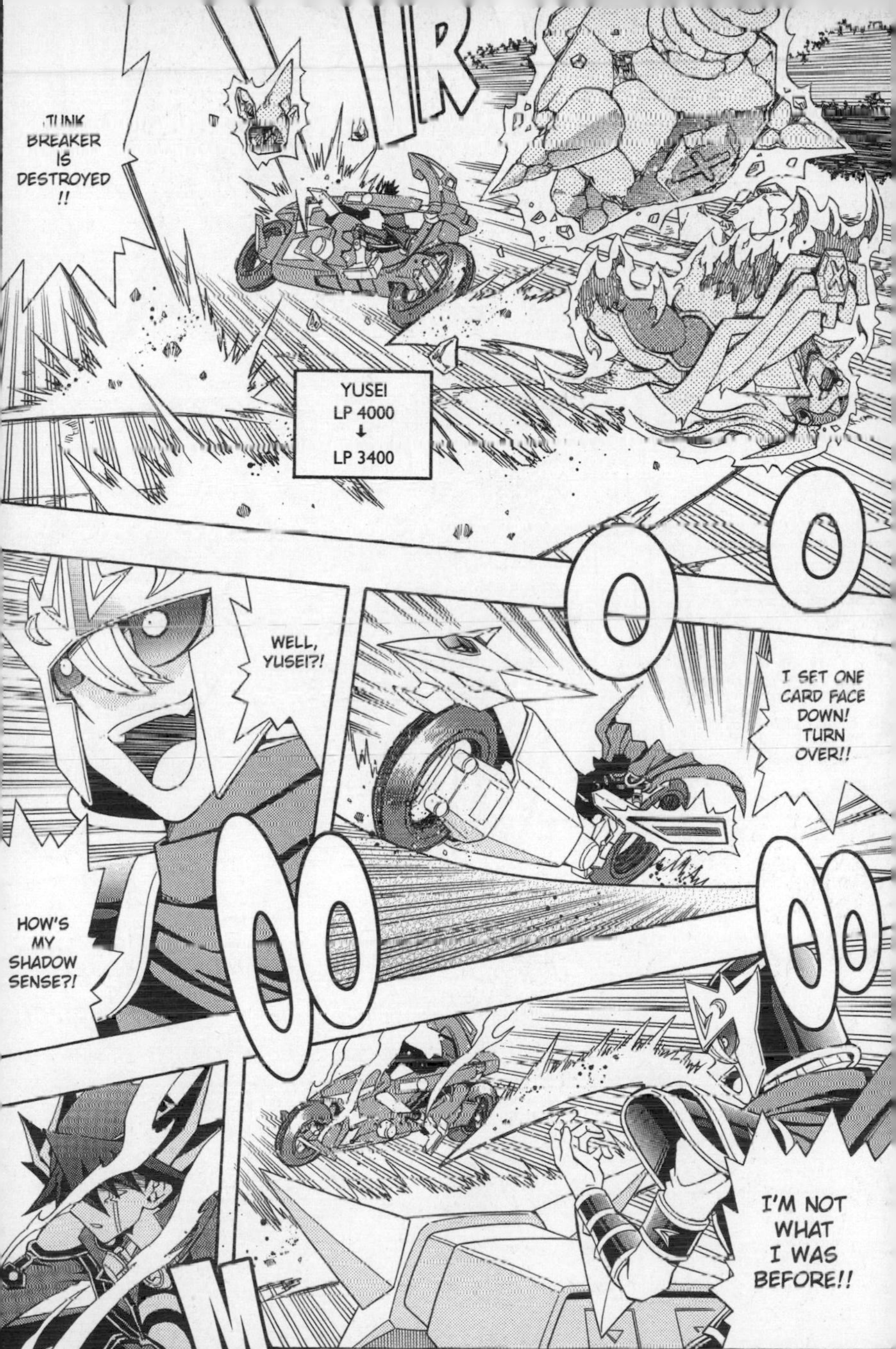
YUSEI
LP 4000
↓
LP 3400
JUNK BREAKER IS DESTROYED!!
I SET ONE CARD FACE DOWN! TURN OVER!!
WELL, YUSEI?!
HOW'S MY SHADOW SENSE?!
I'M NOT WHAT I WAS BEFORE!!

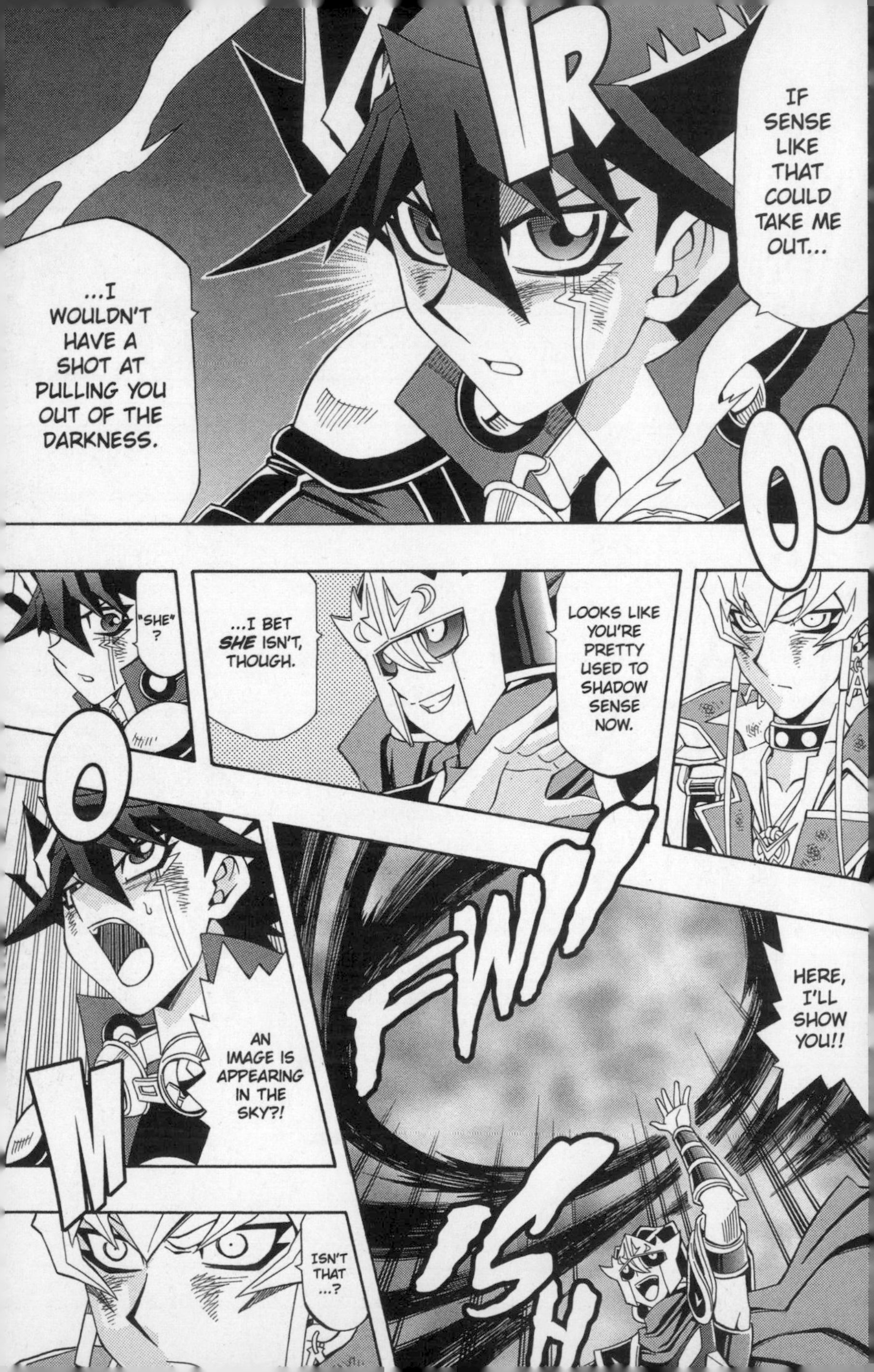
IF SENSE LIKE THAT COULD TAKE ME OUT...
...I WOULDN'T HAVE A SHOT AT PULLING YOU OUT OF THE DARKNESS.
LOOKS LIKE YOU'RE PRETTY USED TO SHADOW SENSE NOW.
...I BET *SHE* ISN'T, THOUGH.
"SHE"?
HERE, I'LL SHOW YOU!!
AN IMAGE IS APPEARING IN THE SKY?!
ISN'T THAT ...?

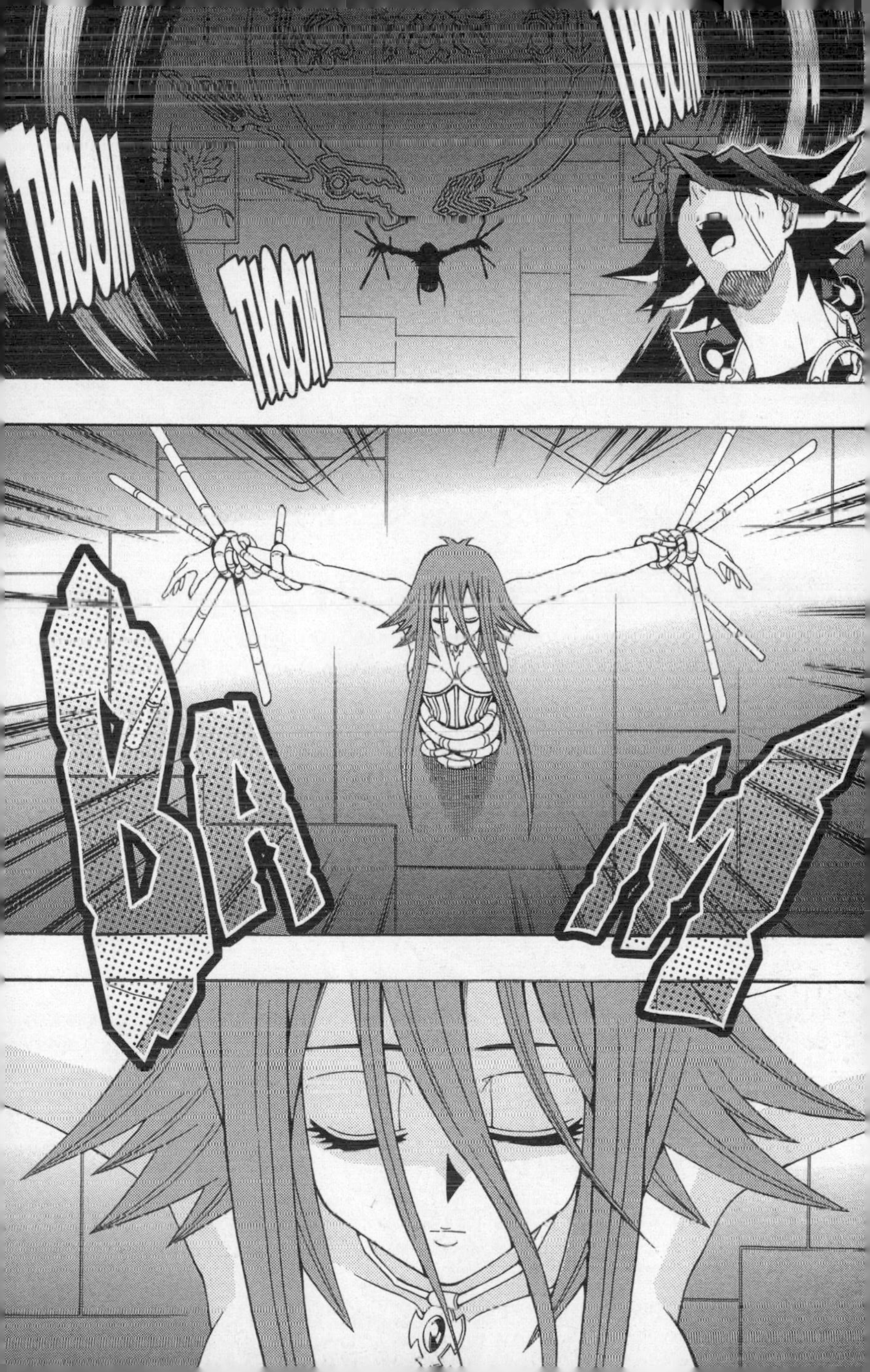
THOOM
THOOM
THOOM
BAM

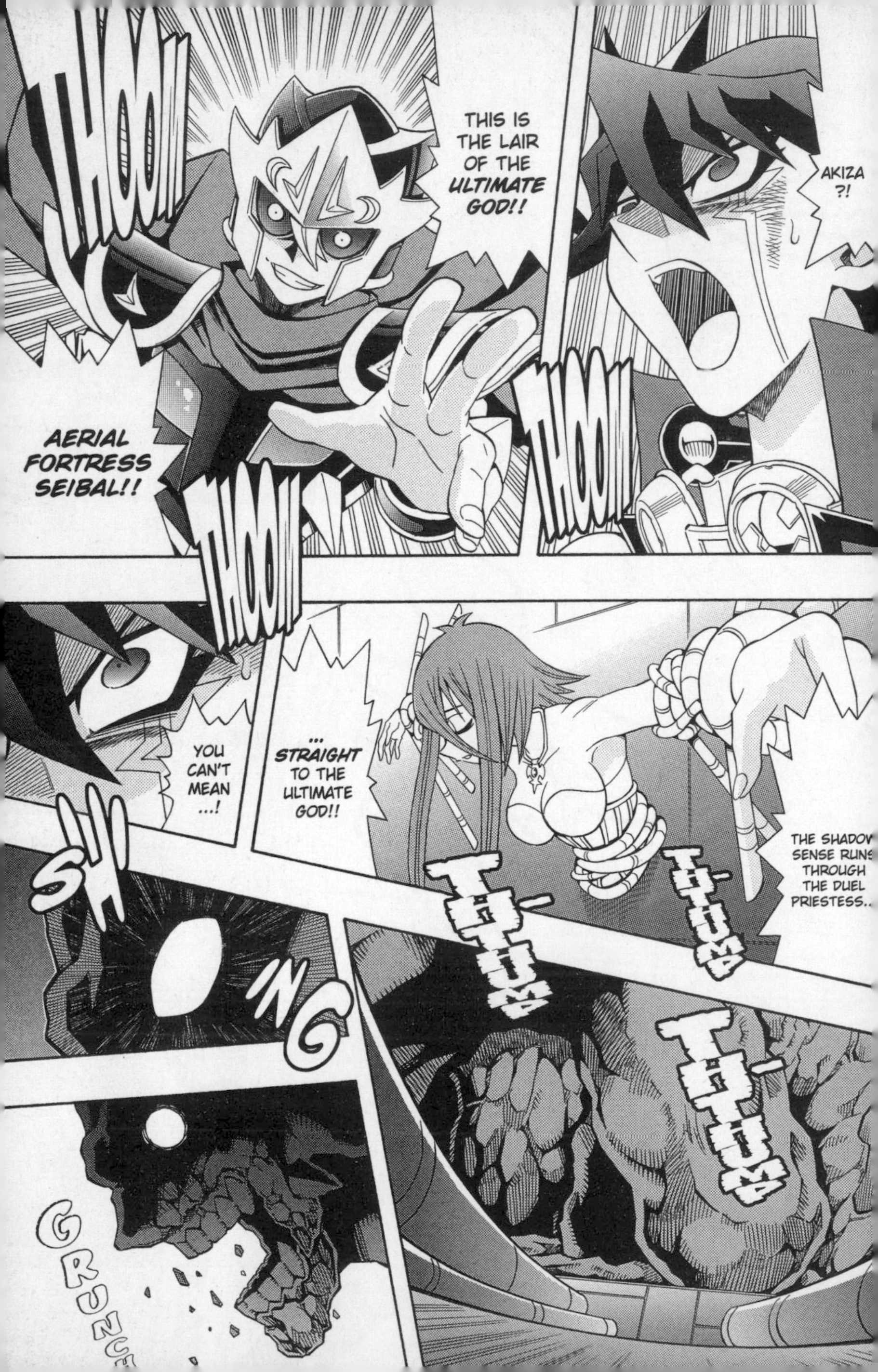
THOOM
AKIZA ?!
THIS IS THE LAIR OF THE ULTIMATE GOD!!
THOOM
AERIAL FORTRESS SEIBAL!!
THOOM
THE SHADOW SENSE RUNS THROUGH THE DUEL PRIESTESS...
TH-THUMP
TH-THUMP
... STRAIGHT TO THE ULTIMATE GOD!!
YOU CAN'T MEAN ...!
SHING
TH-THUMP
GRUNCH

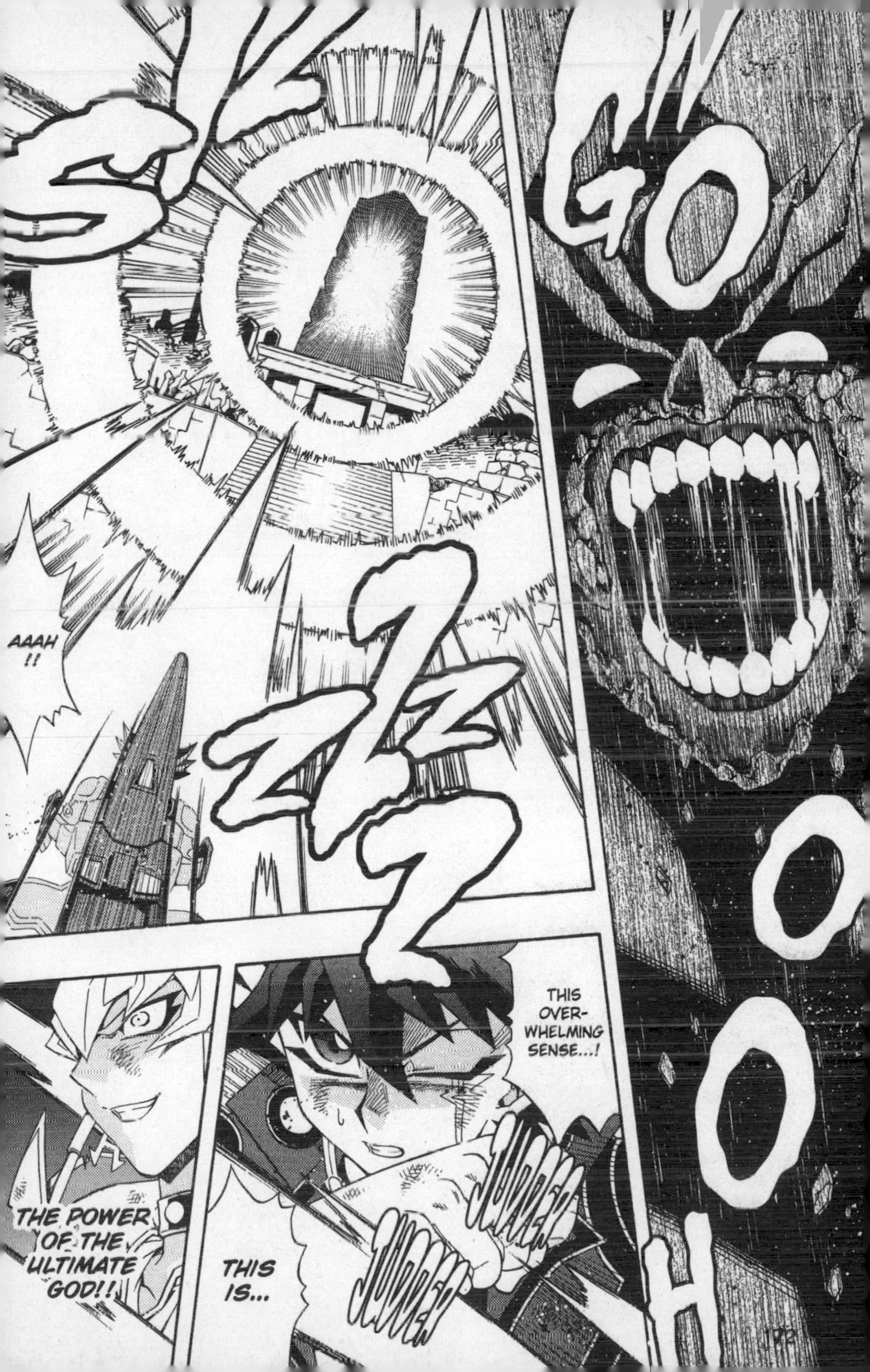
GOOOOH
AAAH !!
THIS OVER-WHELMING SENSE...!
THIS IS...
THE POWER OF THE ULTIMATE GOD!!

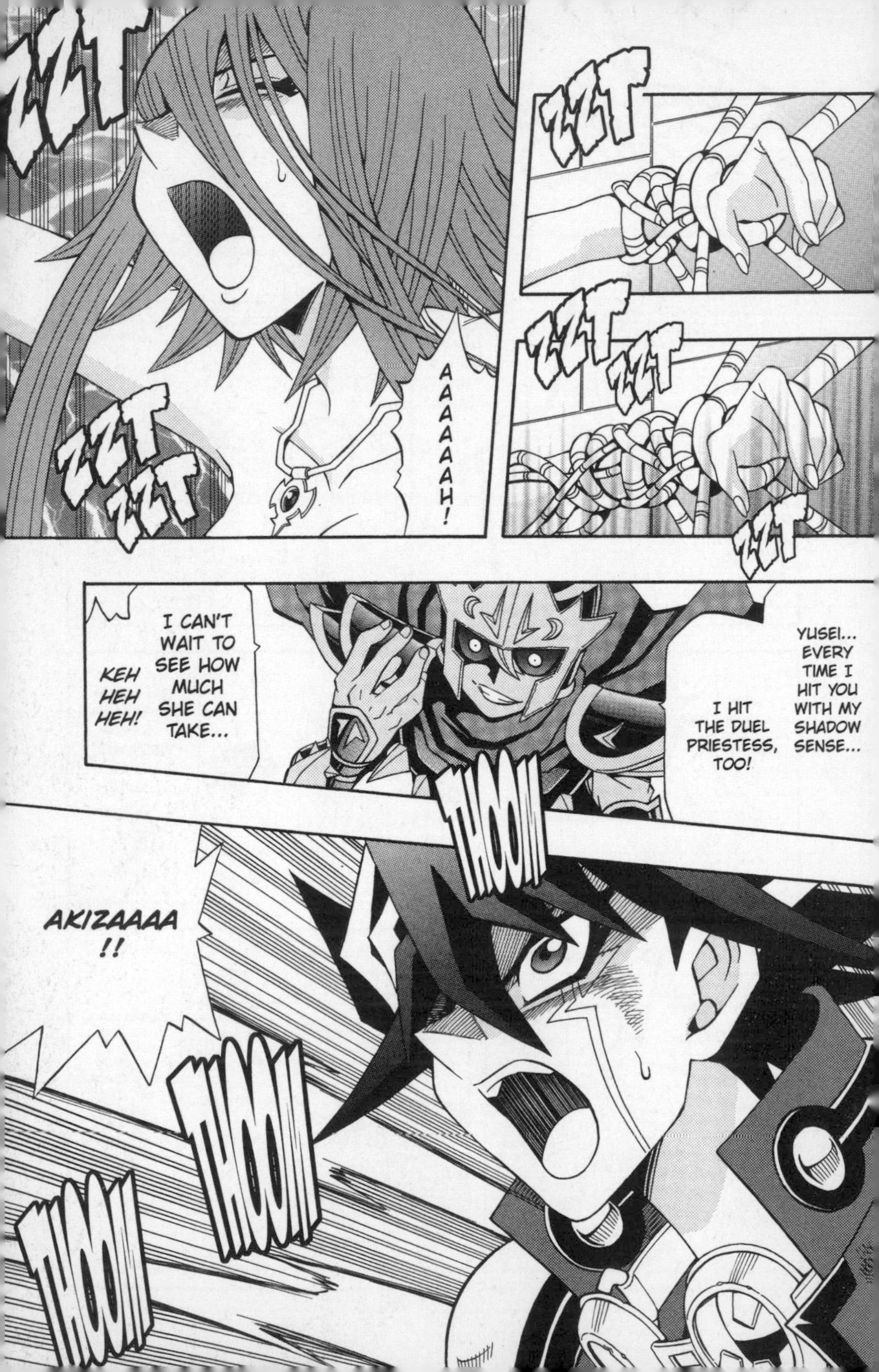
ZZZT
ZZZT
ZZZT
ZZZT
ZZZT
AAAAAAAH!
ZZZT
ZZZT
YUSEI... EVERY TIME I HIT YOU WITH MY SHADOW SENSE...
I HIT THE DUEL PRIESTESS, TOO!
I CAN'T WAIT TO SEE HOW MUCH SHE CAN TAKE...
KEH HEH HEH!
THOOM
AKIZAAAA!!
THOOM
THOOM

5D's TRACKS

THE 51ST

BY SATOMASA

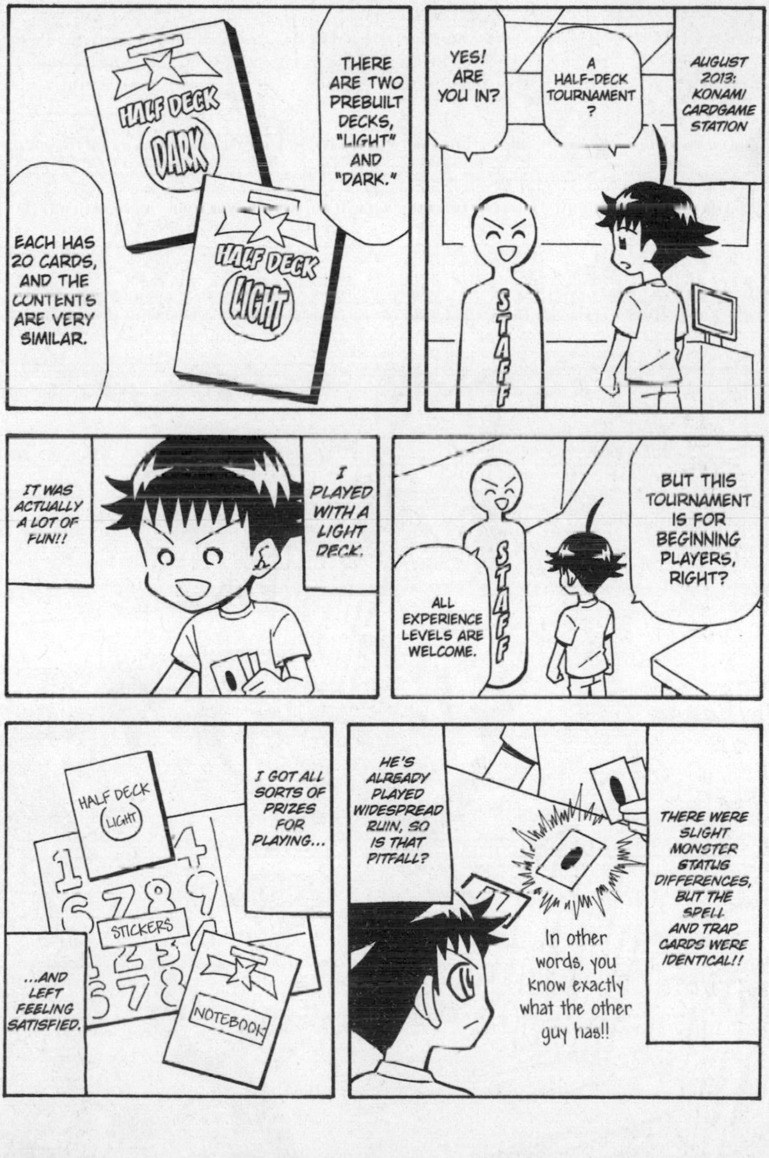
AUGUST 2013: KONAMI CARDGAME STATION
A HALF-DECK TOURNAMENT?
YES! ARE YOU IN?
STAFF
THERE ARE TWO PREBUILT DECKS, "LIGHT" AND "DARK."
HALF DECK DARK
HALF DECK LIGHT
EACH HAS 20 CARDS, AND THE CONTENTS ARE VERY SIMILAR.
BUT THIS TOURNAMENT IS FOR BEGINNING PLAYERS, RIGHT?
STAFF
ALL EXPERIENCE LEVELS ARE WELCOME.
I PLAYED WITH A LIGHT DECK.
IT WAS ACTUALLY A LOT OF FUN!!
THERE WERE SLIGHT MONSTER STATUS DIFFERENCES, BUT THE SPELL AND TRAP CARDS WERE IDENTICAL!!
HE'S ALREADY PLAYED WIDESPREAD RUIN, SO IS THAT PITFALL?
In other words, you know exactly what the other guy has!!
I GOT ALL SORTS OF PRIZES FOR PLAYING...
HALF DECK LIGHT
STICKERS
NOTEBOOK
...AND LEFT FEELING SATISFIED.

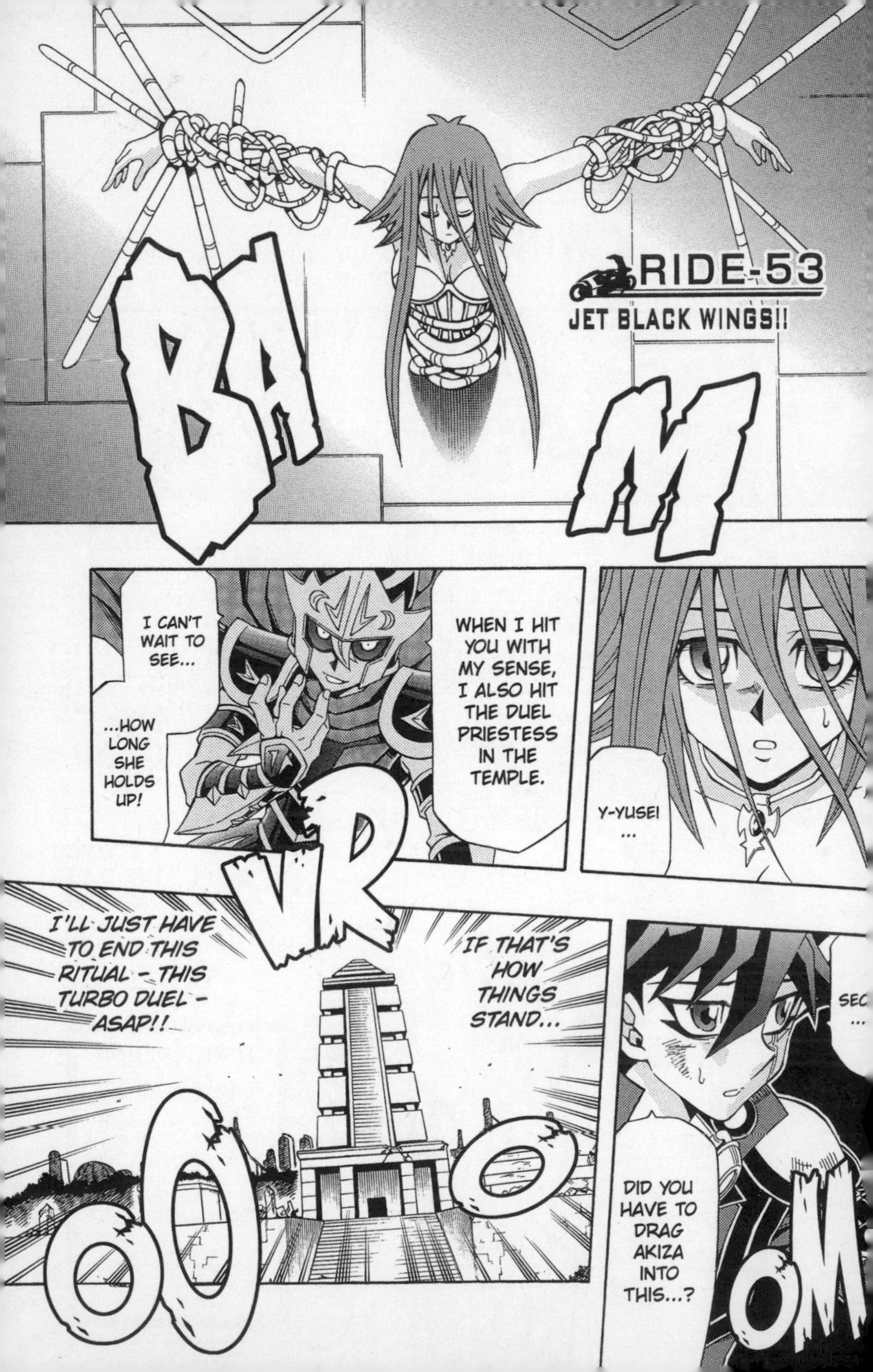
RIDE-53
JET BLACK WINGS!!
BAM
Y-YUSEI ...
WHEN I HIT YOU WITH MY SENSE, I ALSO HIT THE DUEL PRIESTESS IN THE TEMPLE.
I CAN'T WAIT TO SEE...
...HOW LONG SHE HOLDS UP!
VR
SEC ...
DID YOU HAVE TO DRAG AKIZA INTO THIS...?
IF THAT'S HOW THINGS STAND...
I'LL JUST HAVE TO END THIS RITUAL - THIS TURBO DUEL - ASAP!!
OOO
OM

RIDE-53
JET BLACK WINGS!!

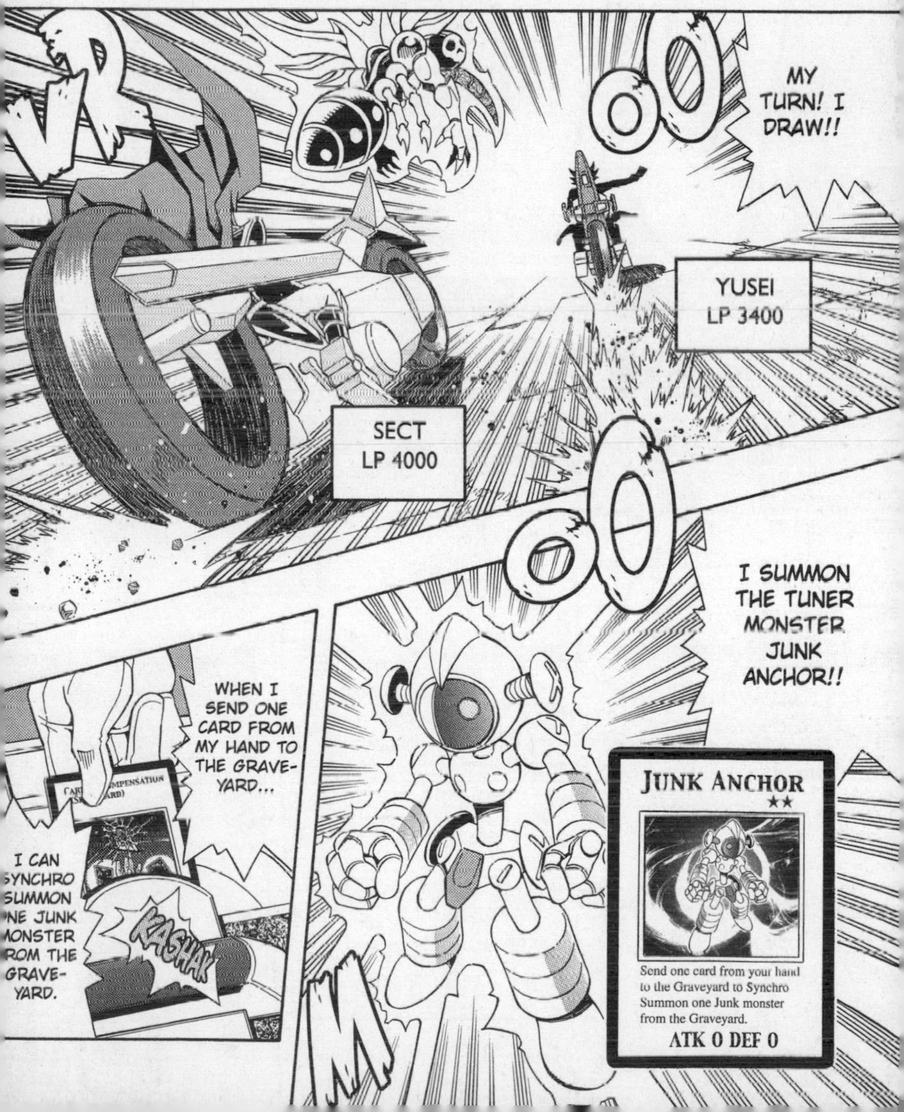

MY TURN! I DRAW!!
YUSEI
LP 3400
SECT
LP 4000
I SUMMON THE TUNER MONSTER JUNK ANCHOR!!
JUNK ANCHOR
Send one card from your hand to the Graveyard to Synchro Summon one Junk monster from the Graveyard.
ATK 0 DEF 0
WHEN I SEND ONE CARD FROM MY HAND TO THE GRAVE-YARD...
I CAN YNCHRO UMMON NE JUNK ONSTER ROM THE GRAVE-YARD.
KASHAK

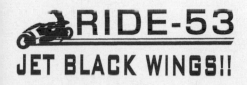

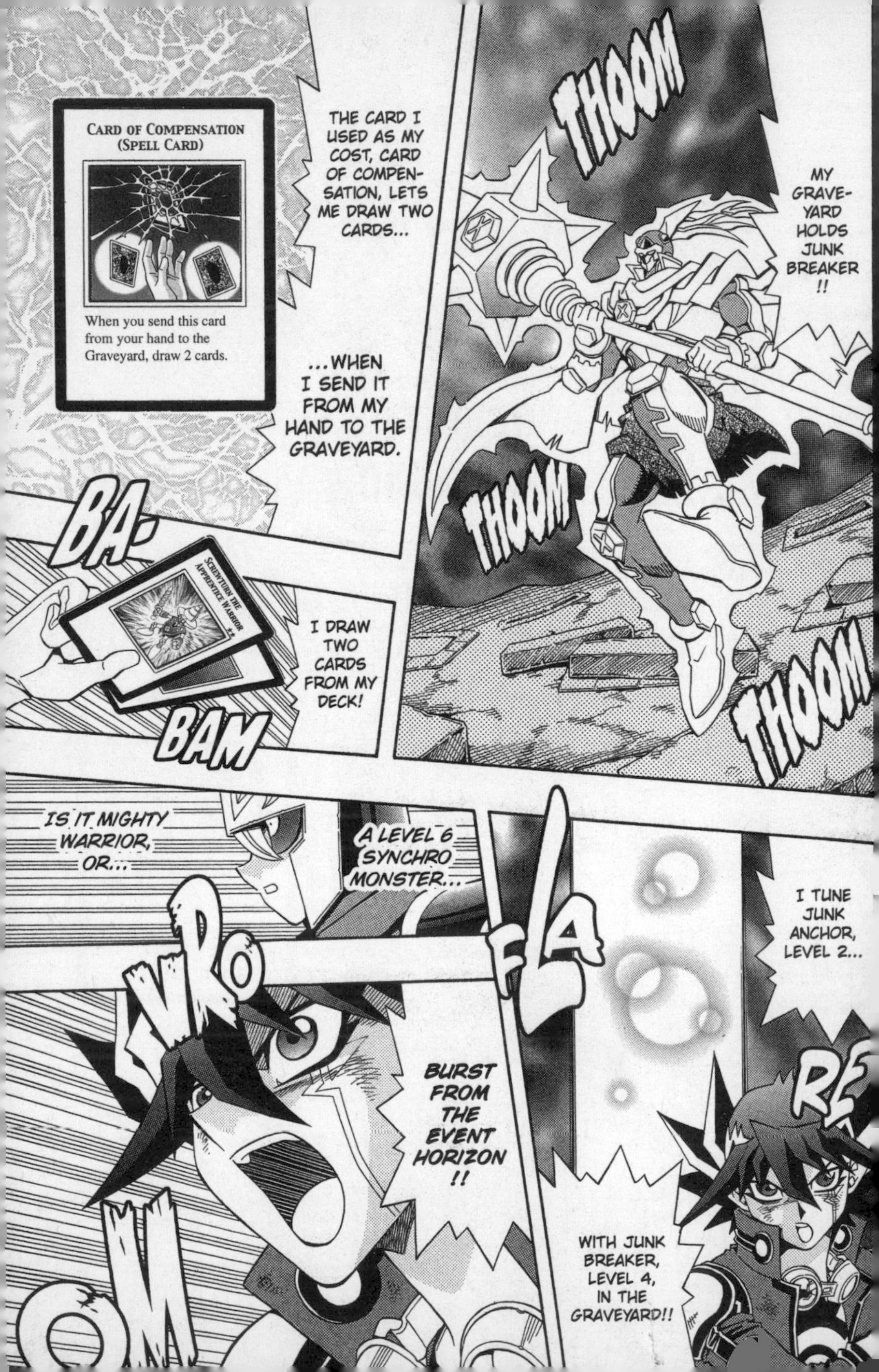
THOOM
MY GRAVEYARD HOLDS JUNK BREAKER!!
THOOM
THOOM
CARD OF COMPENSATION
(SPELL CARD)
When you send this card from your hand to the Graveyard, draw 2 cards.
THE CARD I USED AS MY COST, CARD OF COMPENSATION, LETS ME DRAW TWO CARDS...
...WHEN I SEND IT FROM MY HAND TO THE GRAVEYARD.
BA-
SCREWTURN THE APPRENTICE WARRIOR
I DRAW TWO CARDS FROM MY DECK!
BAM
I TUNE JUNK ANCHOR, LEVEL 2...
RE
WITH JUNK BREAKER, LEVEL 4, IN THE GRAVEYARD!!
FLA
A LEVEL 6 SYNCHRO MONSTER...
IS IT MIGHTY WARRIOR, OR...
VROOM
BURST FROM THE EVENT HORIZON!!

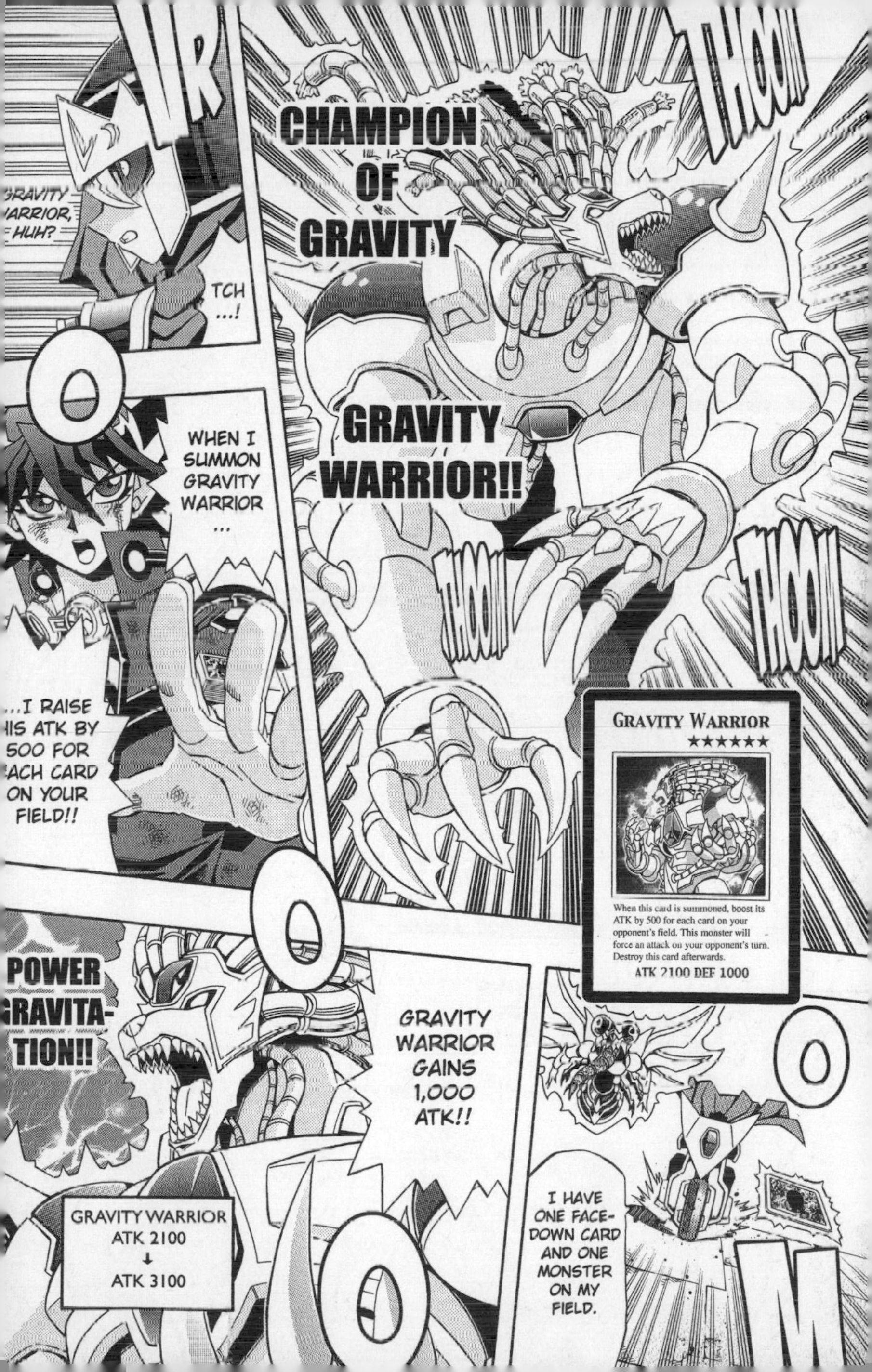
THOOM
CHAMPION OF GRAVITY
GRAVITY WARRIOR!!
THOOM
THOOM
GRAVITY WARRIOR
★★★★★★
When this card is summoned, boost its ATK by 500 for each card on your opponent's field. This monster will force an attack on your opponent's turn. Destroy this card afterwards.
ATK 2100 DEF 1000
VR
GRAVITY WARRIOR, HUH?
TCH ...!
WHEN I SUMMON GRAVITY WARRIOR ...
...I RAISE HIS ATK BY 500 FOR EACH CARD ON YOUR FIELD!!
I HAVE ONE FACE-DOWN CARD AND ONE MONSTER ON MY FIELD.
M
GRAVITY WARRIOR GAINS 1,000 ATK!!
POWER GRAVITA-TION!!
GRAVITY WARRIOR ATK 2100 ↓ ATK 3100

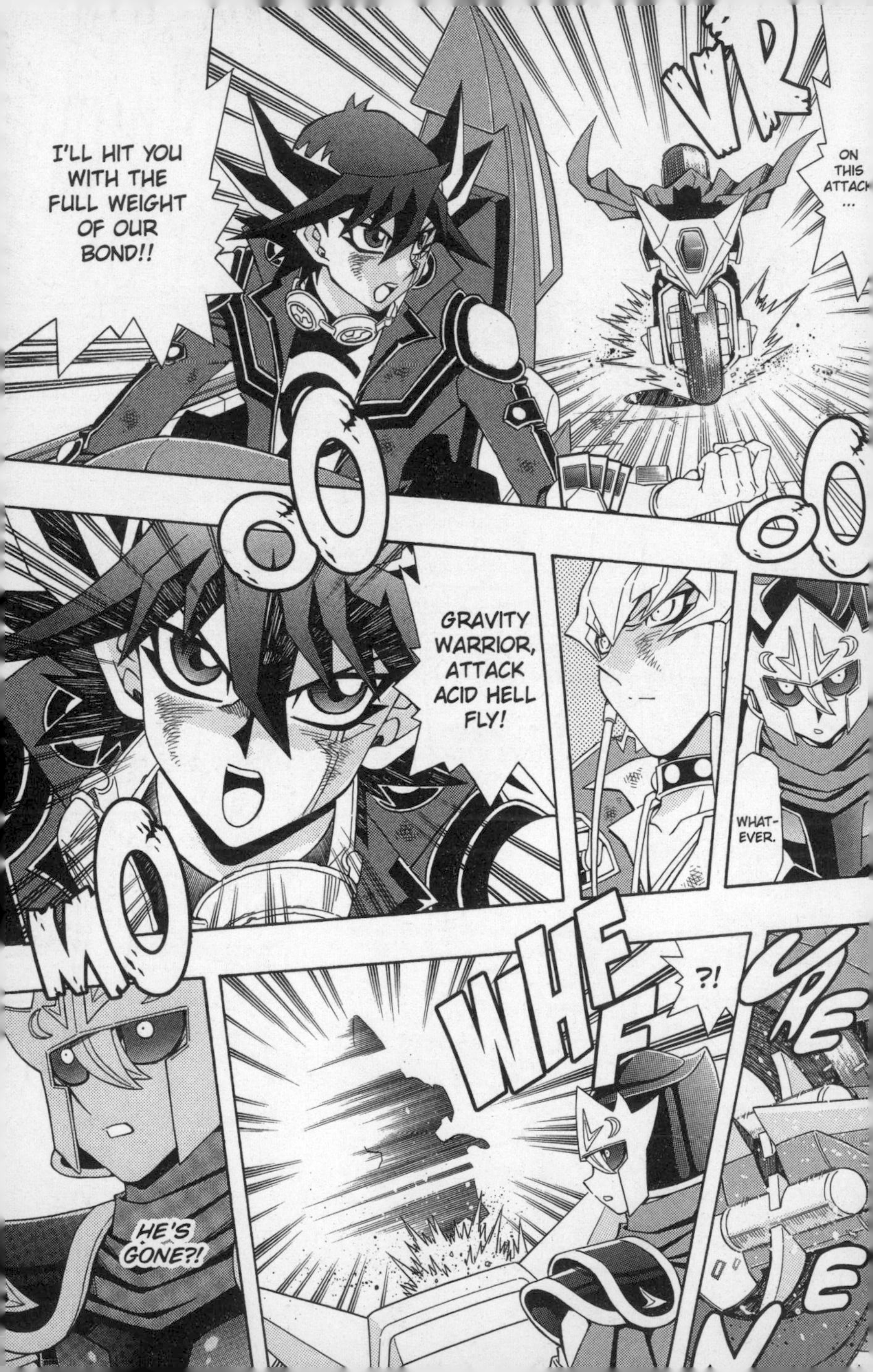
VR
ON THIS ATTACK...
I'LL HIT YOU WITH THE FULL WEIGHT OF OUR BOND!!
WHAT-EVER.
GRAVITY WARRIOR, ATTACK ACID HELL FLY!
MOOO
?!
WHFF
HE'S GONE?!

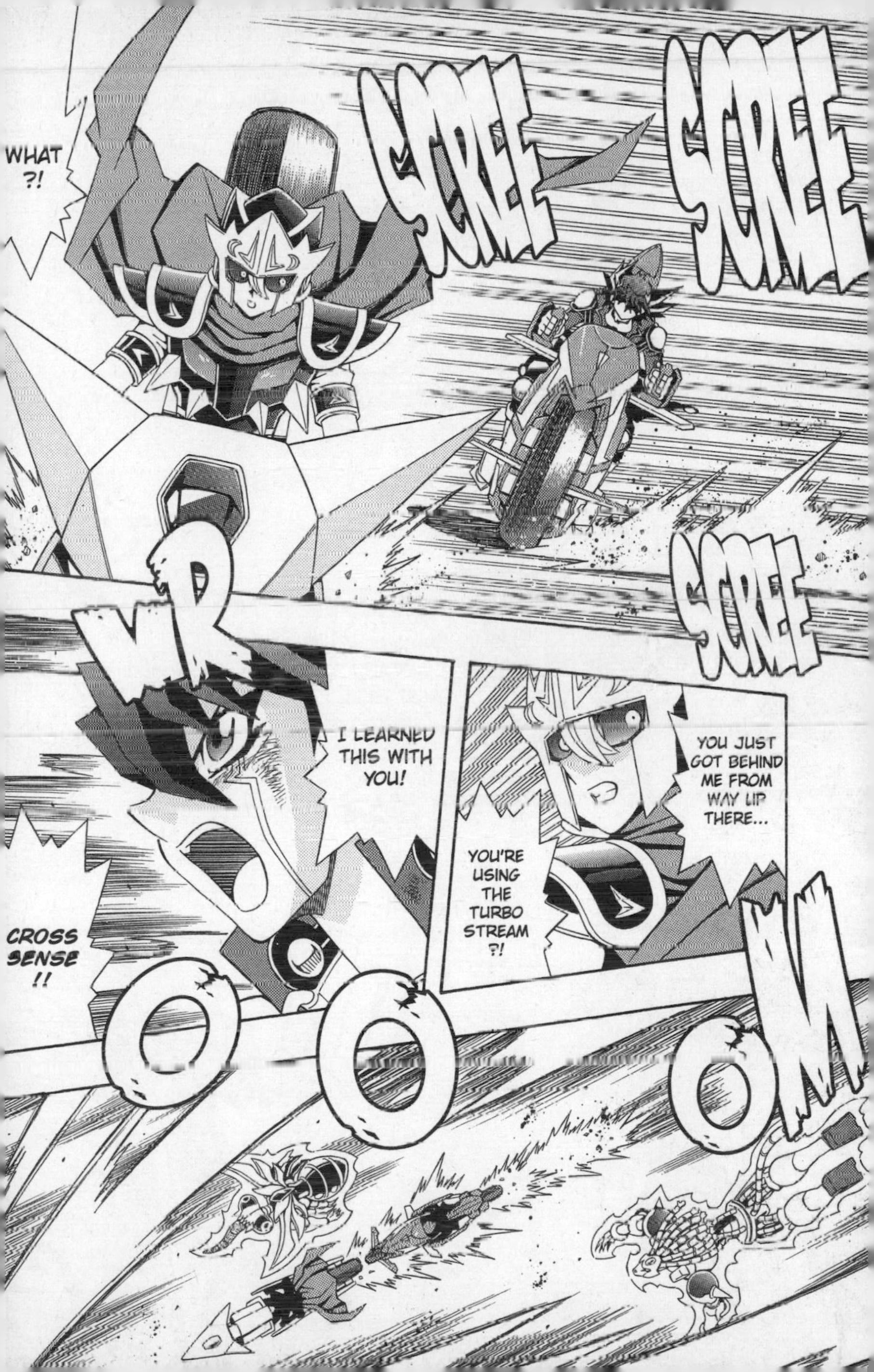
SCREE
SCREE
WHAT ?!
SCREE
YOU JUST GOT BEHIND ME FROM WAY UP THERE...
YOU'RE USING THE TURBO STREAM ?!
I LEARNED THIS WITH YOU!
CROSS SENSE !!
VROOOM

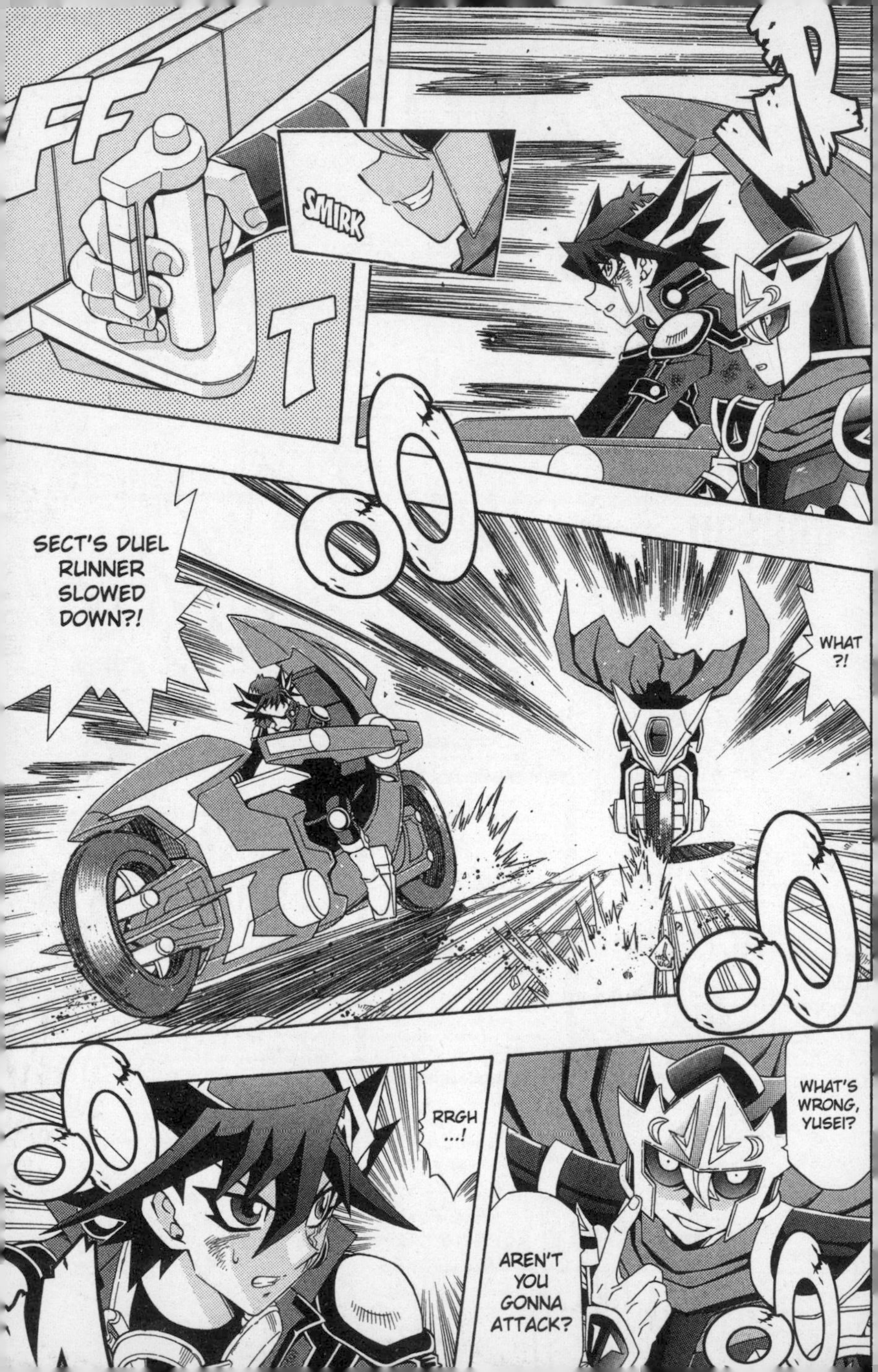
SMIRK
WHAT ?!
SECT'S DUEL RUNNER SLOWED DOWN?!
WHAT'S WRONG, YUSEI?
AREN'T YOU GONNA ATTACK?
RRGH ...!

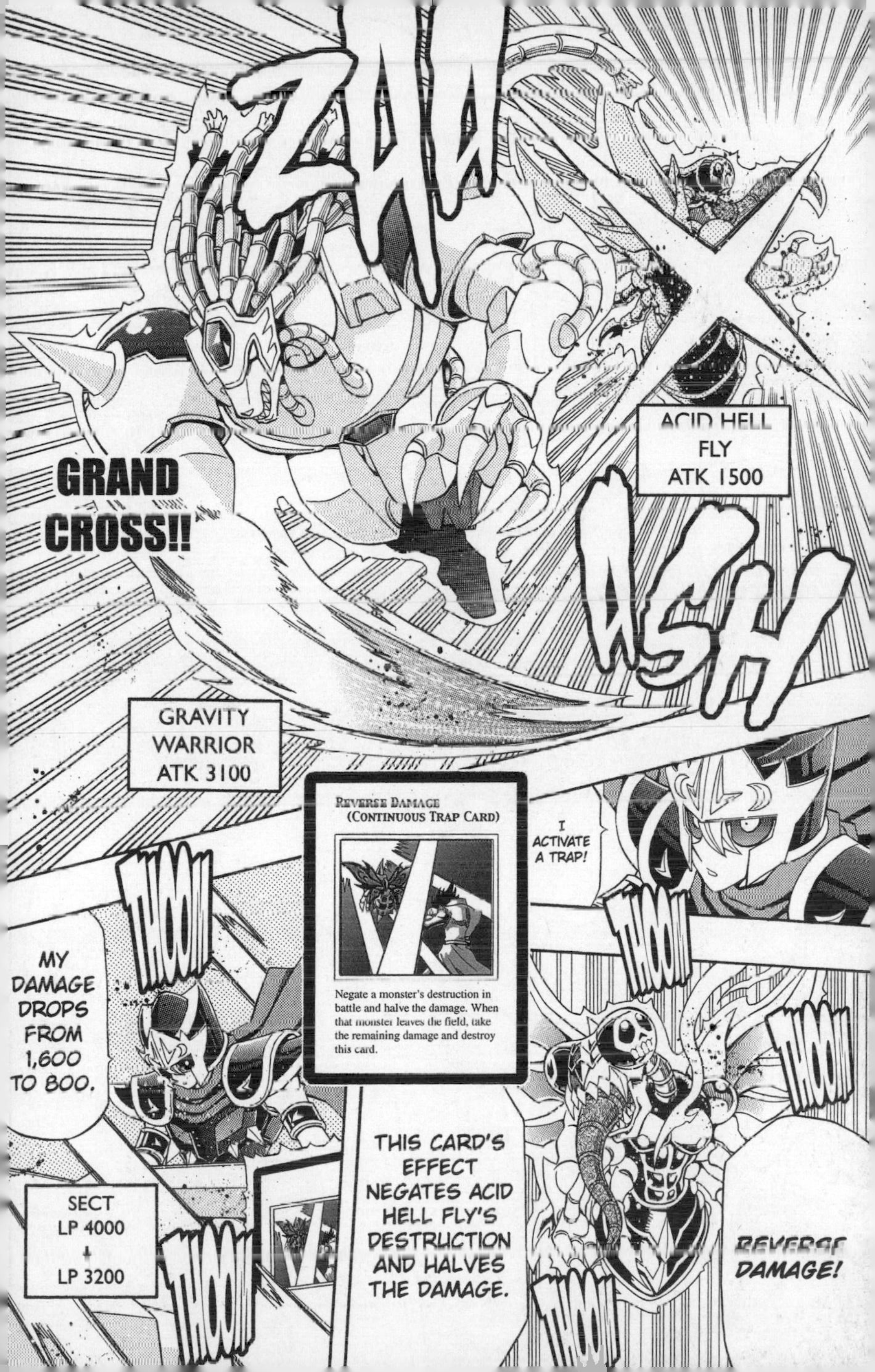
ZAA
ASH
ACID HELL FLY ATK 1500
GRAND CROSS!!
GRAVITY WARRIOR ATK 3100
I ACTIVATE A TRAP!
THOOM
REVERSE DAMAGE (CONTINUOUS TRAP CARD)
Negate a monster's destruction in battle and halve the damage. When that monster leaves the field, take the remaining damage and destroy this card.
THOOM
MY DAMAGE DROPS FROM 1,600 TO 800.
THOOM
REVERSE DAMAGE!
THIS CARD'S EFFECT NEGATES ACID HELL FLY'S DESTRUCTION AND HALVES THE DAMAGE.
THOOM
SECT LP 4000 → LP 3200
THOOM

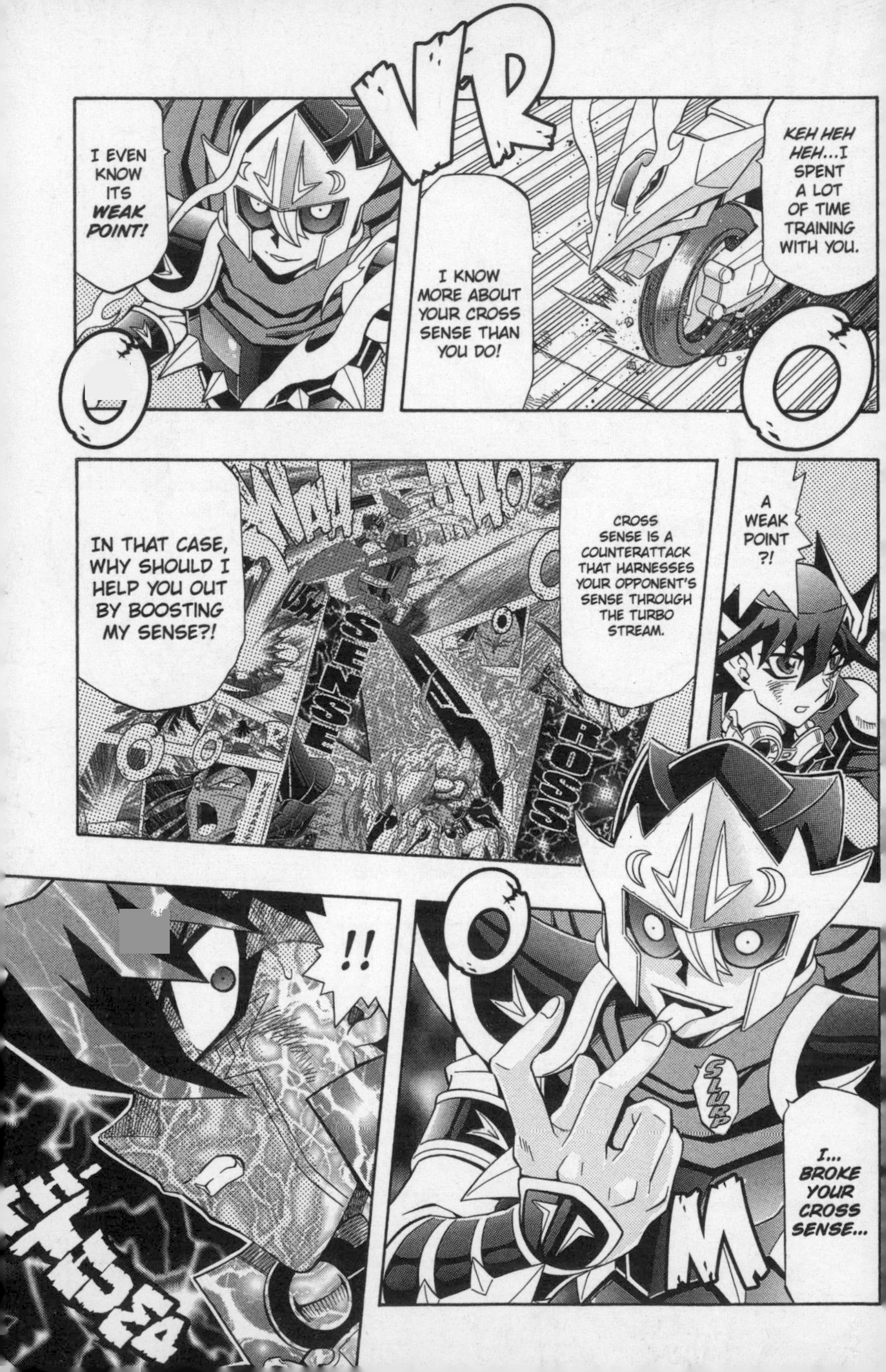
VR
KEH HEH HEH...I SPENT A LOT OF TIME TRAINING WITH YOU.
I KNOW MORE ABOUT YOUR CROSS SENSE THAN YOU DO!
I EVEN KNOW ITS WEAK POINT!
A WEAK POINT ?!
CROSS SENSE IS A COUNTERATTACK THAT HARNESSES YOUR OPPONENT'S SENSE THROUGH THE TURBO STREAM.
SENSE
IN THAT CASE, WHY SHOULD I HELP YOU OUT BY BOOSTING MY SENSE?!
SLURP
I... BROKE YOUR CROSS SENSE...
!!

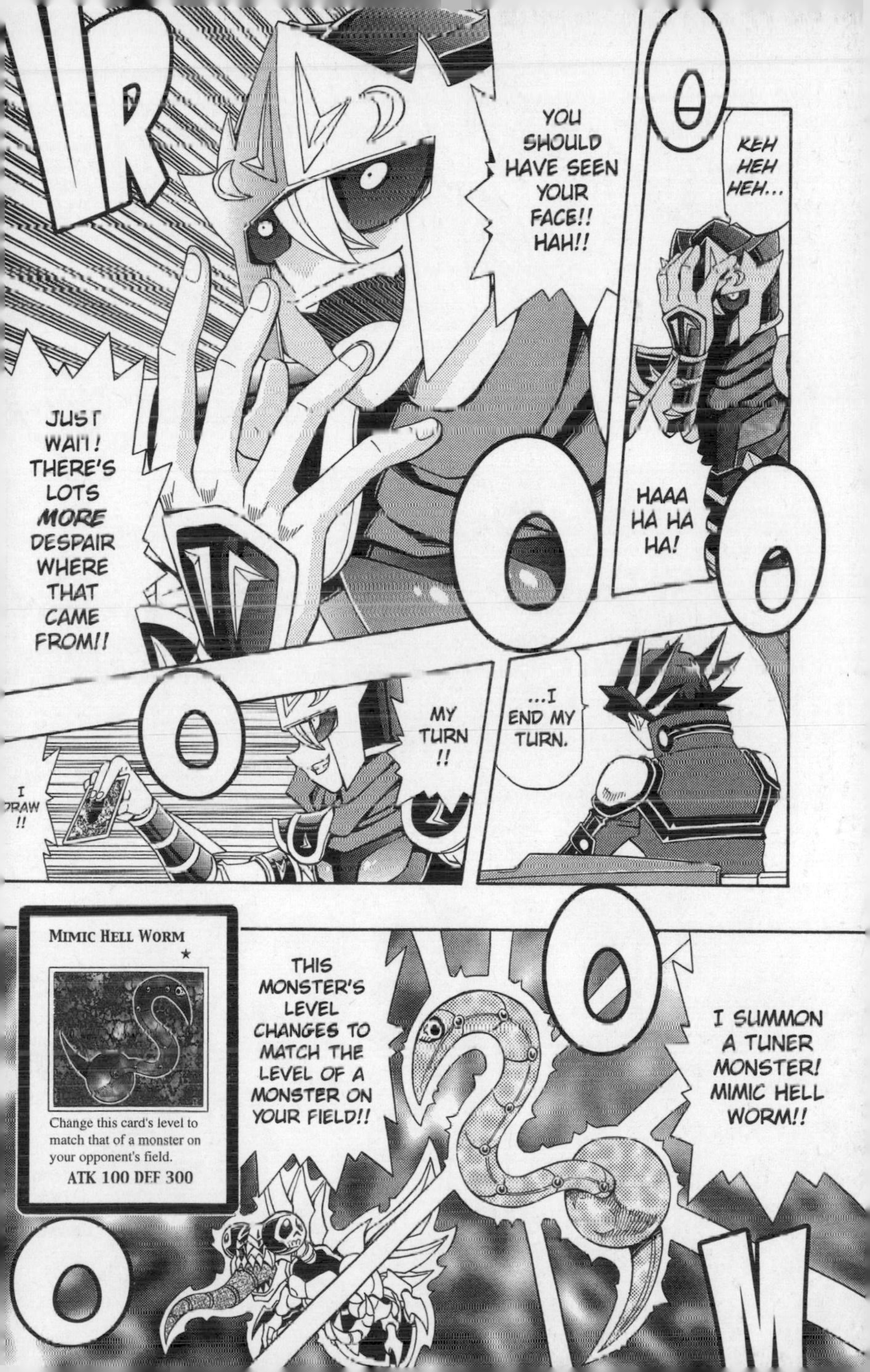
KEH HEH HEH...
HAAA HA HA HA!
YOU SHOULD HAVE SEEN YOUR FACE!! HAH!!
JUST WAIT! THERE'S LOTS MORE DESPAIR WHERE THAT CAME FROM!!
...I END MY TURN.
MY TURN!!
I DRAW!!
I SUMMON A TUNER MONSTER! MIMIC HELL WORM!!
THIS MONSTER'S LEVEL CHANGES TO MATCH THE LEVEL OF A MONSTER ON YOUR FIELD!!
MIMIC HELL WORM
Change this card's level to match that of a monster on your opponent's field.
ATK 100 DEF 300

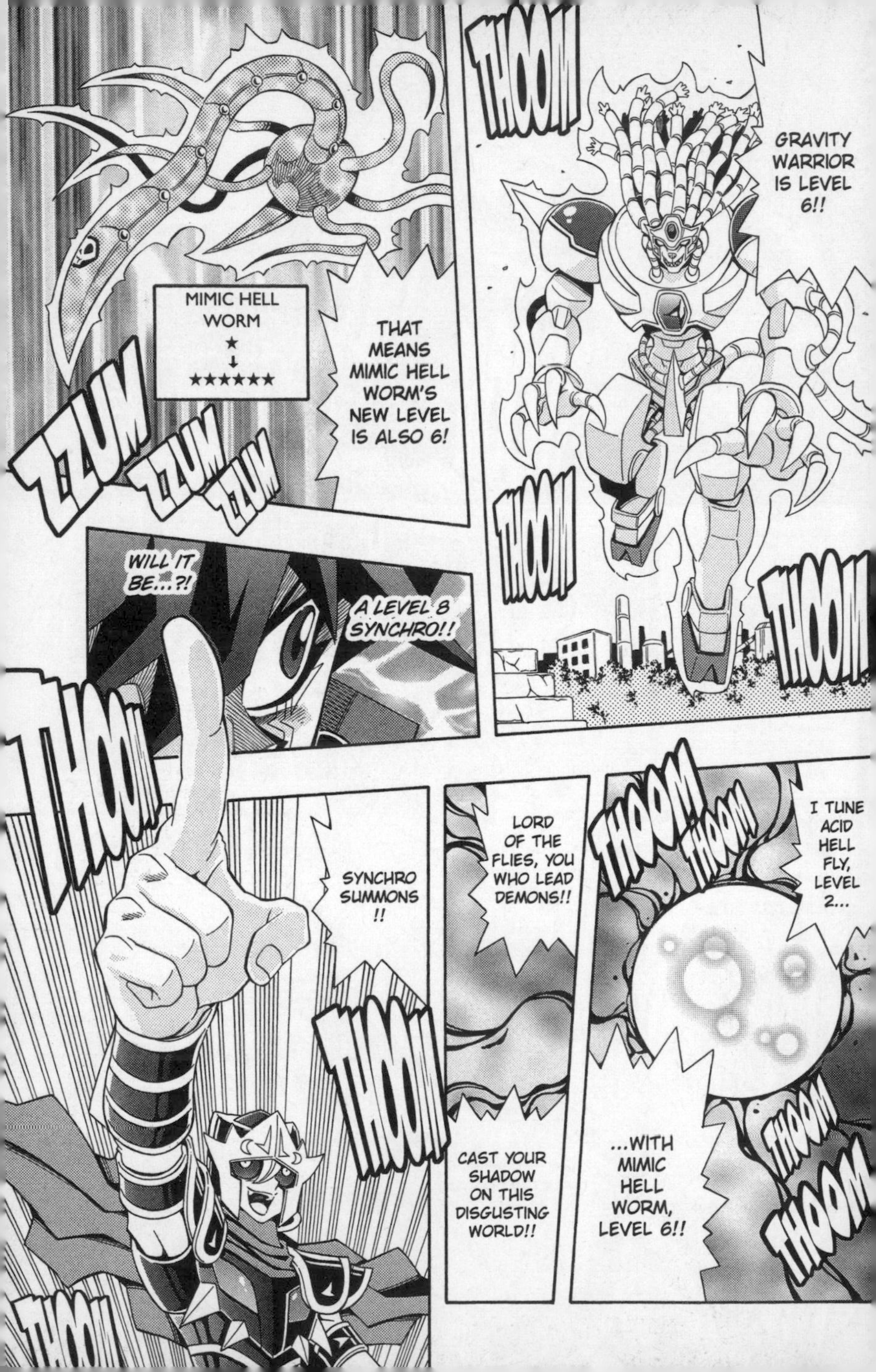
THOOM
GRAVITY WARRIOR IS LEVEL 6!!
THOOM
THOOM
THAT MEANS MIMIC HELL WORM'S NEW LEVEL IS ALSO 6!
MIMIC HELL WORM ★ ↓ ★★★★★★
ZZUM
ZZUM
ZZUM
A LEVEL 8 SYNCHRO!!
WILL IT BE...?!
THOOM
THOOM
THOOM
I TUNE ACID HELL FLY, LEVEL 2...
THOOM
THOOM
...WITH MIMIC HELL WORM, LEVEL 6!!
LORD OF THE FLIES, YOU WHO LEAD DEMONS!!
CAST YOUR SHADOW ON THIS DISGUSTING WORLD!!
SYNCHRO SUMMONS !!
THOOM
THOOM

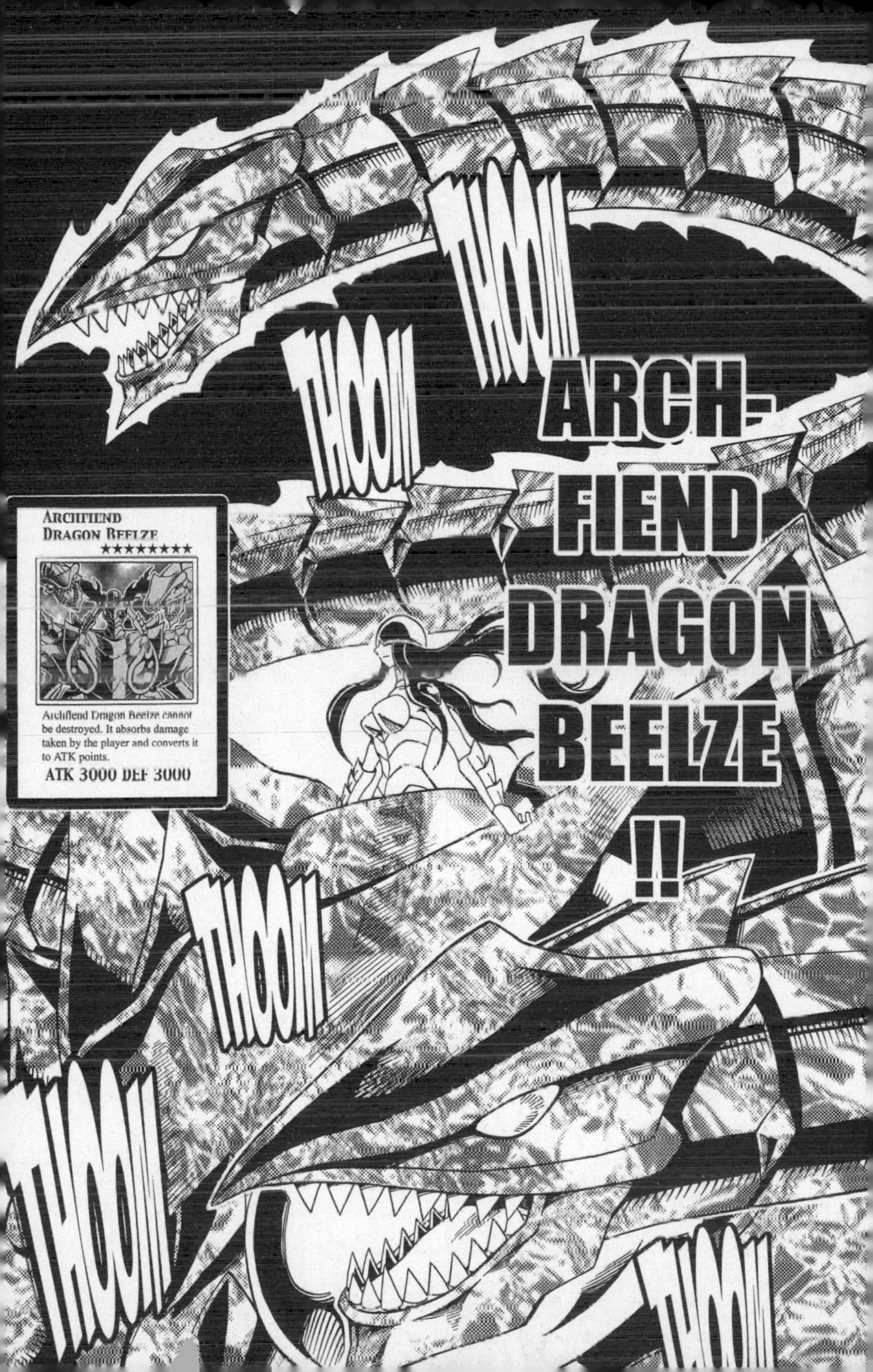
THOOM
THOOM
ARCH-FIEND DRAGON BEELZE!!
ARCHFIEND DRAGON BEELZE
Archfiend Dragon Beelze cannot be destroyed. It absorbs damage taken by the player and converts it to ATK points.
ATK 3000 DEF 3000
THOOM
THOOM
THOOM

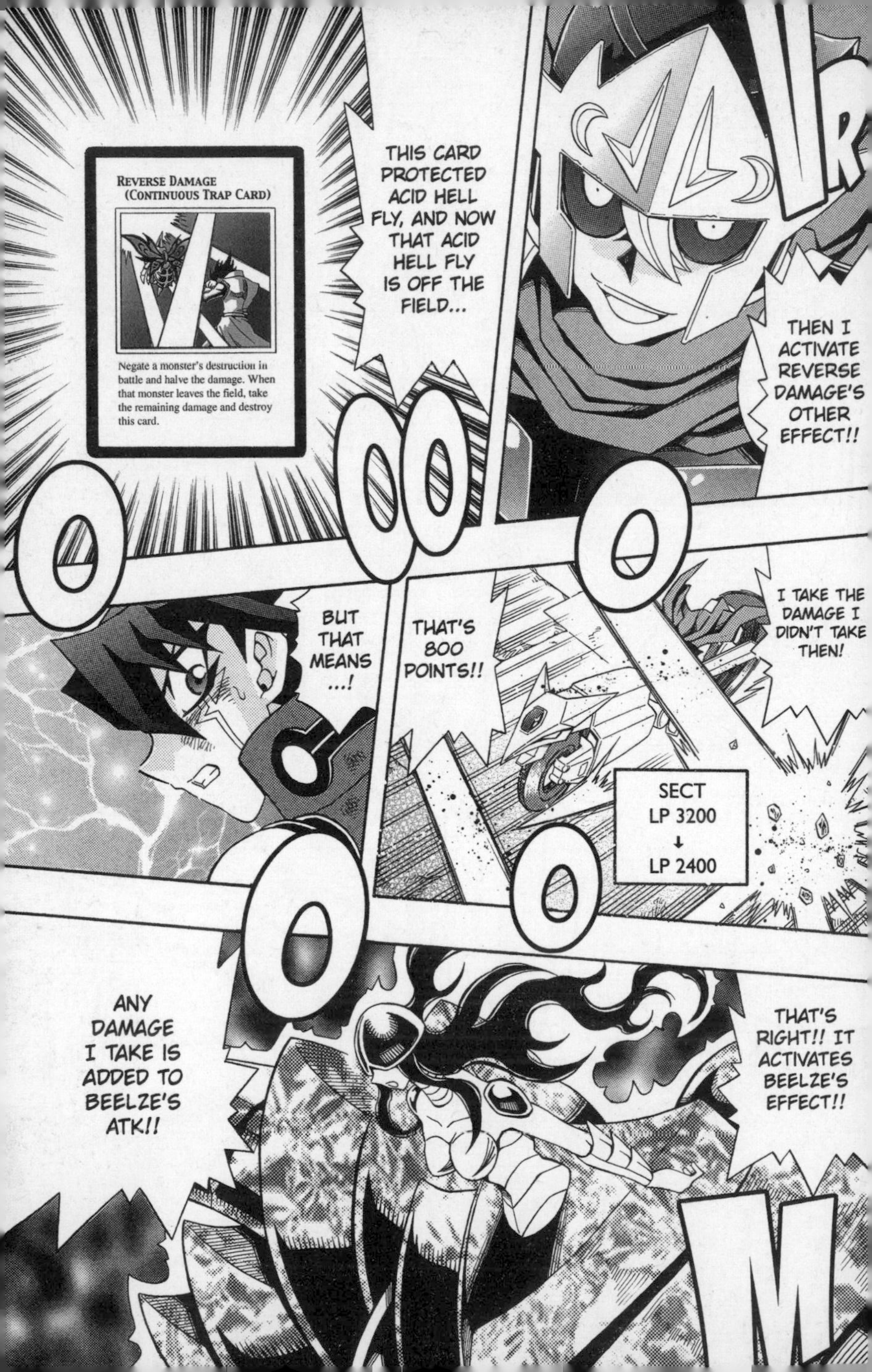
THIS CARD PROTECTED ACID HELL FLY, AND NOW THAT ACID HELL FLY IS OFF THE FIELD...
THEN I ACTIVATE REVERSE DAMAGE'S OTHER EFFECT!!
REVERSE DAMAGE
(CONTINUOUS TRAP CARD)
Negate a monster's destruction in battle and halve the damage. When that monster leaves the field, take the remaining damage and destroy this card.
I TAKE THE DAMAGE I DIDN'T TAKE THEN!
THAT'S 800 POINTS!!
SECT
LP 3200
↓
LP 2400
BUT THAT MEANS ...!
THAT'S RIGHT!! IT ACTIVATES BEELZE'S EFFECT!!
ANY DAMAGE I TAKE IS ADDED TO BEELZE'S ATK!!

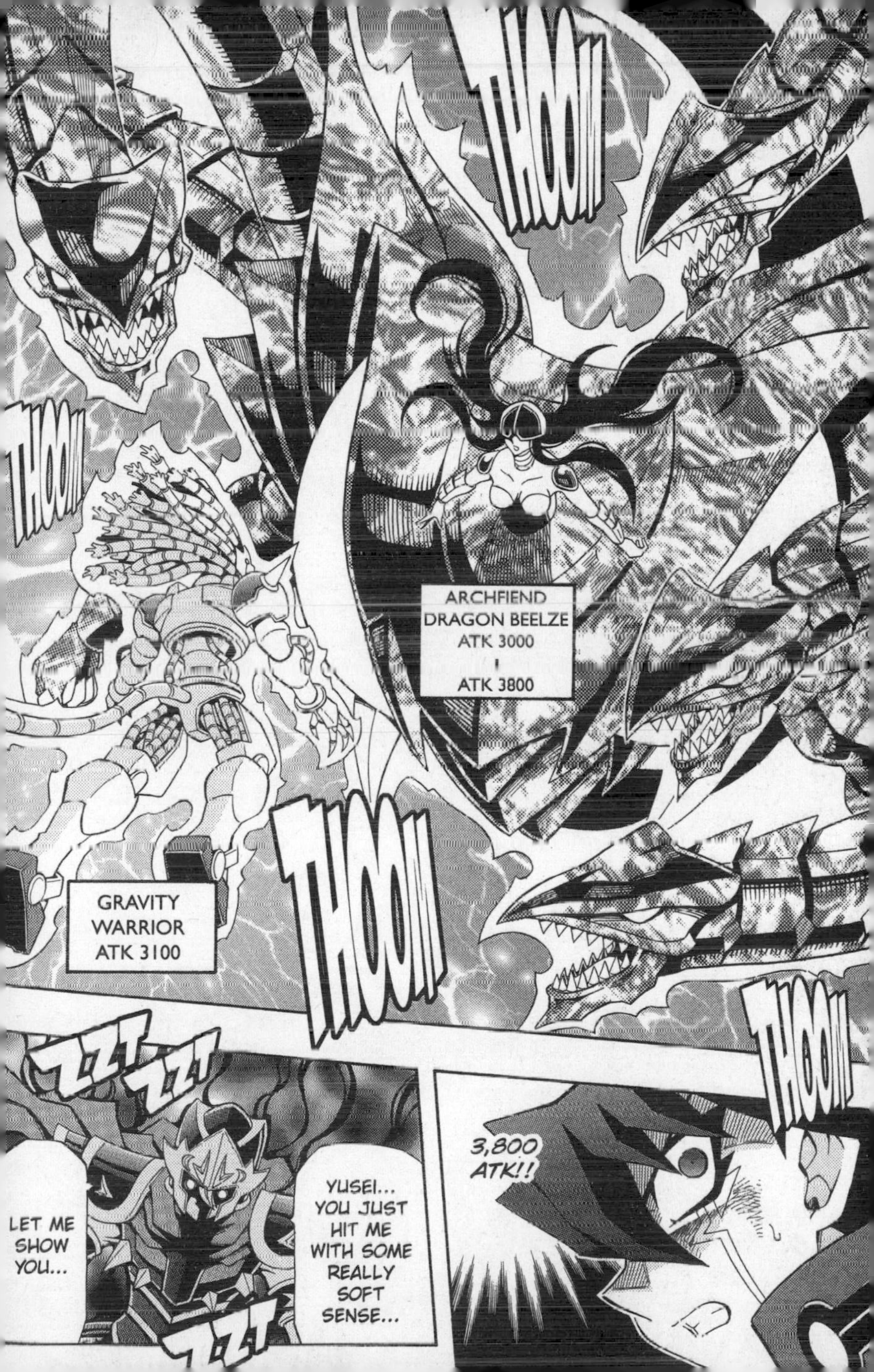
THOOM
ARCHFIEND DRAGON BEELZE ATK 3000
↓
ATK 3800
THOOM
THOOM
GRAVITY WARRIOR ATK 3100
THOOM
3,800 ATK!!
YUSEI... YOU JUST HIT ME WITH SOME REALLY SOFT SENSE...
LET ME SHOW YOU...
ZZZT
ZZZT
ZZZT

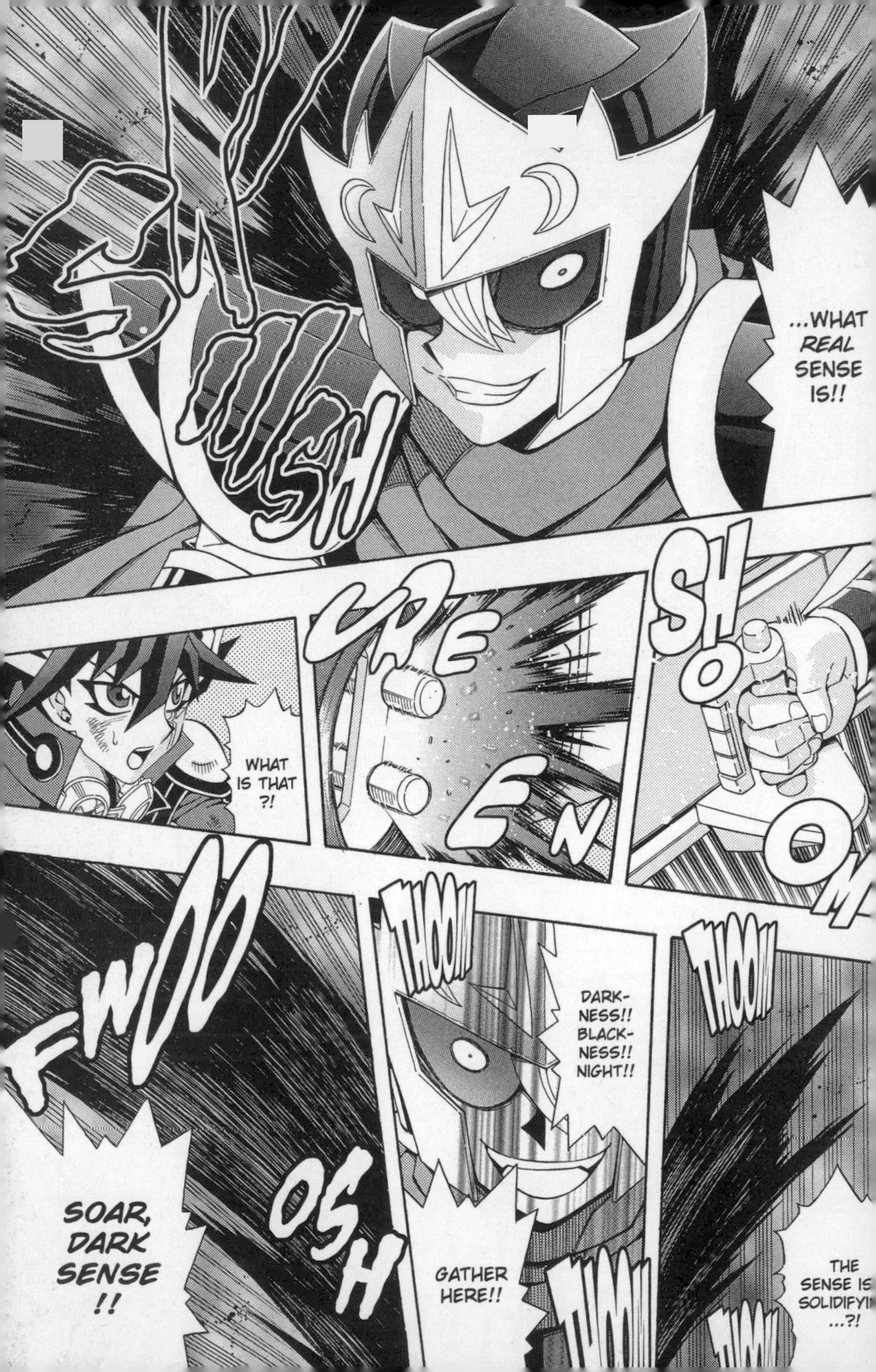
...WHAT REAL SENSE IS!!
SWISH
SHOOM
CREEN
WHAT IS THAT ?!
THOOM
THE SENSE IS SOLIDIFYI ...?!
THOOM
DARK-NESS!! BLACK-NESS!! NIGHT!!
GATHER HERE!!
FWOOSH
SOAR, DARK SENSE !!

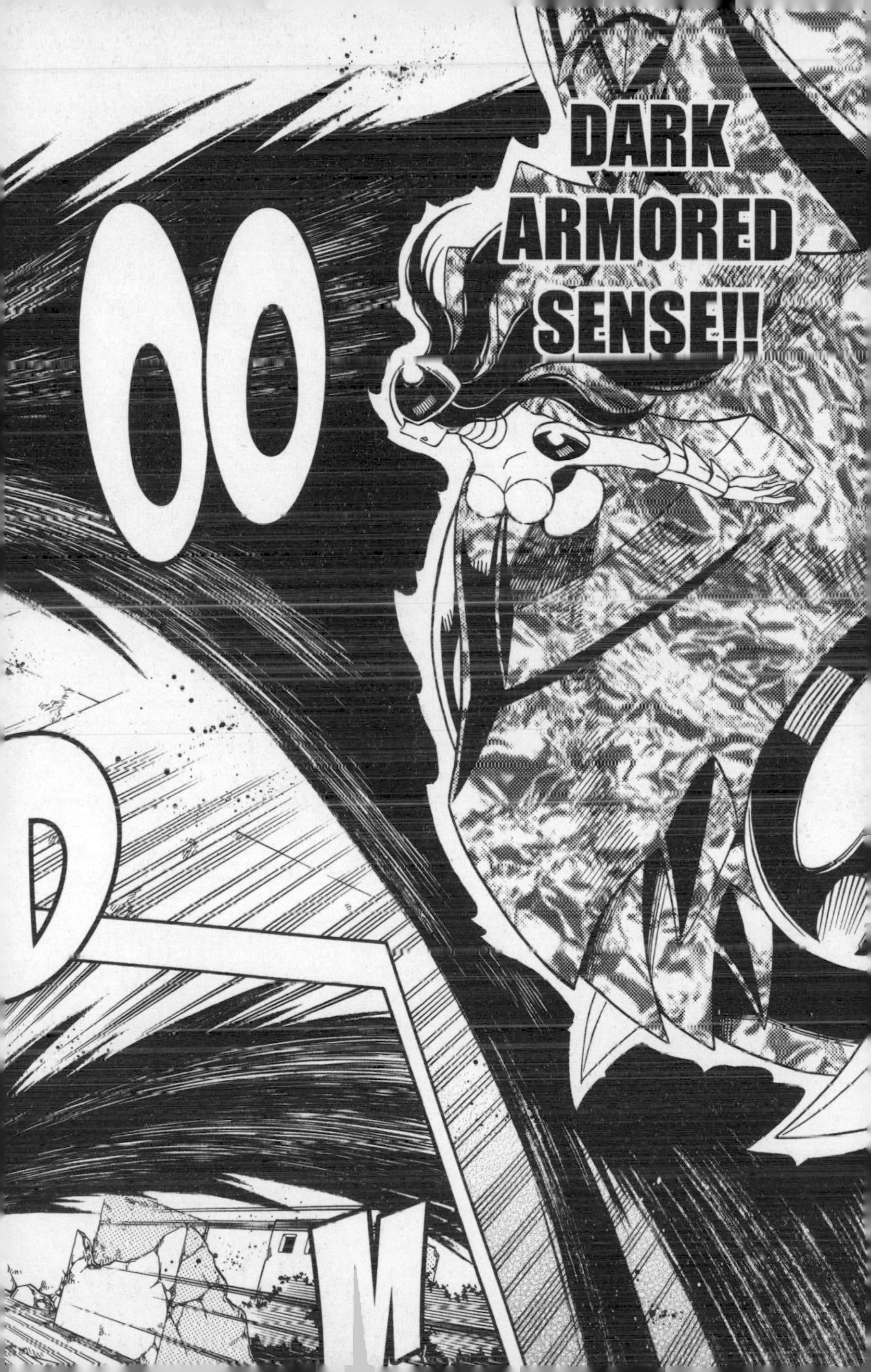
DARK ARMORED SENSE!!

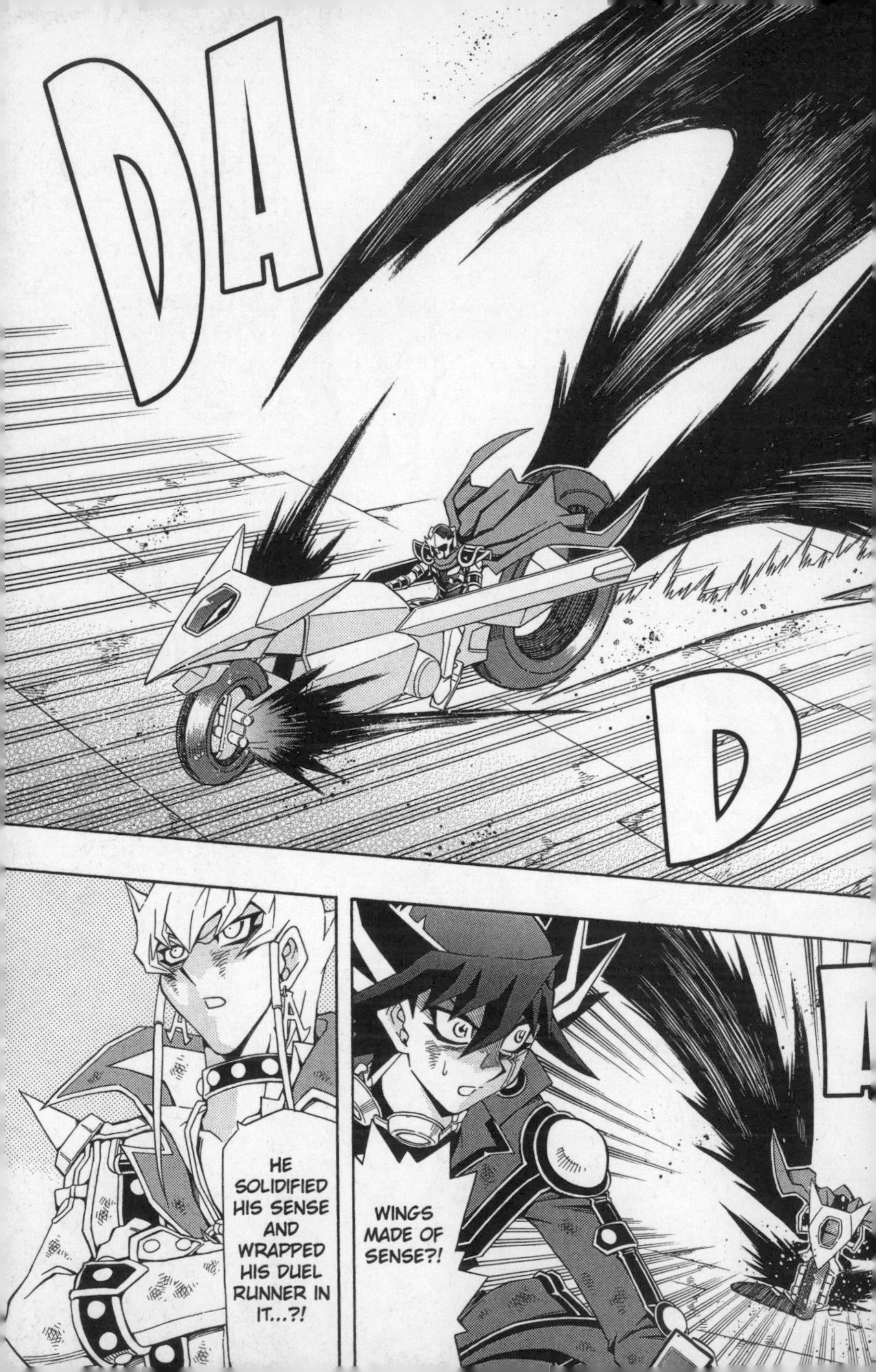
DA
D
A
WINGS MADE OF SENSE?!
HE SOLIDIFIED HIS SENSE AND WRAPPED HIS DUEL RUNNER IN IT...?!

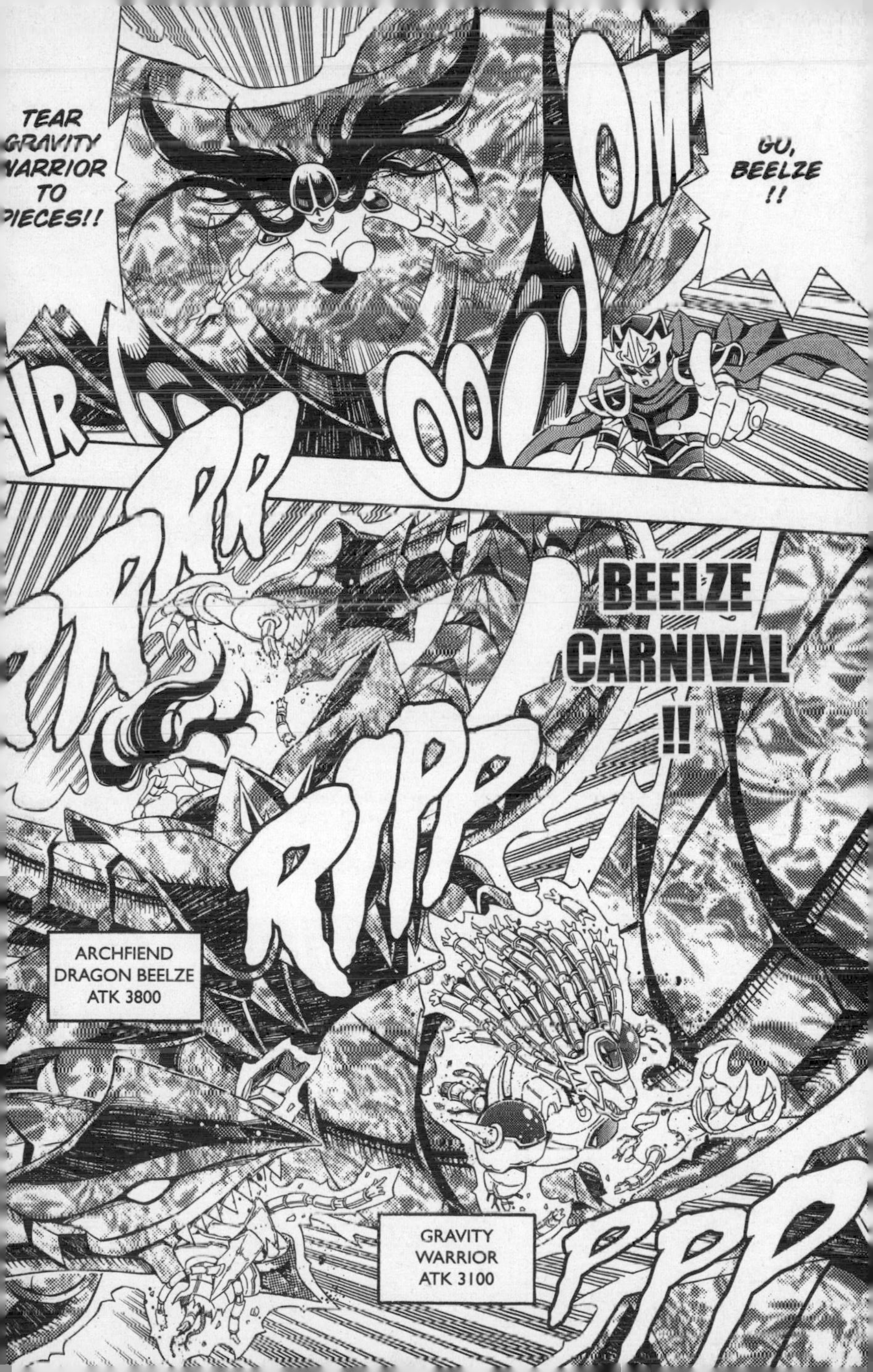

GO, BEELZE!!
VROOOOM
TEAR GRAVITY WARRIOR TO PIECES!!
BEELZE CARNIVAL!!
RIPP
PPPP
RRR
GRAVITY WARRIOR ATK 3100
ARCHFIEND DRAGON BEELZE ATK 3800

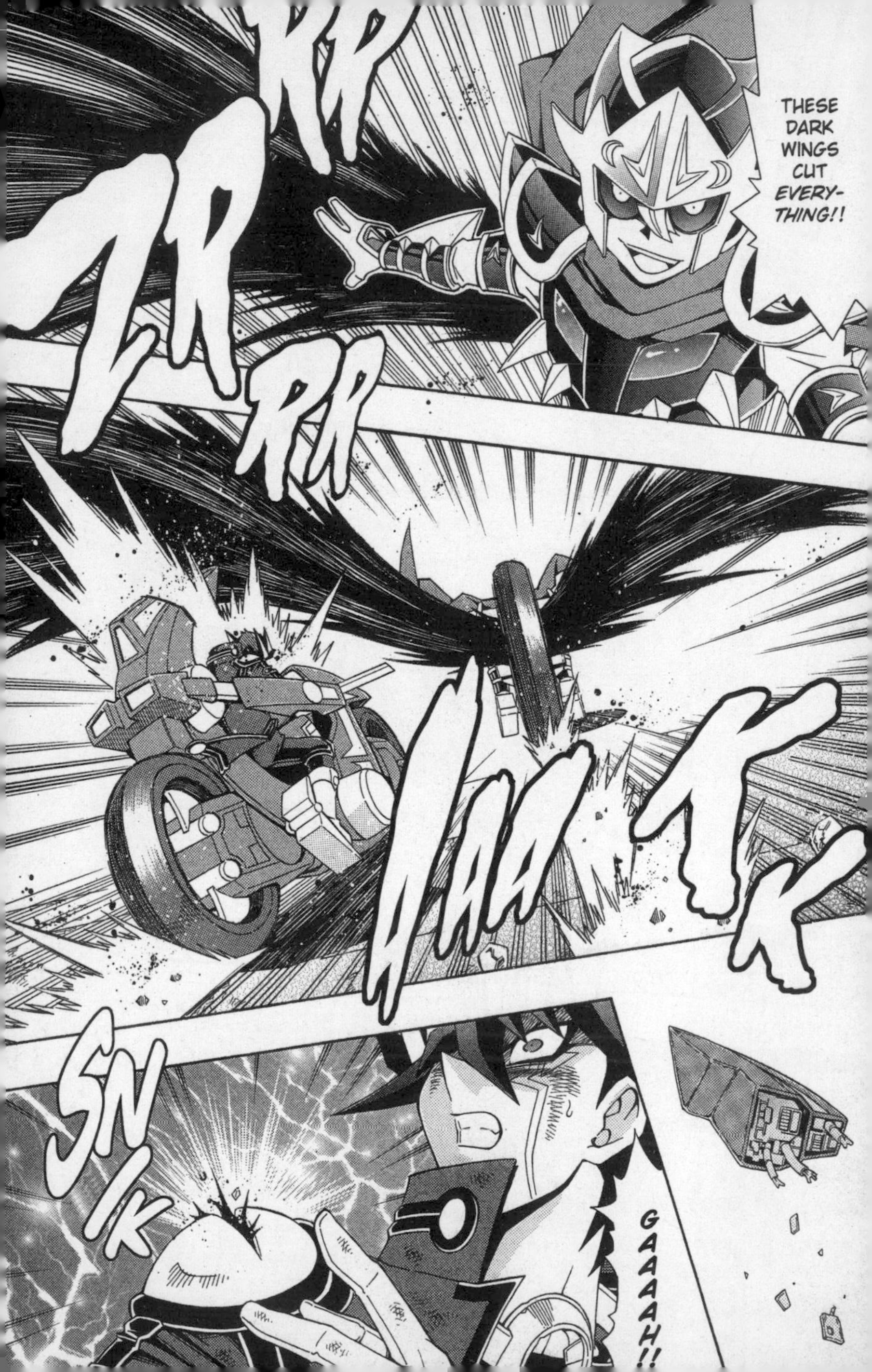
THESE DARK WINGS CUT EVERYTHING!!
ZRRRRP
WHAAAK
SNIK
GAAAAAH!!

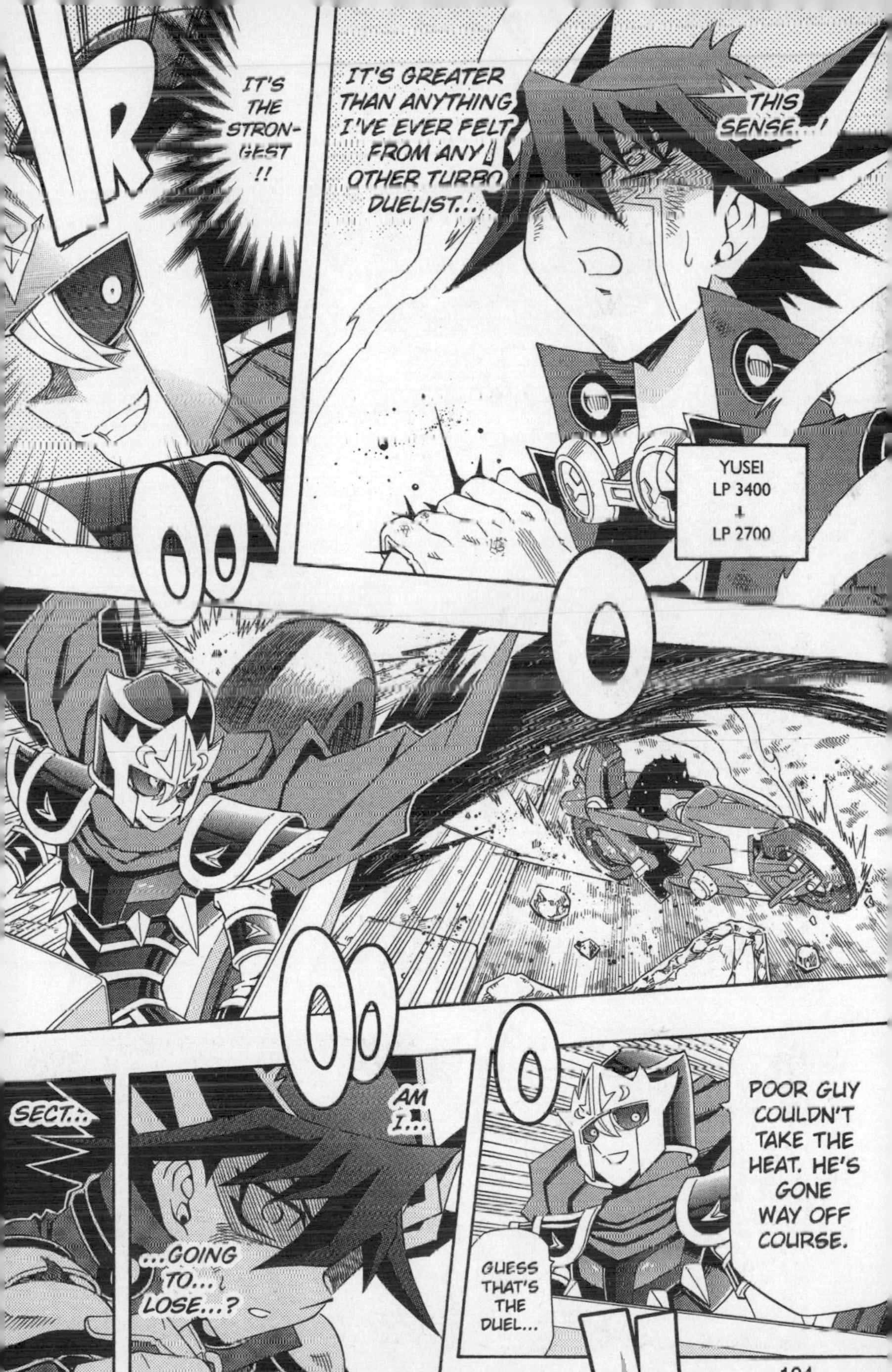
THIS SENSE...!
IT'S GREATER THAN ANYTHING I'VE EVER FELT FROM ANY OTHER TURBO DUELIST...!
YUSEI LP 3400 ↓ LP 2700
IT'S THE STRONGEST!!
POOR GUY COULDN'T TAKE THE HEAT. HE'S GONE WAY OFF COURSE.
GUESS THAT'S THE DUEL...
AM I...
...GOING TO... LOSE...?
SECT...

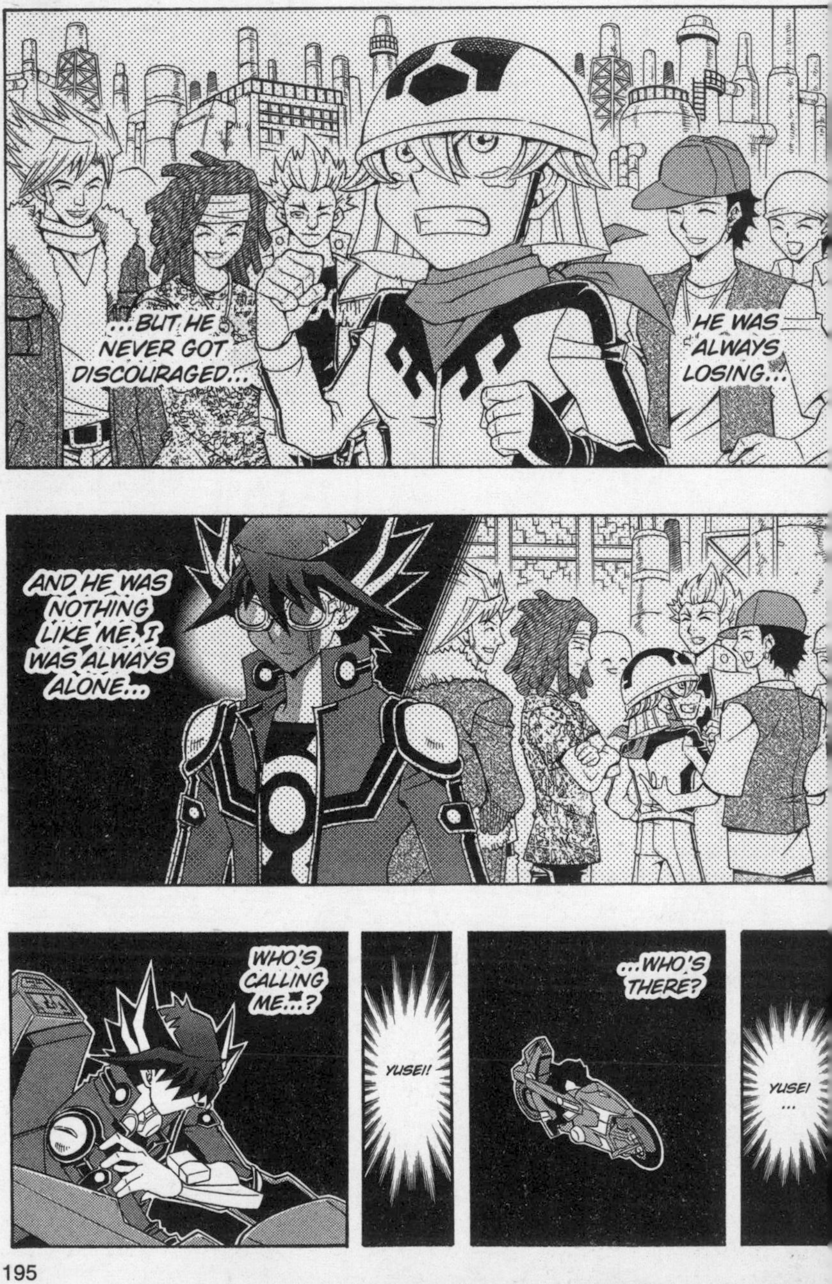
HE WAS ALWAYS LOSING...
...BUT HE NEVER GOT DISCOURAGED...
AND HE WAS NOTHING LIKE ME. I WAS ALWAYS ALONE...
YUSEI ...
...WHO'S THERE?
YUSEI!
WHO'S CALLING ME...?

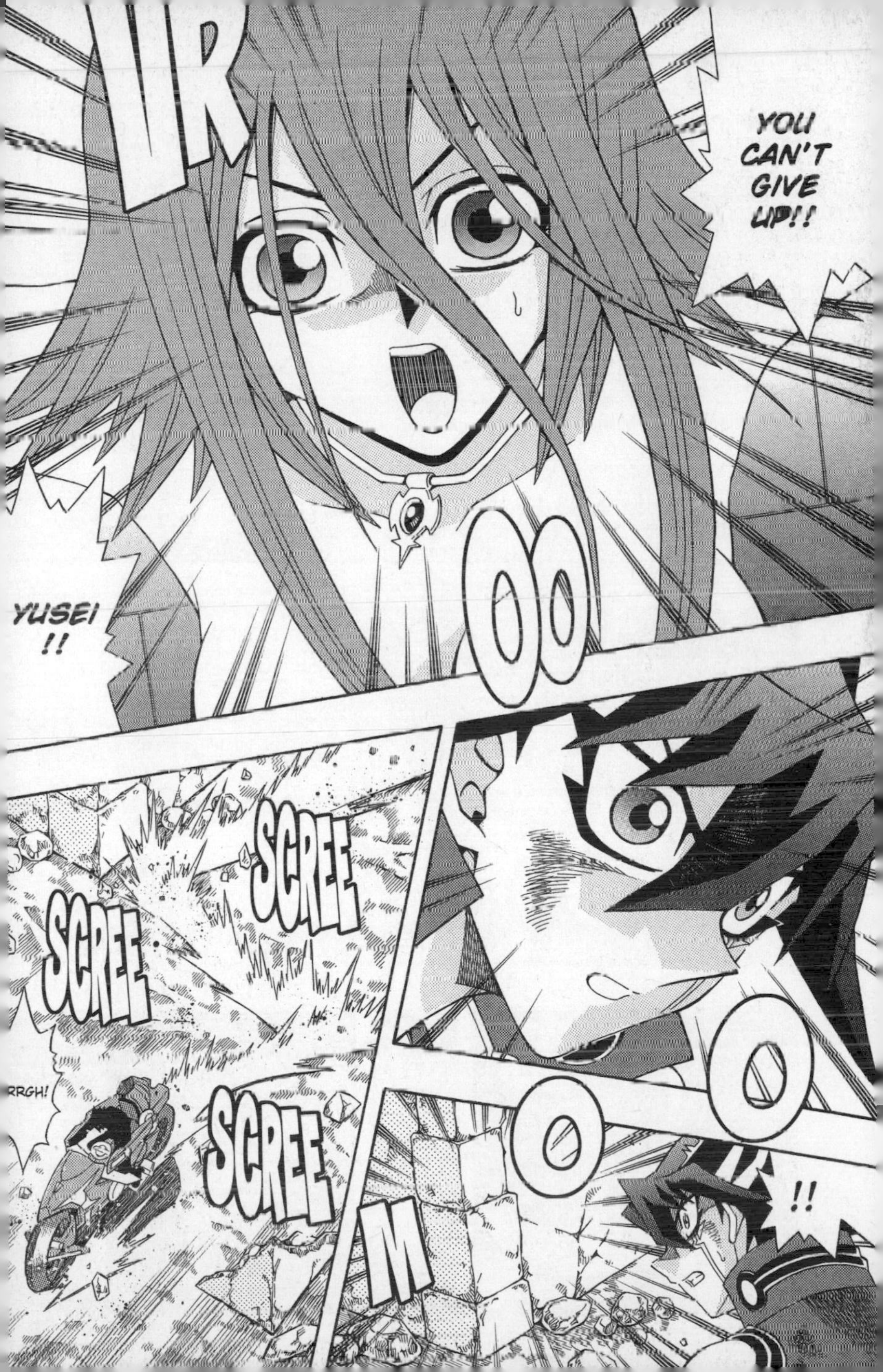
VR
YOU CAN'T GIVE UP!!
YUSEI !!
OO
OO
SCREE
SCREE
SCREE
RRGH!
!!
M

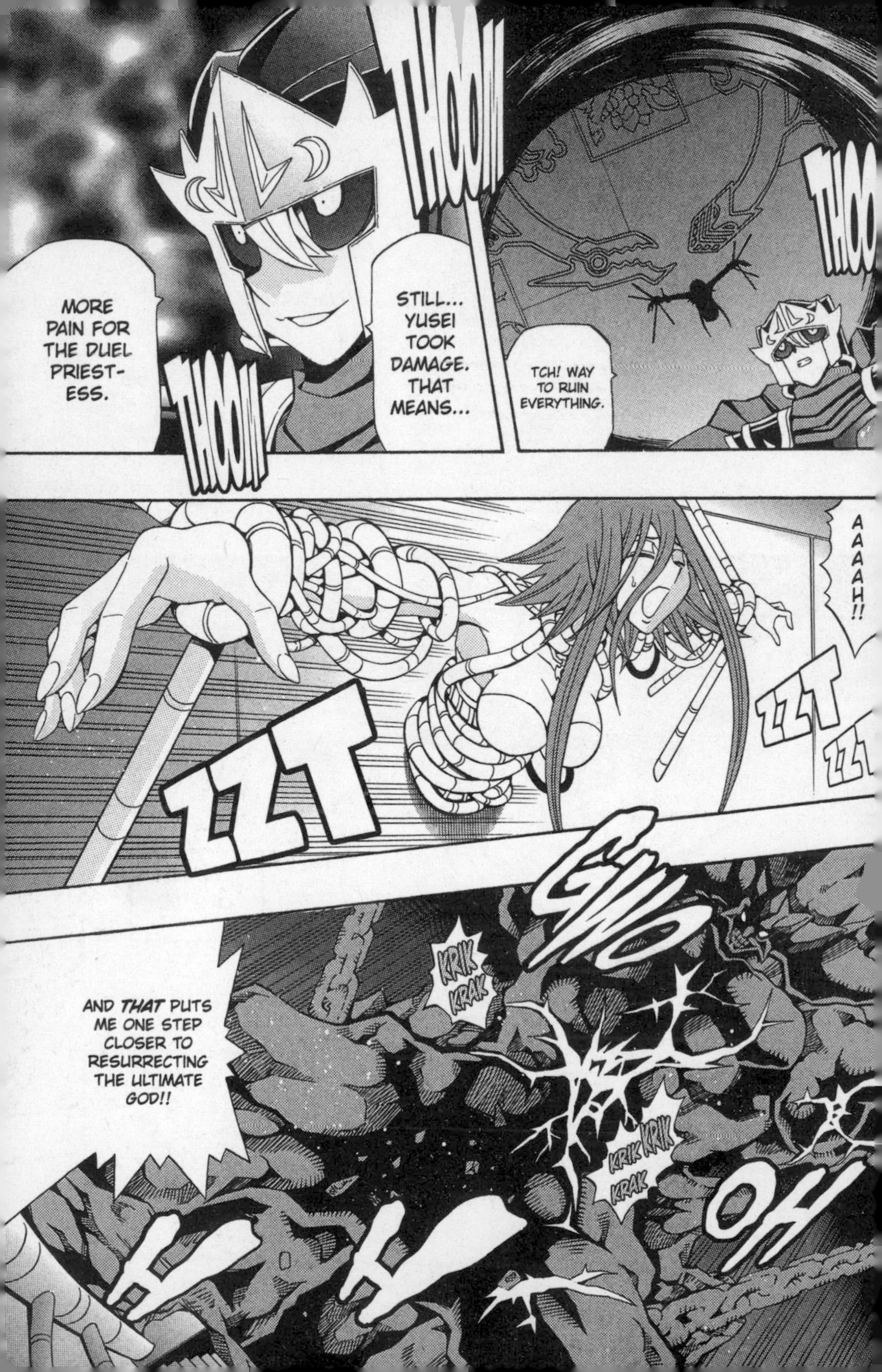
THOOM
TCH! WAY TO RUIN EVERYTHING.
THOOM
STILL... YUSEI TOOK DAMAGE. THAT MEANS...
MORE PAIN FOR THE DUEL PRIEST-ESS.
THOOM
AAAAAH!!
ZZT
ZZT
ZZT
GWO
KRIK KRAK
AND *THAT* PUTS ME ONE STEP CLOSER TO RESURRECTING THE ULTIMATE GOD!!
KRIK KRIK KRAK
OH

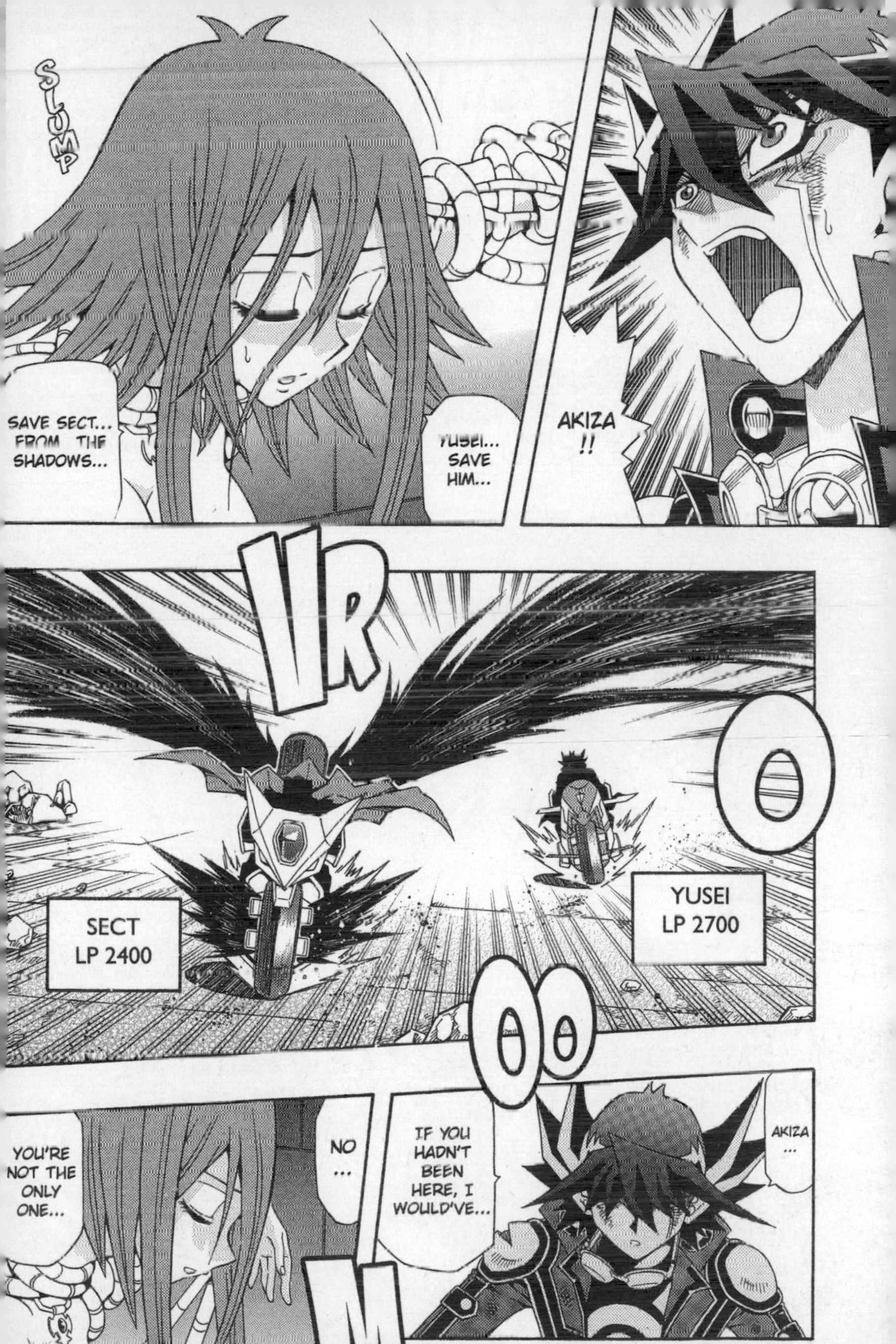
AKIZA !!
SLUMP
YUSEI... SAVE HIM...
SAVE SECT... FROM THE SHADOWS...
VROOOM
YUSEI LP 2700
SECT LP 2400
AKIZA ...
IF YOU HADN'T BEEN HERE, I WOULD'VE...
NO ...
YOU'RE NOT THE ONLY ONE...

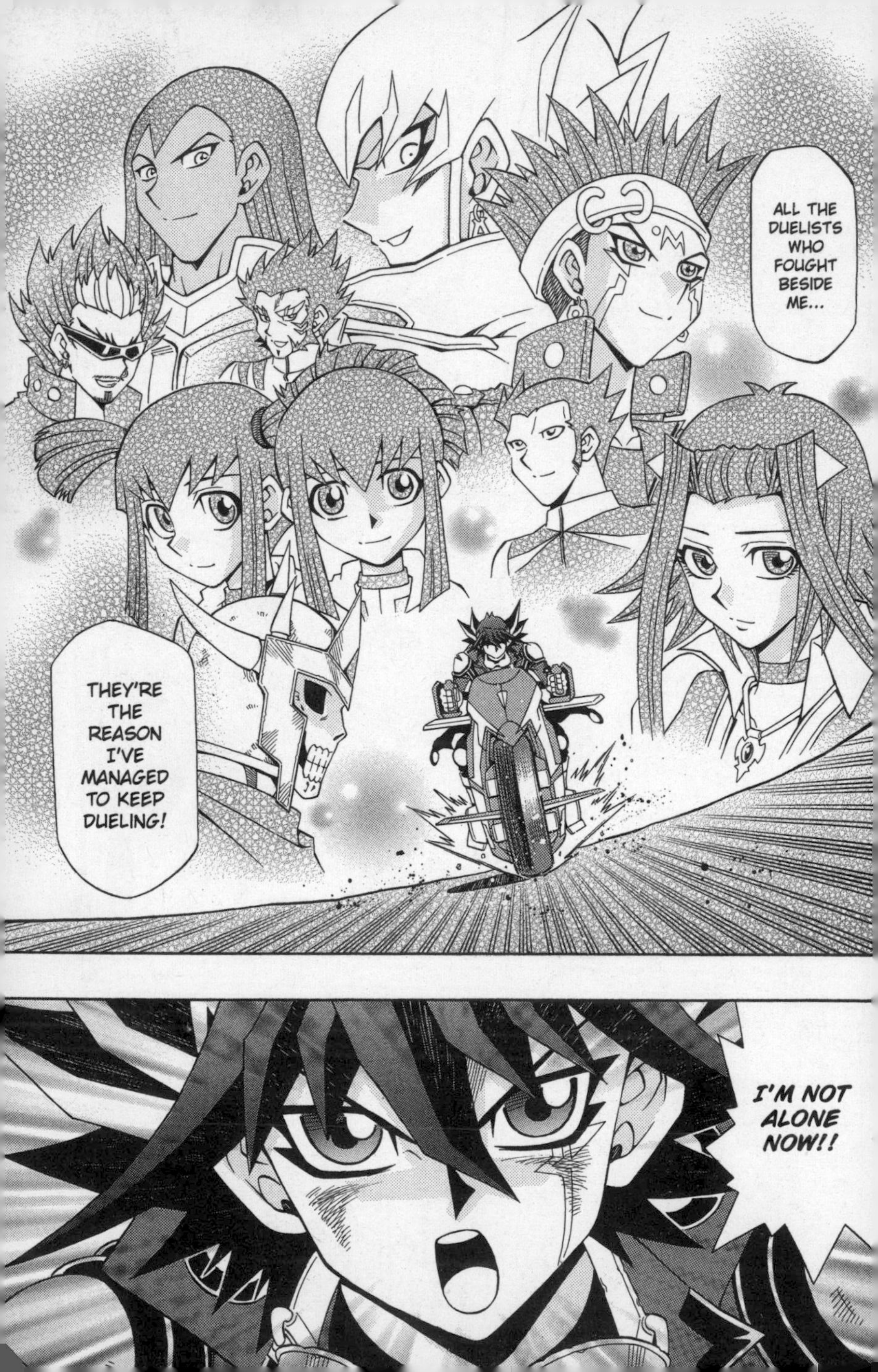
ALL THE DUELISTS WHO FOUGHT BESIDE ME...
THEY'RE THE REASON I'VE MANAGED TO KEEP DUELING!
I'M NOT ALONE NOW!!

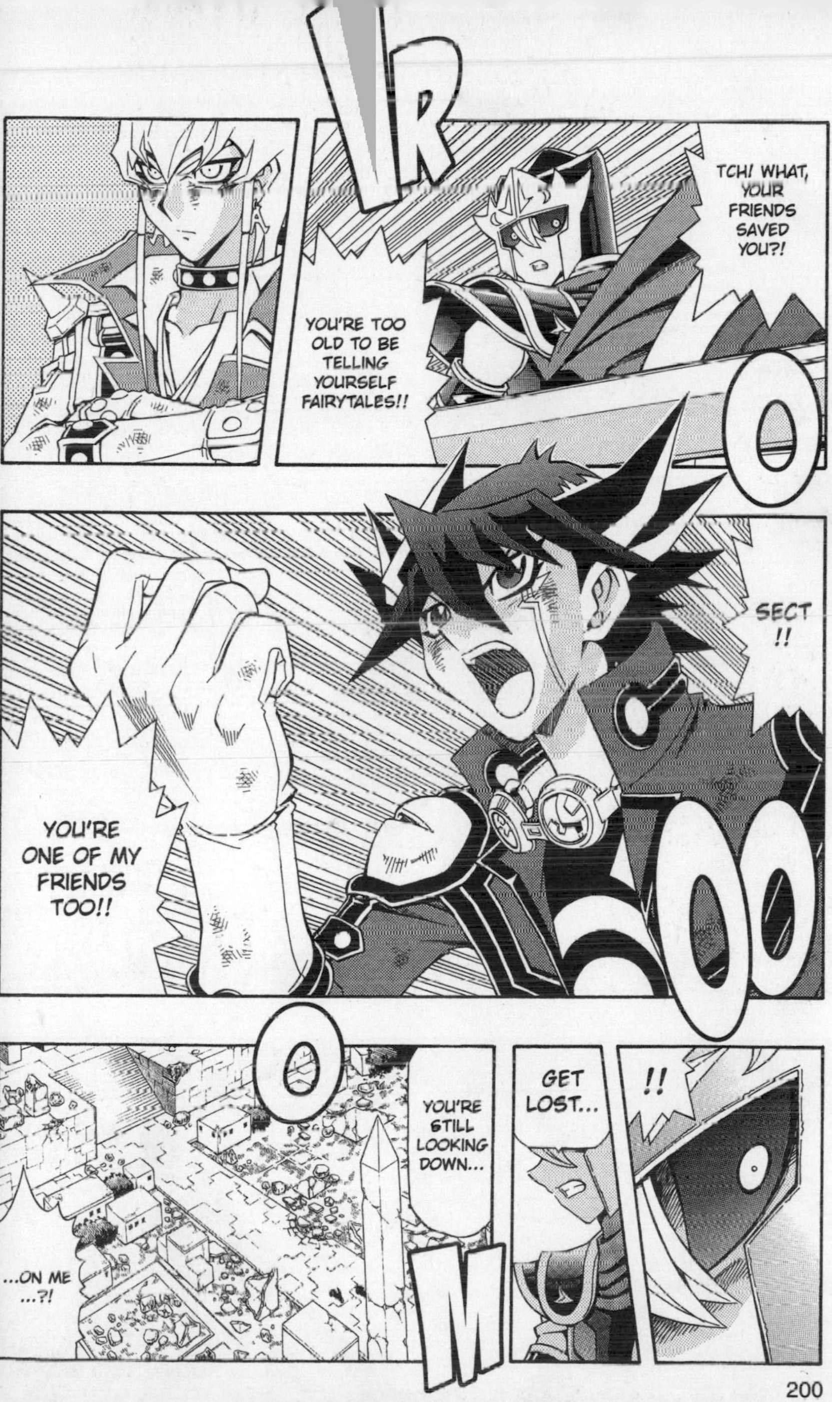
VR
TCH! WHAT, YOUR FRIENDS SAVED YOU?!
YOU'RE TOO OLD TO BE TELLING YOURSELF FAIRYTALES!!
O
SECT !!
OO
YOU'RE ONE OF MY FRIENDS TOO!!
O
!!
GET LOST...
YOU'RE STILL LOOKING DOWN...
...ON ME ...?!
M

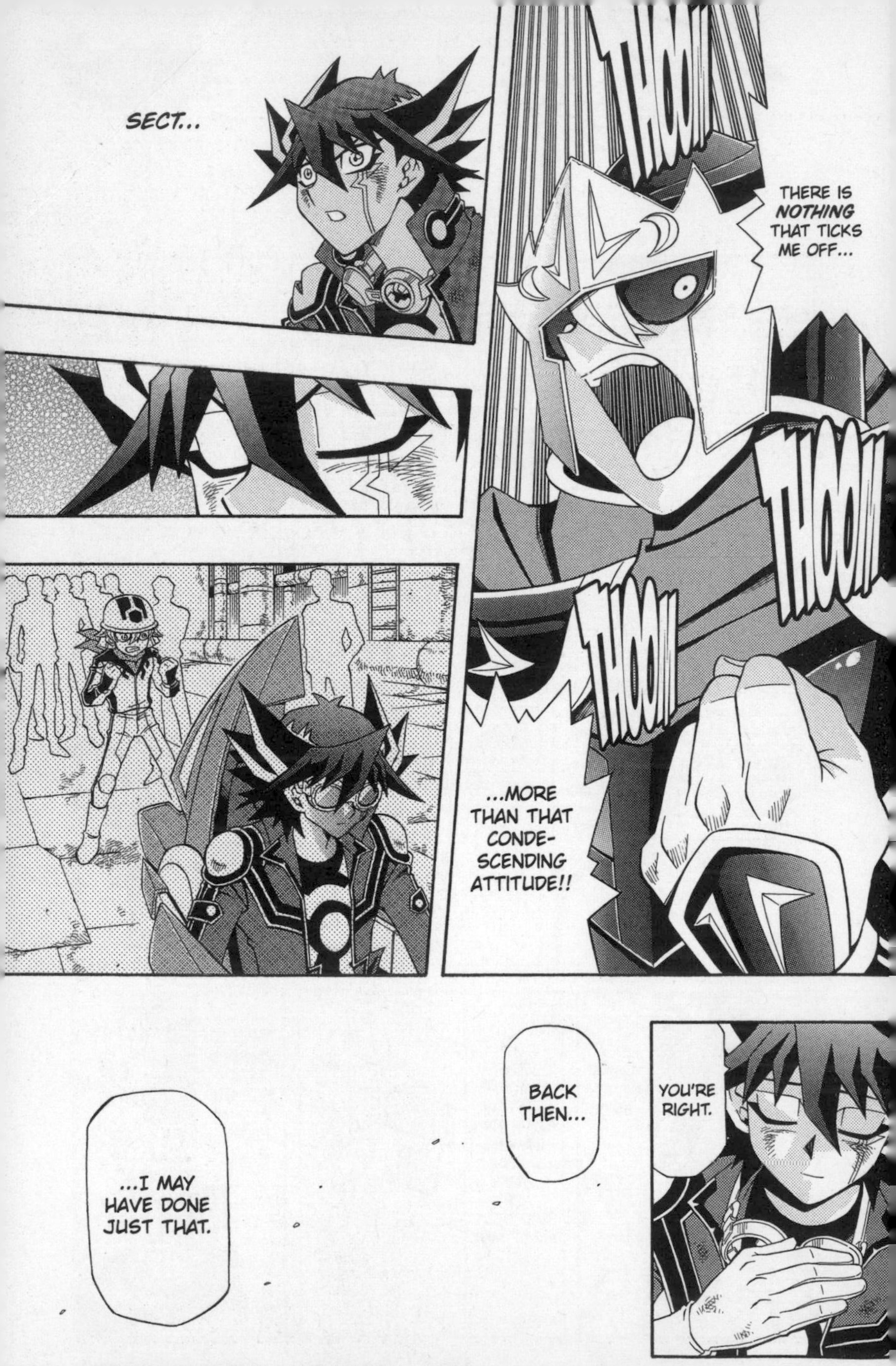
THOOM
THERE IS NOTHING THAT TICKS ME OFF...
THOOM
THOOM
...MORE THAN THAT CONDE- SCENDING ATTITUDE!!
SECT...
YOU'RE RIGHT.
BACK THEN...
...I MAY HAVE DONE JUST THAT.

YU-GI-OH! 5D'S - VOLUME 7 - END

5D's TRACKS

THE 52ND

BY SATOMASA

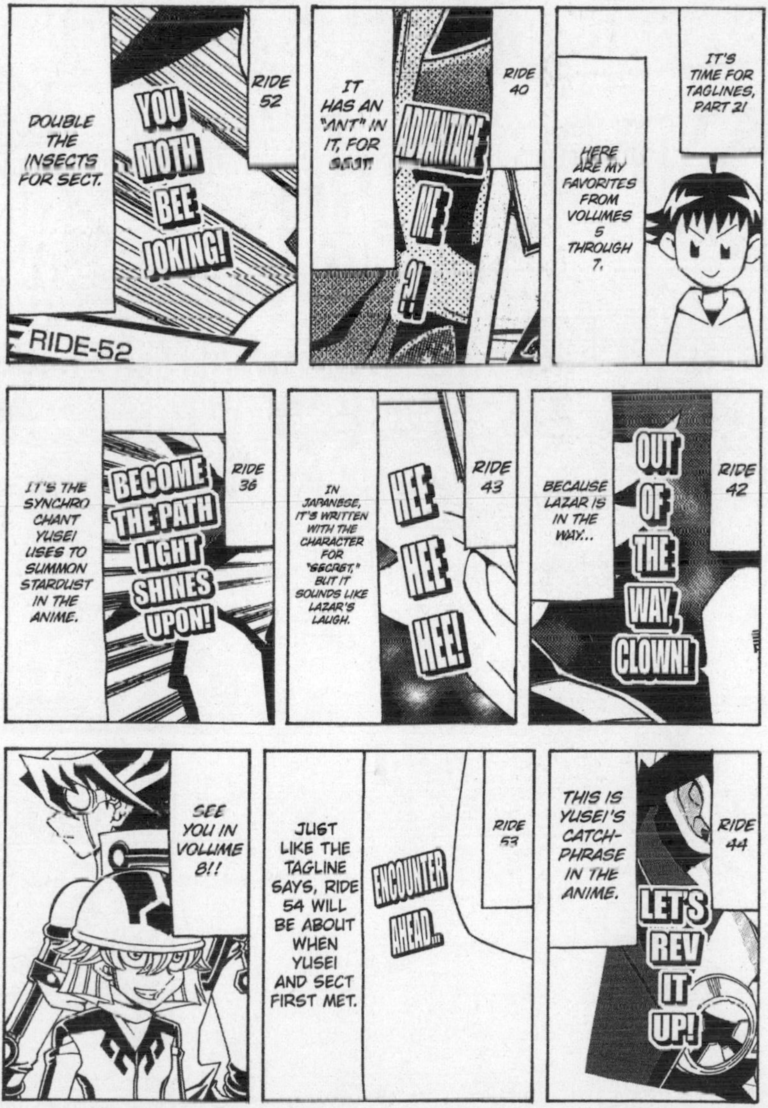
IT'S TIME FOR TAGLINES, PART 21
HERE ARE MY FAVORITES FROM VOLUMES 5 THROUGH 7.
RIDE 40
ADVANTAGE ME?!
IT HAS AN "ANT" IN IT, FOR SECT.
RIDE 52
YOU MOTH BEE JOKING!
DOUBLE THE INSECTS FOR SECT.
RIDE-52
RIDE 42
OUT OF THE WAY, CLOWN!
BECAUSE LAZAR IS IN THE WAY...
RIDE 43
HEE HEE HEE!
IN JAPANESE, IT'S WRITTEN WITH THE CHARACTER FOR "SECRET," BUT IT SOUNDS LIKE LAZAR'S LAUGH.
RIDE 36
BECOME THE PATH LIGHT SHINES UPON!
IT'S THE SYNCHRO CHANT YUSEI USES TO SUMMON STARDUST IN THE ANIME.
RIDE 44
LET'S REV IT UP!
THIS IS YUSEI'S CATCHPHRASE IN THE ANIME.
RIDE 53
ENCOUNTER AHEAD...
JUST LIKE THE TAGLINE SAYS, RIDE 54 WILL BE ABOUT WHEN YUSEI AND SECT FIRST MET.
SEE YOU IN VOLUME 8!!

IN THE NEXT VOLUME...

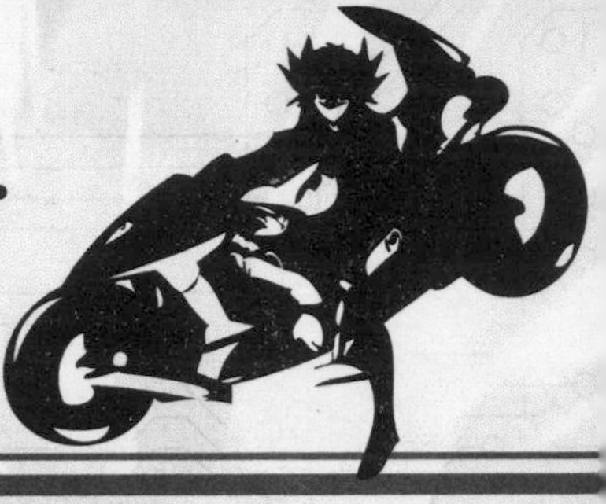

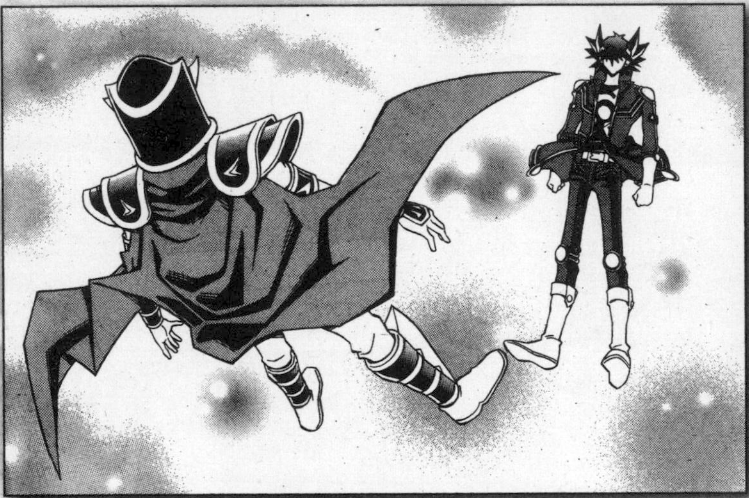

Forced to duel his friend Sect, Yusei plays his most powerful cards. Will the duel end their friendship, or their lives?

COMING SOON!!

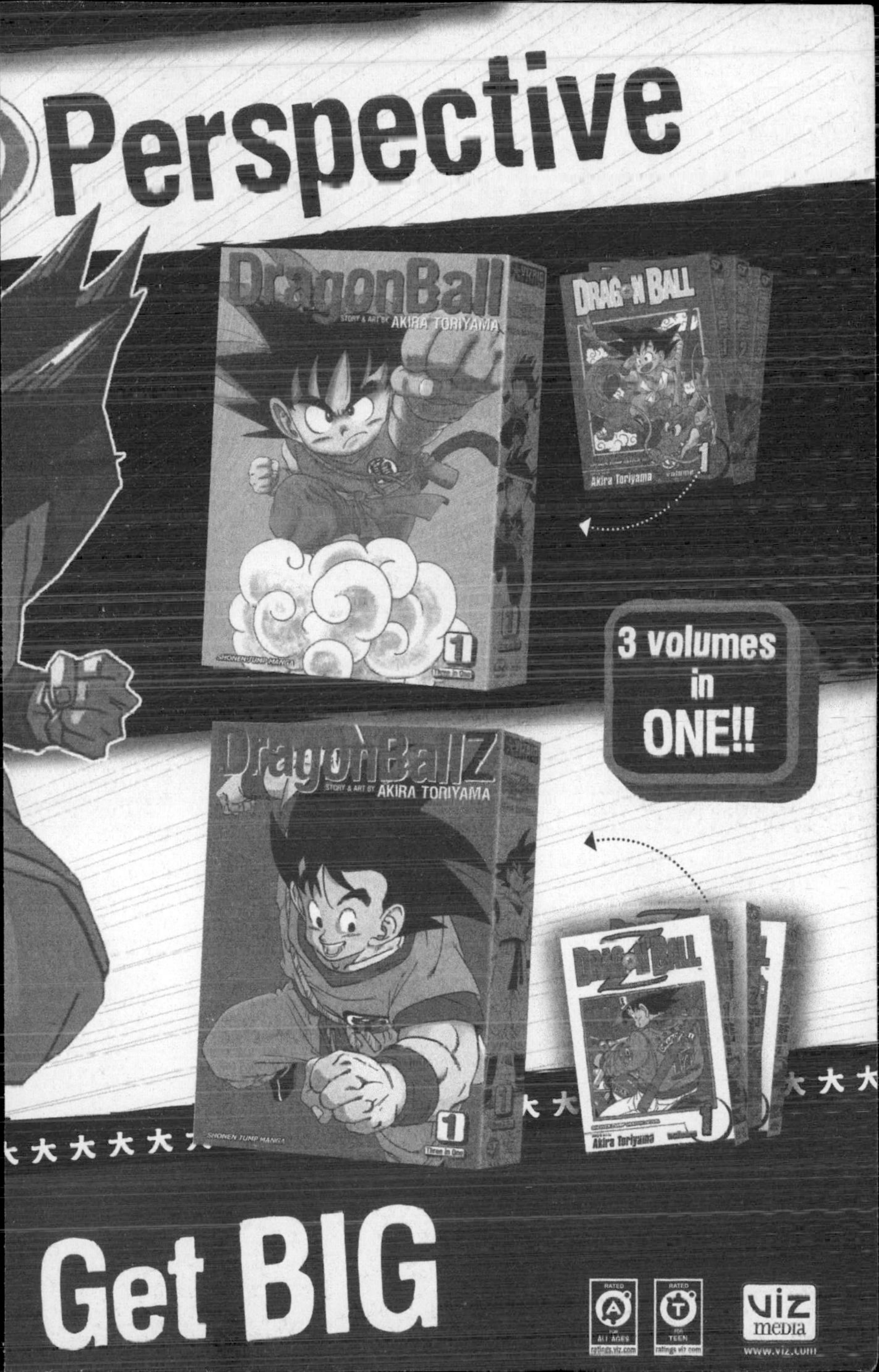

Perspective
DragonBall
STORY & ART BY AKIRA TORIYAMA
SHONEN JUMP MANGA
1
Three in One
DRAGON BALL
Akira Toriyama
3 volumes in ONE!!
DragonBall Z
STORY & ART BY AKIRA TORIYAMA
SHONEN JUMP MANGA
1
Three in One
Akira Toriyama
Get BIG
RATED A FOR ALL AGES ratings.viz.com
RATED T FOR TEEN ratings.viz.com
viz media
www.viz.com

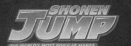
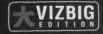

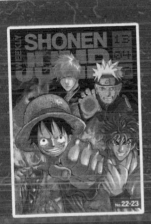

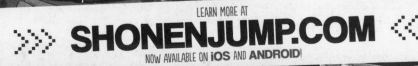

YOU ARE READING IN THE WRONG DIRECTION!!

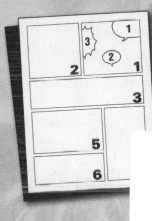

Whoops!
Guess what?
You're starting at the wrong end of the comic!

...it's true! In keeping with the original Japanese format, *Yu-Gi-Oh! 5Ds* is meant to be read from right to left, starting in the upper-right corner.

Unlike English, which is read from left to right, Japanese is read from right to left, meaning that action, sound effects and word-balloon order are completely reversed... something which can make readers unfamiliar with Japanese feel pretty backwards themselves. For this reason, manga or Japanese comics published in the U.S. in English have sometimes been published "flopped"—that is, printed in exact reverse order, as though seen from the other side of a mirror.

By flopping pages, U.S. publishers can avoid confusing readers, but the compromise is not without its downside. For one thing, a character in a flopped manga series who once wore in the original Japanese version a T-shirt emblazoned with "M A Y" (as in "the merry month of") now wears one which reads "Y A M"! Additionally, many manga creators in Japan are themselves unhappy with the process, as some feel the mirror-imaging of their art alters their original intentions.

We are proud to bring you Masahiro Hikokubo and Masashi Sato's *Yu-Gi-Oh! 5D's* in the original unflopped format. For now, though, turn to the other side of the book and let the duel begin...!

—Editor